PREACHER

Book One

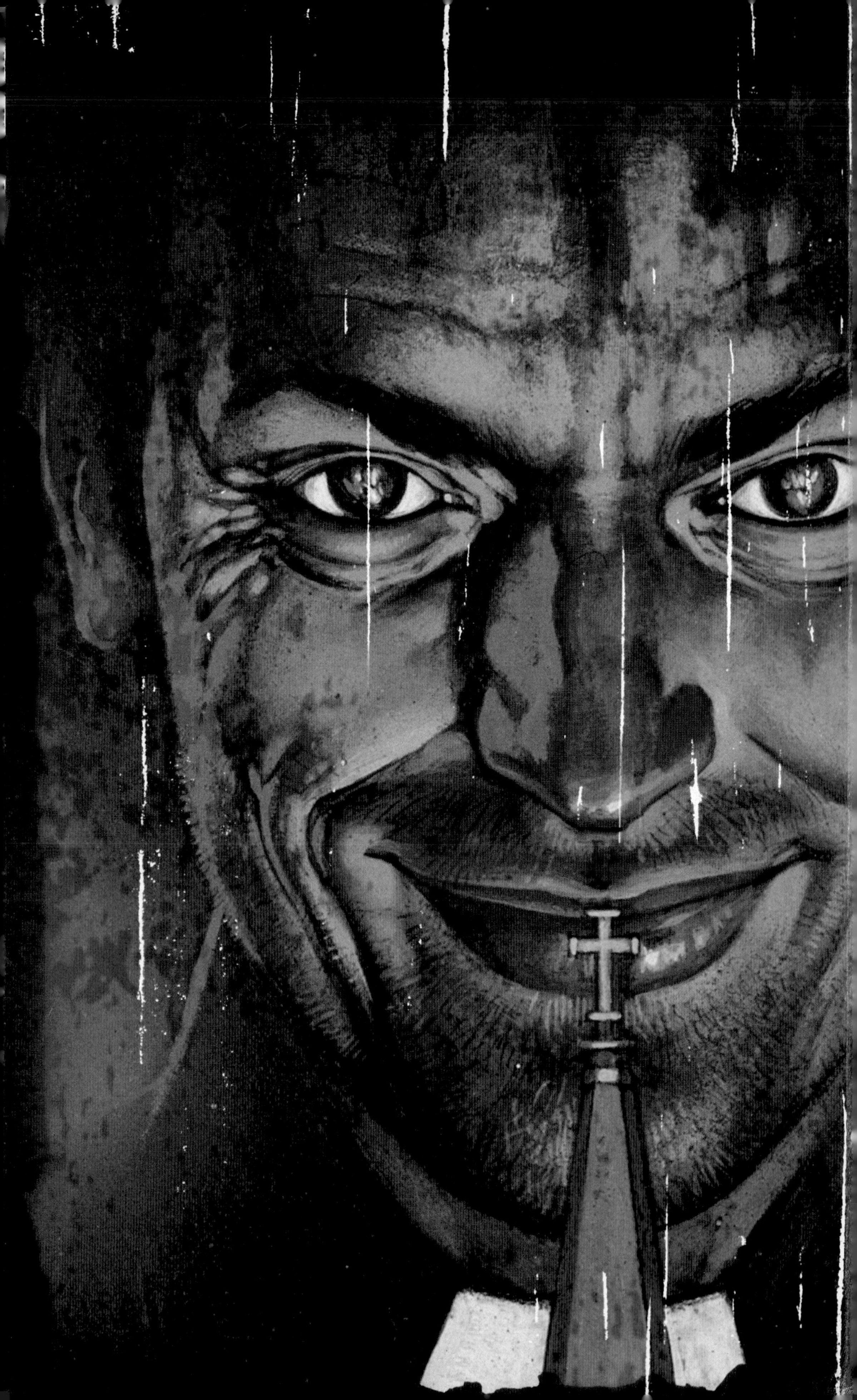

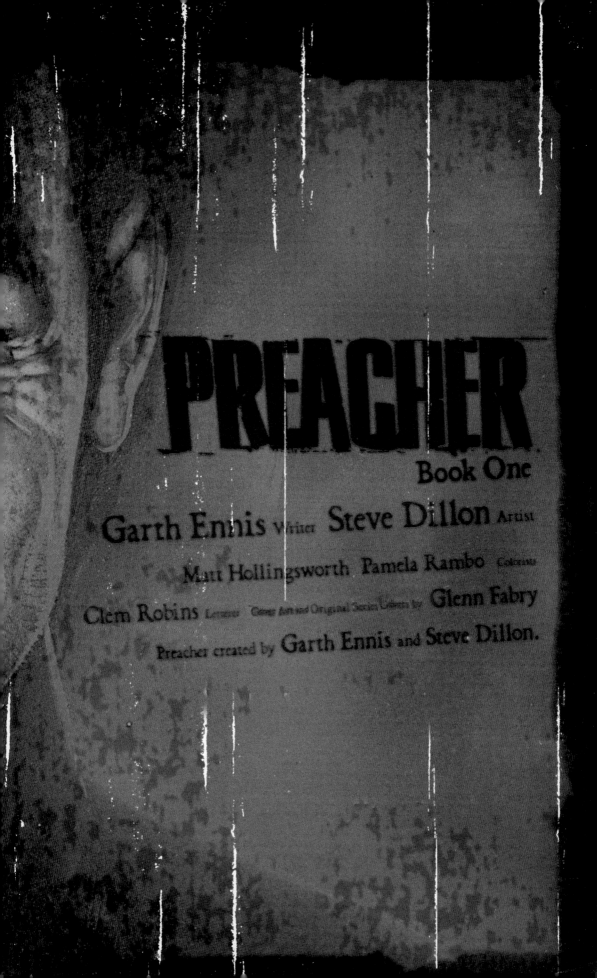

PREACHER

Book One

Garth Ennis Writer **Steve Dillon** Artist

Matt Hollingsworth Pamela Rambo Colorists

Clem Robins Letterer Cover Art and Original Series Covers by **Glenn Fabry**

Preacher created by **Garth Ennis** and **Steve Dillon**.

Stuart Moore Axel Alonso Editors – Original Series Julie Rottenberg Associate Editor – Original Sseries Scott Nybakken Editor Robbin Brosterman
Design Director – Books Louis Prandi Publication Design Shelly Bond Executive Editor – Vertigo Hank Kanalz Senior VP – Vertigo & Integrated Publishing
Diane Nelson President Dan DiDio and Jim Lee Co-Publishers Geoff Johns Chief Creative Officer Amit Desai Senior VP – Marketing & Franchise Management
Amy Genkins Senior VP – Business & Legal Affairs Nairi Gardiner Senior VP – Finance Jeff Boison VP – Publishing Planning
Mark Chiarello VP – Art Direction & Design John Cunningham VP – Marketing Terri Cunningham VP – Editorial Administration
Larry Ganem VP – Talent Relations & Services Alison Gill Senior VP – Manufacturing & Operations Jay Kogan VP – Business & Legal Affairs, Publishing
Jack Mahan VP – Business Affairs, Talent Nick Napolitano VP – Manufacturing Administration Sue Pohja VP – Book Sales
Fred Ruiz VP – Manufacturing Operations Courtney Simmons Senior VP – Publicity Bob Wayne Senior VP – Sales

PREACHER BOOK ONE

Library of Congress Cataloging-in-Publication Data

Ennis, Garth.
    Preacher, book one / Garth Ennis, Steve Dillon.
        pages cm
    "Originally published in single magazine form in Preacher 1-12."
    ISBN 978-1-4012-4045-5
    1. Custer, Jesse (Fictitious character)--Comic books, strips, etc. 2. Vigilantes--Comic books, strips, etc. 3. Clergy--Comic books, strips, etc. 4. Graphic novels.
    I. Dillon, Steve. II. Title.
    PN6727.E56P73 2013
    741.5'973--dc23
                        2013003531

TABLE OF CONTENTS

6 INTRODUCTION BY GARTH ENNIS

9 CHAPTER ONE: THE TIME OF THE PREACHER

51 CHAPTER TWO: AND HELL FOLLOWED WITH HIM

77 CHAPTER THREE: AND THE HORSE YOU RODE IN ON

103 CHAPTER FOUR: STANDING TALL

129 CHAPTER FIVE: SAY A PRAYER FOR SEVEN BULLETS

155 CHAPTER SIX: NEW YORK'S FINEST

181 CHAPTER SEVEN: N.Y.P.D. BLUE

207 CHAPTER EIGHT: ALL IN THE FAMILY

233 CHAPTER NINE: WHEN THE STORY BEGAN

259 CHAPTER TEN: HOW I LEARNED TO LOVE THE LORD

285 CHAPTER ELEVEN: PARDNERS

311 CHAPTER TWELVE: UNTIL THE END OF THE WORLD

337 WANTED: A PREACHER GALLERY

The Greatest Thing Since Sliced Bread

Memorably described by British comics old contemptible Dave
Gibbons as "uncalled for," and by Marvel Comics editor-in-chief
Joe Quesada as "a good, one-dump read," PREACHER was
many things to many people. Some liked it, some loathed it. A
few constantly railed against it, realizing too late that their howls
of protest translated directly into increased sales for the object of
their frustration. Most understood that we were going all the way
to issue 66 come hell or high water, and that the smart thing to do
was either bale out or come along for the ride.

What does PREACHER mean to me? Enormous enjoyment is
the expression that first comes to mind; there are far, far worse ways
to spend five years than writing a story you love about characters
you've created yourself. "Whopping great wodges of cash" is
another relevant phrase; there seems little point in trying to deny it.
Finally, the book established my name in a way that led to many
more enjoyable projects, and continues to do to this day. So big
thumbs-up all round, that would be my verdict.

Now, as I stroll the battlements of La Casa delle Pistole di
Navarone, enjoying the Tuscan evening with my mongoose Charlie at
my heels, my thoughts drift back to those heady times and to the
people that I shared them with. I watch the sun sink behind a line of
trees on the horizon, those ones that always seem so perfectly aligned
for a nice stock establishing shot of the Italian countryside, and I
recall the comrades with whom I embarked on that extraordinary
journey. Where are they now, my dearest PREACHER chums?
Gone, all gone. All swept away and scattered to the winds, each one
individually violated by the fickle finger of fate. I take another sip of
whatever wizard Eyetie plonk it is I'm quaffing... and I remember.

Original editor *Stuart Moore's* career in stand-up comedy went
nowhere, largely due to his crippling inability to tell a joke. The
Mother-In-Law stuff was one thing, but the infamous "Flintstone
Incident" was the final nail in his coffin. Soon afterwards, he
joined the Legion to forget.

His replacement *Axel Alonso* runs D-Block in Riker's now.
"Don't be messin' wit' the Double-A," newcomers are told, "or
he be all up in yo' shit wit' a quickness." For the price of twenty
menthol Kools a day, a sensible inmate can usually avoid Alonso's
ire; but woe betide the "hapless muthafucka" whom he decides to
make his "bitch."

Dreadful oik and, yes, I suppose, talented colorist *Matt Hollingsworth* has left his native land for pastures new, where he lies in wait for the credulous. Obviously there's always been trouble in the Balkans, but the granting of his permanent visa seems like an act of pure recklessness. Any Archdukes in the vicinity are advised to keep a wary eye out.

We were all delighted when good egg and ace talent *Pam Rambo* took over from the beastly Hollingsworth. Personally, I can't decide if the best bit was when the giant bomb went off, or if it was when the truck driver slid out of the cab in several wet, meaty slices. But a splendid return to form, I think we can all agree on that.

Clem Robbins succumbed to a drubbing.

Glenn Fabry's ghastly wraith haunts the barren moorlands of Brighton to this day. Charming and debonair even in undeath, somehow his tormented howls retain the good humor, split-second comic timing and sheer wit that always made the man such splendid company. His specter is available for private commissions. Still a hell of a talent.

And *Steve Dillon*? Co-creator, artistic genius, storyteller without compare, Steve's contribution to the success of PREACHER cannot be overestimated. It was all very well for me to script the madness one week out of every month and then move on to another project, but Steve had to live with it — *and make it work* — day in, day out, for five and a half years. I have, indeed, always gone to some lengths to make this very point, so it is with some sadness that I must acknowledge the low esteem with which my former oppo now regards me. Hanging in the cum-dungeons of Lord Flarg The Octo-Cocked, his lot is obviously not a happy one, but in my defense I would just like to establish that a) the contract clearly said "eternal *soul*" (singular), and b) of course that wasn't a doubled-headed coin. Whoever heard of such a thing, outside the pages of some penny dreadful or similar flight of fiction?

But enough of this cloying sentimentality, this sugar-coated scamper down the paths of yesteryear. Why let misplaced guilt interfere with such a perfect evening? Twilight settles on the land like a pissed-up fat lad sprawling on his couch, and soon the chorus of the night begins. The rabbit drops a euro in the jukebox. The badger kicks the living shit out of the weasel. The nightjar fills itself with jam. All is well.

The sensible thing to do would be to open another bottle, but that would make eight for the day. Hmm... heads I do, tails I don't... well, well.

Heads again.

— Garth Ennis
Wombling free, February 2009

PREACHER

Book One

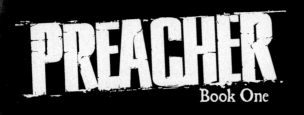

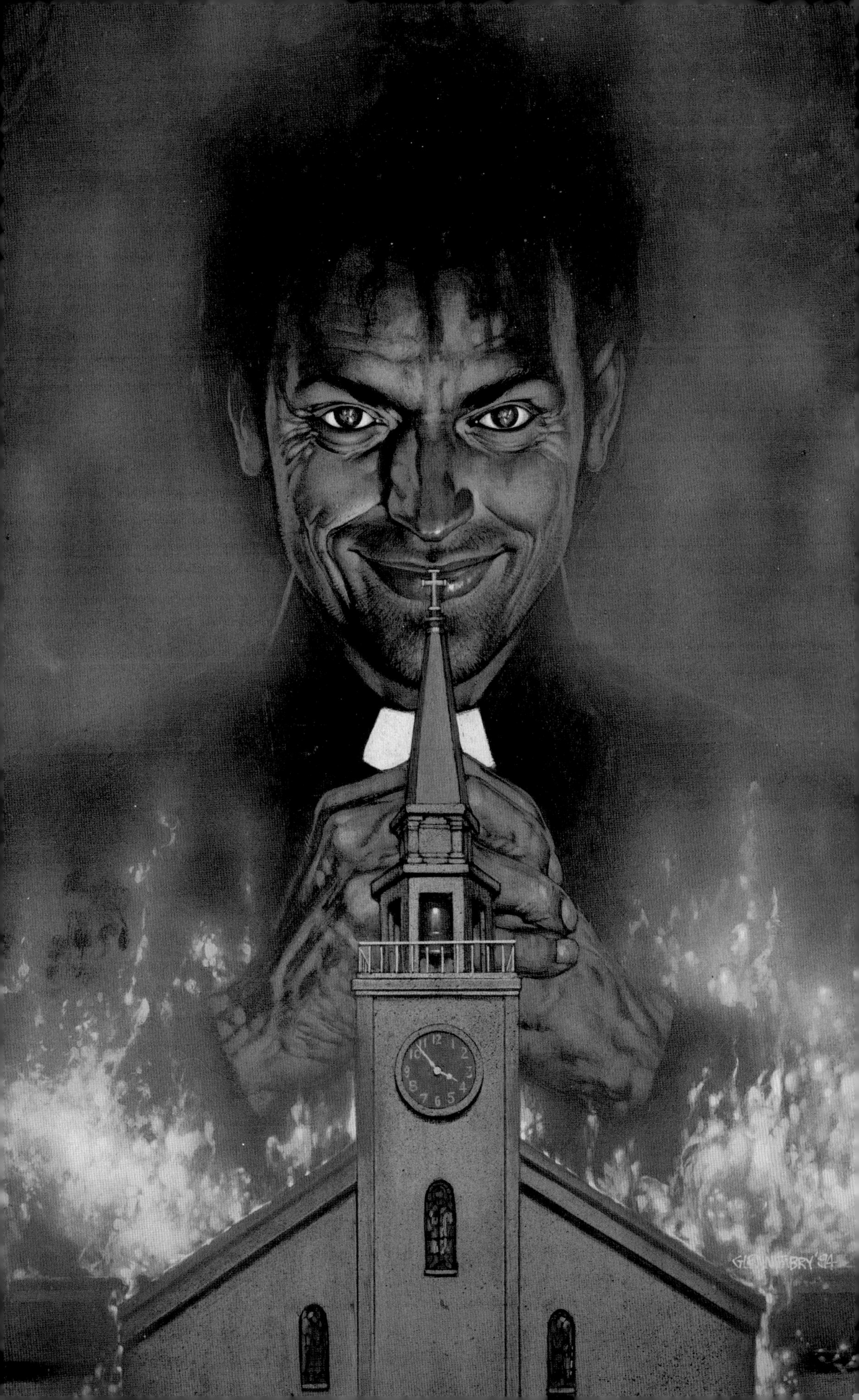

"Whatever it tells me, whatever it says —
it sounds like the word of God."

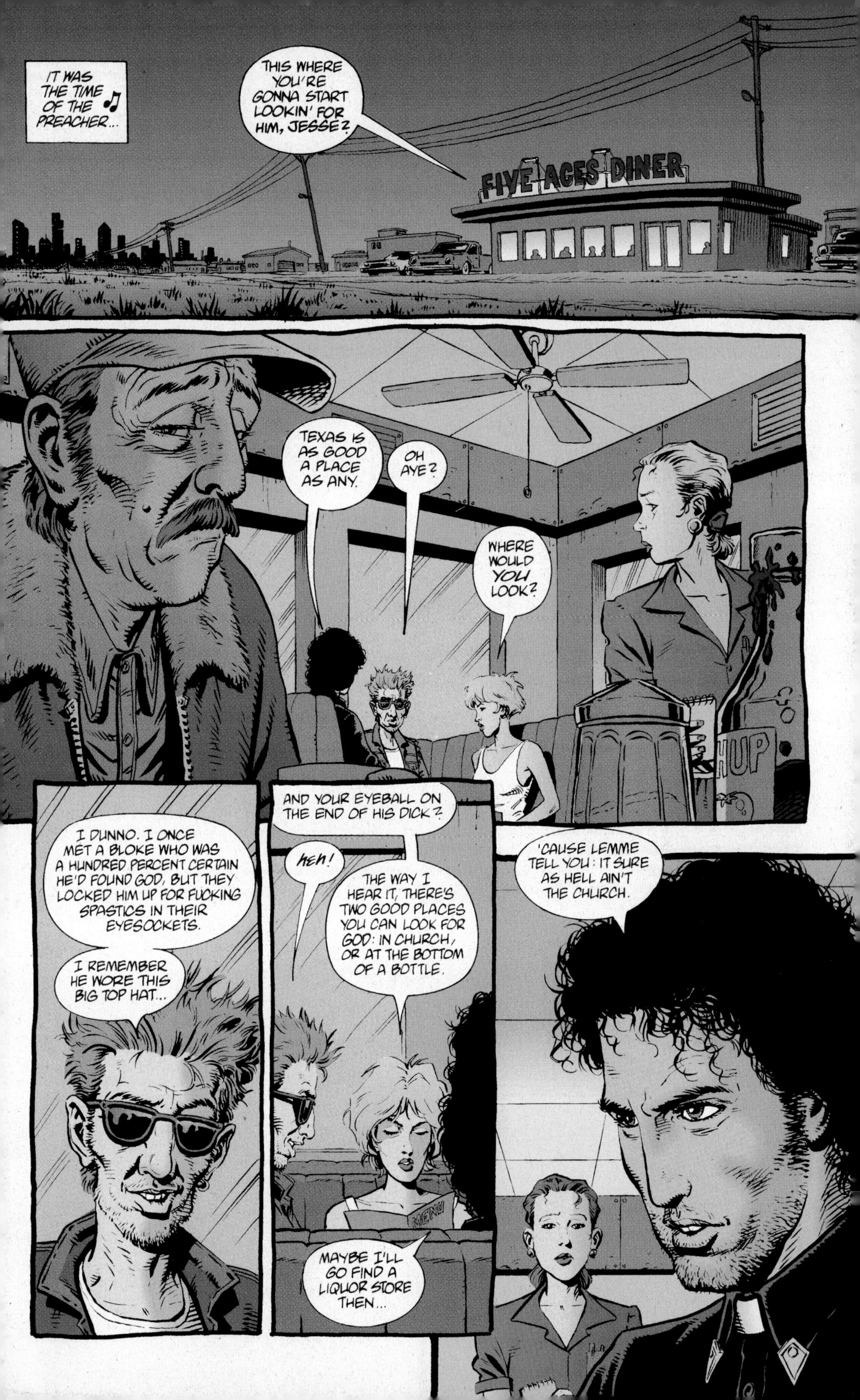
IT WAS THE TIME OF THE PREACHER...
THIS WHERE YOU'RE GONNA START LOOKIN' FOR HIM, JESSE?
FIVE ACES DINER
TEXAS IS AS GOOD A PLACE AS ANY.
OH AYE?
WHERE WOULD YOU LOOK?
I DUNNO. I ONCE MET A BLOKE WHO WAS A HUNDRED PERCENT CERTAIN HE'D FOUND GOD, BUT THEY LOCKED HIM UP FOR FUCKING SPASTICS IN THEIR EYESOCKETS.
I REMEMBER HE WORE THIS BIG TOP HAT...
AND YOUR EYEBALL ON THE END OF HIS DICK?
HEH!
THE WAY I HEAR IT, THERE'S TWO GOOD PLACES YOU CAN LOOK FOR GOD: IN CHURCH, OR AT THE BOTTOM OF A BOTTLE.
MAYBE I'LL GO FIND A LIQUOR STORE THEN...
'CAUSE LEMME TELL YOU: IT SURE AS HELL AIN'T THE CHURCH.

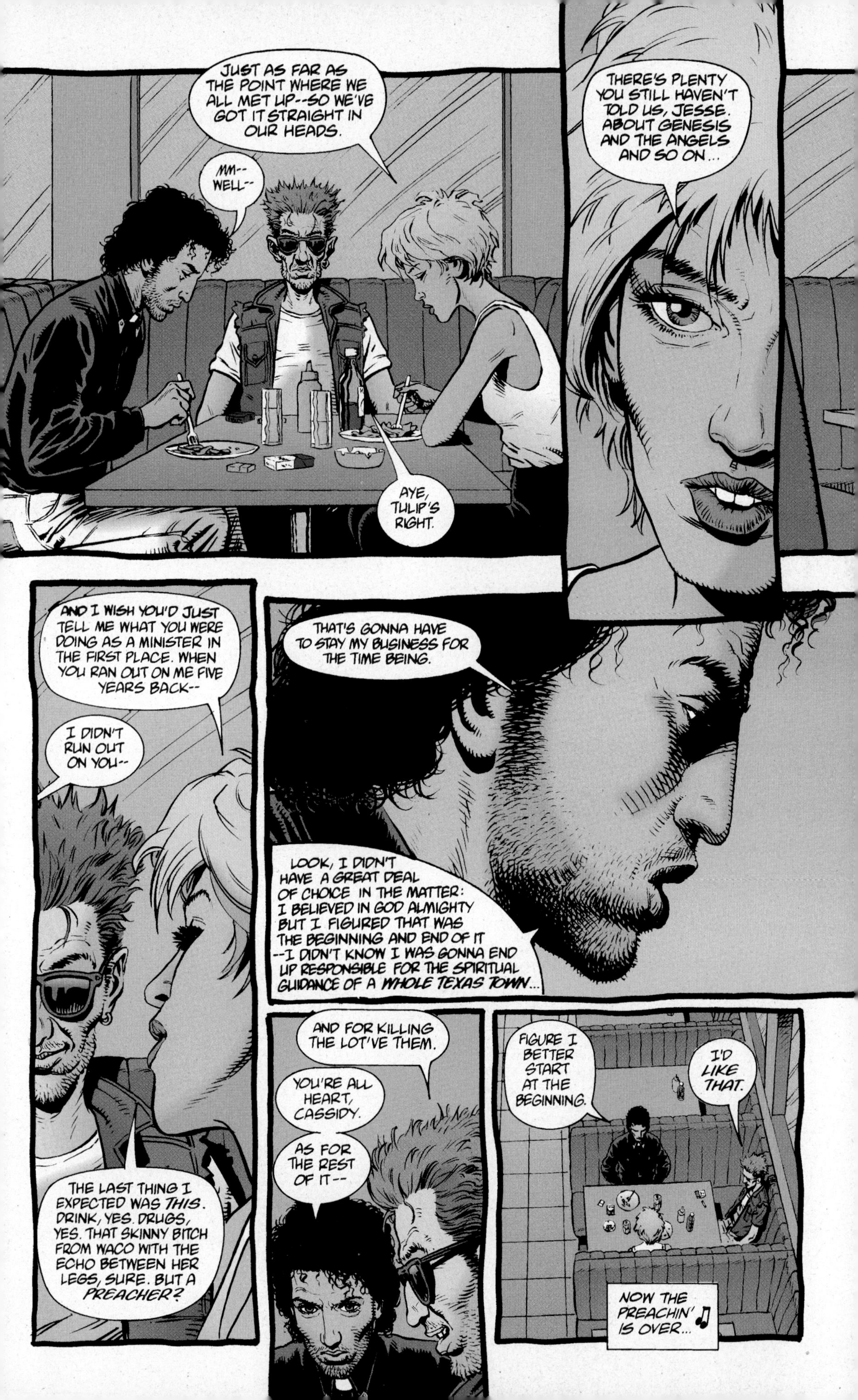
JUST AS FAR AS THE POINT WHERE WE ALL MET UP--SO WE'VE GOT IT STRAIGHT IN OUR HEADS.
MM--WELL--
AYE, TULIP'S RIGHT.
THERE'S PLENTY YOU STILL HAVEN'T TOLD US, JESSE. ABOUT GENESIS AND THE ANGELS AND SO ON...
AND I WISH YOU'D JUST TELL ME WHAT YOU WERE DOING AS A MINISTER IN THE FIRST PLACE. WHEN YOU RAN OUT ON ME FIVE YEARS BACK--
I DIDN'T RUN OUT ON YOU--
THE LAST THING I EXPECTED WAS *THIS*. DRINK, YES. DRUGS, YES. THAT SKINNY BITCH FROM WACO WITH THE ECHO BETWEEN HER LEGS, SURE. BUT A *PREACHER?*
THAT'S GONNA HAVE TO STAY MY BUSINESS FOR THE TIME BEING.
LOOK, I DIDN'T HAVE A GREAT DEAL OF CHOICE IN THE MATTER: I BELIEVED IN GOD ALMIGHTY BUT I FIGURED THAT WAS THE BEGINNING AND END OF IT --I DIDN'T KNOW I WAS GONNA END UP RESPONSIBLE FOR THE SPIRITUAL GUIDANCE OF A *WHOLE TEXAS TOWN*...
AND FOR KILLING THE LOT'VE THEM.
YOU'RE ALL HEART, CASSIDY.
AS FOR THE REST OF IT--
FIGURE I BETTER START AT THE BEGINNING.
I'D LIKE THAT.
NOW THE PREACHIN' IS OVER...♫

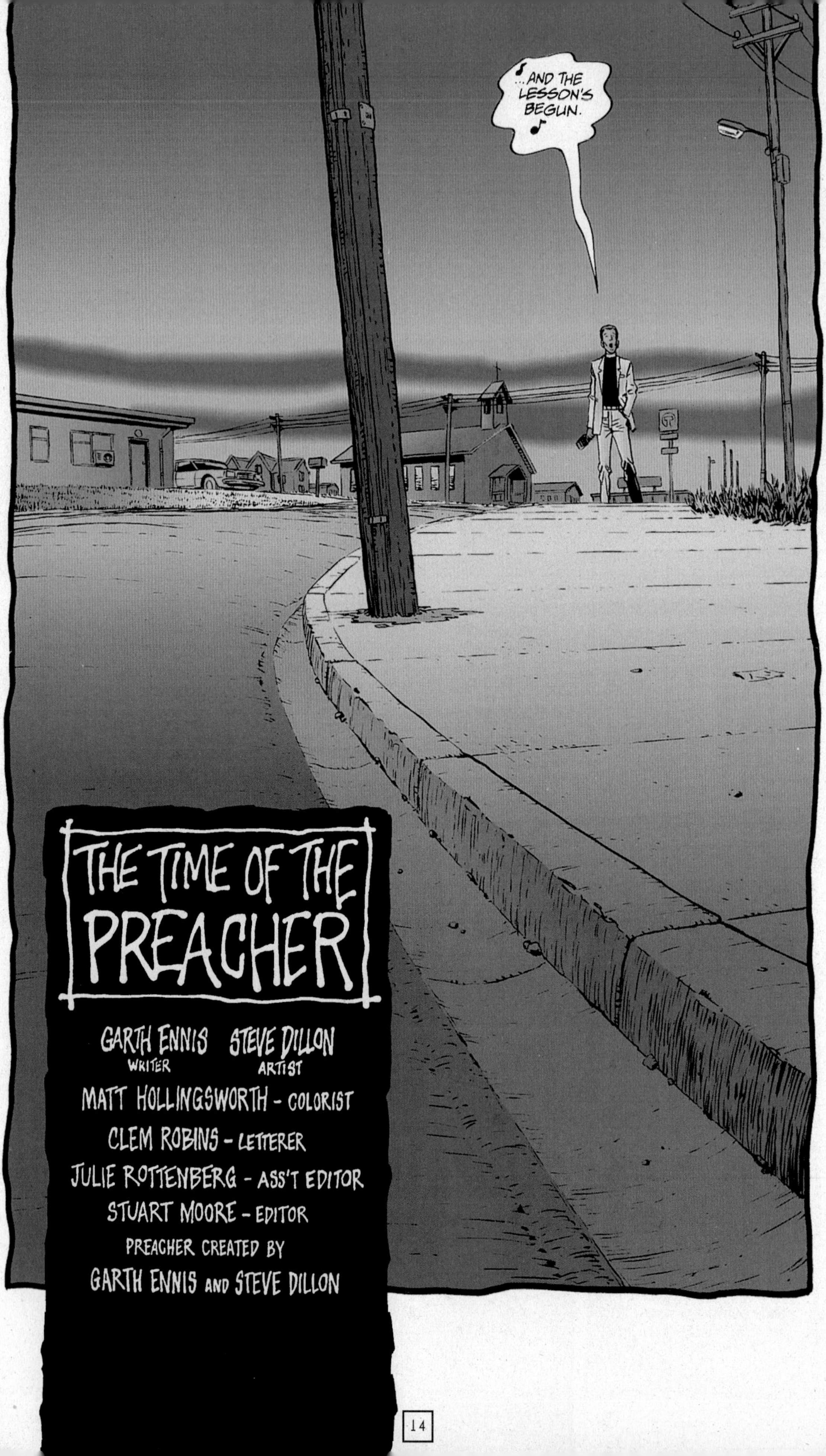
...AND THE LESSON'S BEGUN.
THE TIME OF THE PREACHER
GARTH ENNIS WRITER
STEVE DILLON ARTIST
MATT HOLLINGSWORTH - COLORIST
CLEM ROBINS - LETTERER
JULIE ROTTENBERG - ASS'T EDITOR
STUART MOORE - EDITOR
PREACHER CREATED BY GARTH ENNIS AND STEVE DILLON

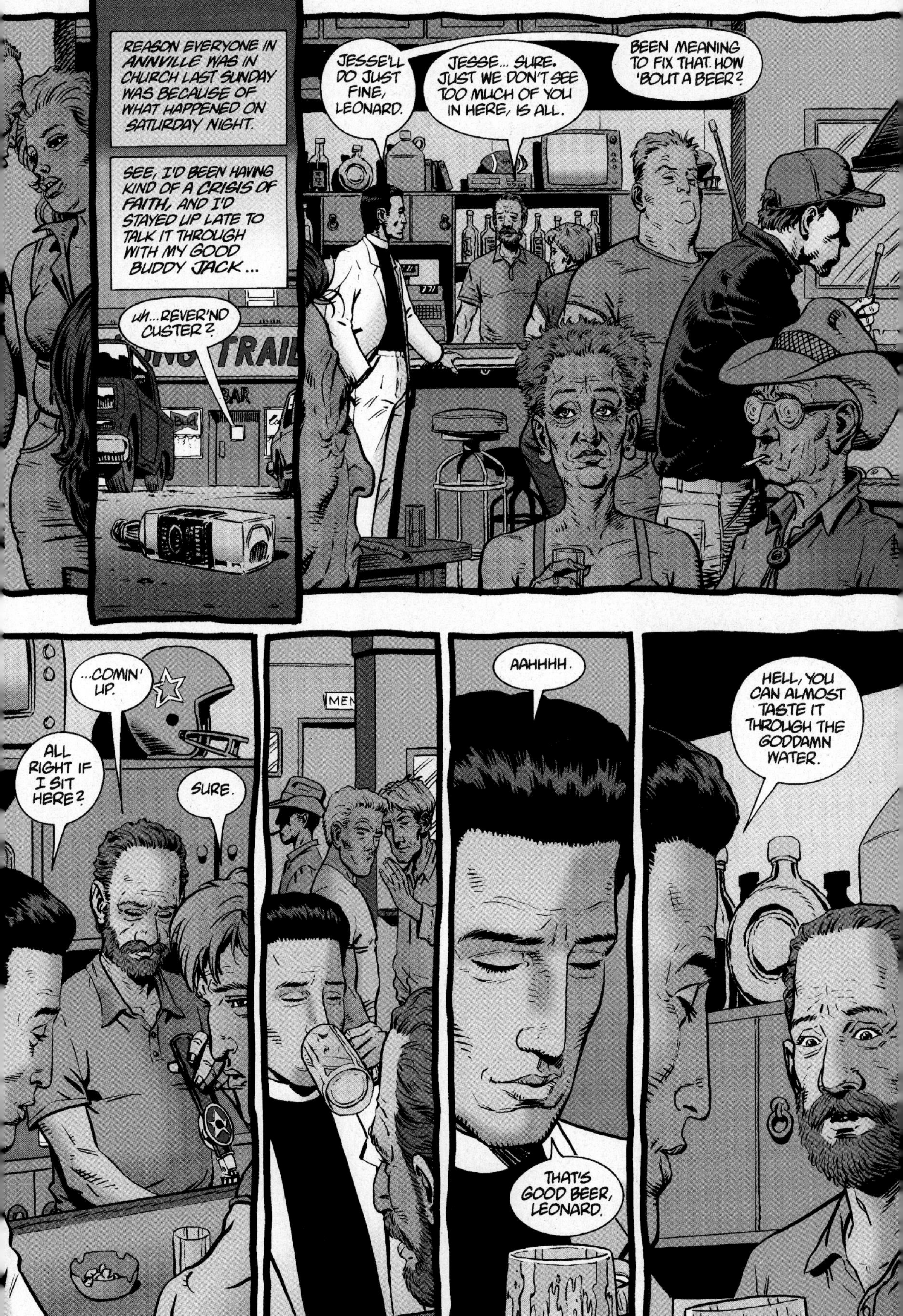
REASON EVERYONE IN ANNVILLE WAS IN CHURCH LAST SUNDAY WAS BECAUSE OF WHAT HAPPENED ON SATURDAY NIGHT.
SEE, I'D BEEN HAVING KIND OF A CRISIS OF FAITH, AND I'D STAYED UP LATE TO TALK IT THROUGH WITH MY GOOD BUDDY JACK...
uh...REVER'ND CUSTER?
JESSE'LL DO JUST FINE, LEONARD.
JESSE... SURE. JUST WE DON'T SEE TOO MUCH OF YOU IN HERE, IS ALL.
BEEN MEANING TO FIX THAT. HOW 'BOUT A BEER?
ALL RIGHT IF I SIT HERE?
...COMIN' UP.
SURE.
AAHHHH.
THAT'S GOOD BEER, LEONARD.
HELL, YOU CAN ALMOST TASTE IT THROUGH THE GODDAMN WATER.

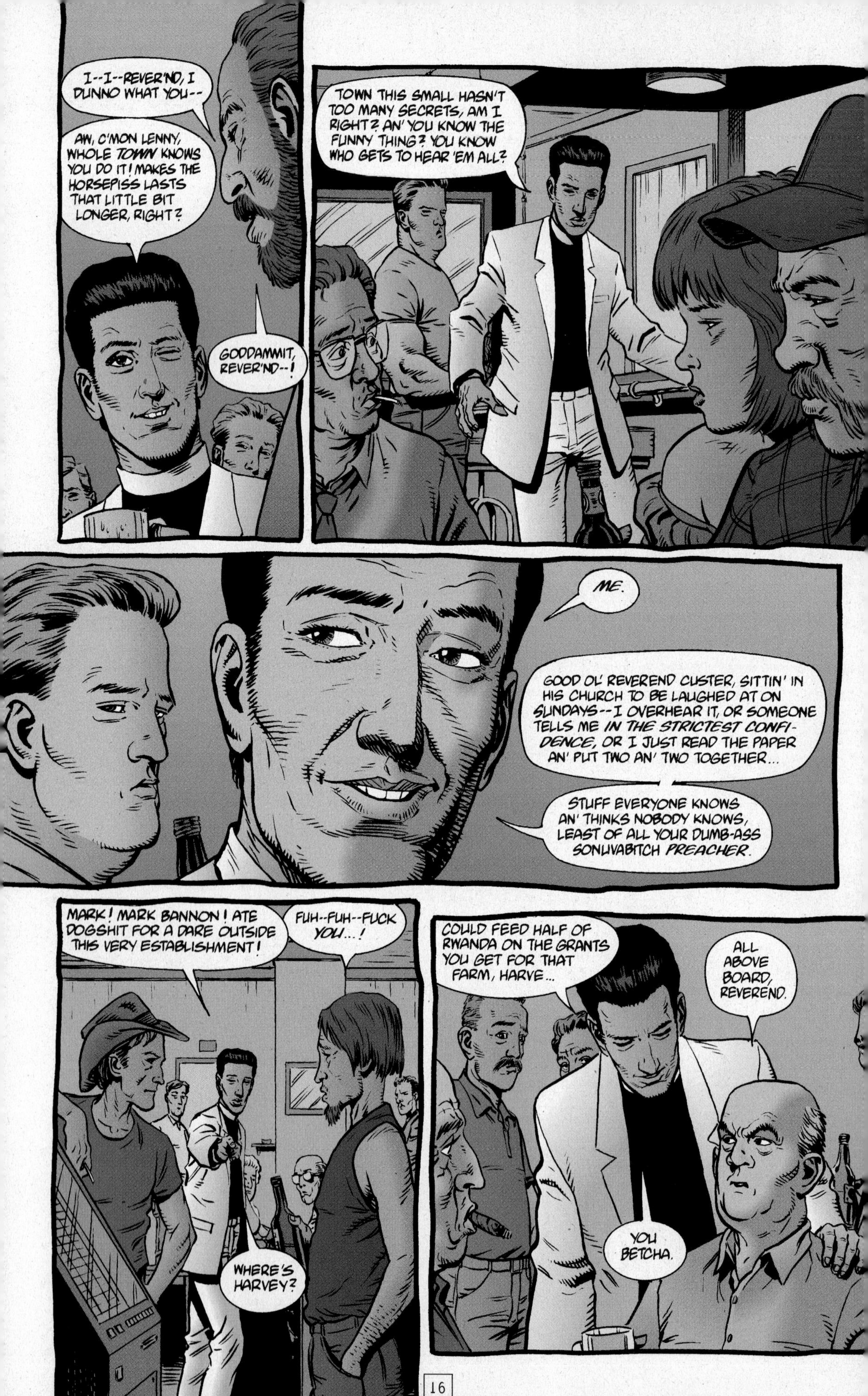
I--I--REVER'ND, I DUNNO WHAT YOU--
AW, C'MON LENNY, WHOLE *TOWN* KNOWS YOU DO IT! MAKES THE HORSEPISS LASTS THAT LITTLE BIT LONGER, RIGHT?
GODDAMMIT, REVER'ND--!
TOWN THIS SMALL HASN'T TOO MANY SECRETS, AM I RIGHT? AN' YOU KNOW THE FUNNY THING? YOU KNOW WHO GETS TO HEAR 'EM ALL?
ME.
GOOD OL' REVEREND CUSTER, SITTIN' IN HIS CHURCH TO BE LAUGHED AT ON SUNDAYS--I OVERHEAR IT, OR SOMEONE TELLS ME *IN THE STRICTEST CONFIDENCE*, OR I JUST READ THE PAPER AN' PUT TWO AN' TWO TOGETHER...
STUFF EVERYONE KNOWS AN' THINKS NOBODY KNOWS, LEAST OF ALL YOUR DUMB-ASS SONUVABITCH *PREACHER*.
MARK! MARK BANNON! ATE DOGSHIT FOR A DARE OUTSIDE THIS VERY ESTABLISHMENT!
FUH--FUH--FUCK *YOU*...!
WHERE'S HARVEY?
COULD FEED HALF OF RWANDA ON THE GRANTS YOU GET FOR THAT FARM, HARVE...
YOU BETCHA.
ALL ABOVE BOARD, REVEREND.

LIKE THE MOVIE KATE SHOT IN YOUR BARN, HUH? JUST HER AN' A PIEBALD STALLION-- WENT STRAIGHT TO VIDEO, WAY I HEAR IT.

I'VE NEVER SEEN THIS WOMAN BEFORE IN MY LIFE--

uh--

BUT LEAVIN' ASIDE MICHAEL HERE--WHO'S GOTTA BE THE ONLY MAN FROM ANNVILLE THAT EVER WENT TO CALIFORNIA --LET'S MEET THE STARS OF THE SHOW...

REVER'ND, YOU'VE HAD A LITTLE TOO MUCH TO--REVER'ND--

PAT AN' TERRY MORROW.

NOW YOU BETTER JUST WATCH YOUR FUCKIN' MOUTH, CUSTER...

WHO RAPED THAT HITCHER GIRL NO MATTER WHAT THEIR DADDY PAID JUDGE SHEBIN.

I SEE YOU EVERY SUNDAY, THE FEW OF YOU BOTHER TO SHOW UP, AN' YOU THINK YOU CAN SING A FEW GOD-DAMN HYMNS AN' THEN ACT LIKE SAVAGES FOR THE REST OF THE WEEK?

OR HOW MANY TIMES THIS TOWN CAN CHANGE THE GODDAMN SUBJECT.

YOU'RE FUCKIN' DRIVIN' ME INSANE AN' I'M HERE TO TELL YOU, THAT AIN'T THE WAY IT WORKS--

17

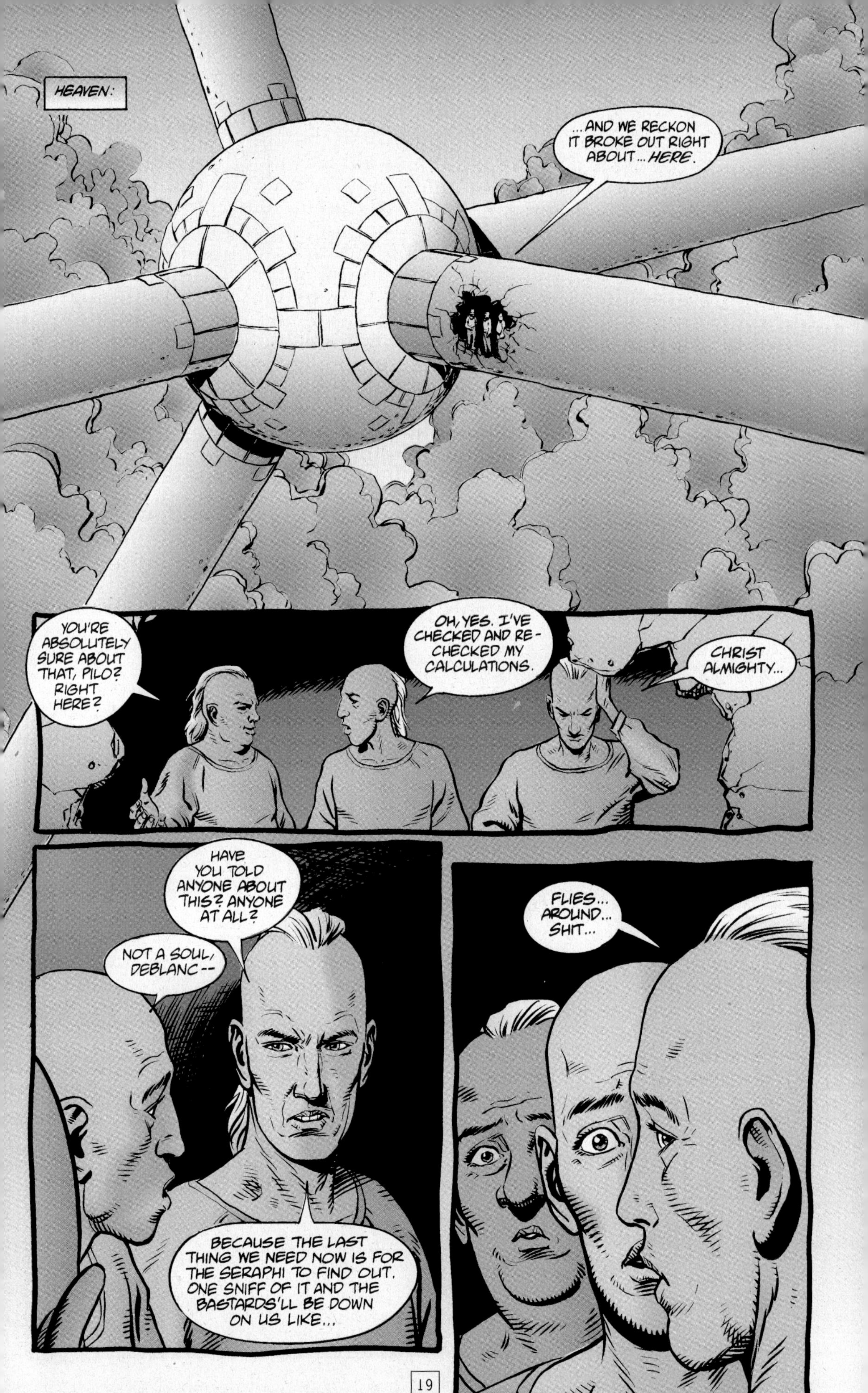
HEAVEN:
...AND WE RECKON IT BROKE OUT RIGHT ABOUT... HERE.
YOU'RE ABSOLUTELY SURE ABOUT THAT, PILO? RIGHT HERE?
OH, YES. I'VE CHECKED AND RE-CHECKED MY CALCULATIONS.
CHRIST ALMIGHTY...
HAVE YOU TOLD ANYONE ABOUT THIS? ANYONE AT ALL?
NOT A SOUL, DEBLANC--
BECAUSE THE LAST THING WE NEED NOW IS FOR THE SERAPHI TO FIND OUT. ONE SNIFF OF IT AND THE BASTARDS'LL BE DOWN ON US LIKE...
FLIES... AROUND... SHIT...

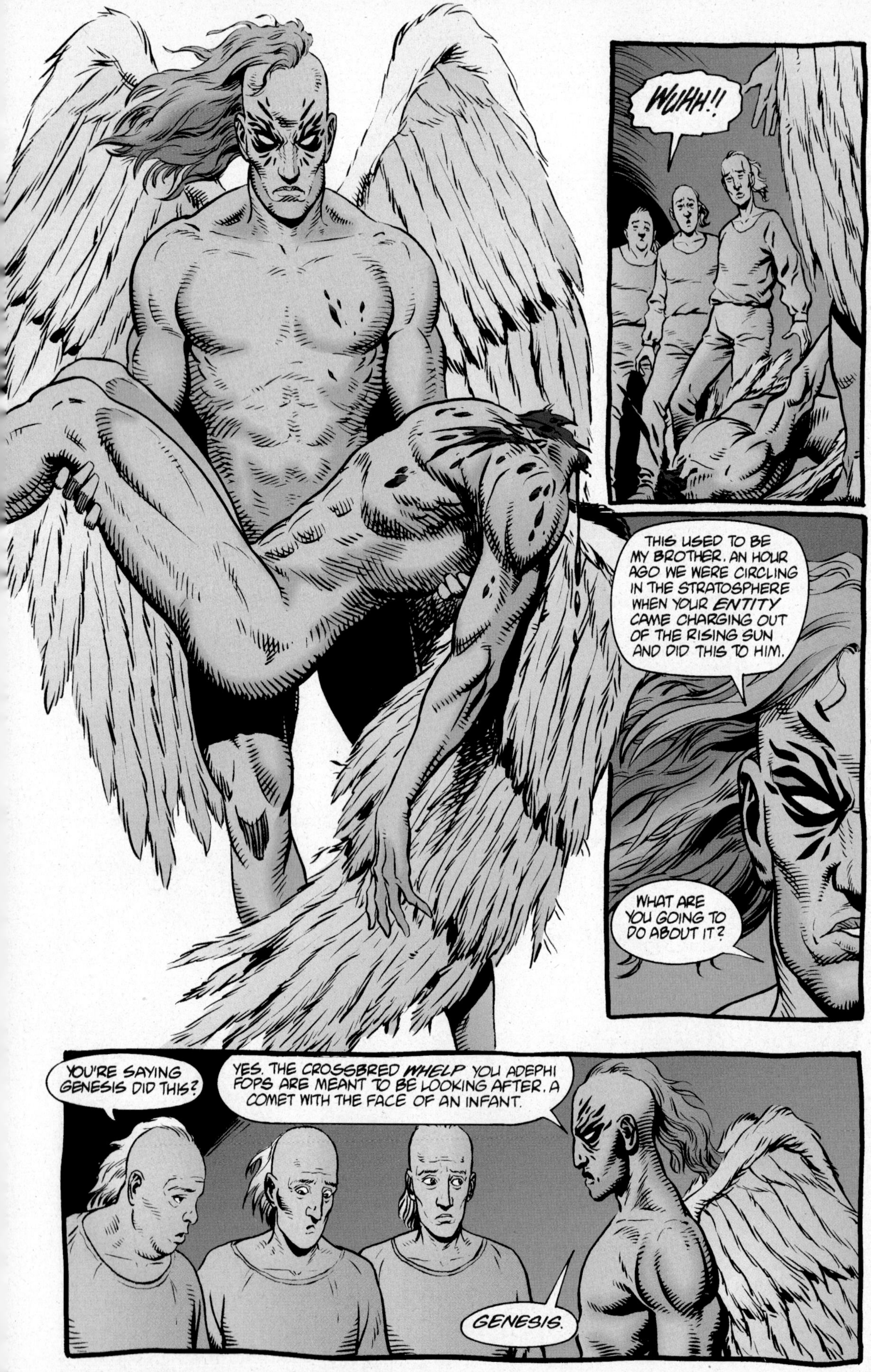
WUHH!!
THIS USED TO BE MY BROTHER. AN HOUR AGO WE WERE CIRCLING IN THE STRATOSPHERE WHEN YOUR ENTITY CAME CHARGING OUT OF THE RISING SUN AND DID THIS TO HIM.
WHAT ARE YOU GOING TO DO ABOUT IT?
YOU'RE SAYING GENESIS DID THIS?
YES. THE CROSSBRED WHELP YOU ADEPHI FOPS ARE MEANT TO BE LOOKING AFTER. A COMET WITH THE FACE OF AN INFANT.
GENESIS.

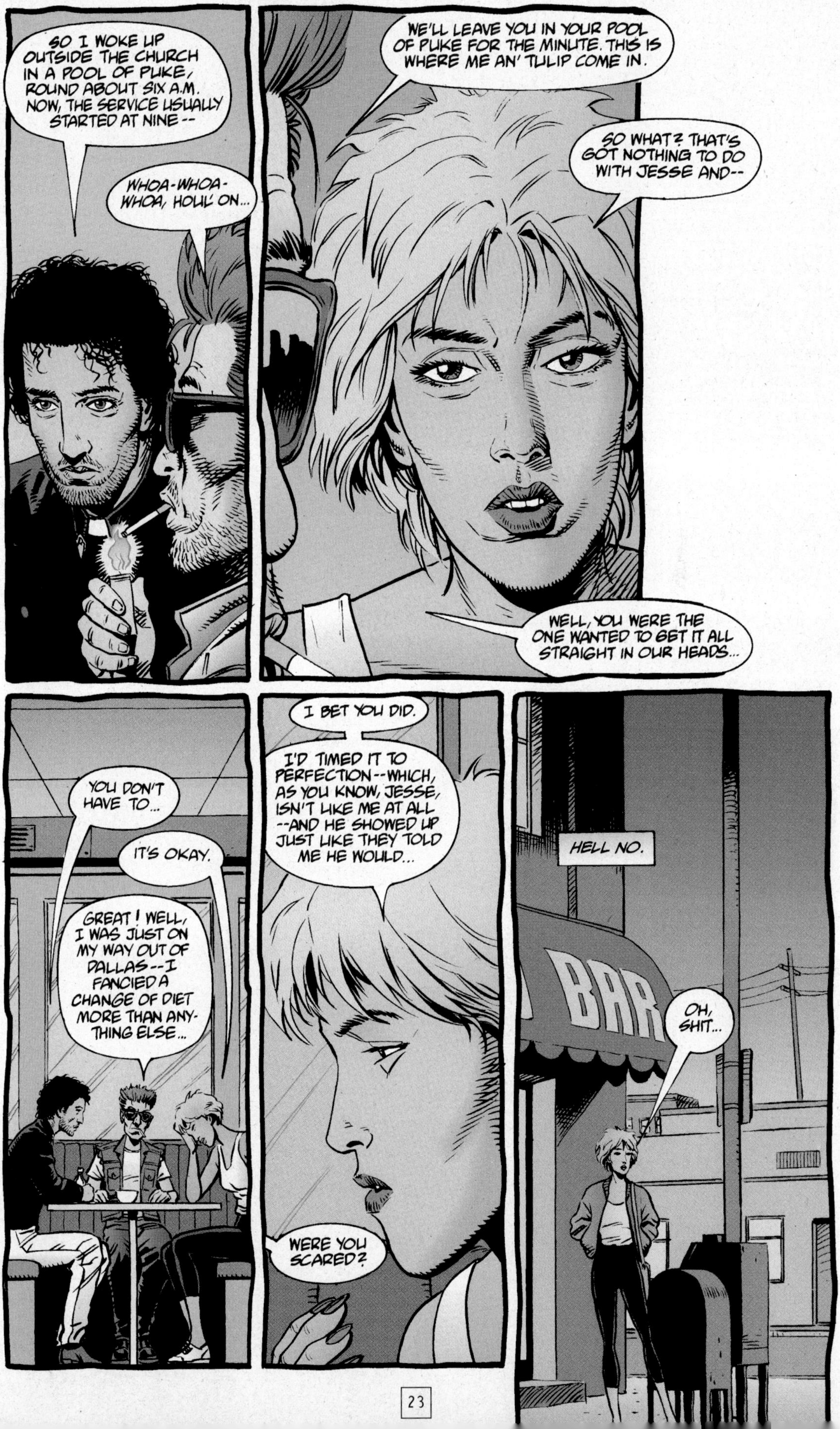
SO I WOKE UP OUTSIDE THE CHURCH IN A POOL OF PUKE, ROUND ABOUT SIX A.M. NOW, THE SERVICE USUALLY STARTED AT NINE --
WHOA-WHOA-WHOA, HOUL' ON...
WE'LL LEAVE YOU IN YOUR POOL OF PUKE FOR THE MINUTE. THIS IS WHERE ME AN' TULIP COME IN.
SO WHAT? THAT'S GOT NOTHING TO DO WITH JESSE AND--
WELL, YOU WERE THE ONE WANTED TO GET IT ALL STRAIGHT IN OUR HEADS...
YOU DON'T HAVE TO...
IT'S OKAY.
GREAT! WELL, I WAS JUST ON MY WAY OUT OF DALLAS--I FANCIED A CHANGE OF DIET MORE THAN ANY-THING ELSE...
I BET YOU DID.
I'D TIMED IT TO PERFECTION--WHICH, AS YOU KNOW, JESSE, ISN'T LIKE ME AT ALL --AND HE SHOWED UP JUST LIKE THEY TOLD ME HE WOULD...
WERE YOU SCARED?
HELL NO.
BAR
OH, SHIT...

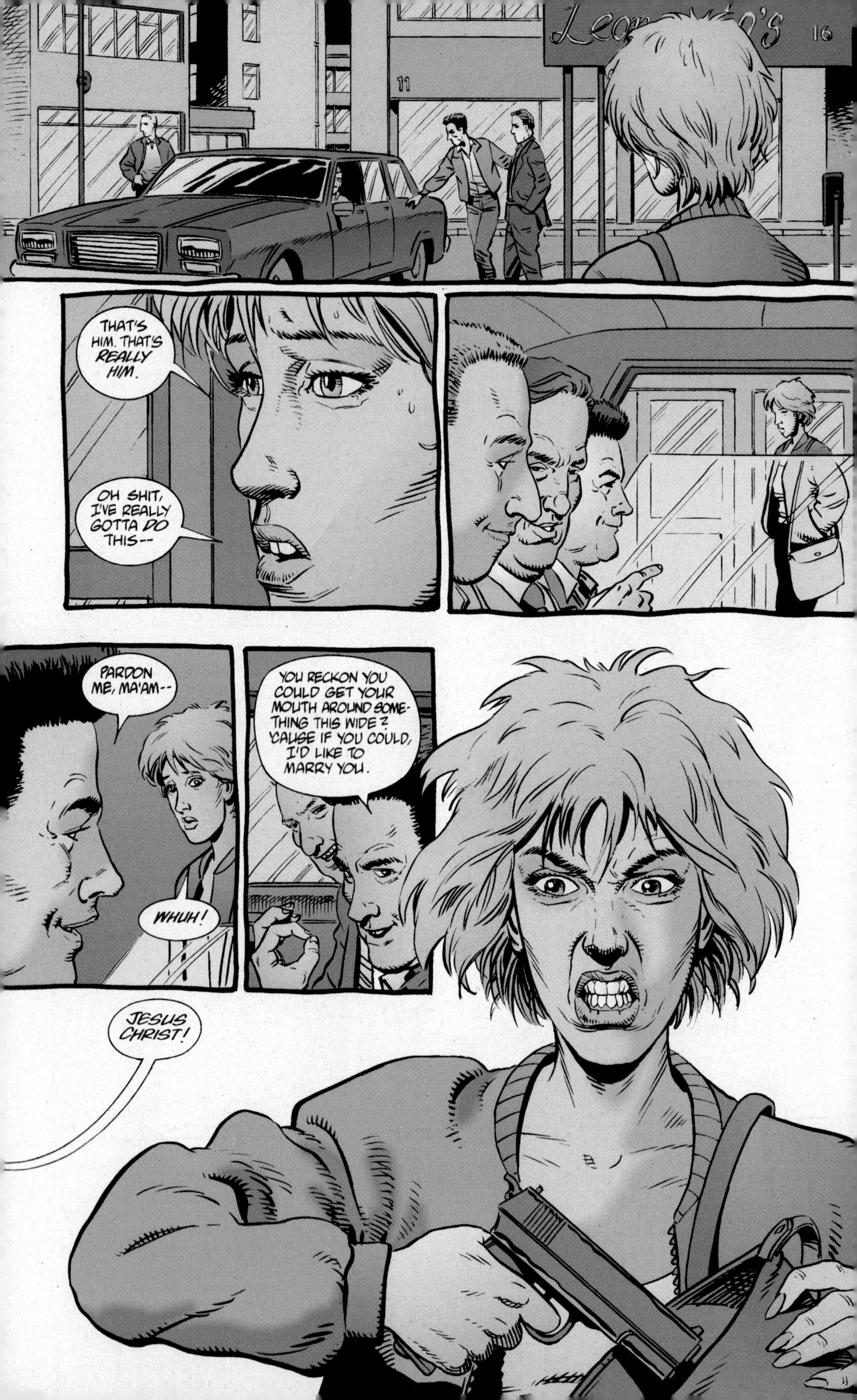
THAT'S HIM. THAT'S REALLY HIM.
OH SHIT, I'VE REALLY GOTTA DO THIS--
PARDON ME, MA'AM--
WHUH!
YOU RECKON YOU COULD GET YOUR MOUTH AROUND SOME-THING THIS WIDE? 'CAUSE IF YOU COULD, I'D LIKE TO MARRY YOU.
JESUS CHRIST!

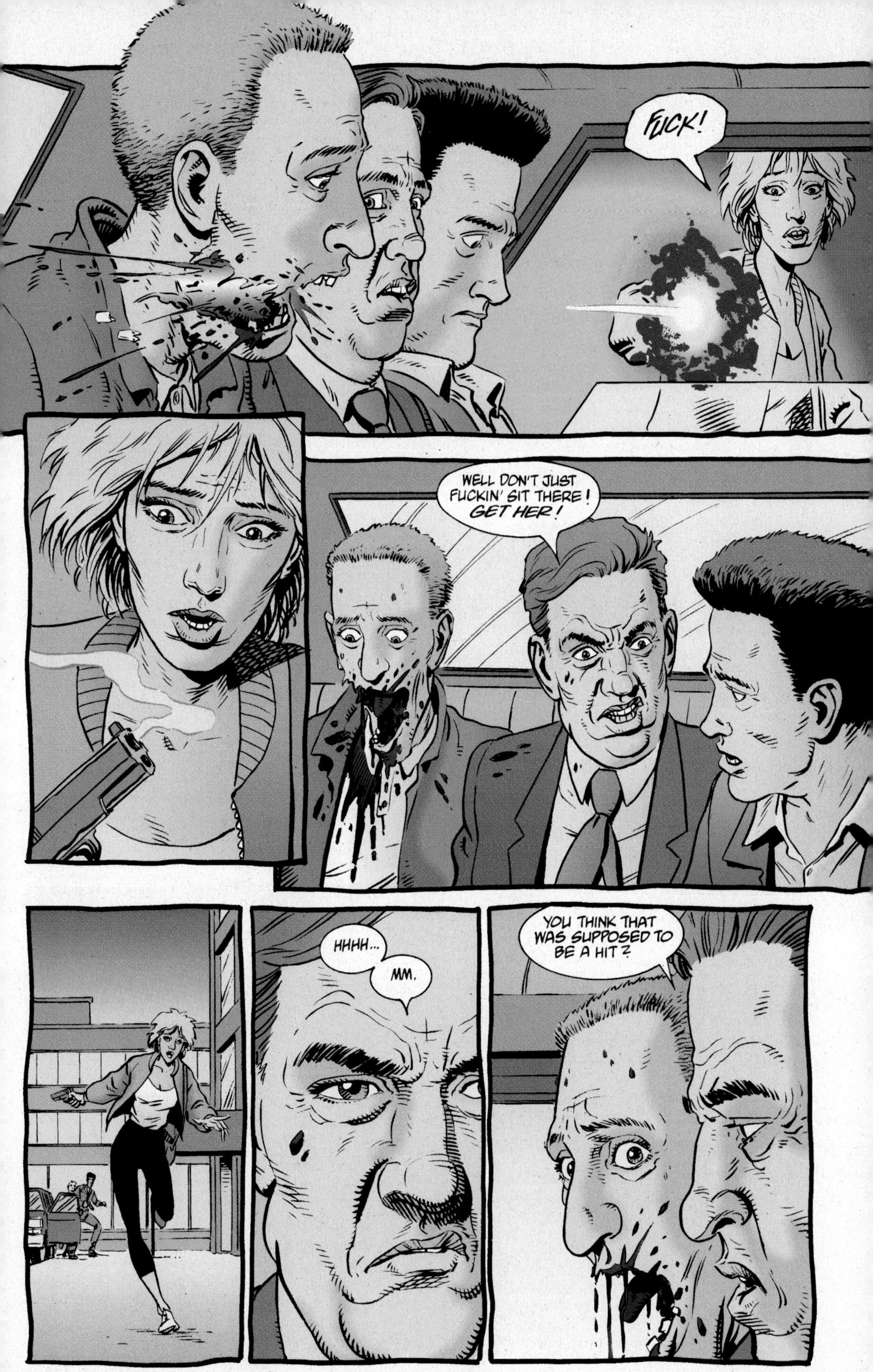
FUCK!
WELL DON'T JUST FUCKIN' SIT THERE! GET HER!
HHHH...
MM.
YOU THINK THAT WAS SUPPOSED TO BE A HIT?

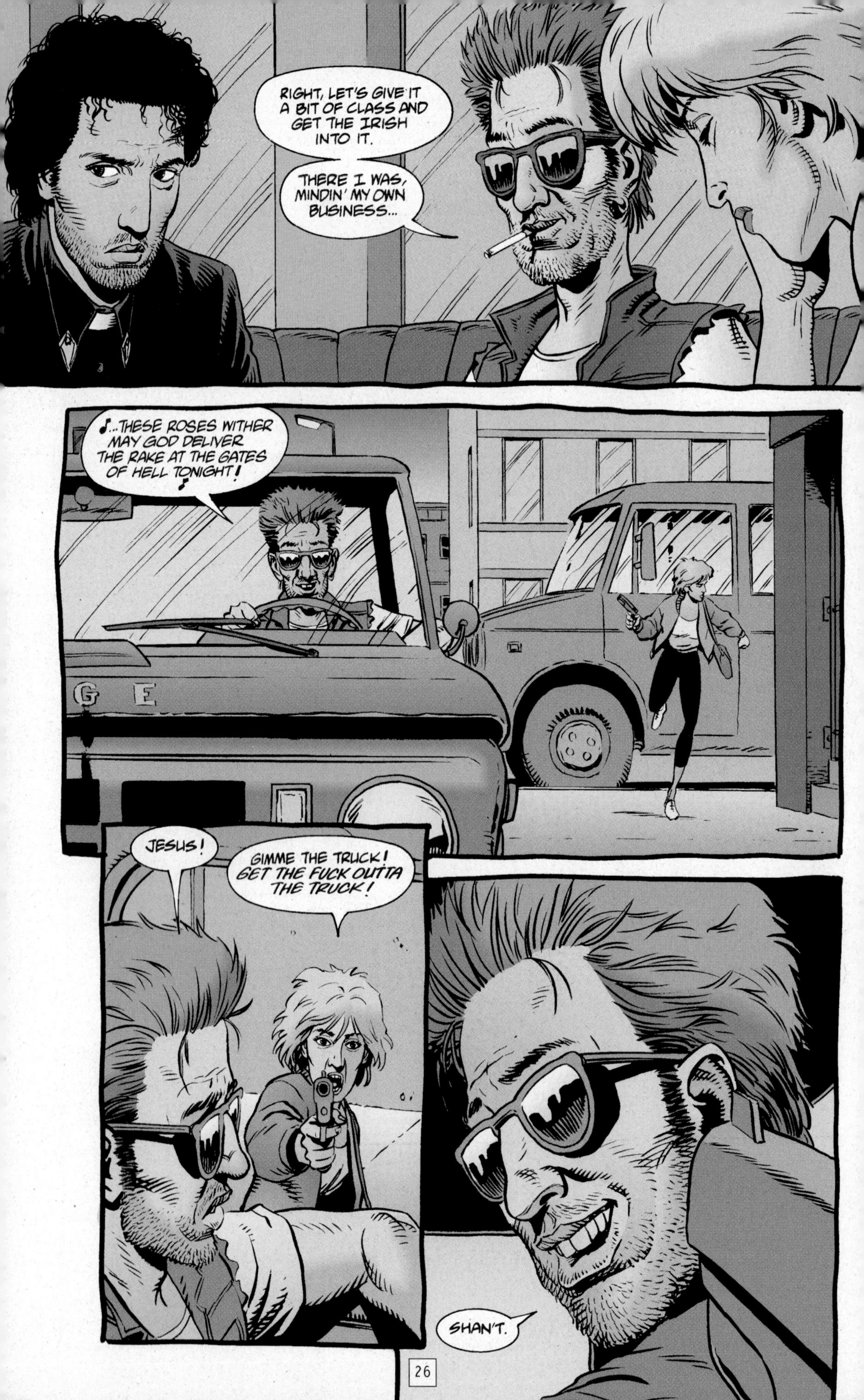
RIGHT, LET'S GIVE IT A BIT OF CLASS AND GET THE IRISH INTO IT.
THERE I WAS, MINDIN' MY OWN BUSINESS...
♪...THESE ROSES WITHER MAY GOD DELIVER THE RAKE AT THE GATES OF HELL TONIGHT! ♪
G E
JESUS!
GIMME THE TRUCK! GET THE FUCK OUTTA THE TRUCK!
SHAN'T.

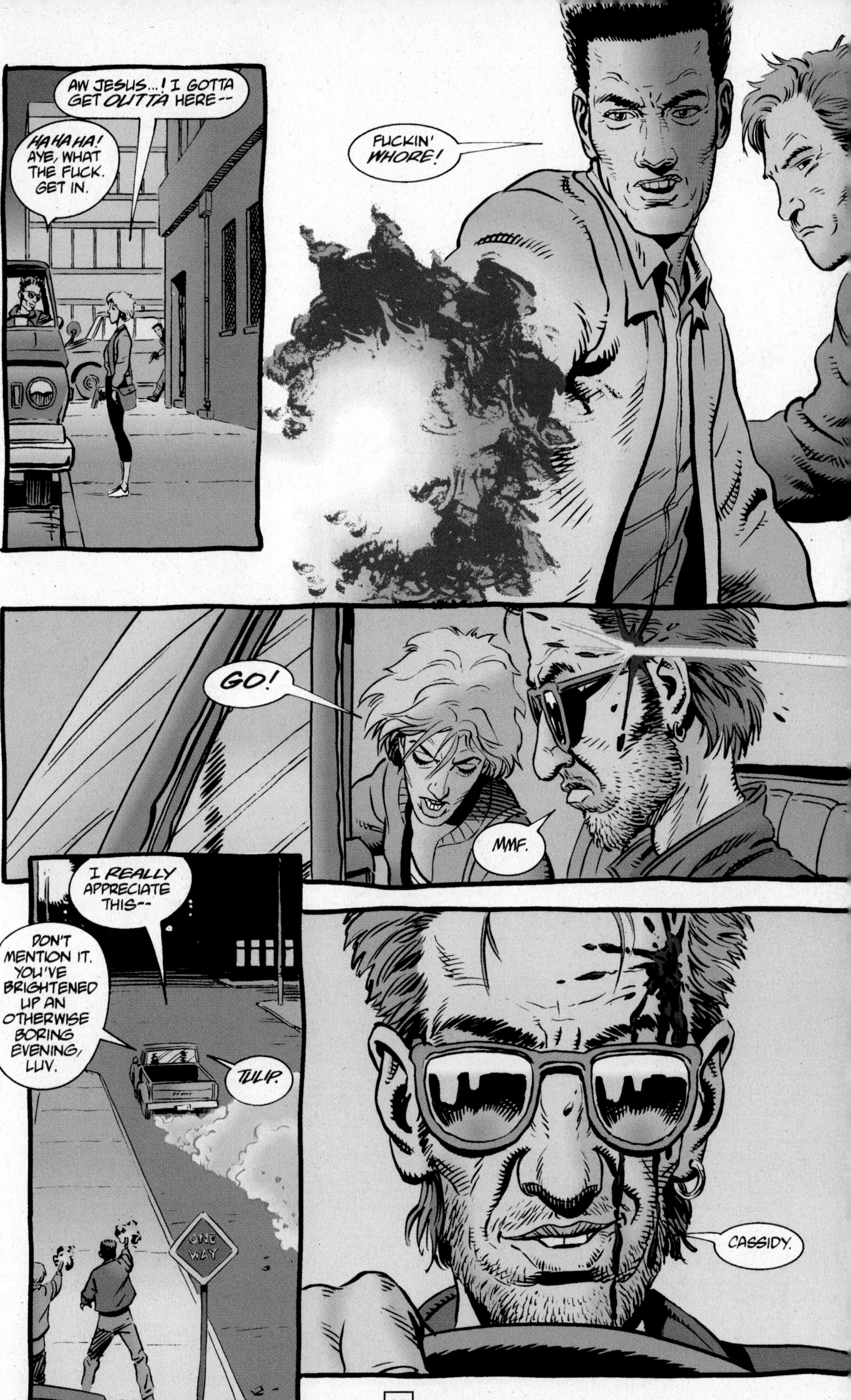
AW JESUS...! I GOTTA GET OUTTA HERE--
HAHAHA! AYE, WHAT THE FUCK. GET IN.
FUCKIN' WHORE!
GO!
MMF.
I REALLY APPRECIATE THIS--
DON'T MENTION IT. YOU'VE BRIGHTENED UP AN OTHERWISE BORING EVENING, LUV.
TULIP.
CASSIDY.
ONE WAY

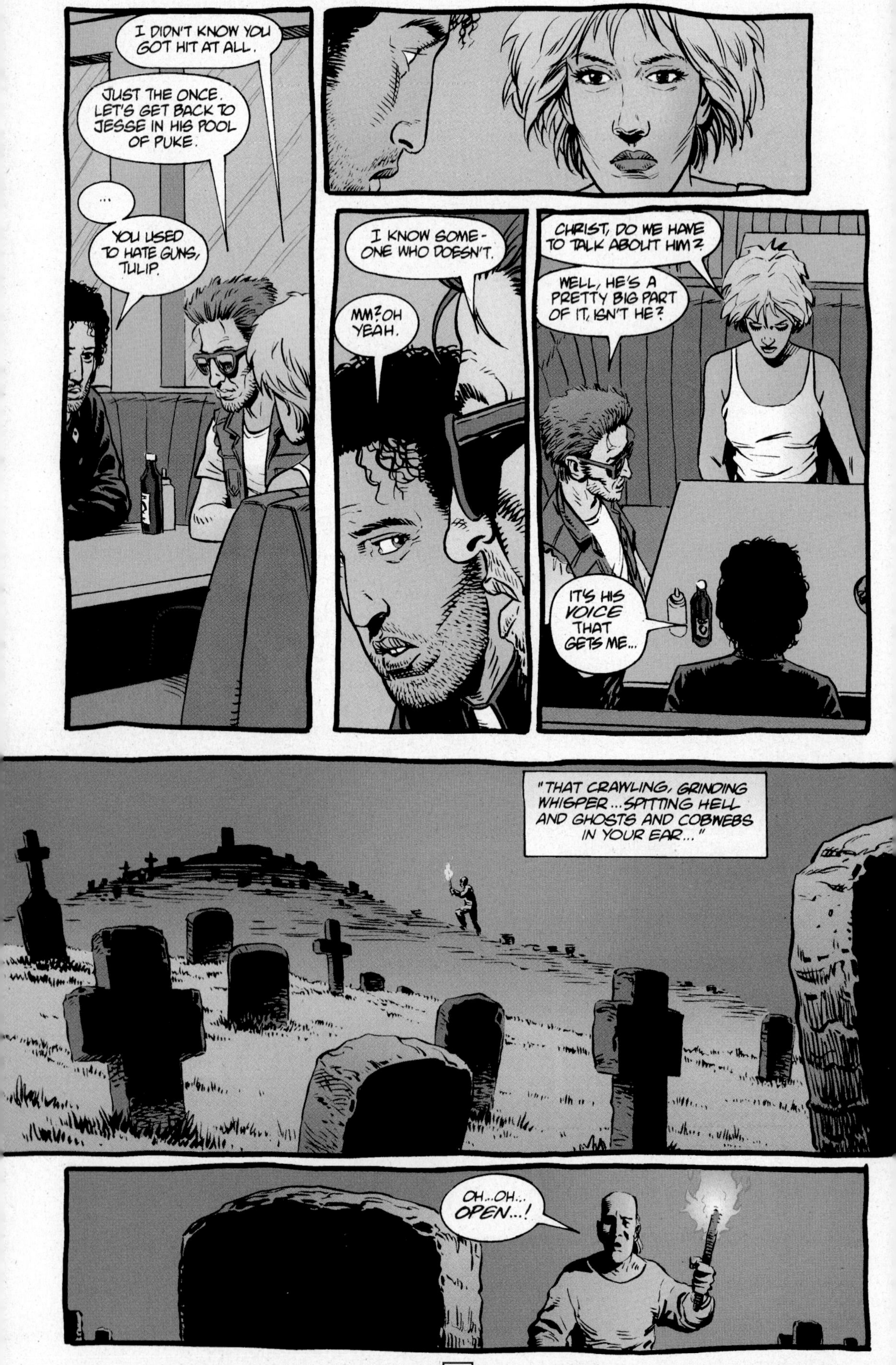

I DIDN'T KNOW YOU GOT HIT AT ALL.
JUST THE ONCE. LET'S GET BACK TO JESSE IN HIS POOL OF PUKE.
...
YOU USED TO HATE GUNS, TULIP.
I KNOW SOME-ONE WHO DOESN'T.
MM? OH YEAH.
CHRIST, DO WE HAVE TO TALK ABOUT HIM?
WELL, HE'S A PRETTY BIG PART OF IT, ISN'T HE?
IT'S HIS VOICE THAT GETS ME...
"THAT CRAWLING, GRINDING WHISPER... SPITTING HELL AND GHOSTS AND COBWEBS IN YOUR EAR..."
OH...OH... OPEN...!

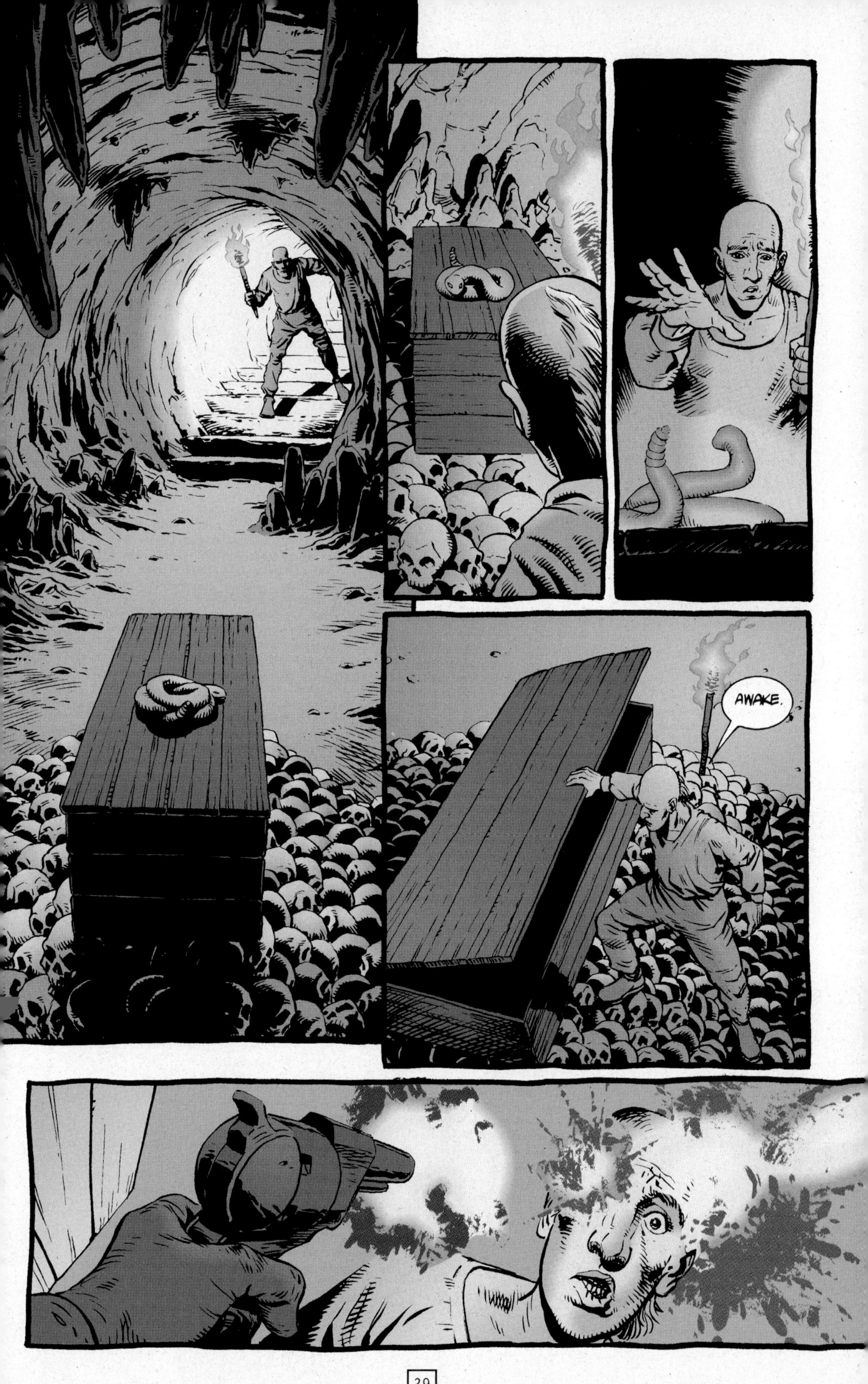
AWAKE.

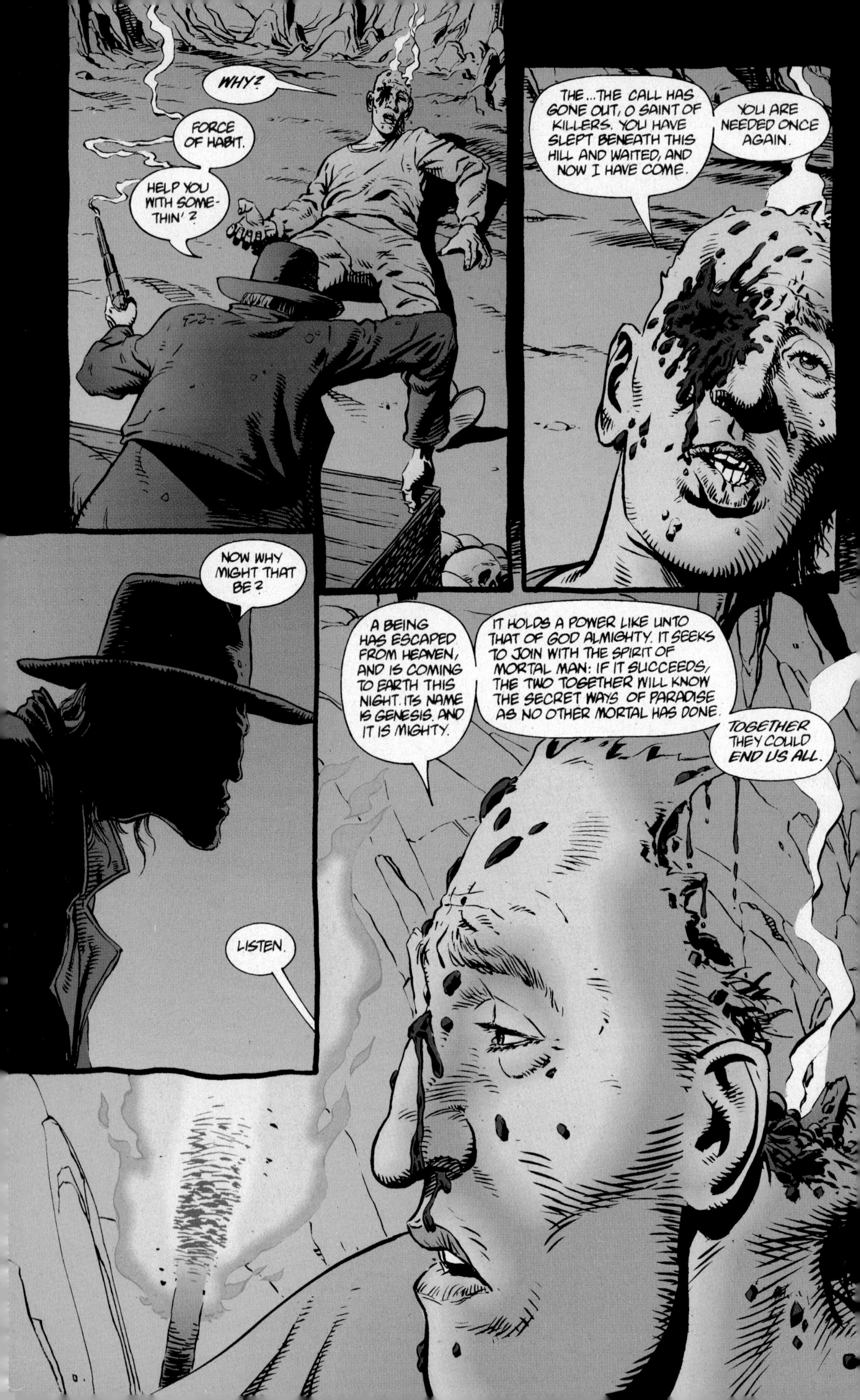
WHY?
FORCE OF HABIT.
HELP YOU WITH SOME-THIN'?
THE...THE CALL HAS GONE OUT, O SAINT OF KILLERS. YOU HAVE SLEPT BENEATH THIS HILL AND WAITED, AND NOW I HAVE COME.
YOU ARE NEEDED ONCE AGAIN.
NOW WHY MIGHT THAT BE?
A BEING HAS ESCAPED FROM HEAVEN, AND IS COMING TO EARTH THIS NIGHT. ITS NAME IS GENESIS. AND IT IS MIGHTY.
IT HOLDS A POWER LIKE UNTO THAT OF GOD ALMIGHTY. IT SEEKS TO JOIN WITH THE SPIRIT OF MORTAL MAN: IF IT SUCCEEDS, THE TWO TOGETHER WILL KNOW THE SECRET WAYS OF PARADISE AS NO OTHER MORTAL HAS DONE.
TOGETHER THEY COULD END US ALL.
LISTEN.

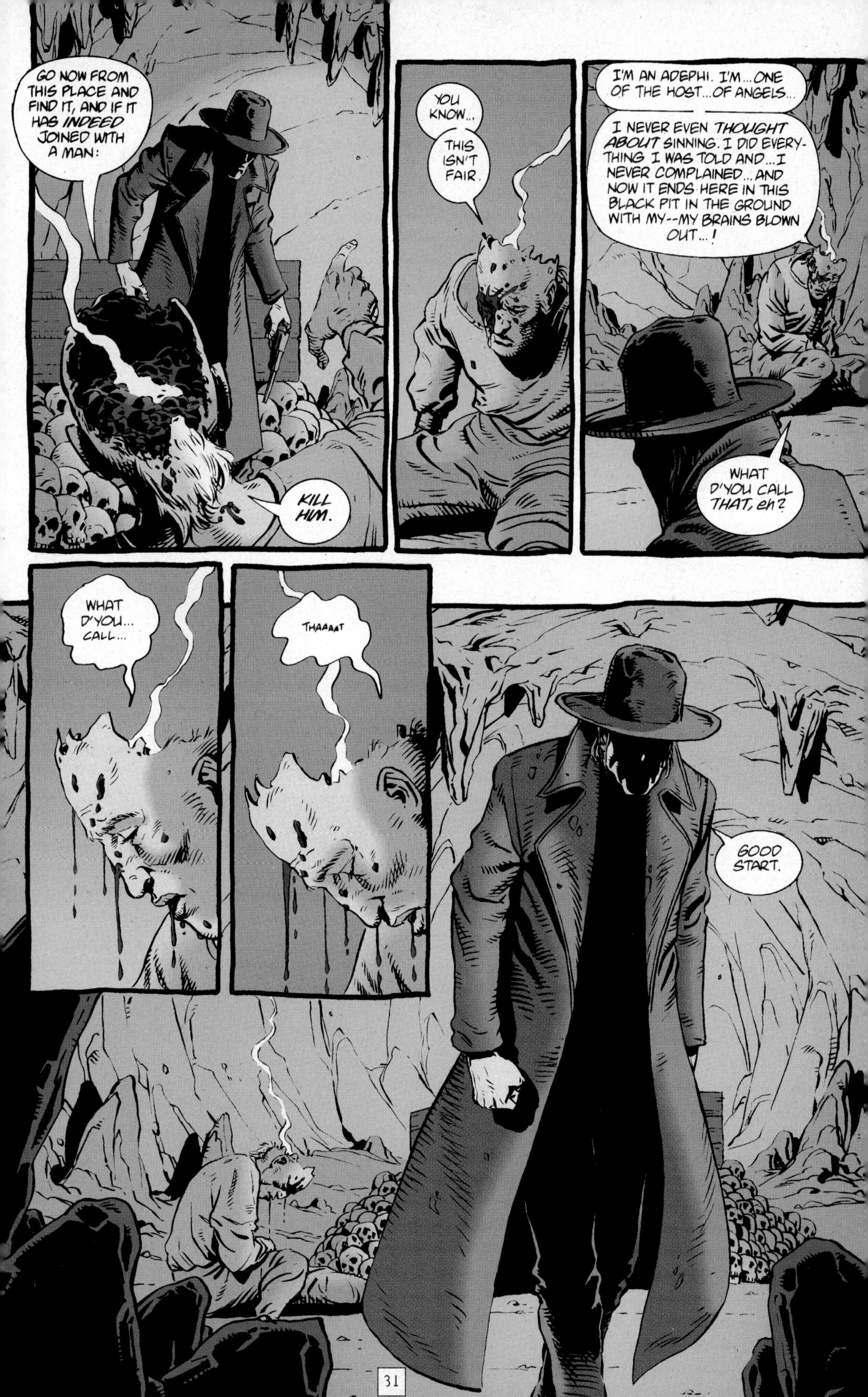
GO NOW FROM THIS PLACE AND FIND IT, AND IF IT HAS *INDEED* JOINED WITH A MAN:
KILL HIM.
YOU KNOW...
THIS ISN'T FAIR.
I'M AN ADEPHI. I'M...ONE OF THE HOST...OF ANGELS...
I NEVER EVEN *THOUGHT ABOUT* SINNING. I DID EVERYTHING I WAS TOLD AND...I NEVER COMPLAINED...AND NOW IT ENDS HERE IN THIS BLACK PIT IN THE GROUND WITH MY--MY BRAINS BLOWN OUT...!
WHAT D'YOU CALL *THAT*, eh?
WHAT D'YOU... CALL...
THAAAAT
GOOD START.

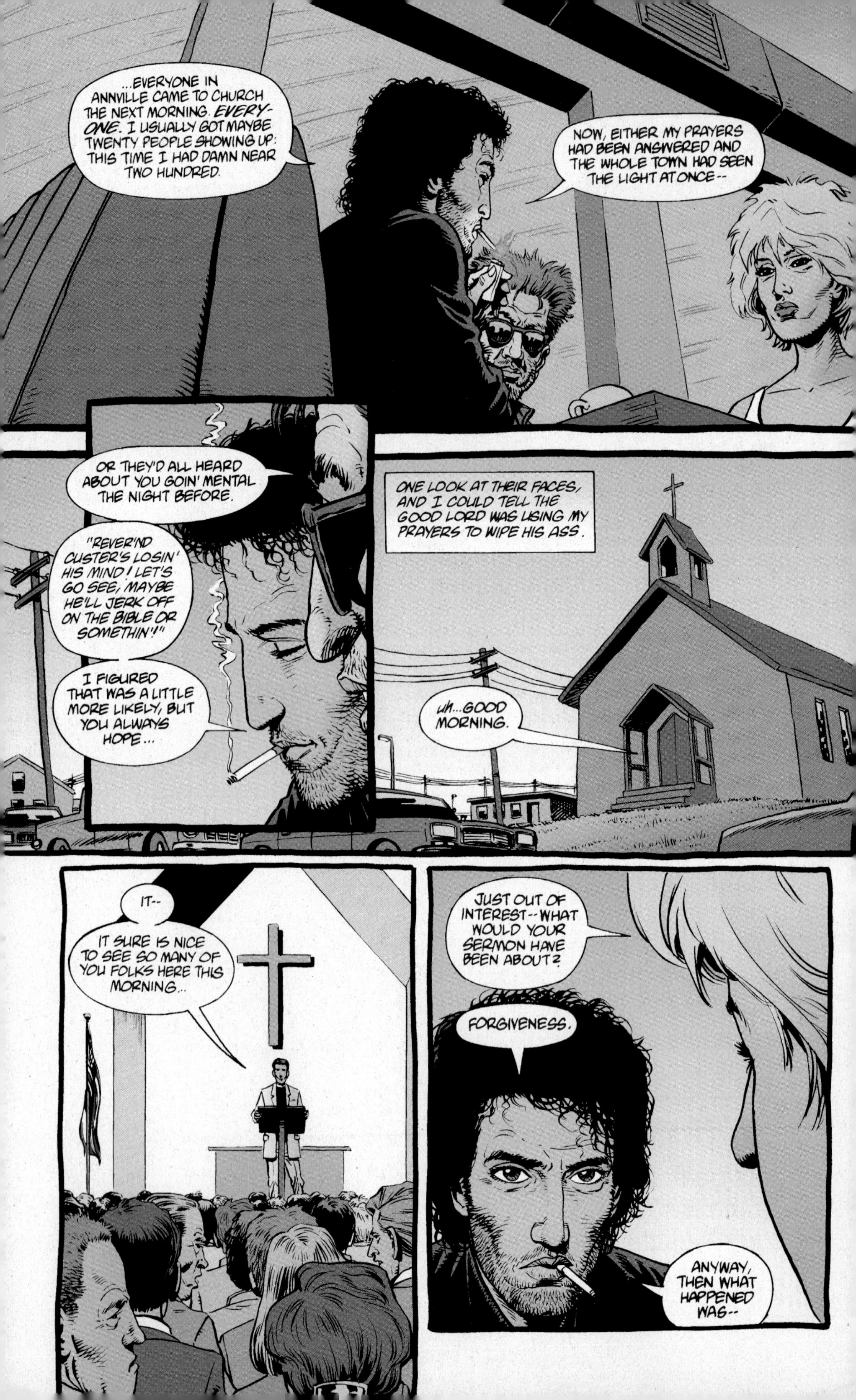
...EVERYONE IN ANNVILLE CAME TO CHURCH THE NEXT MORNING. EVERY-ONE. I USUALLY GOT MAYBE TWENTY PEOPLE SHOWING UP: THIS TIME I HAD DAMN NEAR TWO HUNDRED.
NOW, EITHER MY PRAYERS HAD BEEN ANSWERED AND THE WHOLE TOWN HAD SEEN THE LIGHT AT ONCE--
OR THEY'D ALL HEARD ABOUT YOU GOIN' MENTAL THE NIGHT BEFORE.
"REVER'ND CUSTER'S LOSIN' HIS MIND! LET'S GO SEE; MAYBE HE'LL JERK OFF ON THE BIBLE OR SOMETHIN'!"
I FIGURED THAT WAS A LITTLE MORE LIKELY, BUT YOU ALWAYS HOPE...
ONE LOOK AT THEIR FACES, AND I COULD TELL THE GOOD LORD WAS USING MY PRAYERS TO WIPE HIS ASS.
uh...GOOD MORNING.
IT--
IT SURE IS NICE TO SEE SO MANY OF YOU FOLKS HERE THIS MORNING...
JUST OUT OF INTEREST--WHAT WOULD YOUR SERMON HAVE BEEN ABOUT?
FORGIVENESS.
ANYWAY, THEN WHAT HAPPENED WAS--

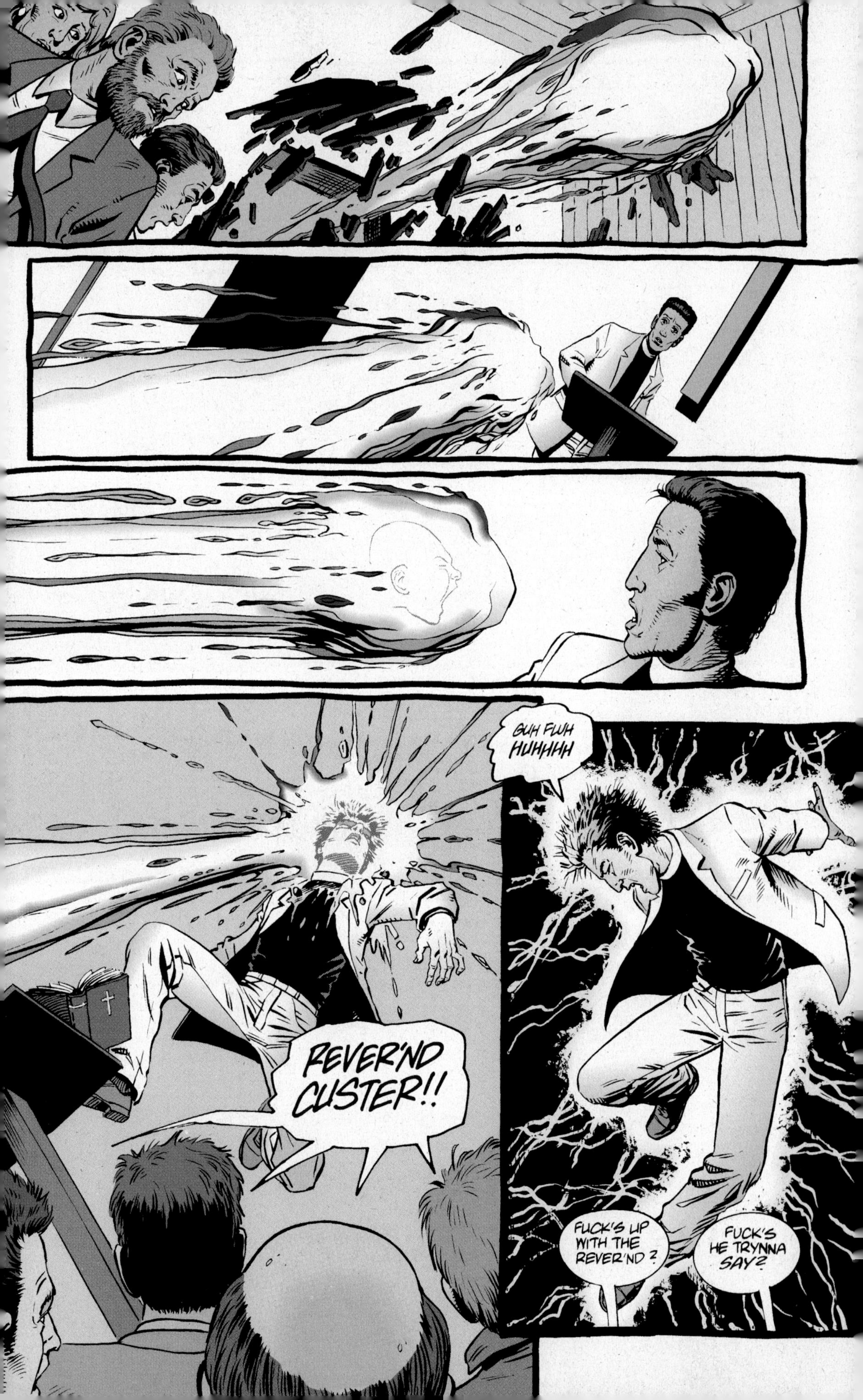
REVER'ND CUSTER!!
GUH FLUH HUHHHH
FUCK'S UP WITH THE REVER'ND ?
FUCK'S HE TRYNNA SAY?

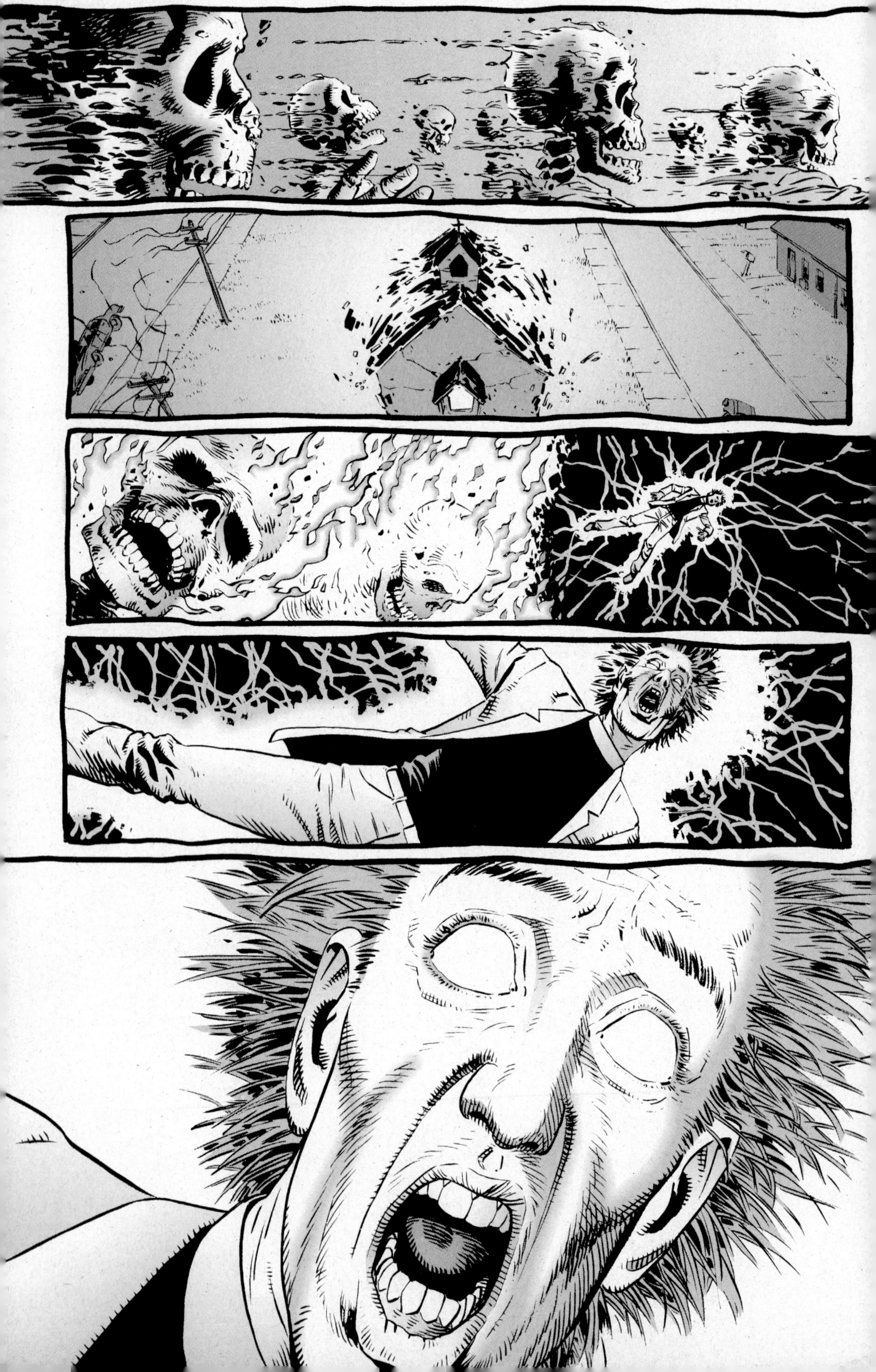

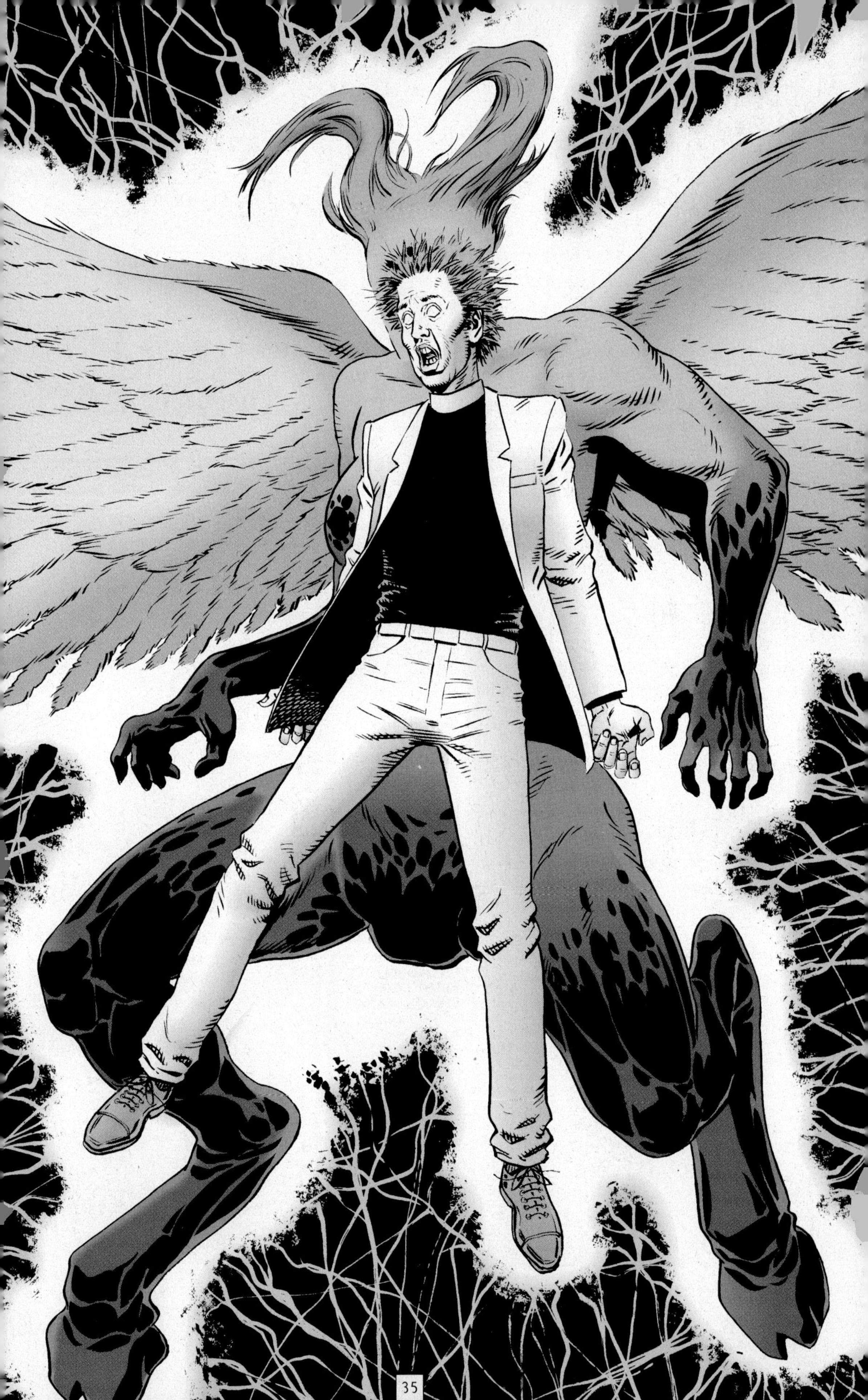

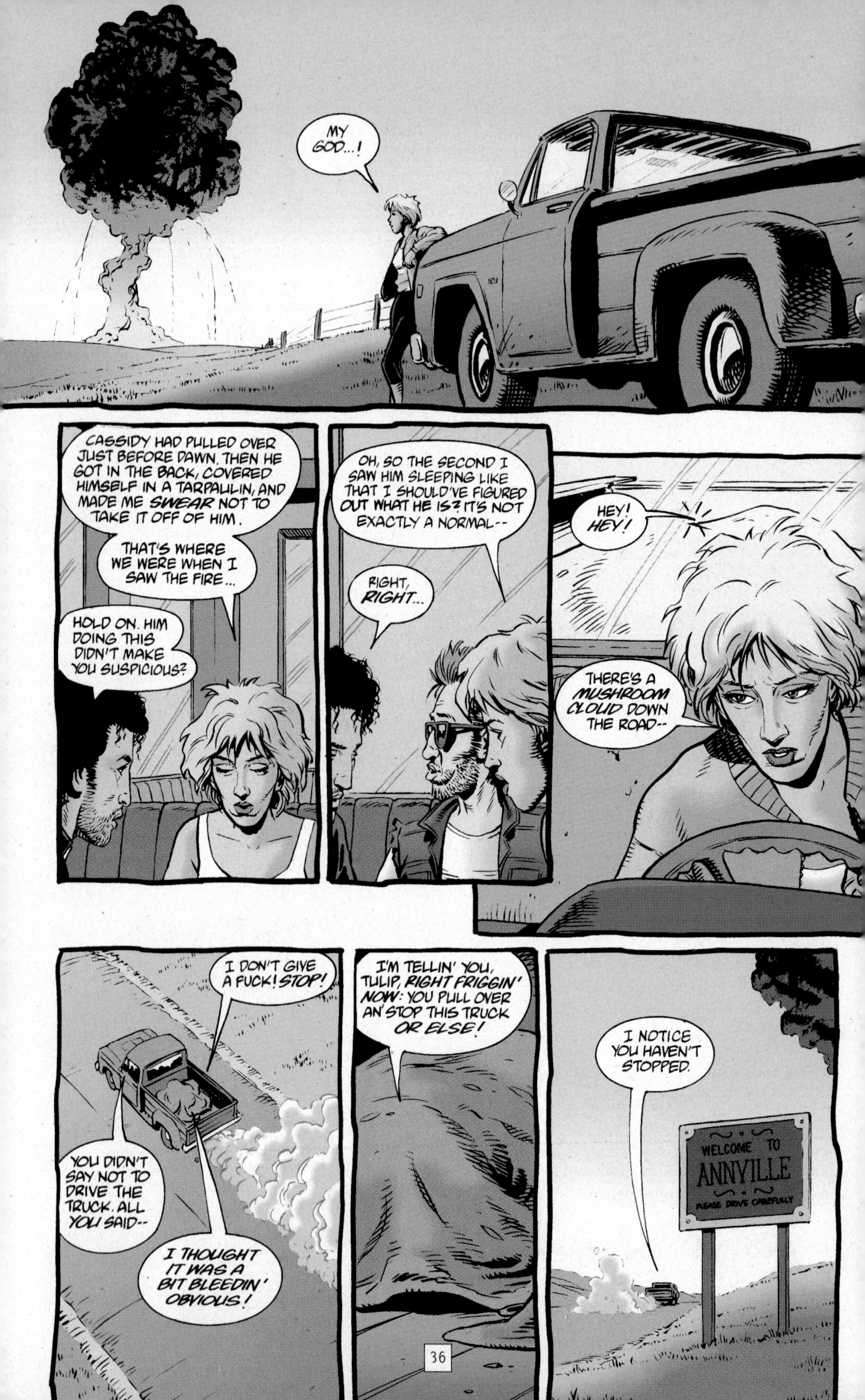

MY GOD...!
CASSIDY HAD PULLED OVER JUST BEFORE DAWN. THEN HE GOT IN THE BACK, COVERED HIMSELF IN A TARPAULIN, AND MADE ME SWEAR NOT TO TAKE IT OFF OF HIM.
THAT'S WHERE WE WERE WHEN I SAW THE FIRE...
HOLD ON. HIM DOING THIS DIDN'T MAKE YOU SUSPICIOUS?
OH, SO THE SECOND I SAW HIM SLEEPING LIKE THAT I SHOULD'VE FIGURED OUT WHAT HE IS? IT'S NOT EXACTLY A NORMAL--
RIGHT, RIGHT...
HEY! HEY!
THERE'S A MUSHROOM CLOUD DOWN THE ROAD--
I DON'T GIVE A FUCK! STOP!
YOU DIDN'T SAY NOT TO DRIVE THE TRUCK. ALL YOU SAID--
I THOUGHT IT WAS A BIT BLEEDIN' OBVIOUS!
I'M TELLIN' YOU, TULIP, RIGHT FRIGGIN' NOW: YOU PULL OVER AN' STOP THIS TRUCK OR ELSE!
I NOTICE YOU HAVEN'T STOPPED.
WELCOME TO
ANNVILLE
PLEASE DRIVE CAREFULLY

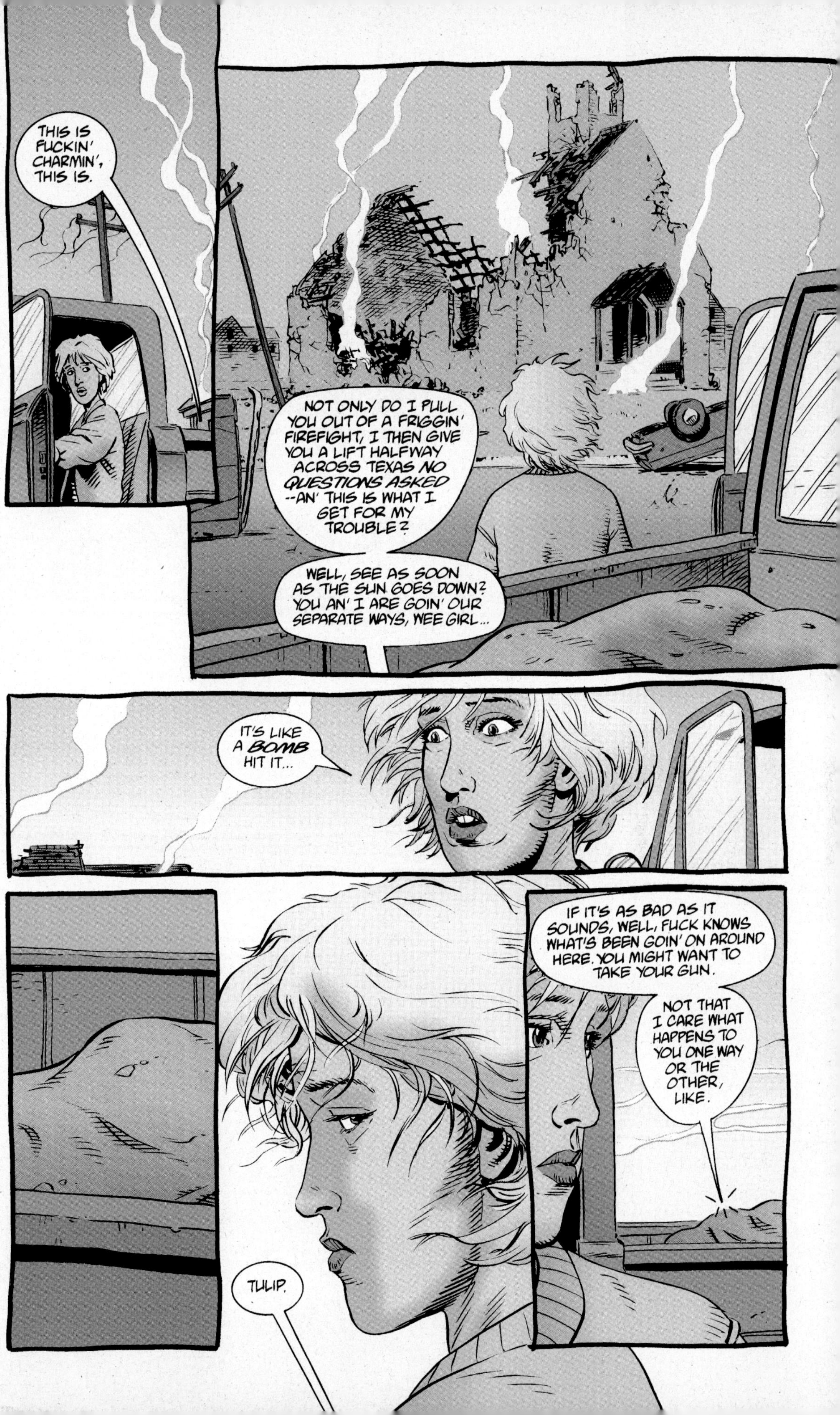
THIS IS FUCKIN' CHARMIN', THIS IS.
NOT ONLY DO I PULL YOU OUT OF A FRIGGIN' FIREFIGHT, I THEN GIVE YOU A LIFT HALFWAY ACROSS TEXAS NO QUESTIONS ASKED --AN' THIS IS WHAT I GET FOR MY TROUBLE?
WELL, SEE AS SOON AS THE SUN GOES DOWN? YOU AN' I ARE GOIN' OUR SEPARATE WAYS, WEE GIRL...
IT'S LIKE A BOMB HIT IT...
IF IT'S AS BAD AS IT SOUNDS, WELL, FUCK KNOWS WHAT'S BEEN GOIN' ON AROUND HERE. YOU MIGHT WANT TO TAKE YOUR GUN.
NOT THAT I CARE WHAT HAPPENS TO YOU ONE WAY OR THE OTHER, LIKE.
TULIP.

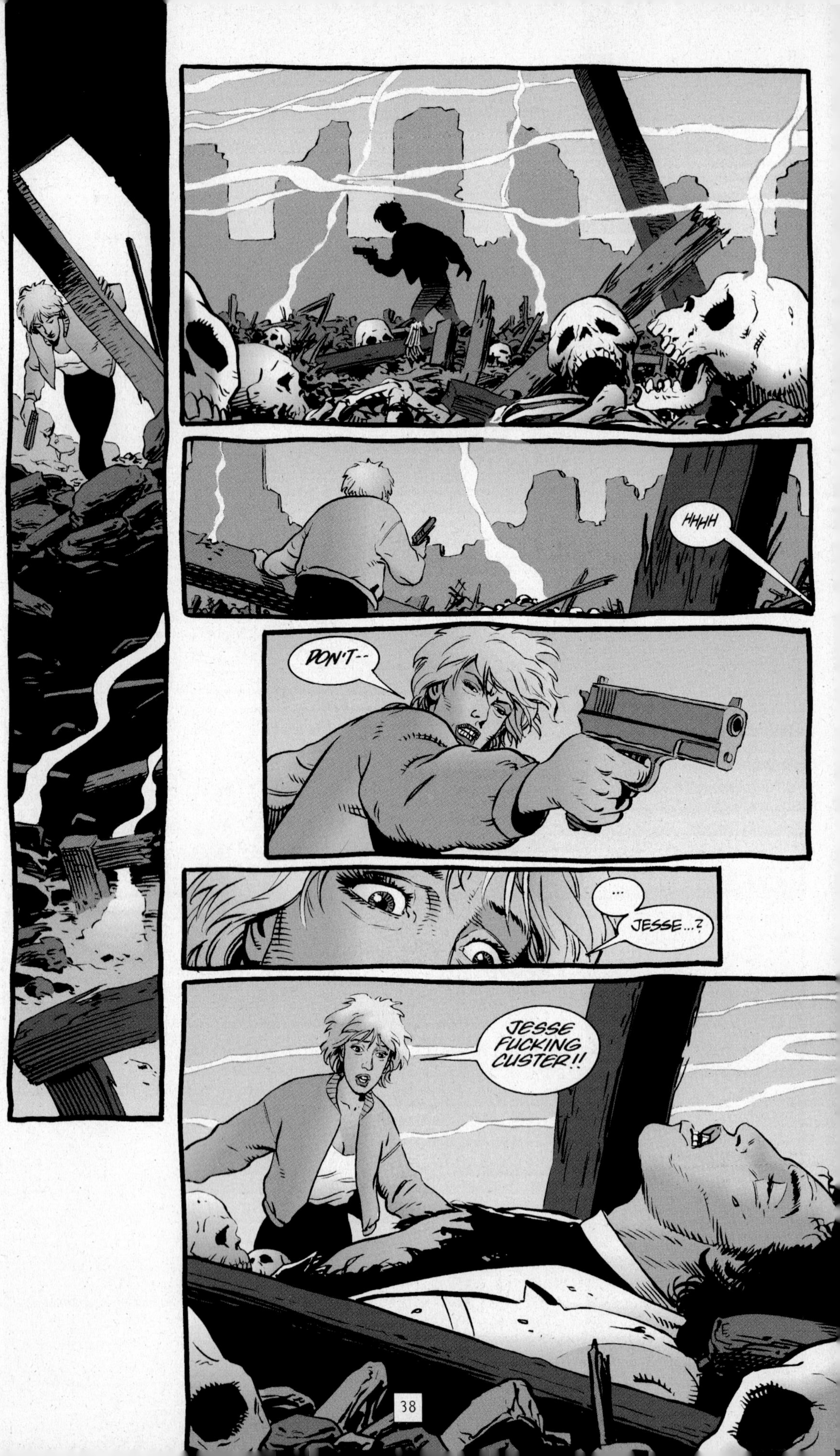
HHHH
DON'T--
...
JESSE...?
JESSE FUCKING CUSTER!!

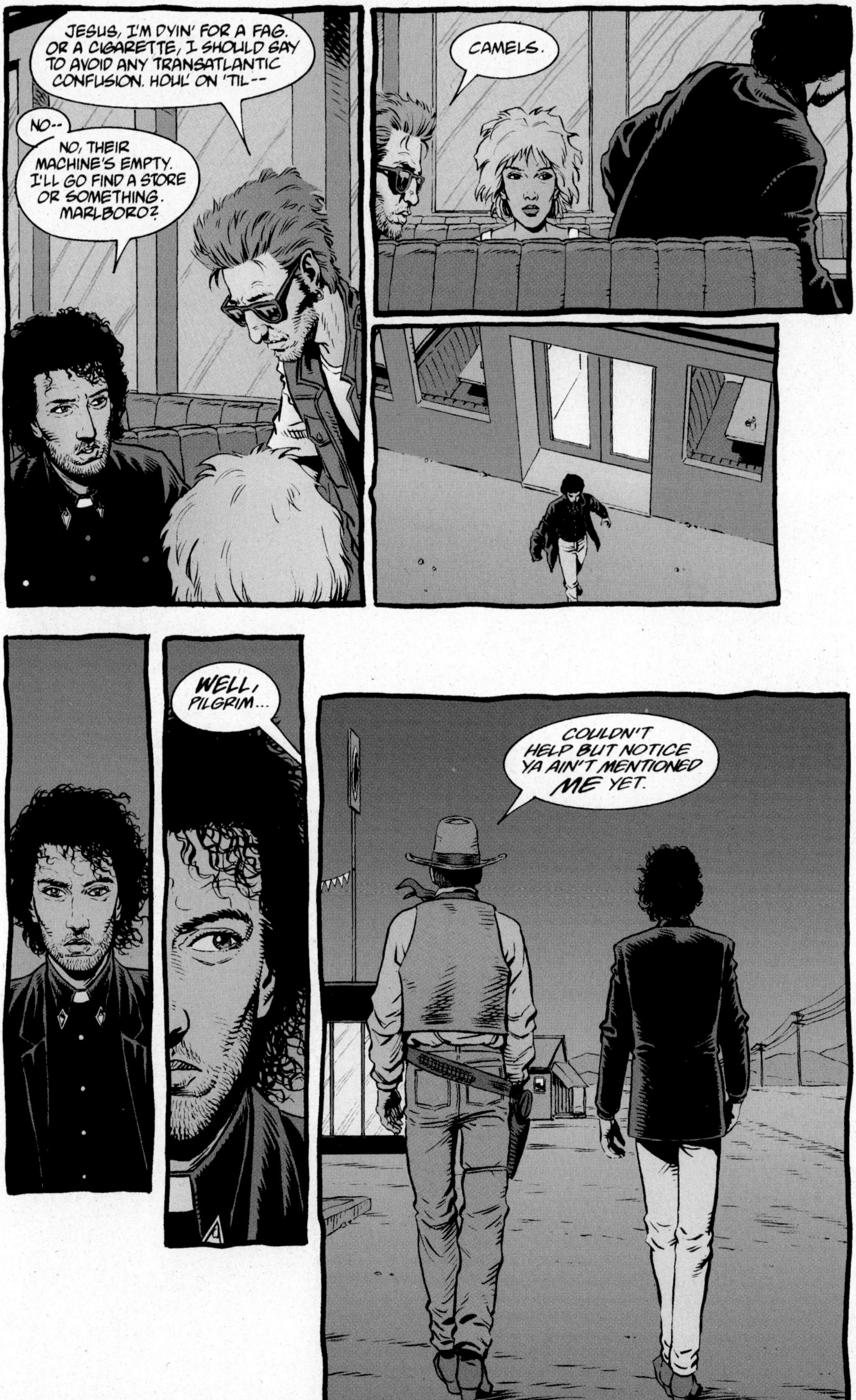
JESUS, I'M DYIN' FOR A FAG. OR A CIGARETTE, I SHOULD SAY TO AVOID ANY TRANSATLANTIC CONFUSION. HOUL' ON 'TIL--
NO--
NO, THEIR MACHINE'S EMPTY. I'LL GO FIND A STORE OR SOMETHING. MARLBORO?
CAMELS.
WELL, PILGRIM...
COULDN'T HELP BUT NOTICE YA AIN'T MENTIONED ME YET.

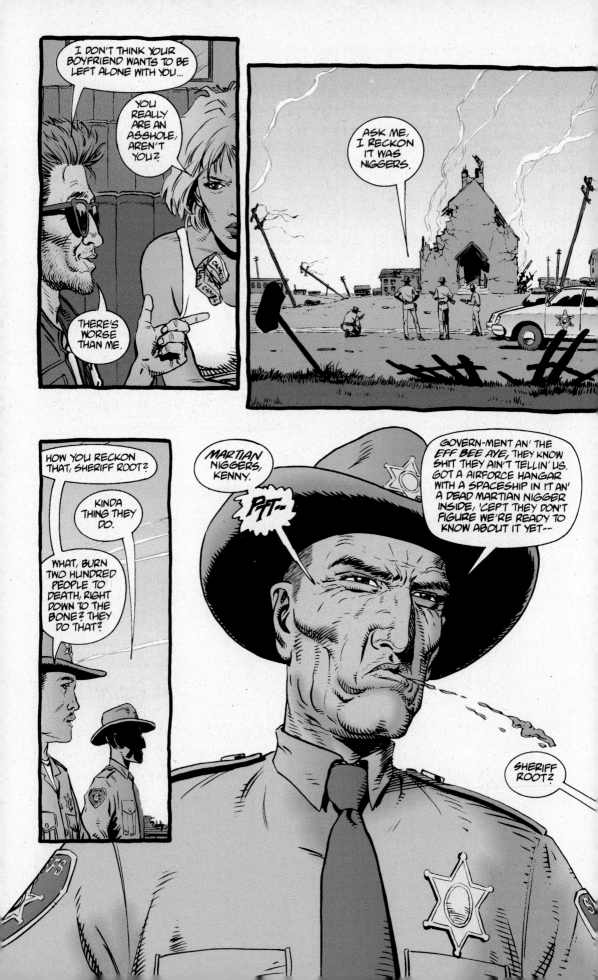

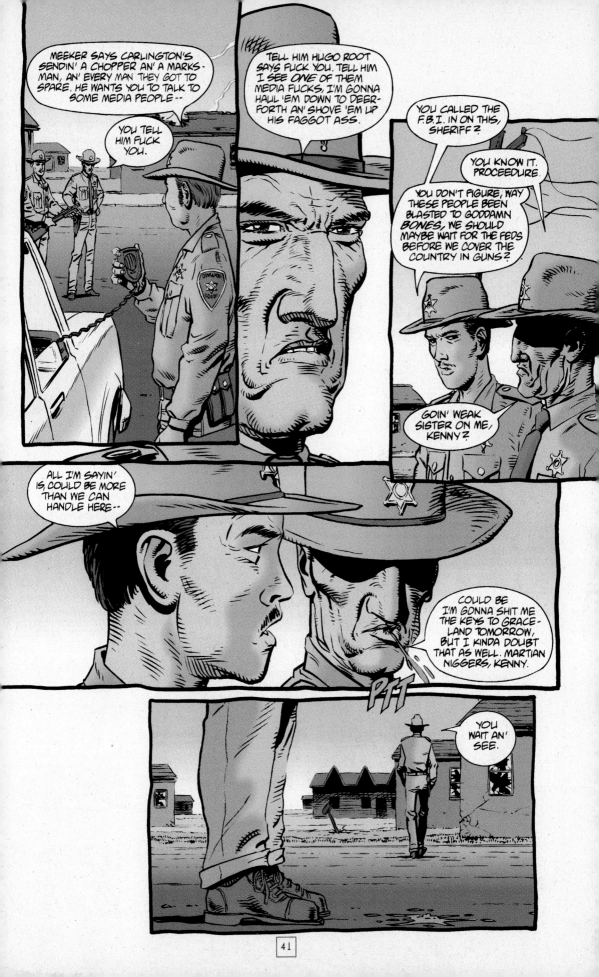

MEEKER SAYS CARLINGTON'S SENDIN' A CHOPPER AN' A MARKS-MAN, AN' EVERY MAN THEY GOT TO SPARE. HE WANTS YOU TO TALK TO SOME MEDIA PEOPLE--

YOU TELL HIM FUCK YOU.

TELL HIM HUGO ROOT SAYS FUCK YOU. TELL HIM I SEE ONE OF THEM MEDIA FUCKS, I'M GONNA HAUL 'EM DOWN TO DEER-FORTH AN' SHOVE 'EM UP HIS FAGGOT ASS.

YOU CALLED THE F.B.I. IN ON THIS, SHERIFF?

YOU KNOW IT. PROCEEDURE.

YOU DON'T FIGURE, WAY THESE PEOPLE BEEN BLASTED TO GODDAMN BONES, WE SHOULD MAYBE WAIT FOR THE FEDS BEFORE WE COVER THE COUNTRY IN GUNS?

GOIN' WEAK SISTER ON ME, KENNY?

ALL I'M SAYIN' IS, COULD BE MORE THAN WE CAN HANDLE HERE--

COULD BE I'M GONNA SHIT ME THE KEYS TO GRACE-LAND TOMORROW, BUT I KINDA DOUBT THAT AS WELL. MARTIAN NIGGERS, KENNY.

PTT

YOU WAIT AN' SEE.

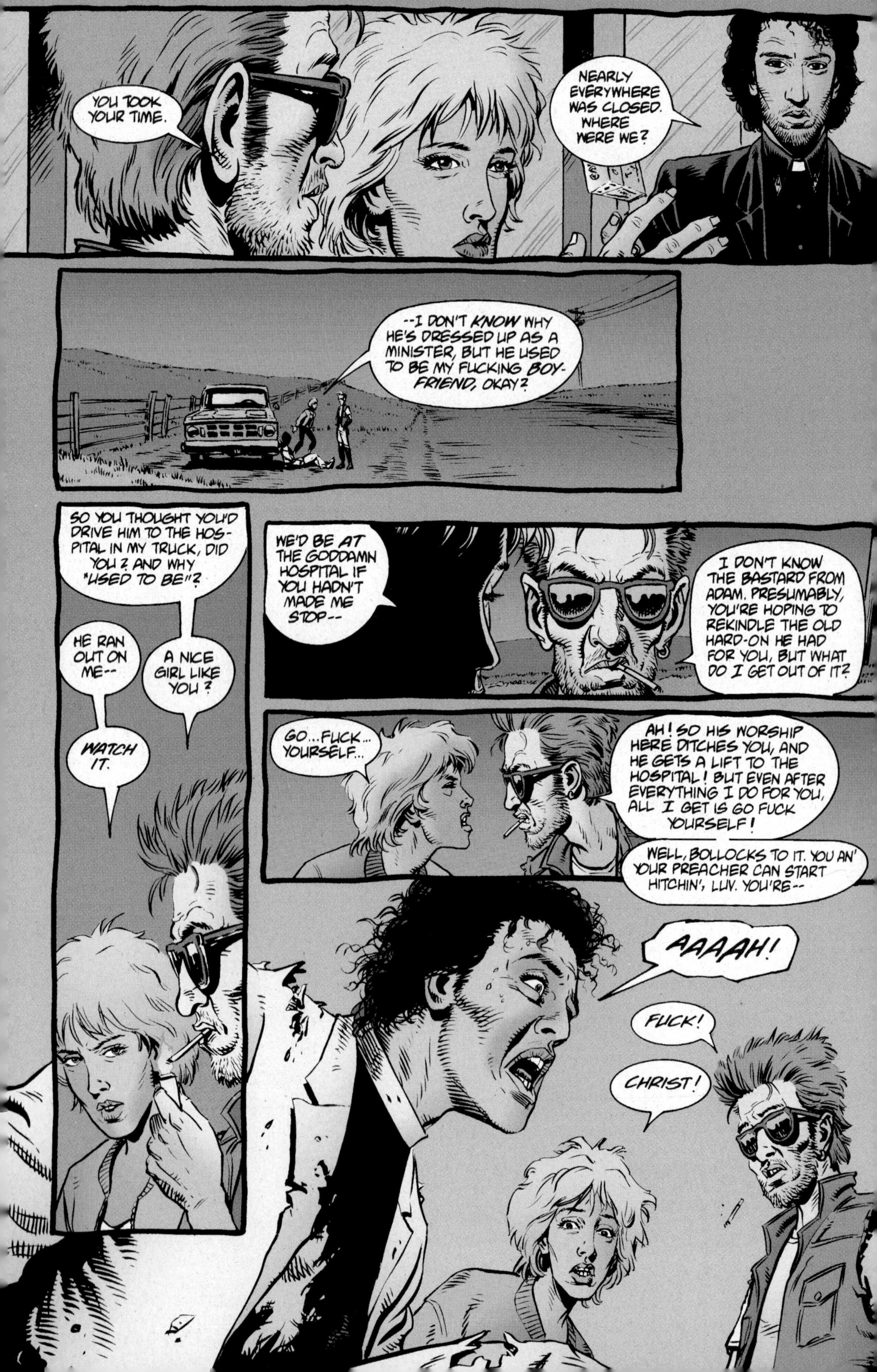
YOU TOOK YOUR TIME.
NEARLY EVERYWHERE WAS CLOSED. WHERE WERE WE?
--I DON'T KNOW WHY HE'S DRESSED UP AS A MINISTER, BUT HE USED TO BE MY FUCKING BOY-FRIEND, OKAY?
SO YOU THOUGHT YOU'D DRIVE HIM TO THE HOS-PITAL IN MY TRUCK, DID YOU? AND WHY "USED TO BE"?
HE RAN OUT ON ME--
A NICE GIRL LIKE YOU?
WATCH IT.
WE'D BE AT THE GODDAMN HOSPITAL IF YOU HADN'T MADE ME STOP--
I DON'T KNOW THE BASTARD FROM ADAM. PRESUMABLY, YOU'RE HOPING TO REKINDLE THE OLD HARD-ON HE HAD FOR YOU, BUT WHAT DO I GET OUT OF IT?
GO...FUCK... YOURSELF...
AH! SO HIS WORSHIP HERE DITCHES YOU, AND HE GETS A LIFT TO THE HOSPITAL! BUT EVEN AFTER EVERYTHING I DO FOR YOU, ALL I GET IS GO FUCK YOURSELF!
WELL, BOLLOCKS TO IT. YOU AN' YOUR PREACHER CAN START HITCHIN', LUV. YOU'RE--
AAAAH!
FUCK!
CHRIST!

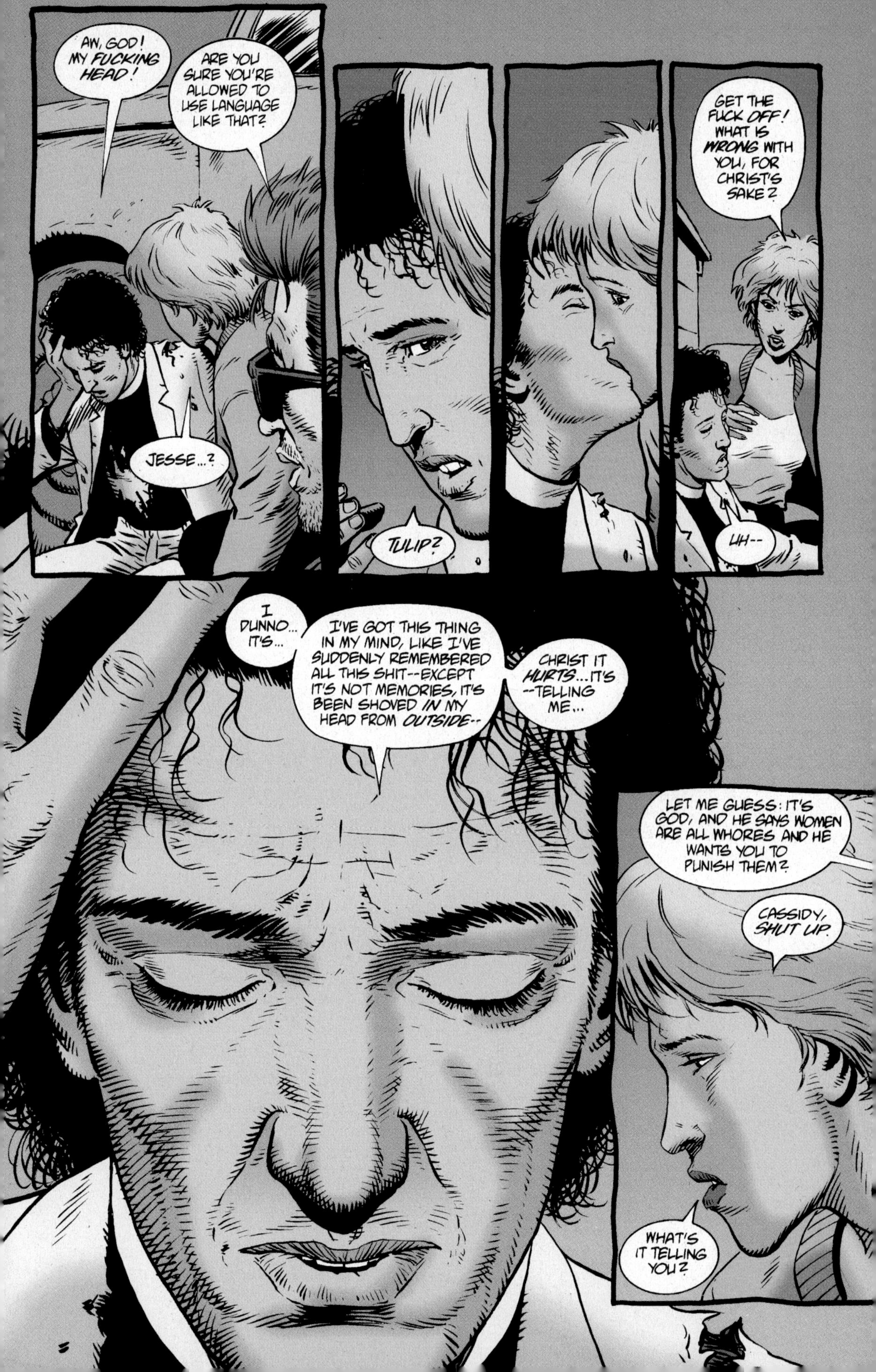
AW, GOD! MY FUCKING HEAD!
ARE YOU SURE YOU'RE ALLOWED TO USE LANGUAGE LIKE THAT?
JESSE...?
TULIP?
GET THE FUCK OFF! WHAT IS WRONG WITH YOU, FOR CHRIST'S SAKE?
UH--
I DUNNO... IT'S...
I'VE GOT THIS THING IN MY MIND, LIKE I'VE SUDDENLY REMEMBERED ALL THIS SHIT--EXCEPT IT'S NOT MEMORIES, IT'S BEEN SHOVED IN MY HEAD FROM OUTSIDE--
CHRIST IT HURTS... IT'S --TELLING ME...
LET ME GUESS: IT'S GOD, AND HE SAYS WOMEN ARE ALL WHORES AND HE WANTS YOU TO PUNISH THEM?
CASSIDY, SHUT UP.
WHAT'S IT TELLING YOU?

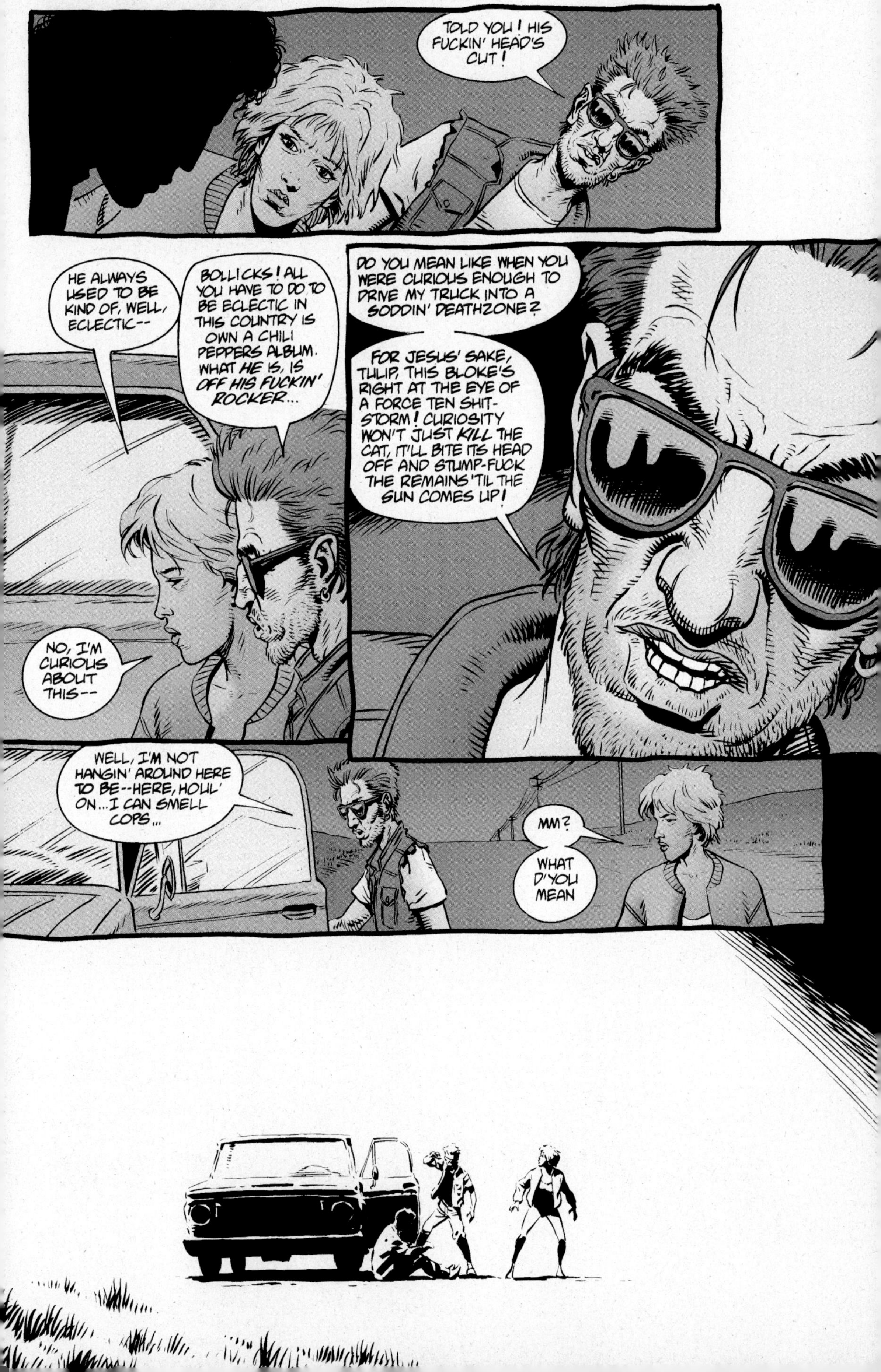
TOLD YOU! HIS FUCKIN' HEAD'S CUT!
HE ALWAYS USED TO BE KIND OF, WELL, ECLECTIC--
BOLLICKS! ALL YOU HAVE TO DO TO BE ECLECTIC IN THIS COUNTRY IS OWN A CHILI PEPPERS ALBUM. WHAT HE IS, IS OFF HIS FUCKIN' ROCKER...
NO, I'M CURIOUS ABOUT THIS--
DO YOU MEAN LIKE WHEN YOU WERE CURIOUS ENOUGH TO DRIVE MY TRUCK INTO A SODDIN' DEATHZONE?
FOR JESUS' SAKE, TULIP, THIS BLOKE'S RIGHT AT THE EYE OF A FORCE TEN SHIT-STORM! CURIOSITY WON'T JUST KILL THE CAT, IT'LL BITE ITS HEAD OFF AND STUMP-FUCK THE REMAINS 'TIL THE SUN COMES UP!
WELL, I'M NOT HANGIN' AROUND HERE TO BE--HERE, HOUL' ON...I CAN SMELL COPS...
MM?
WHAT D'YOU MEAN

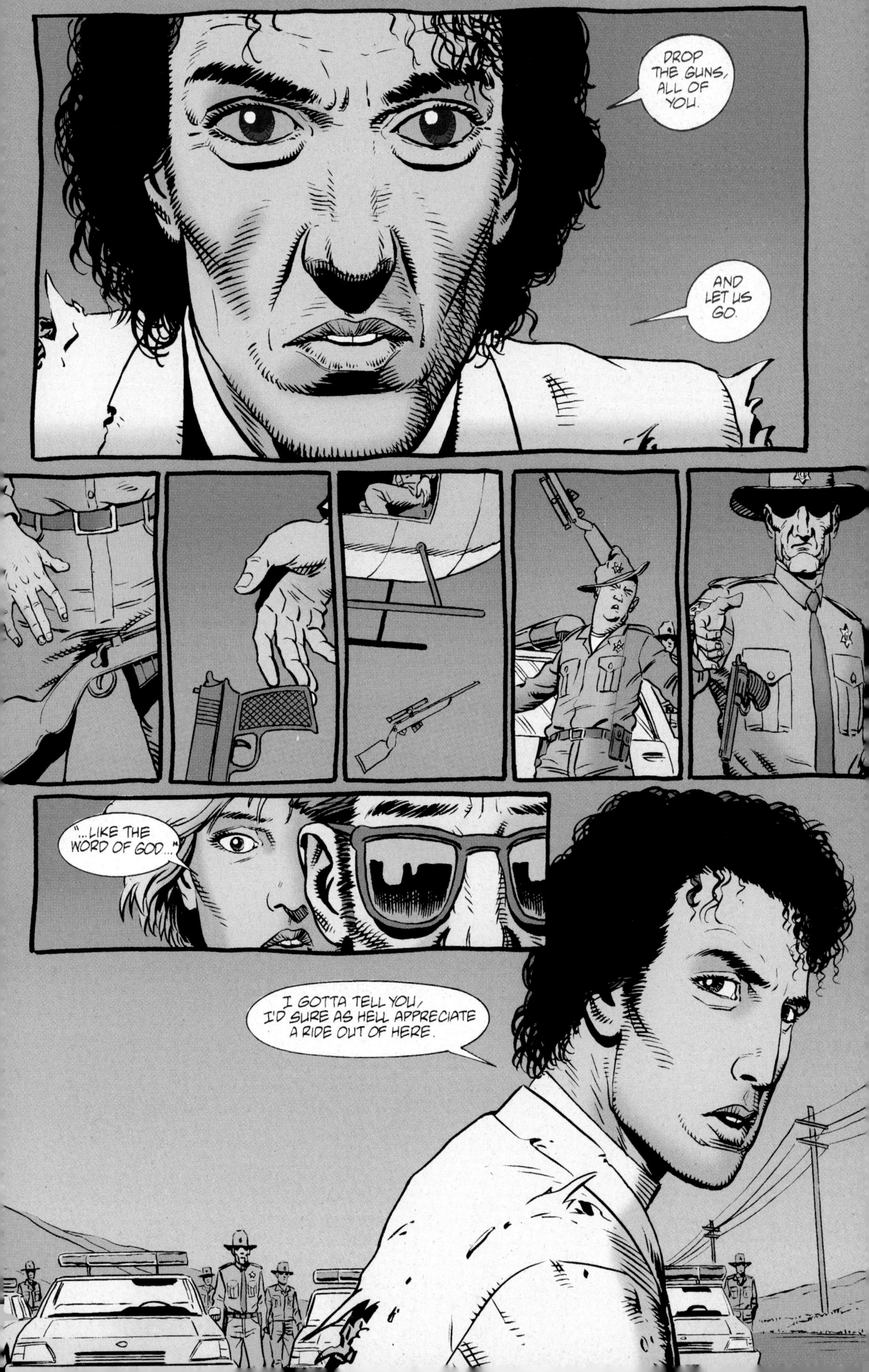
DROP THE GUNS, ALL OF YOU.
AND LET US GO.
"...LIKE THE WORD OF GOD..."
I GOTTA TELL YOU, I'D SURE AS HELL APPRECIATE A RIDE OUT OF HERE.

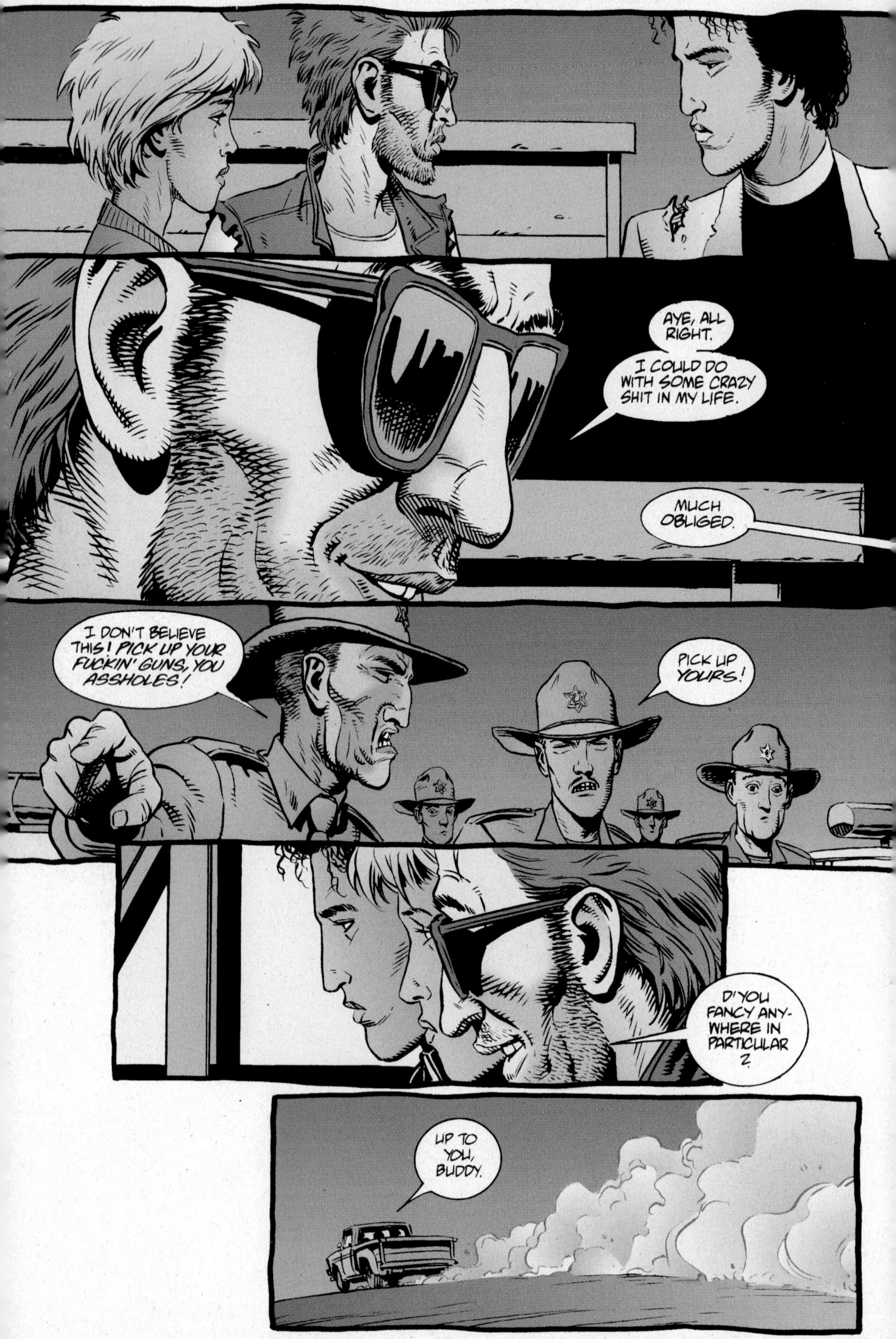
AYE, ALL RIGHT.
I COULD DO WITH SOME CRAZY SHIT IN MY LIFE.
MUCH OBLIGED.
I DON'T BELIEVE THIS! PICK UP YOUR FUCKIN' GUNS, YOU ASSHOLES!
PICK UP YOURS!
D'YOU FANCY ANY-WHERE IN PARTICULAR ?
UP TO YOU, BUDDY.

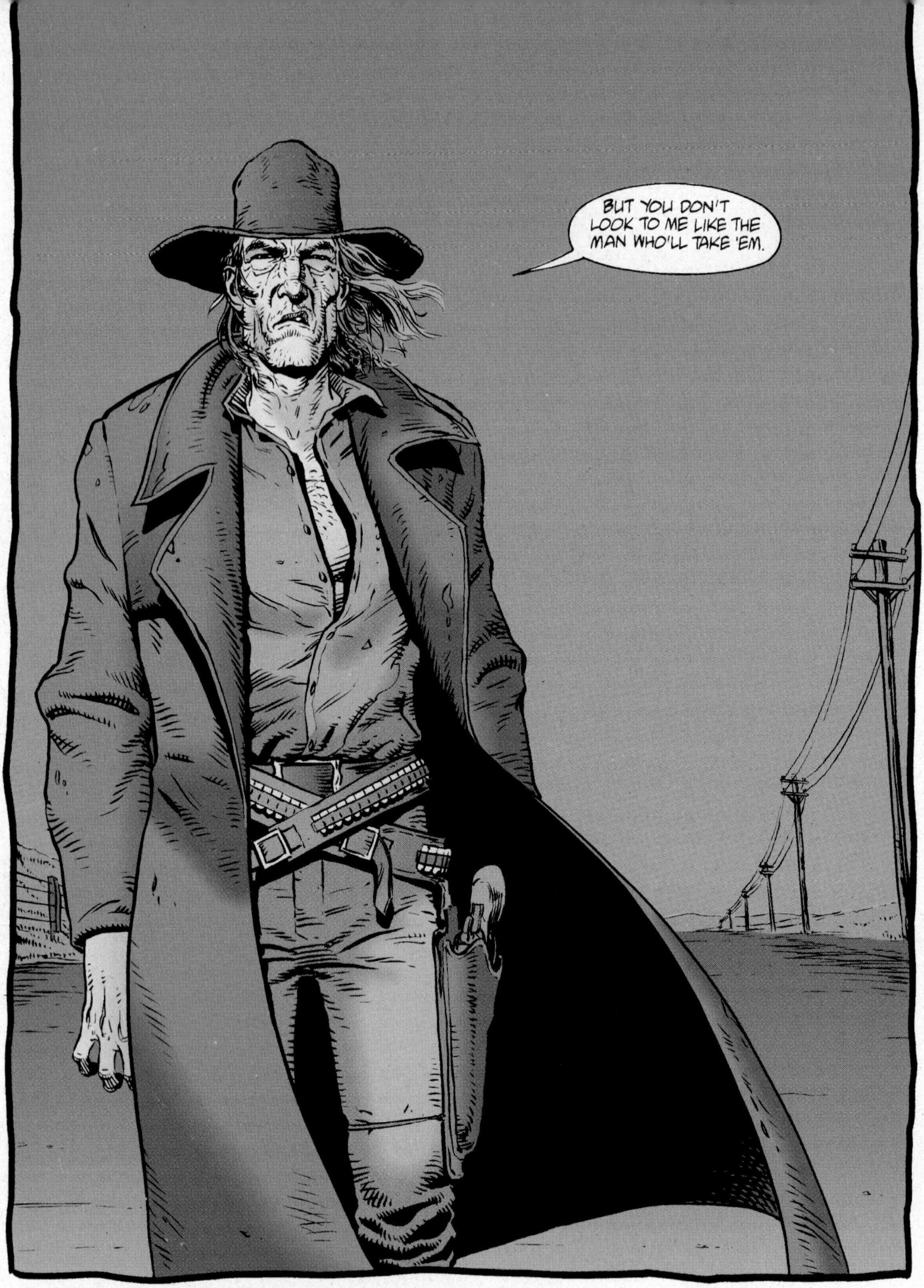
BUT YOU DON'T LOOK TO ME LIKE THE MAN WHO'LL TAKE 'EM.
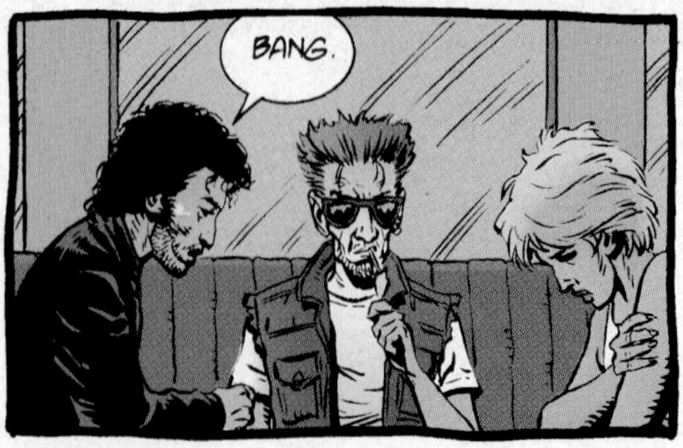
BANG.
NEXT: JUST A FEW COPS

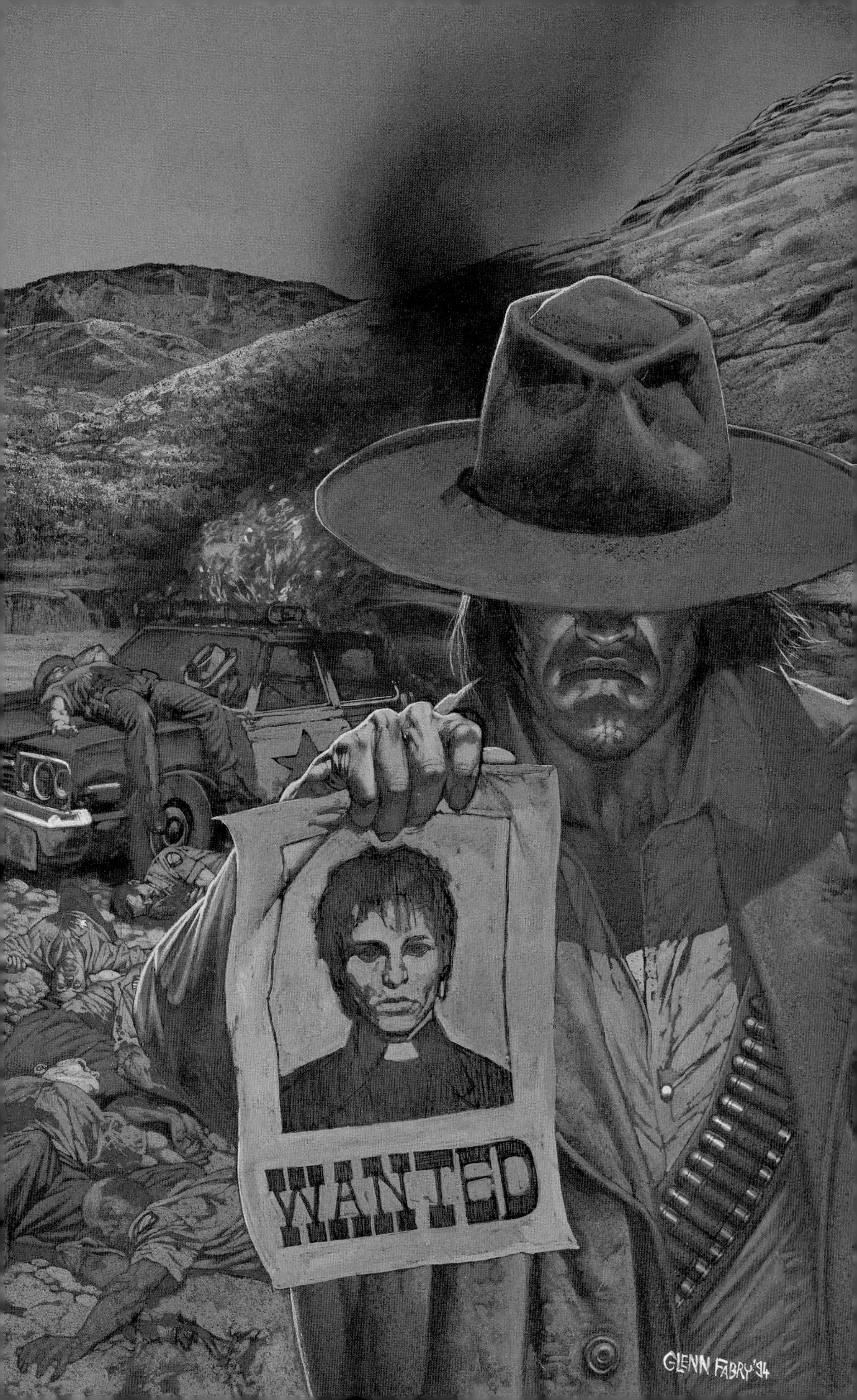
WANTED
GLENN FABRY '94

"He's got a soul so damn cold an' rattlesnake-mean,
Satan himself threw him back outta Hell."

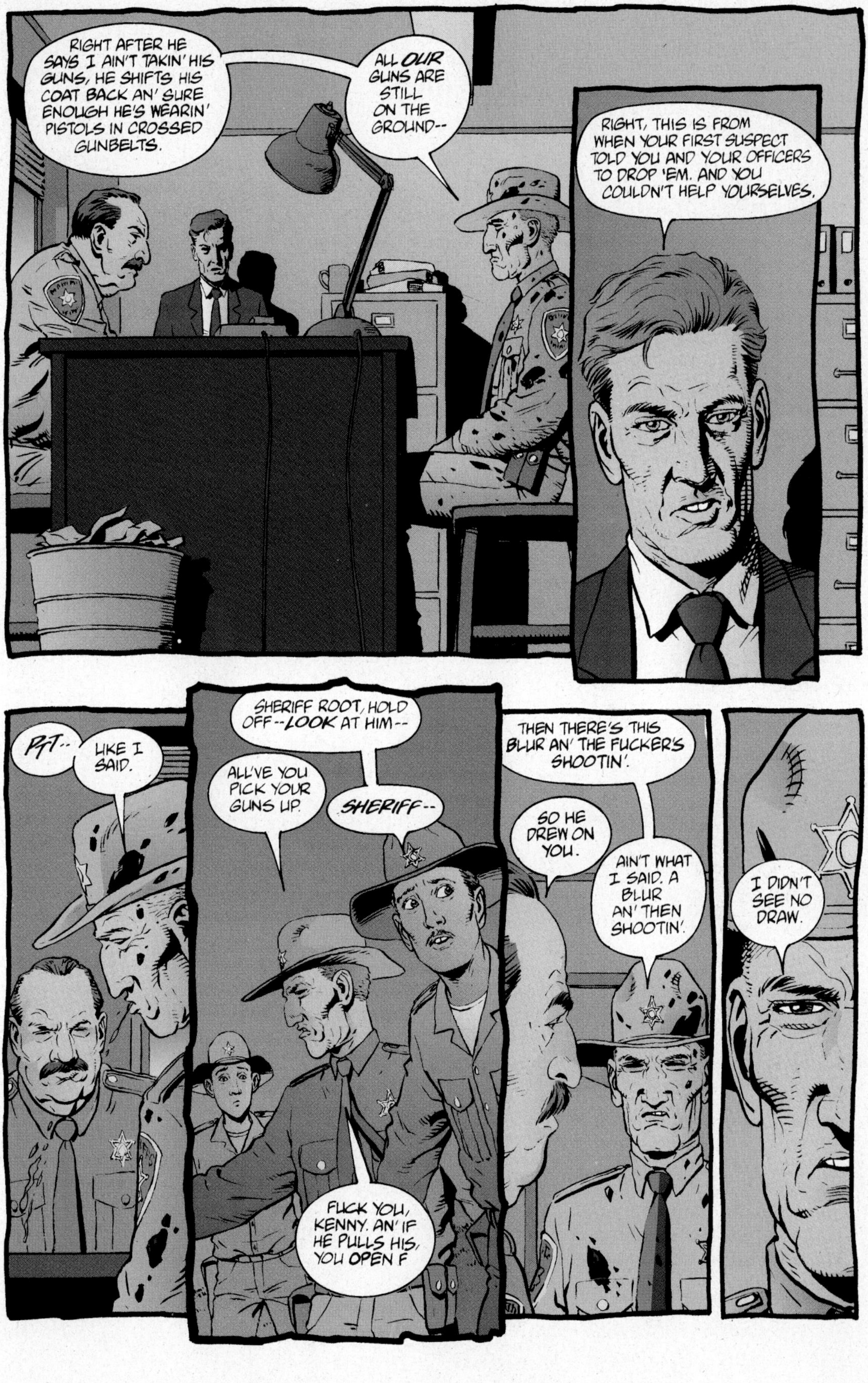
RIGHT AFTER HE SAYS I AIN'T TAKIN' HIS GUNS, HE SHIFTS HIS COAT BACK AN' SURE ENOUGH HE'S WEARIN' PISTOLS IN CROSSED GUNBELTS.
ALL OUR GUNS ARE STILL ON THE GROUND--
RIGHT, THIS IS FROM WHEN YOUR FIRST SUSPECT TOLD YOU AND YOUR OFFICERS TO DROP 'EM. AND YOU COULDN'T HELP YOURSELVES.
PFT..
LIKE I SAID.
SHERIFF ROOT, HOLD OFF--LOOK AT HIM--
ALL'VE YOU PICK YOUR GUNS UP.
SHERIFF--
FUCK YOU, KENNY. AN' IF HE PULLS HIS, YOU OPEN F
THEN THERE'S THIS BLUR AN' THE FUCKER'S SHOOTIN'.
SO HE DREW ON YOU.
AIN'T WHAT I SAID. A BLUR AN' THEN SHOOTIN'.
I DIDN'T SEE NO DRAW.

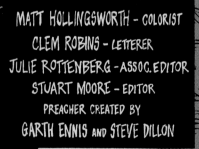

AND HELL FOLLOWED WITH HIM

GARTH ENNIS
WRITER

STEVE DILLON
ARTIST

MATT HOLLINGSWORTH – COLORIST

CLEM ROBINS – LETTERER

JULIE ROTTENBERG – ASSOC. EDITOR

STUART MOORE – EDITOR

PREACHER CREATED BY

GARTH ENNIS AND **STEVE DILLON**

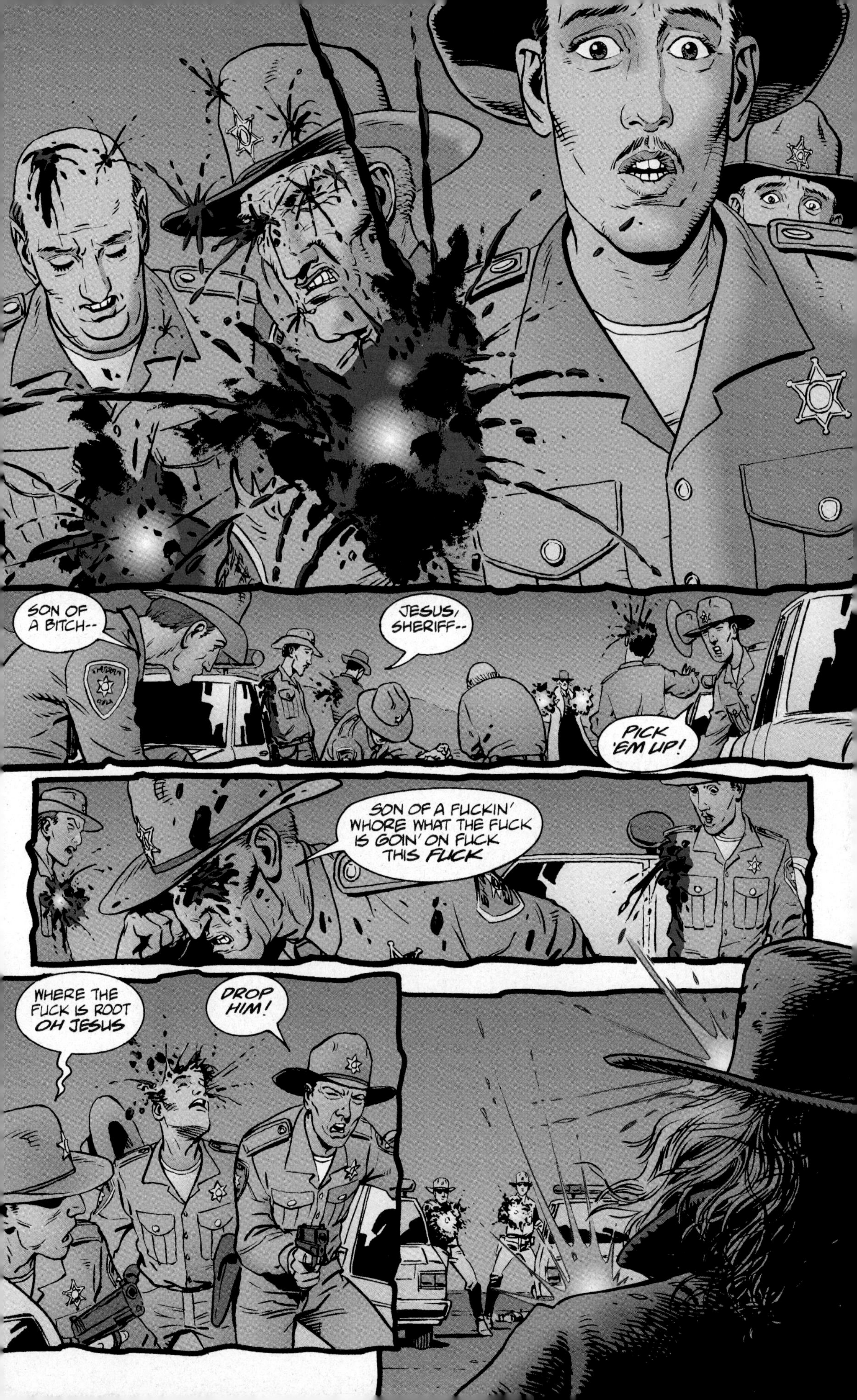
SON OF A BITCH--
JESUS, SHERIFF--
PICK 'EM UP!
SON OF A FUCKIN' WHORE WHAT THE FUCK IS GOIN' ON FUCK THIS FUCK
WHERE THE FUCK IS ROOT OH JESUS
DROP HIM!

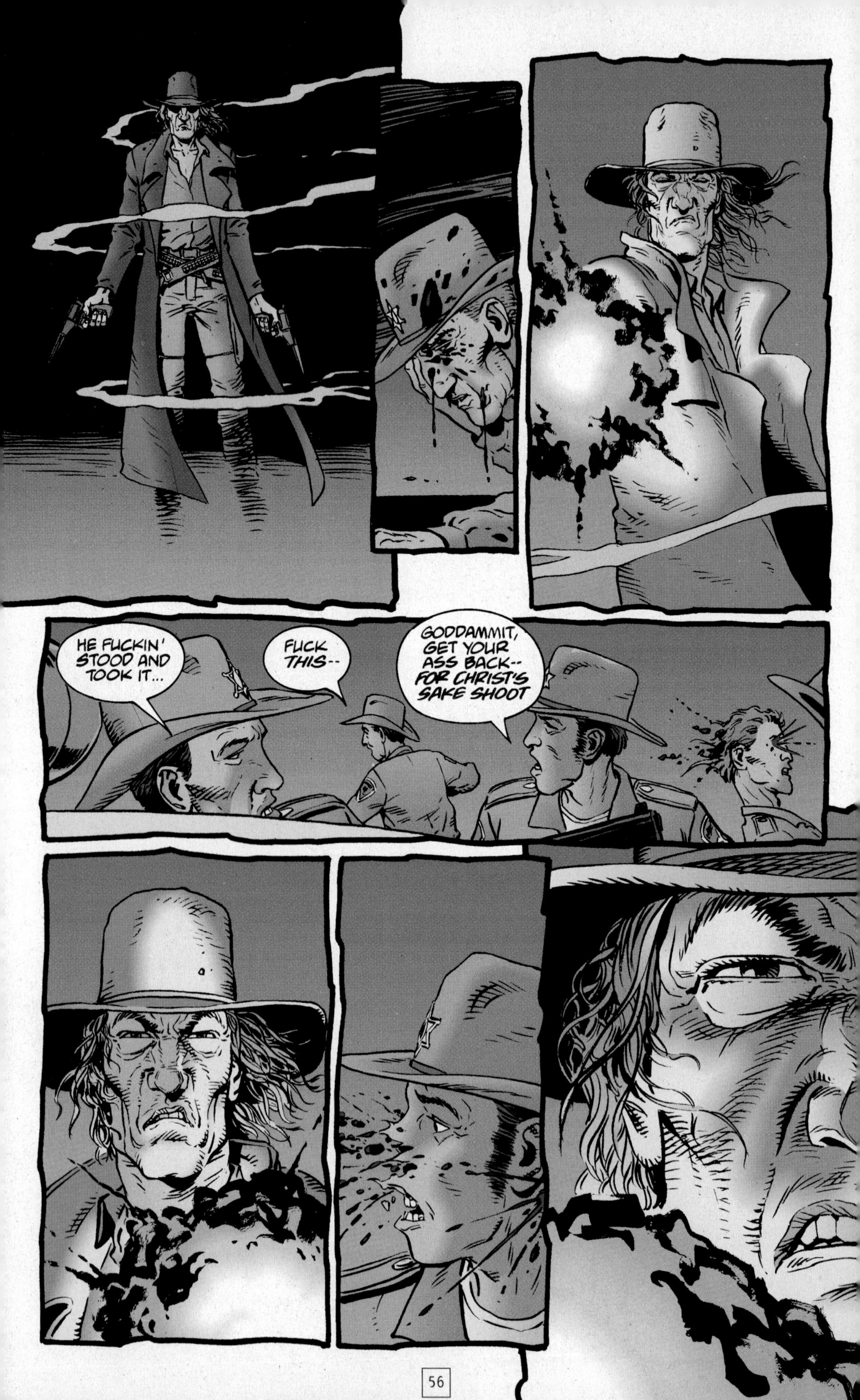
HE FUCKIN' STOOD AND TOOK IT...
FUCK THIS--
GODDAMMIT, GET YOUR ASS BACK-- FOR CHRIST'S SAKE SHOOT

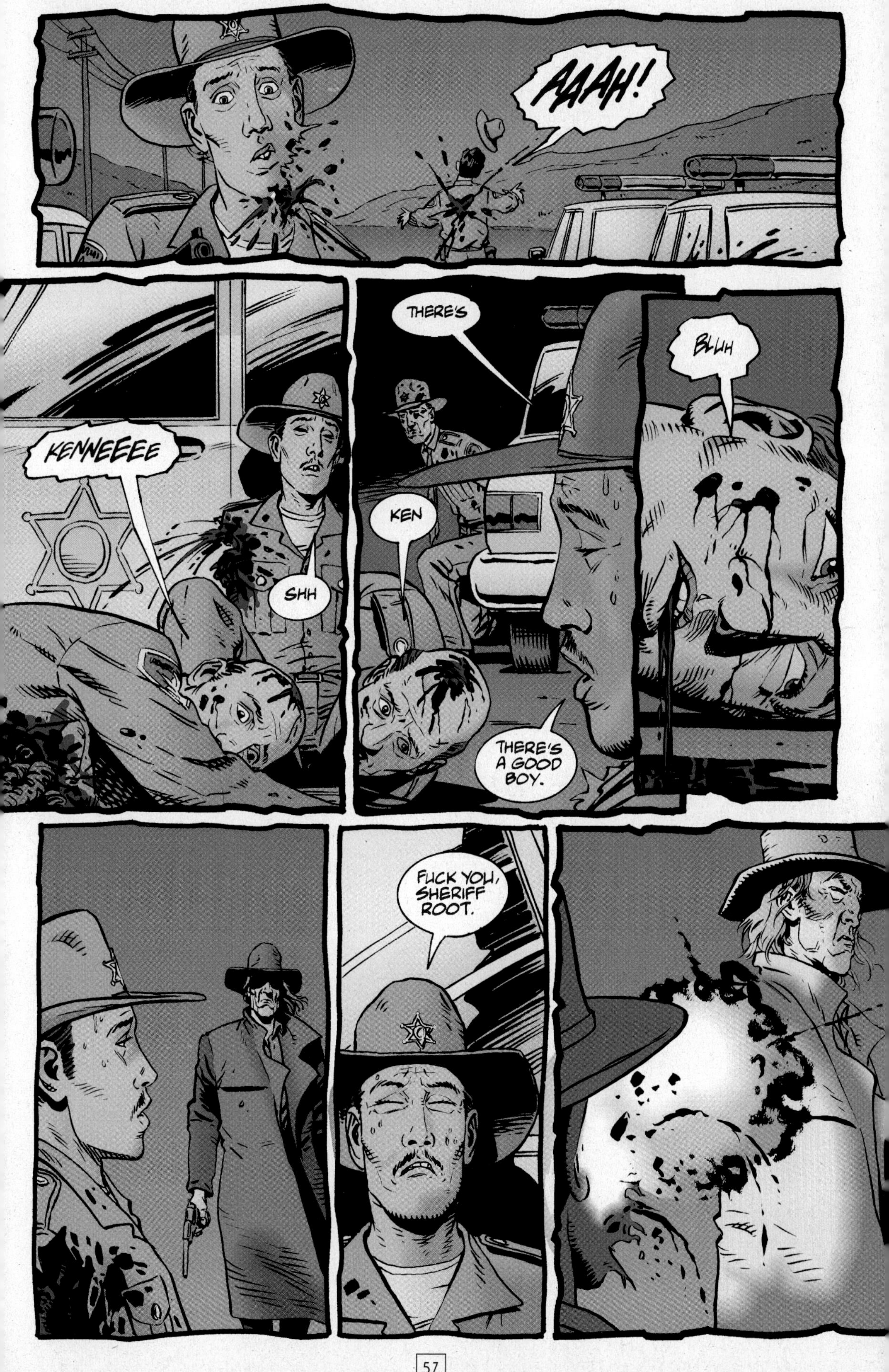
AAAH!
KENNEEEE
SHH
THERE'S
KEN
THERE'S A GOOD BOY.
BLUH
FUCK YOU, SHERIFF ROOT.

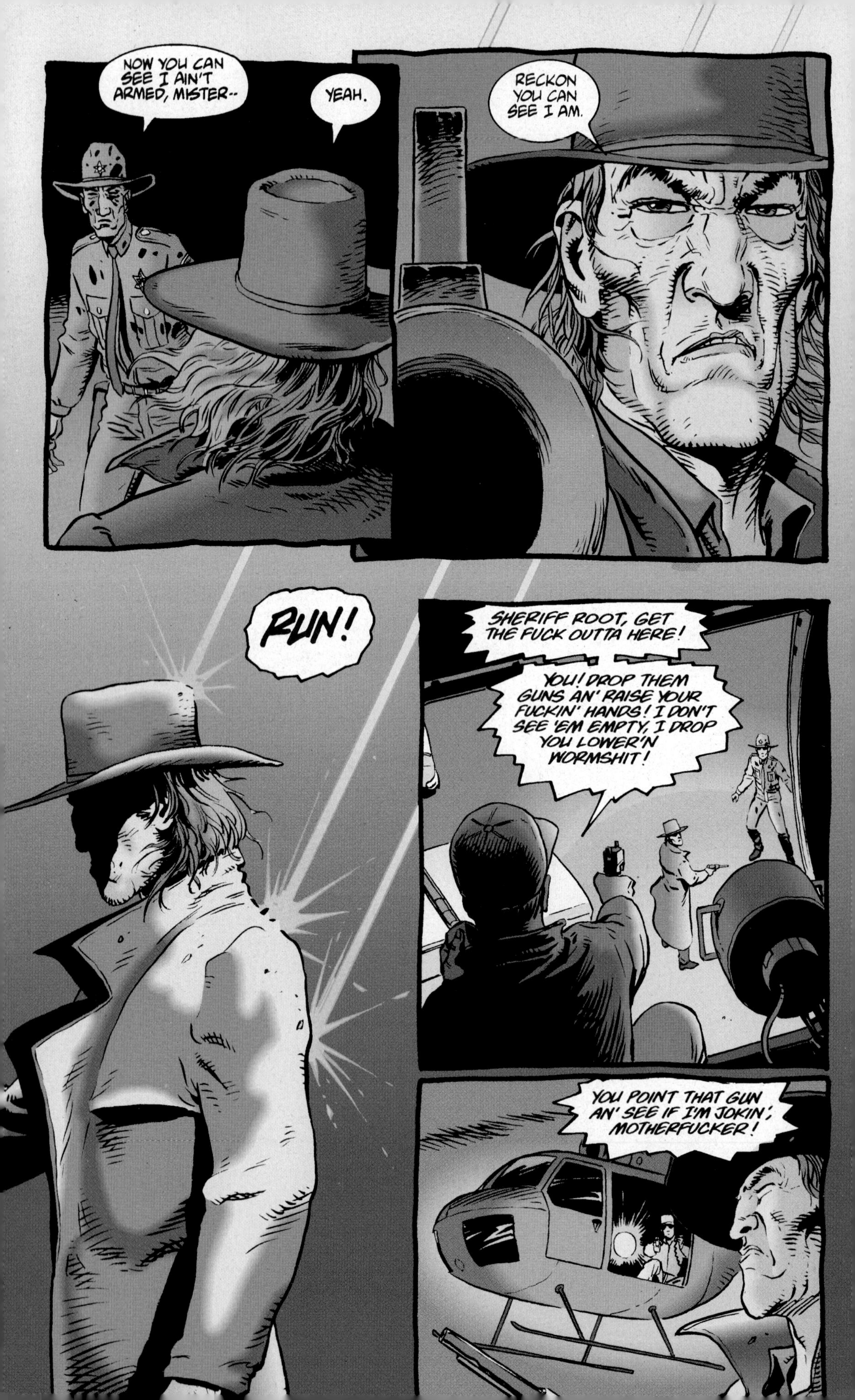
NOW YOU CAN SEE I AIN'T ARMED, MISTER--
YEAH.
RECKON YOU CAN SEE I AM.
RUN!
SHERIFF ROOT, GET THE FUCK OUTTA HERE!
YOU! DROP THEM GUNS AN' RAISE YOUR FUCKIN' HANDS! I DON'T SEE 'EM EMPTY, I DROP YOU LOWER'N WORMSHIT!
YOU POINT THAT GUN AN' SEE IF I'M JOKIN', MOTHERFUCKER!

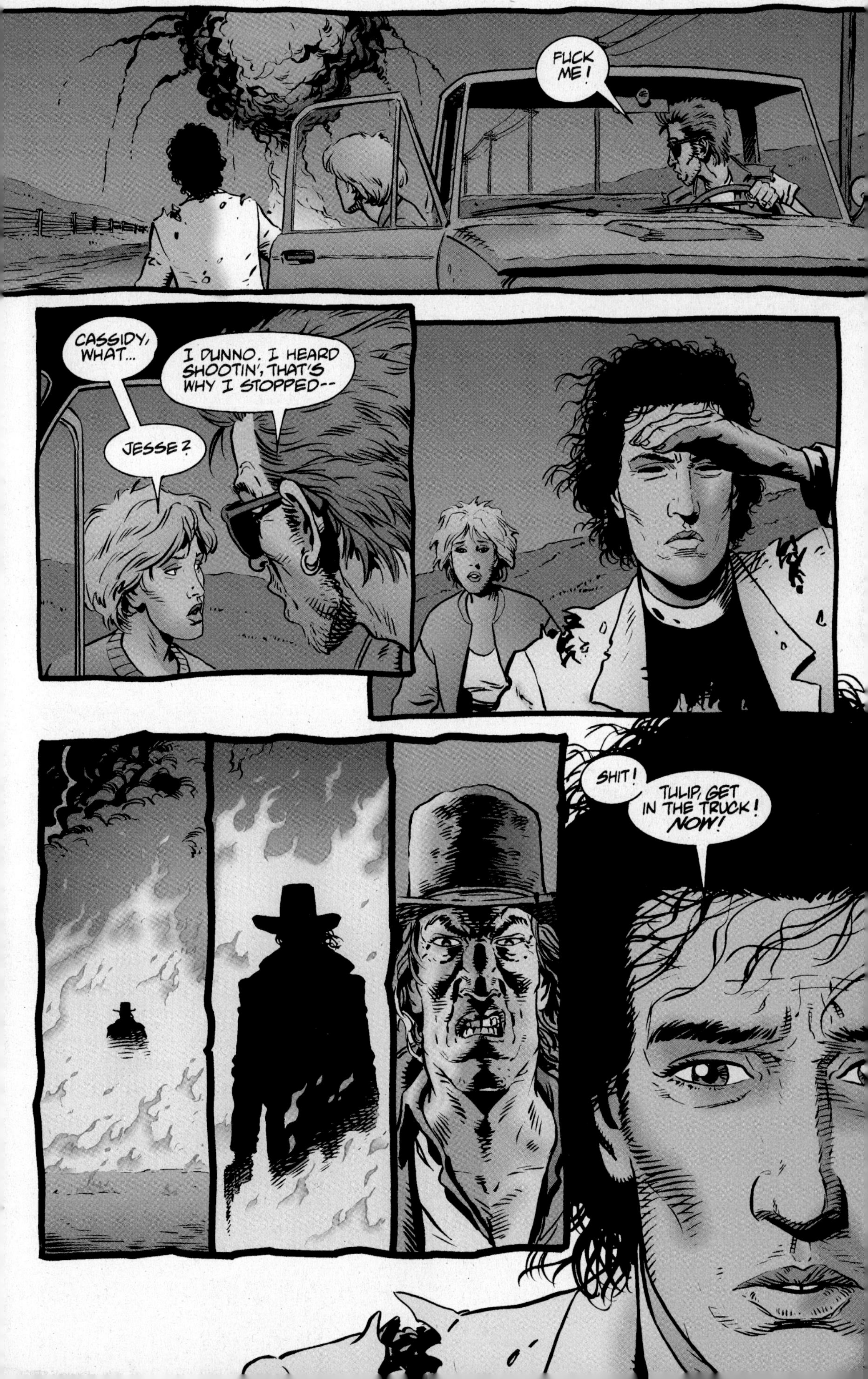
FUCK ME!
CASSIDY, WHAT...
I DUNNO. I HEARD SHOOTIN', THAT'S WHY I STOPPED--
JESSE?
SHIT!
TULIP, GET IN THE TRUCK! NOW!

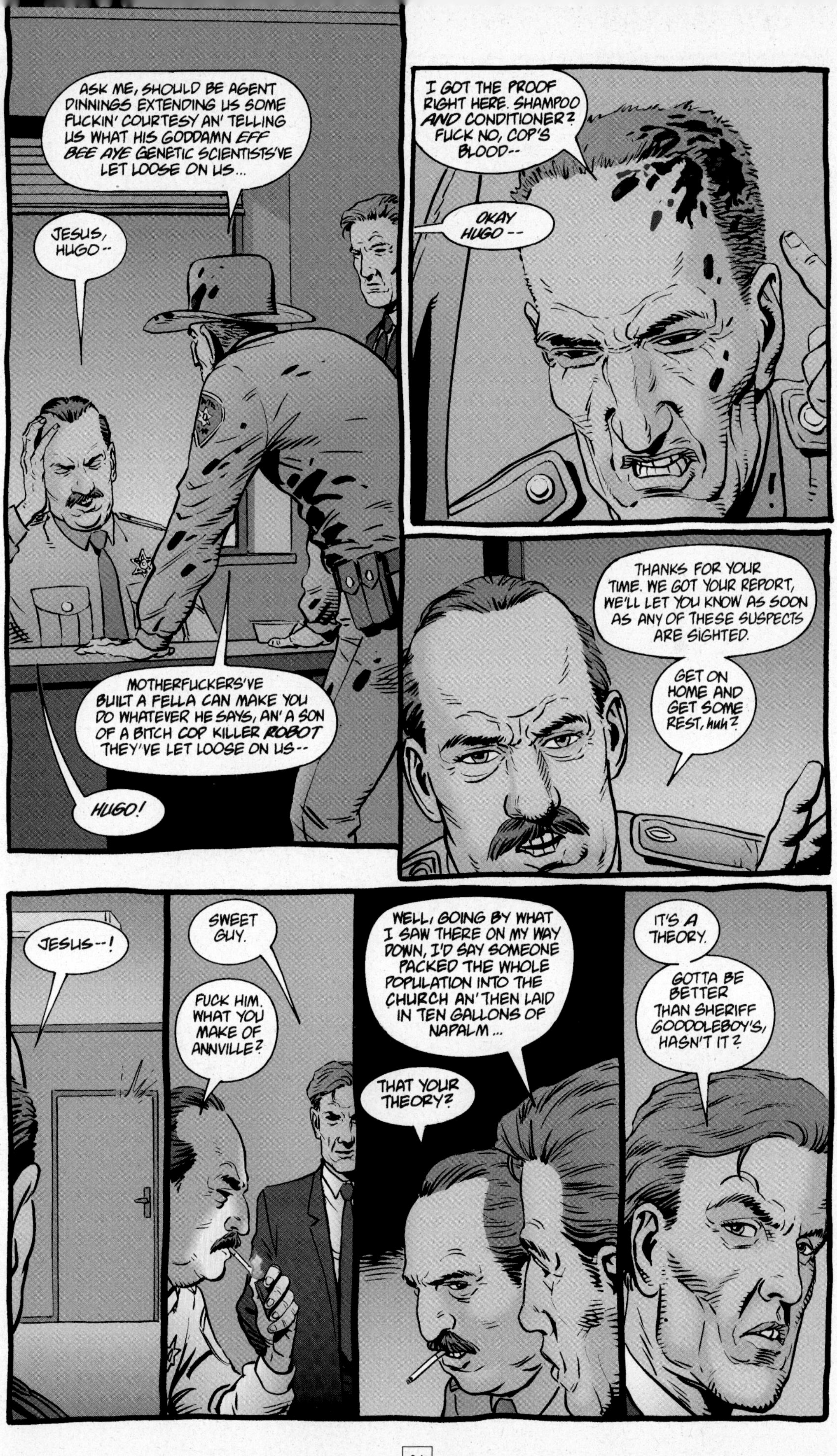
ASK ME, SHOULD BE AGENT DINNINGS EXTENDING US SOME FUCKIN' COURTESY AN' TELLING US WHAT HIS GODDAMN EFF BEE AYE GENETIC SCIENTISTS'VE LET LOOSE ON US...
JESUS, HUGO--
MOTHERFUCKERS'VE BUILT A FELLA CAN MAKE YOU DO WHATEVER HE SAYS, AN' A SON OF A BITCH COP KILLER ROBOT THEY'VE LET LOOSE ON US--
HUGO!
I GOT THE PROOF RIGHT HERE. SHAMPOO AND CONDITIONER? FUCK NO, COP'S BLOOD--
OKAY HUGO--
THANKS FOR YOUR TIME. WE GOT YOUR REPORT, WE'LL LET YOU KNOW AS SOON AS ANY OF THESE SUSPECTS ARE SIGHTED.
GET ON HOME AND GET SOME REST, huh?
JESUS--!
SWEET GUY.
FUCK HIM. WHAT YOU MAKE OF ANNVILLE?
WELL, GOING BY WHAT I SAW THERE ON MY WAY DOWN, I'D SAY SOMEONE PACKED THE WHOLE POPULATION INTO THE CHURCH AN' THEN LAID IN TEN GALLONS OF NAPALM...
THAT YOUR THEORY?
IT'S A THEORY.
GOTTA BE BETTER THAN SHERIFF GOODOLEBOY'S, HASN'T IT?

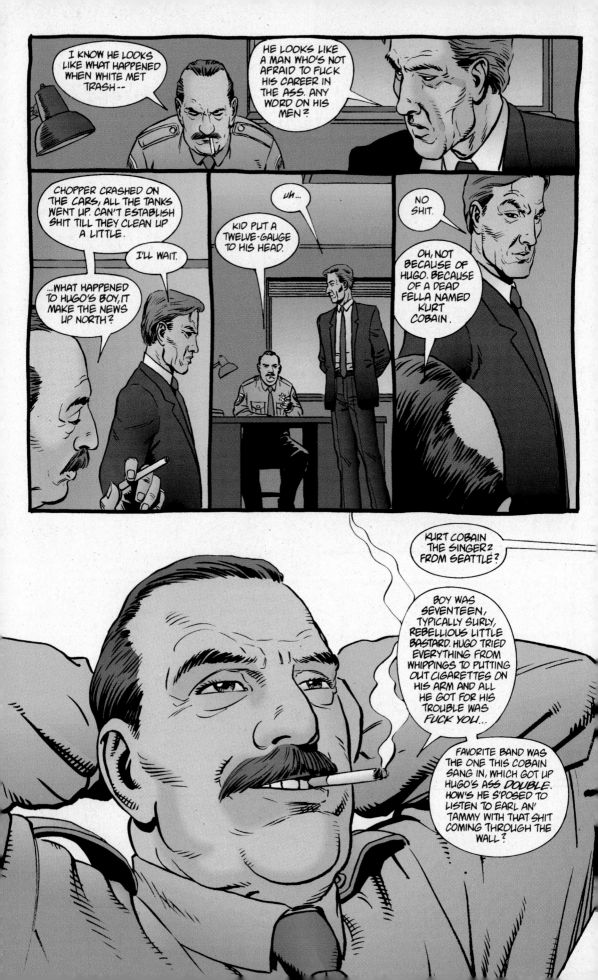

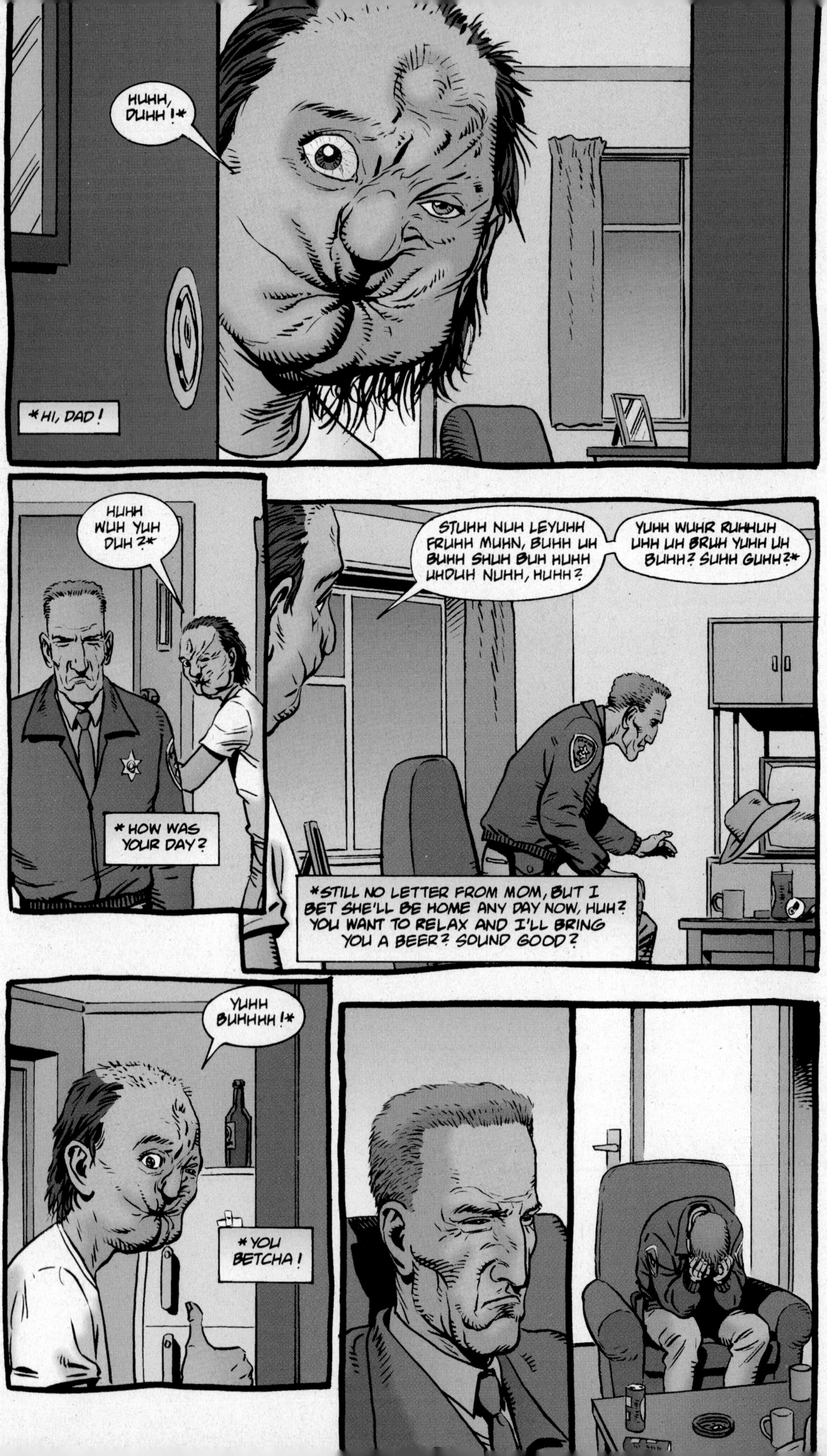

HUHH, DUHH!*
*HI, DAD!
HUHH WUH YUH DUH?*
*HOW WAS YOUR DAY?
STUHH NUH LEYUHH FRUHH MUHN, BUHH UH BUHH SHUH BUH HUHH UHDUH NUHH, HUHH?
YUHH WUHR RUHHUH UHH UH BRUH YUHH UH BUHH? SUHH GUHH?*
*STILL NO LETTER FROM MOM, BUT I BET SHE'LL BE HOME ANY DAY NOW, HUH? YOU WANT TO RELAX AND I'LL BRING YOU A BEER? SOUND GOOD?
YUHH BUHHHH!*
*YOU BETCHA!

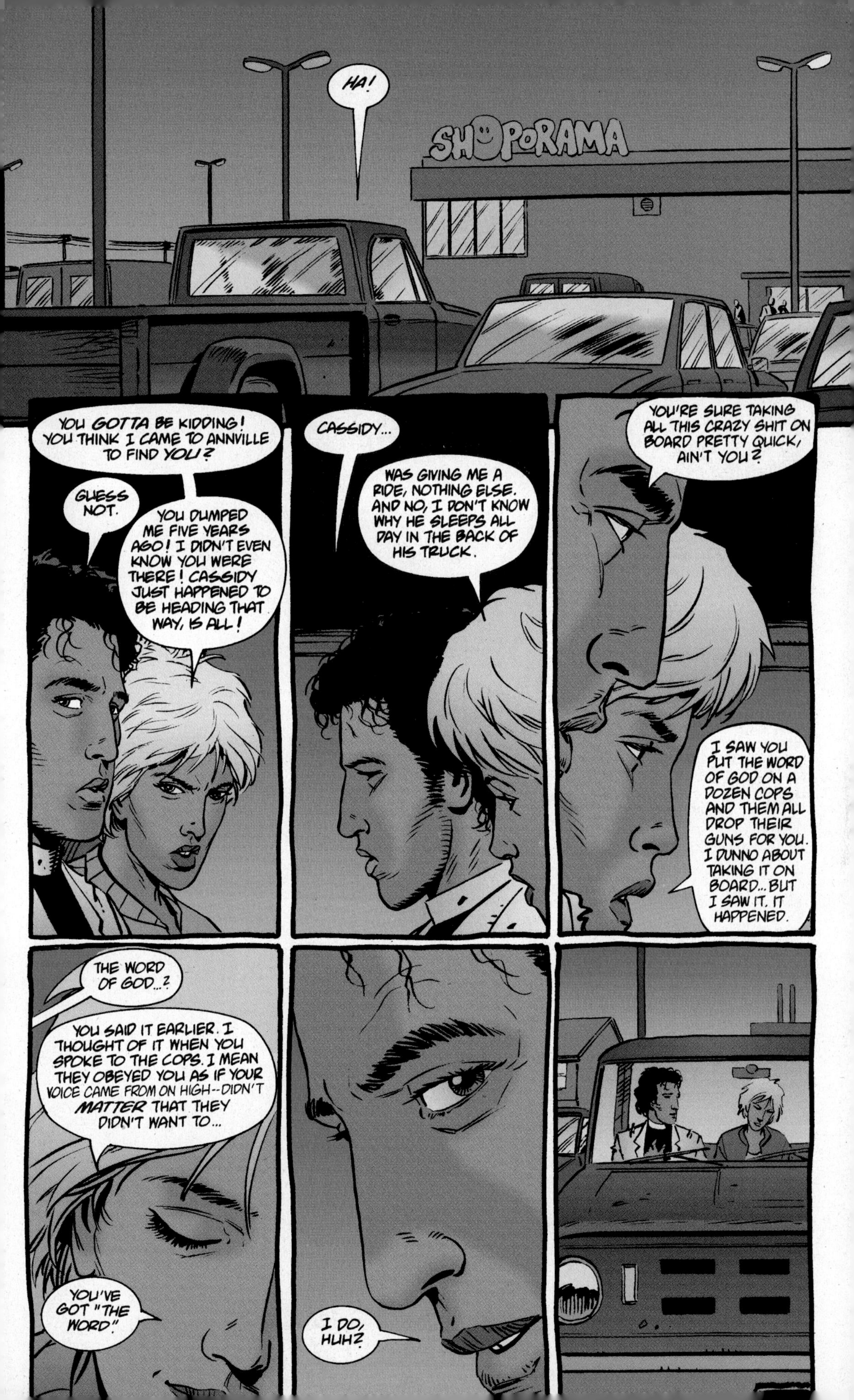
HA!
SHOPORAMA
YOU GOTTA BE KIDDING! YOU THINK I CAME TO ANNVILLE TO FIND YOU?
GUESS NOT.
YOU DUMPED ME FIVE YEARS AGO! I DIDN'T EVEN KNOW YOU WERE THERE! CASSIDY JUST HAPPENED TO BE HEADING THAT WAY, IS ALL!
CASSIDY...
WAS GIVING ME A RIDE, NOTHING ELSE. AND NO, I DON'T KNOW WHY HE SLEEPS ALL DAY IN THE BACK OF HIS TRUCK.
YOU'RE SURE TAKING ALL THIS CRAZY SHIT ON BOARD PRETTY QUICK, AIN'T YOU?
I SAW YOU PUT THE WORD OF GOD ON A DOZEN COPS AND THEM ALL DROP THEIR GUNS FOR YOU. I DUNNO ABOUT TAKING IT ON BOARD... BUT I SAW IT. IT HAPPENED.
THE WORD OF GOD...?
YOU SAID IT EARLIER. I THOUGHT OF IT WHEN YOU SPOKE TO THE COPS. I MEAN THEY OBEYED YOU AS IF YOUR VOICE CAME FROM ON HIGH--DIDN'T MATTER THAT THEY DIDN'T WANT TO...
YOU'VE GOT "THE WORD".
I DO, HUH?

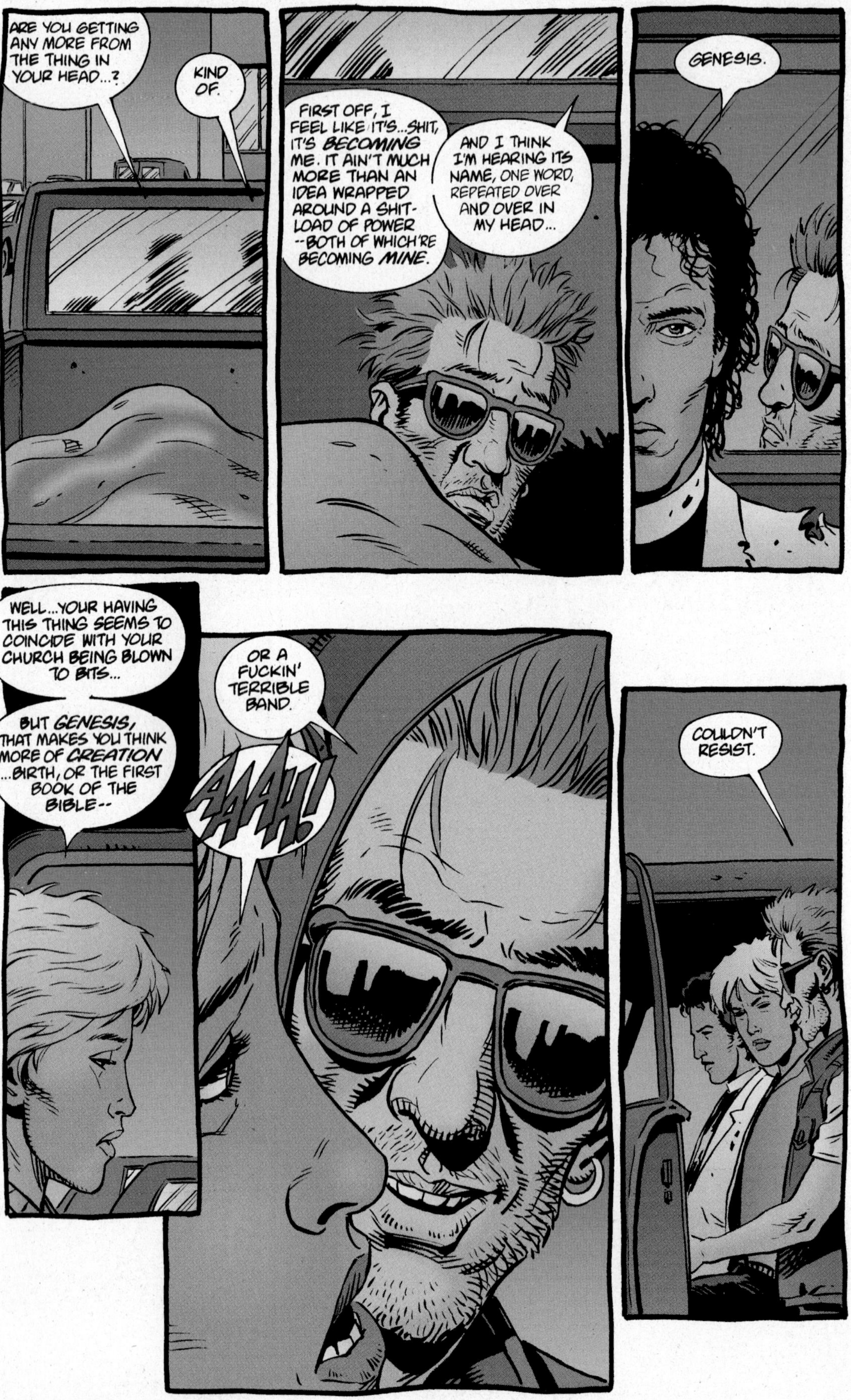
ARE YOU GETTING ANY MORE FROM THE THING IN YOUR HEAD...?
KIND OF.
FIRST OFF, I FEEL LIKE IT'S...SHIT, IT'S BECOMING ME. IT AIN'T MUCH MORE THAN AN IDEA WRAPPED AROUND A SHIT-LOAD OF POWER --BOTH OF WHICH'RE BECOMING MINE.
AND I THINK I'M HEARING ITS NAME, ONE WORD, REPEATED OVER AND OVER IN MY HEAD...
GENESIS.
WELL...YOUR HAVING THIS THING SEEMS TO COINCIDE WITH YOUR CHURCH BEING BLOWN TO BITS...
BUT GENESIS, THAT MAKES YOU THINK MORE OF CREATION ...BIRTH, OR THE FIRST BOOK OF THE BIBLE--
OR A FUCKIN' TERRIBLE BAND.
AAAH!
COULDN'T RESIST.

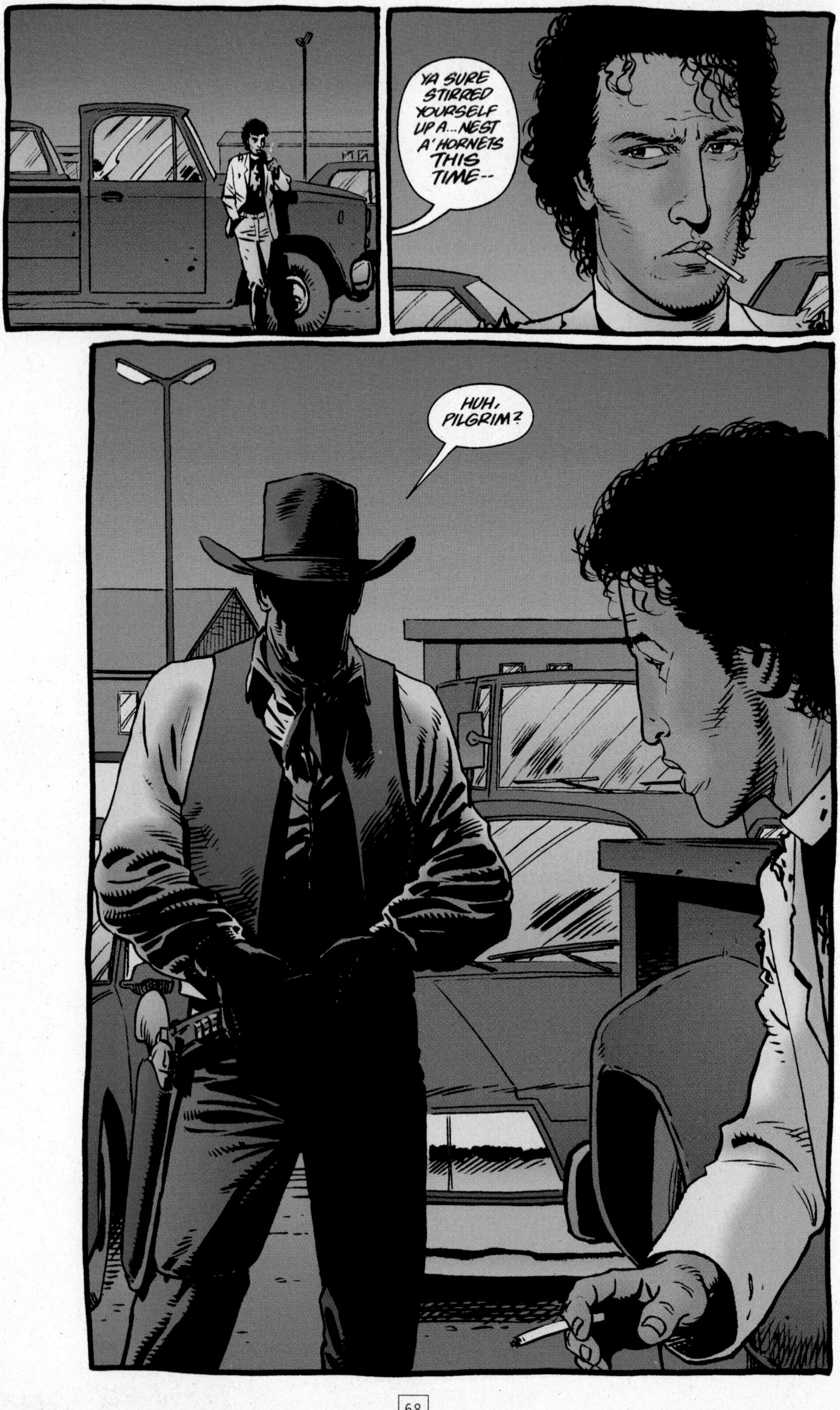
YA SURE STIRRED YOURSELF UP A...NEST A' HORNETS THIS TIME--
HUH, PILGRIM?

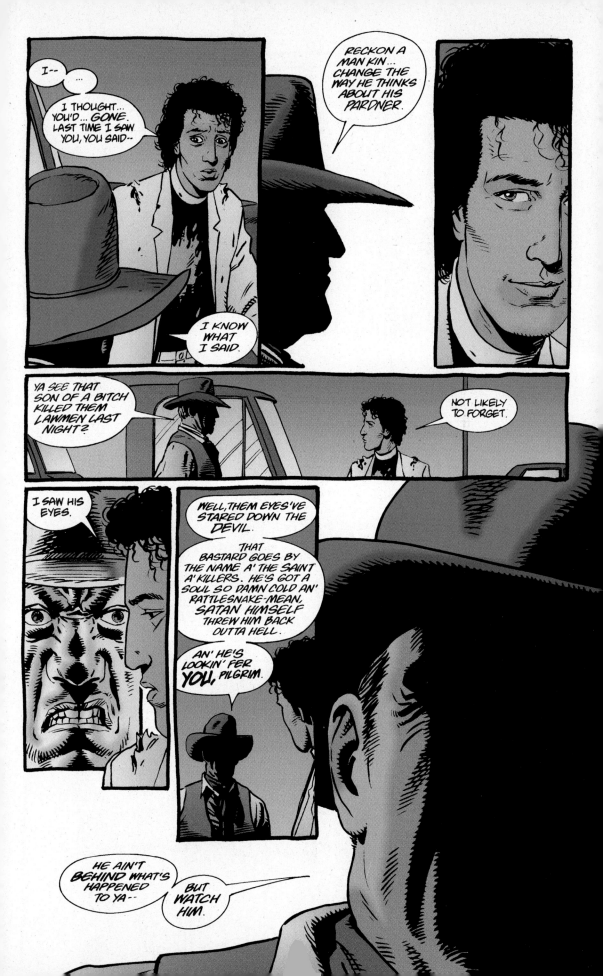

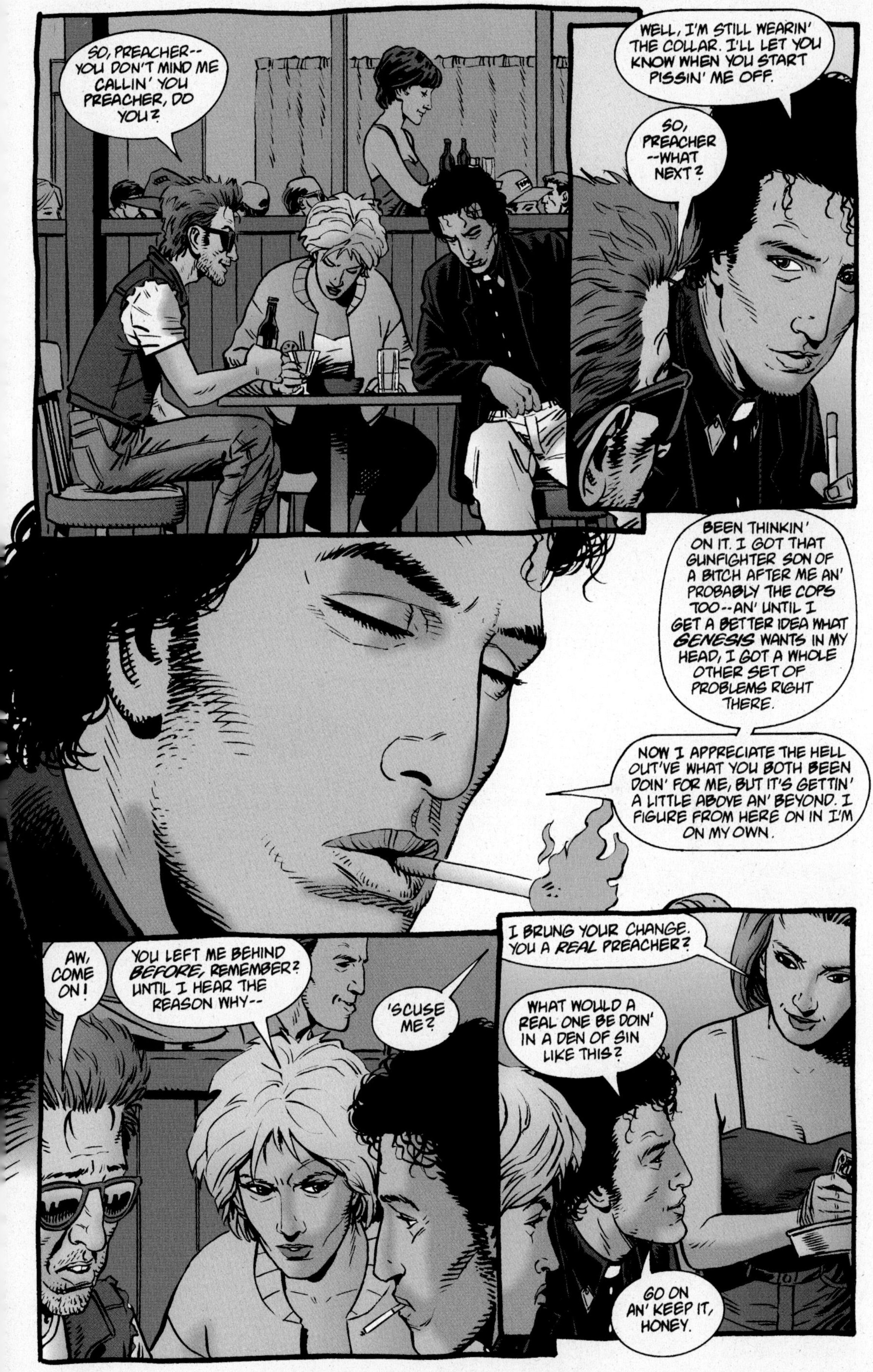
SO, PREACHER-- YOU DON'T MIND ME CALLIN' YOU PREACHER, DO YOU?
WELL, I'M STILL WEARIN' THE COLLAR. I'LL LET YOU KNOW WHEN YOU START PISSIN' ME OFF.
SO, PREACHER --WHAT NEXT?
BEEN THINKIN' ON IT. I GOT THAT GUNFIGHTER SON OF A BITCH AFTER ME AN' PROBABLY THE COPS TOO--AN' UNTIL I GET A BETTER IDEA WHAT GENESIS WANTS IN MY HEAD, I GOT A WHOLE OTHER SET OF PROBLEMS RIGHT THERE.
NOW I APPRECIATE THE HELL OUT'VE WHAT YOU BOTH BEEN DOIN' FOR ME, BUT IT'S GETTIN' A LITTLE ABOVE AN' BEYOND. I FIGURE FROM HERE ON IN I'M ON MY OWN.
AW, COME ON!
YOU LEFT ME BEHIND BEFORE, REMEMBER? UNTIL I HEAR THE REASON WHY--
'SCUSE ME?
I BRUNG YOUR CHANGE. YOU A REAL PREACHER?
WHAT WOULD A REAL ONE BE DOIN' IN A DEN OF SIN LIKE THIS?
GO ON AN' KEEP IT, HONEY.

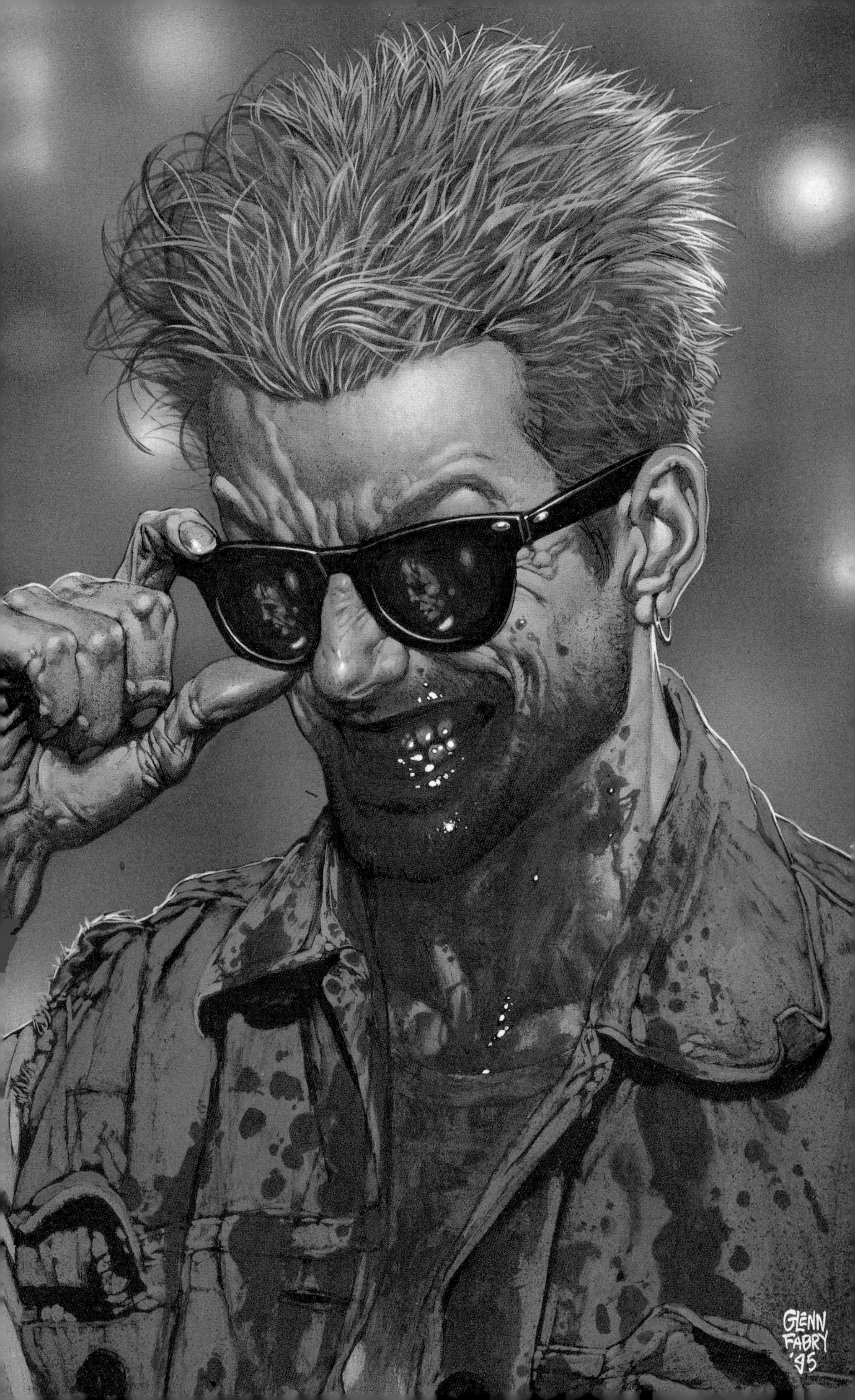
GLENN FABRY '95

"I won't be spoken to like that, not by any son of a bitch alive."

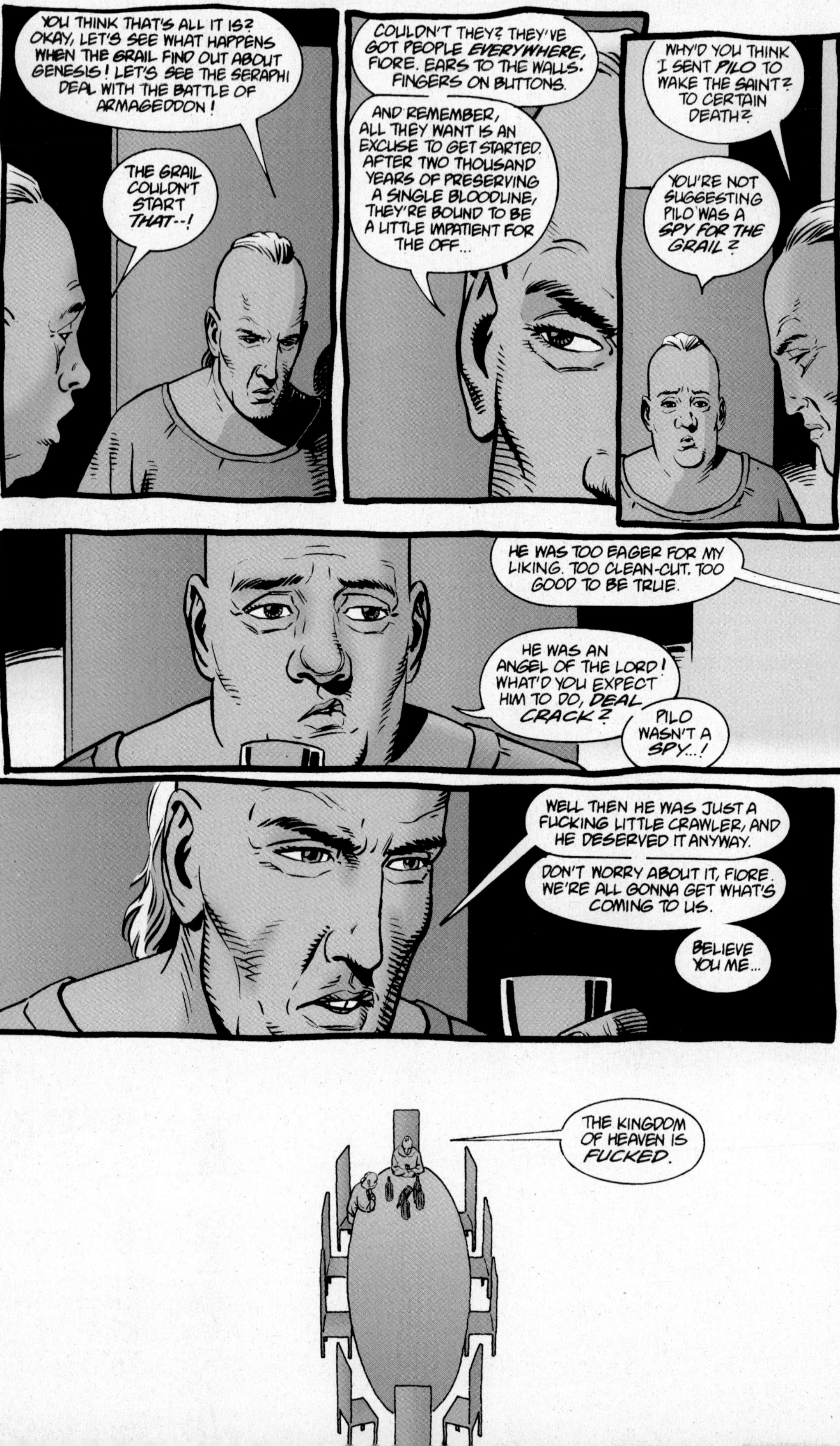
YOU THINK THAT'S ALL IT IS? OKAY, LET'S SEE WHAT HAPPENS WHEN THE GRAIL FIND OUT ABOUT GENESIS! LET'S SEE THE SERAPHI DEAL WITH THE BATTLE OF ARMAGEDDON!
THE GRAIL COULDN'T START THAT--!
COULDN'T THEY? THEY'VE GOT PEOPLE EVERYWHERE, FIORE. EARS TO THE WALLS. FINGERS ON BUTTONS.
AND REMEMBER, ALL THEY WANT IS AN EXCUSE TO GET STARTED. AFTER TWO THOUSAND YEARS OF PRESERVING A SINGLE BLOODLINE, THEY'RE BOUND TO BE A LITTLE IMPATIENT FOR THE OFF...
WHY'D YOU THINK I SENT PILO TO WAKE THE SAINT? TO CERTAIN DEATH?
YOU'RE NOT SUGGESTING PILO WAS A SPY FOR THE GRAIL?
HE WAS TOO EAGER FOR MY LIKING. TOO CLEAN-CUT. TOO GOOD TO BE TRUE.
HE WAS AN ANGEL OF THE LORD! WHAT'D YOU EXPECT HIM TO DO, DEAL CRACK?
PILO WASN'T A SPY...!
WELL THEN HE WAS JUST A FUCKING LITTLE CRAWLER, AND HE DESERVED IT ANYWAY.
DON'T WORRY ABOUT IT, FIORE. WE'RE ALL GONNA GET WHAT'S COMING TO US.
BELIEVE YOU ME...
THE KINGDOM OF HEAVEN IS FUCKED.

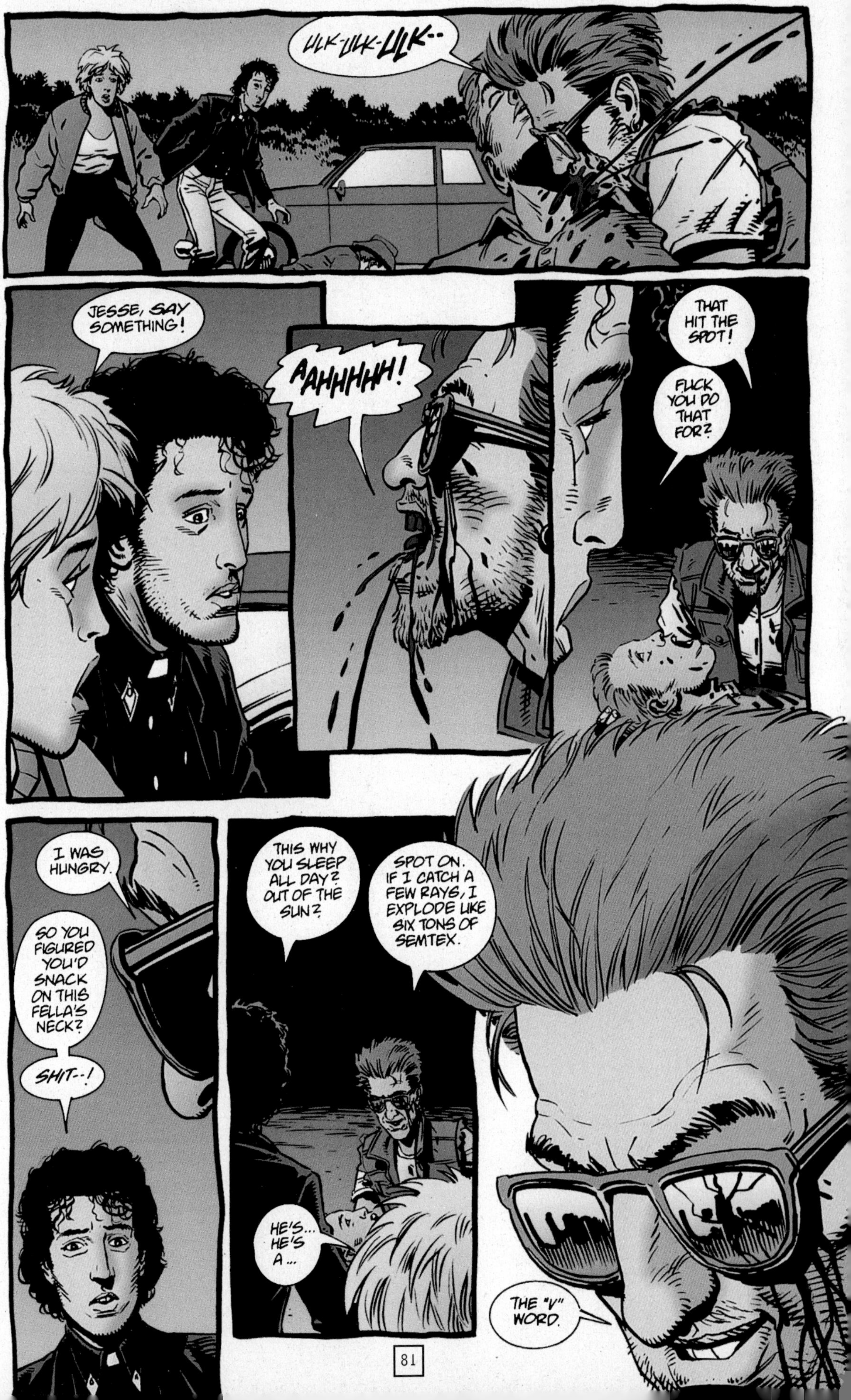
ULK-ULK-ULK--
JESSE, SAY SOMETHING!
AAHHHHH!
THAT HIT THE SPOT!
FUCK YOU DO THAT FOR?
I WAS HUNGRY.
SO YOU FIGURED YOU'D SNACK ON THIS FELLA'S NECK?
SHIT--!
THIS WHY YOU SLEEP ALL DAY? OUT OF THE SUN?
SPOT ON. IF I CATCH A FEW RAYS, I EXPLODE LIKE SIX TONS OF SEMTEX.
HE'S... HE'S A...
THE "V" WORD.

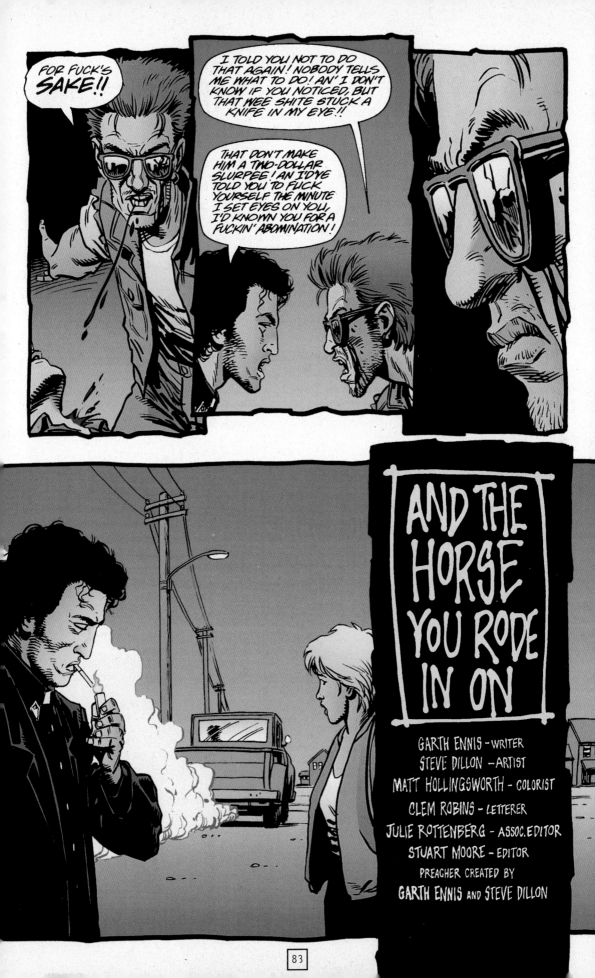

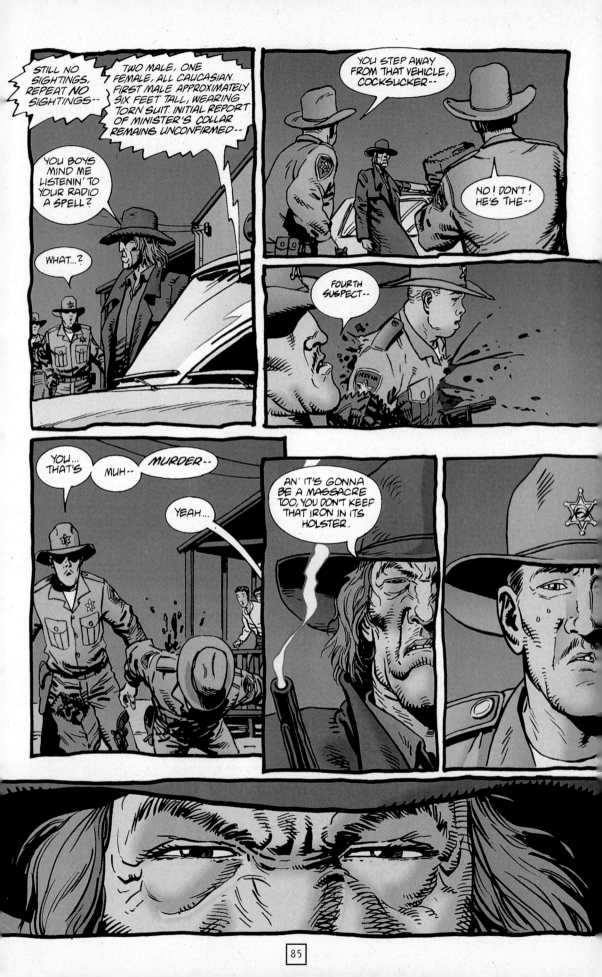

STILL NO SIGHTINGS, REPEAT *NO* SIGHTINGS--

TWO MALE, ONE FEMALE, ALL CAUCASIAN. FIRST MALE APPROXIMATELY SIX FEET TALL, WEARING TORN SUIT. INITIAL REPORT OF MINISTER'S COLLAR REMAINS UNCONFIRMED--

YOU BOYS MIND ME LISTENIN' TO YOUR RADIO A SPELL?

WHAT...?

YOU STEP AWAY FROM THAT VEHICLE, COCKSUCKER--

NO! DON'T! HE'S THE--

FOURTH SUSPECT--

YOU... THAT'S MUH-- *MURDER*--

YEAH...

AN' IT'S GONNA BE A MASSACRE TOO, YOU DON'T KEEP THAT IRON IN ITS HOLSTER.

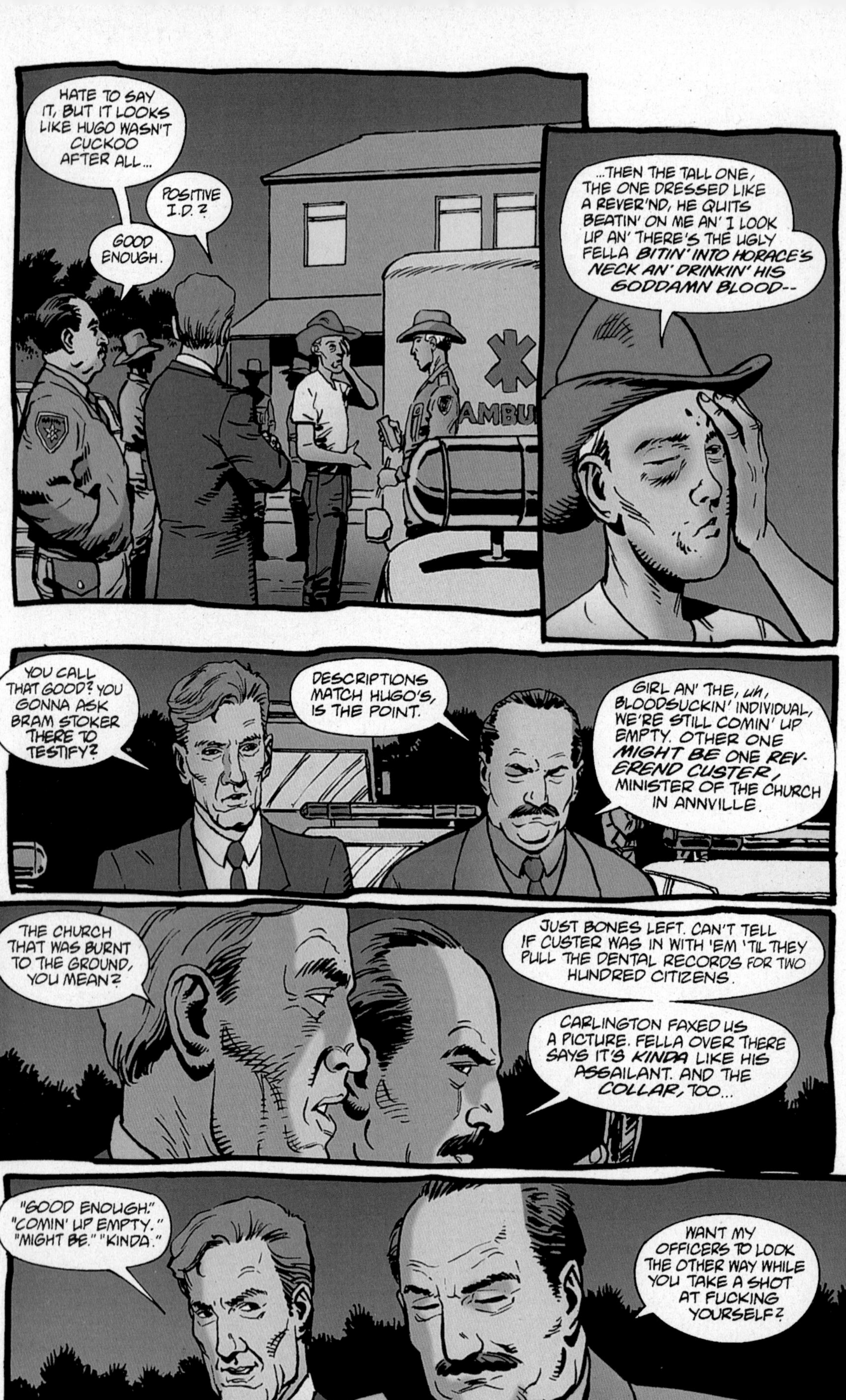
HATE TO SAY IT, BUT IT LOOKS LIKE HUGO WASN'T CUCKOO AFTER ALL...
POSITIVE I.D.?
GOOD ENOUGH.
...THEN THE TALL ONE, THE ONE DRESSED LIKE A REVER'ND, HE QUITS BEATIN' ON ME AN' I LOOK UP AN' THERE'S THE UGLY FELLA BITIN' INTO HORACE'S NECK AN' DRINKIN' HIS GODDAMN BLOOD--
AMBU
YOU CALL THAT GOOD? YOU GONNA ASK BRAM STOKER THERE TO TESTIFY?
DESCRIPTIONS MATCH HUGO'S, IS THE POINT.
GIRL AN' THE, uh, BLOODSUCKIN' INDIVIDUAL, WE'RE STILL COMIN' UP EMPTY. OTHER ONE MIGHT BE ONE REV-EREND CUSTER, MINISTER OF THE CHURCH IN ANNVILLE.
THE CHURCH THAT WAS BURNT TO THE GROUND, YOU MEAN?
JUST BONES LEFT. CAN'T TELL IF CUSTER WAS IN WITH 'EM 'TIL THEY PULL THE DENTAL RECORDS FOR TWO HUNDRED CITIZENS.
CARLINGTON FAXED US A PICTURE. FELLA OVER THERE SAYS IT'S KINDA LIKE HIS ASSAILANT. AND THE COLLAR, TOO...
"GOOD ENOUGH." "COMIN' UP EMPTY." "MIGHT BE." "KINDA."
WANT MY OFFICERS TO LOOK THE OTHER WAY WHILE YOU TAKE A SHOT AT FUCKING YOURSELF?

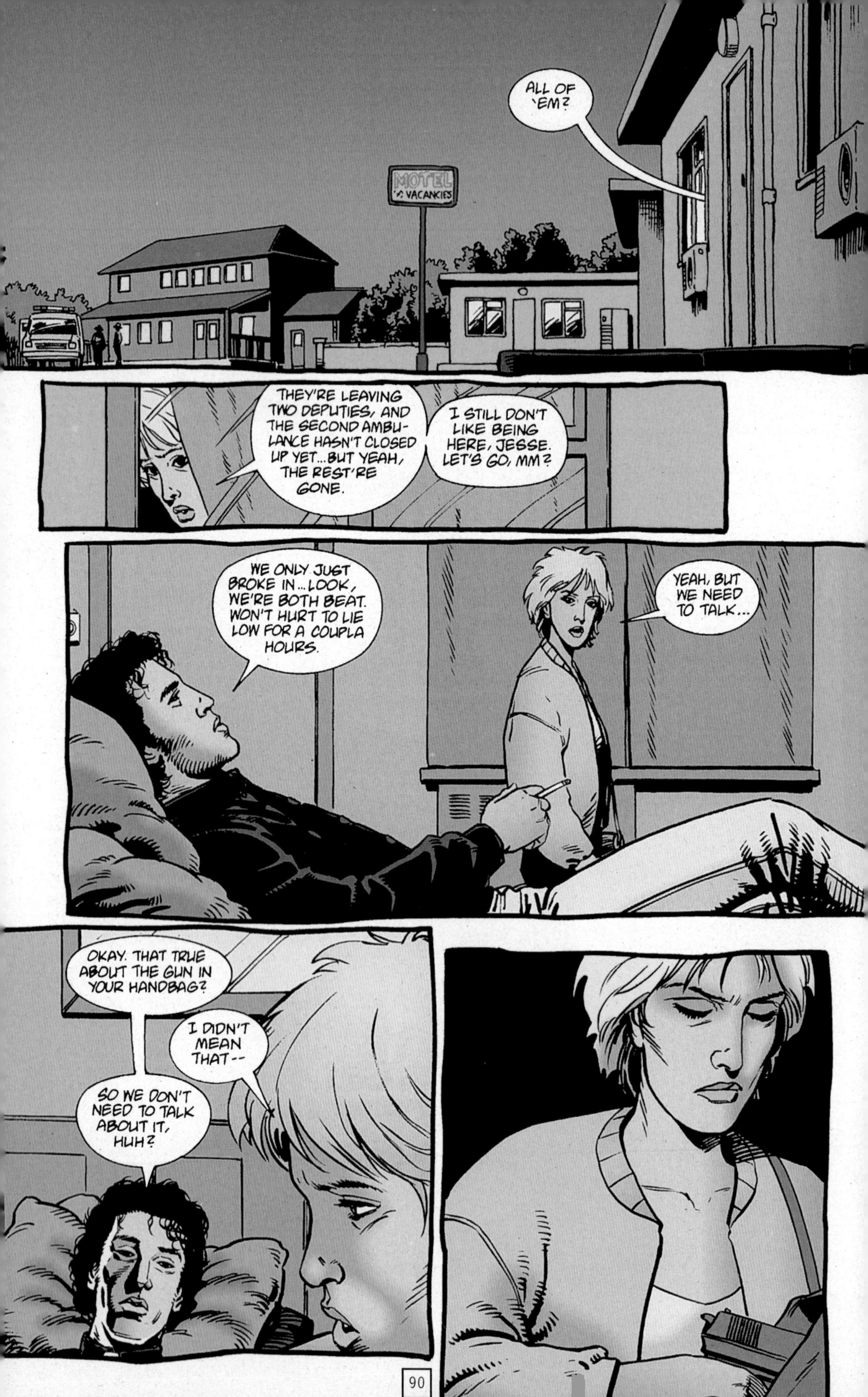
MOTEL
VACANCIES
ALL OF 'EM?
THEY'RE LEAVING TWO DEPUTIES, AND THE SECOND AMBULANCE HASN'T CLOSED UP YET...BUT YEAH, THE REST'RE GONE.
I STILL DON'T LIKE BEING HERE, JESSE. LET'S GO, MM?
WE ONLY JUST BROKE IN...LOOK, WE'RE BOTH BEAT. WON'T HURT TO LIE LOW FOR A COUPLA HOURS.
YEAH, BUT WE NEED TO TALK...
OKAY. THAT TRUE ABOUT THE GUN IN YOUR HANDBAG?
I DIDN'T MEAN THAT--
SO WE DON'T NEED TO TALK ABOUT IT, HUH?

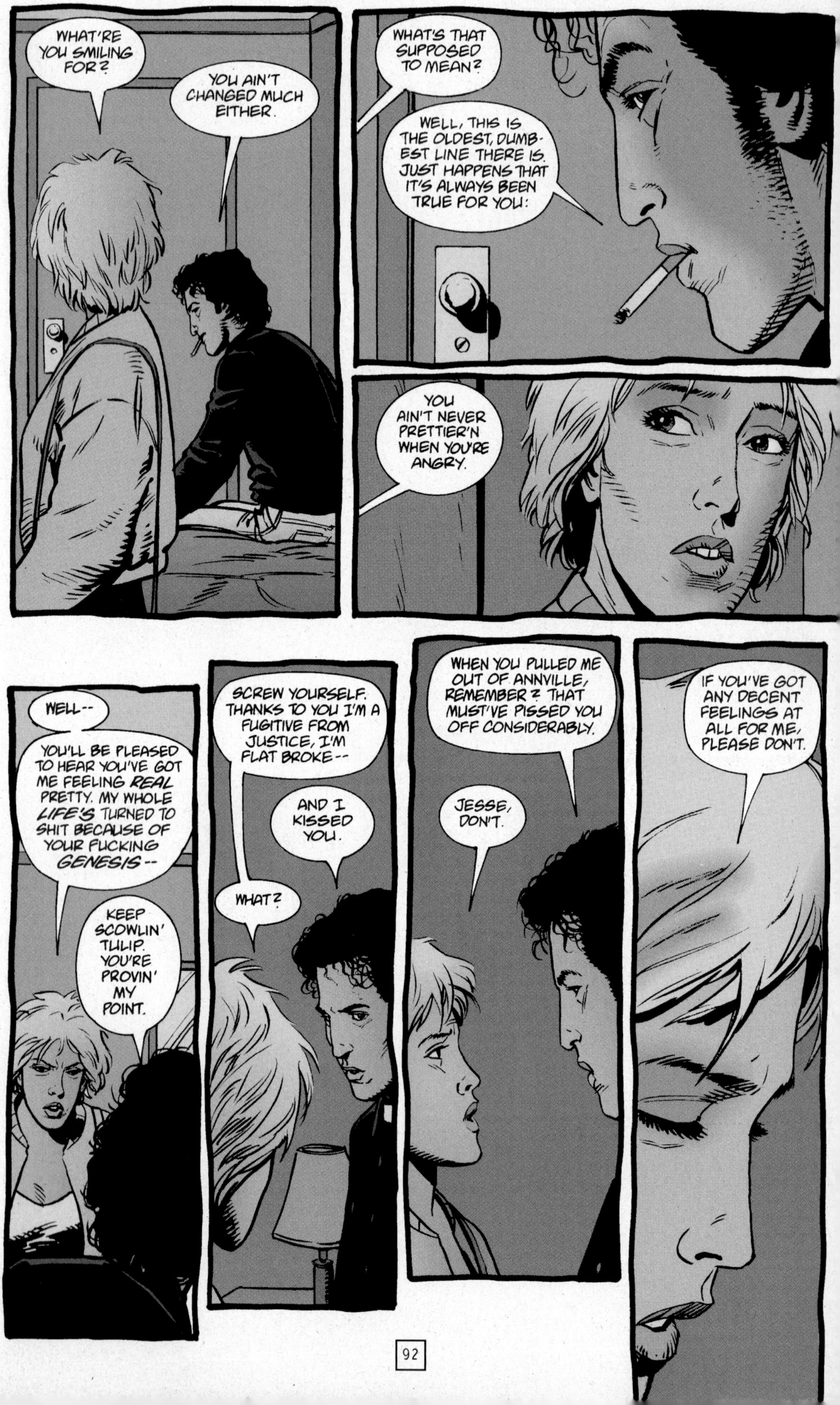

WHAT'RE YOU SMILING FOR?
YOU AIN'T CHANGED MUCH EITHER.
WHAT'S THAT SUPPOSED TO MEAN?
WELL, THIS IS THE OLDEST, DUMB-EST LINE THERE IS. JUST HAPPENS THAT IT'S ALWAYS BEEN TRUE FOR YOU:
YOU AIN'T NEVER PRETTIER'N WHEN YOU'RE ANGRY.
WELL--
YOU'LL BE PLEASED TO HEAR YOU'VE GOT ME FEELING *REAL* PRETTY. MY WHOLE *LIFE'S* TURNED TO SHIT BECAUSE OF YOUR FUCKING *GENESIS*--
KEEP SCOWLIN' TULIP. YOU'RE PROVIN' MY POINT.
SCREW YOURSELF. THANKS TO YOU I'M A FUGITIVE FROM JUSTICE, I'M FLAT BROKE--
AND I KISSED YOU.
WHAT?
WHEN YOU PULLED ME OUT OF ANNVILLE, REMEMBER? THAT MUST'VE PISSED YOU OFF CONSIDERABLY.
JESSE, DON'T.
IF YOU'VE GOT ANY DECENT FEELINGS AT ALL FOR ME, PLEASE DON'T.

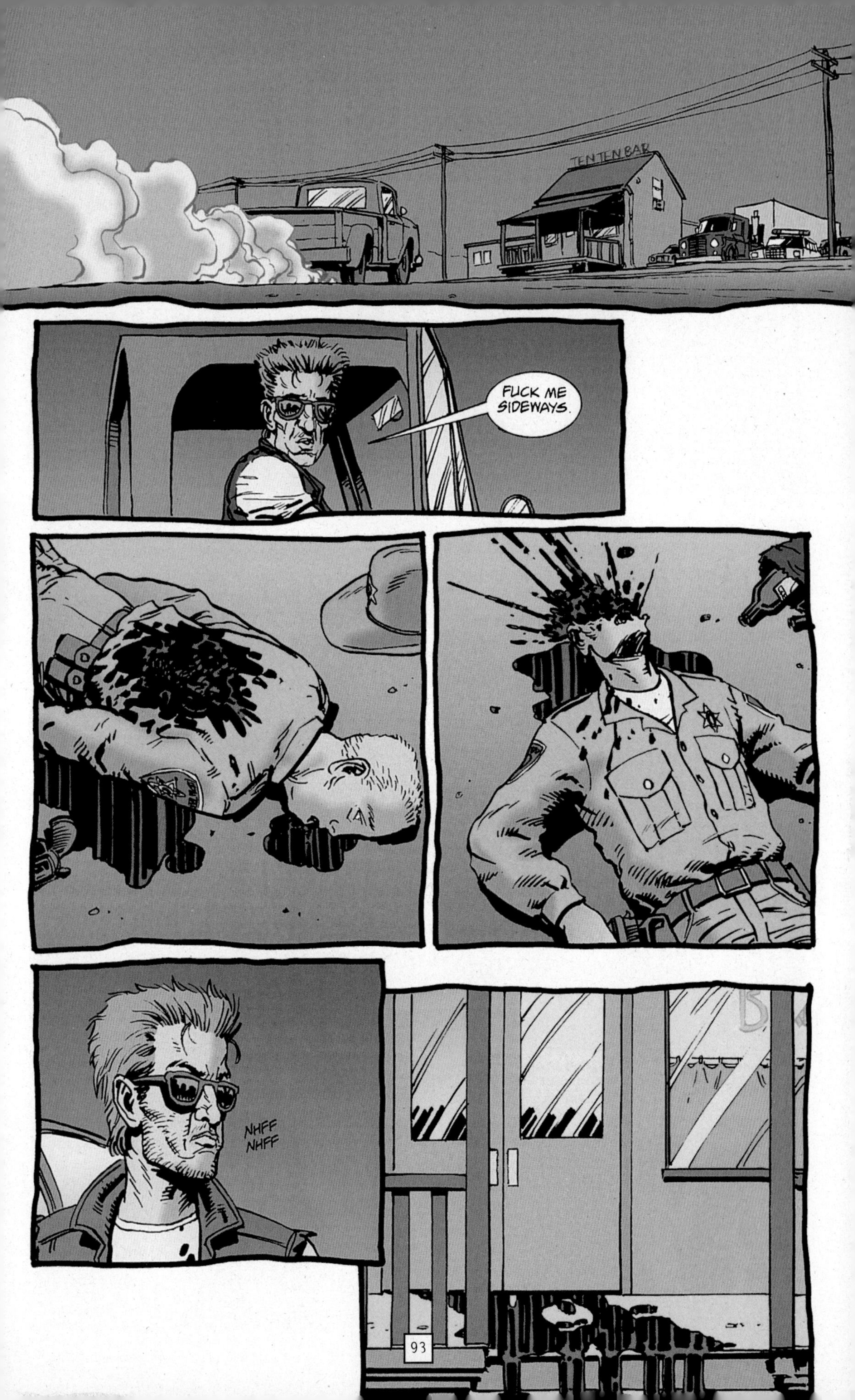
TEN TEN BAR
FUCK ME SIDEWAYS.
NHFF NHFF

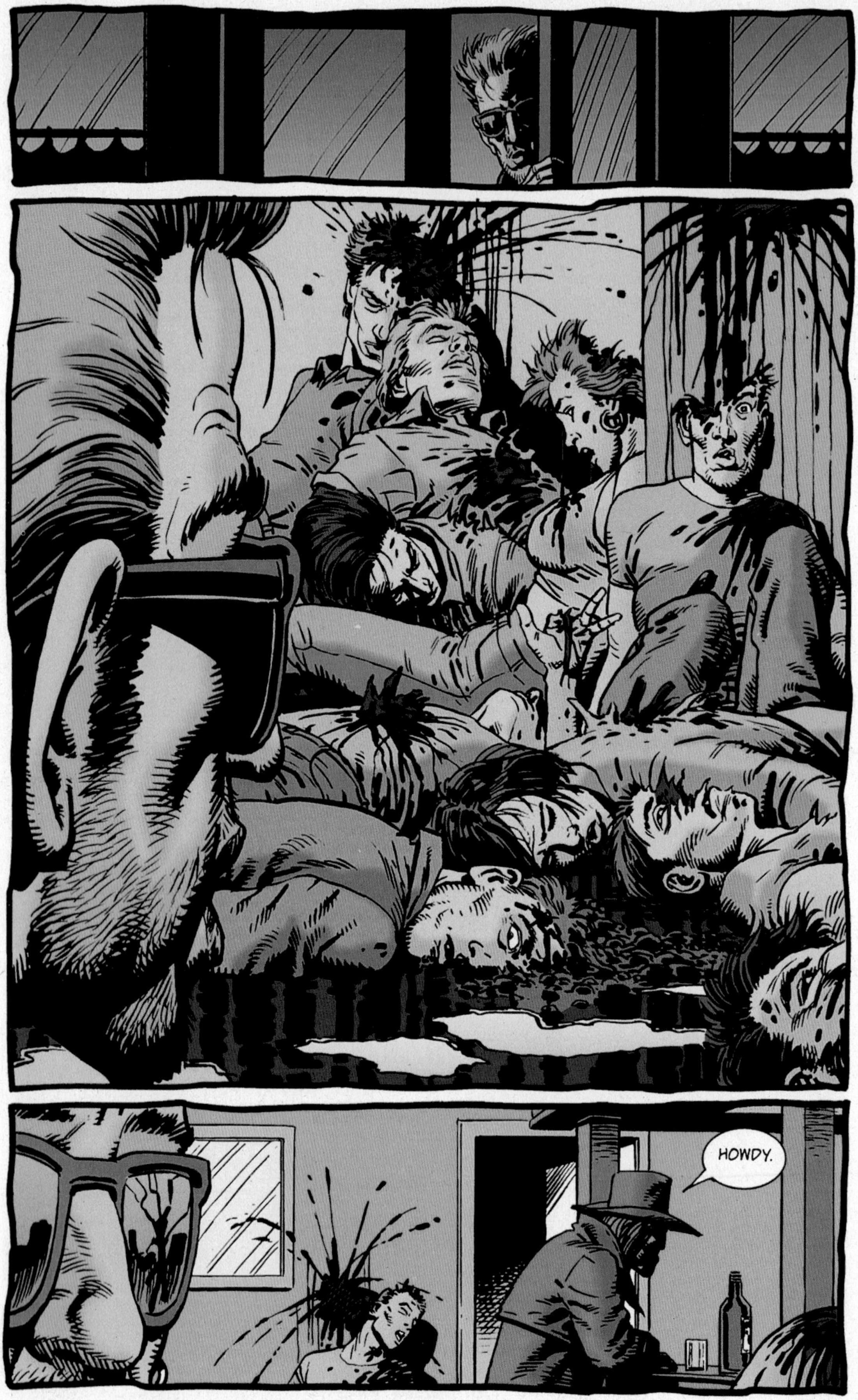
HOWDY.

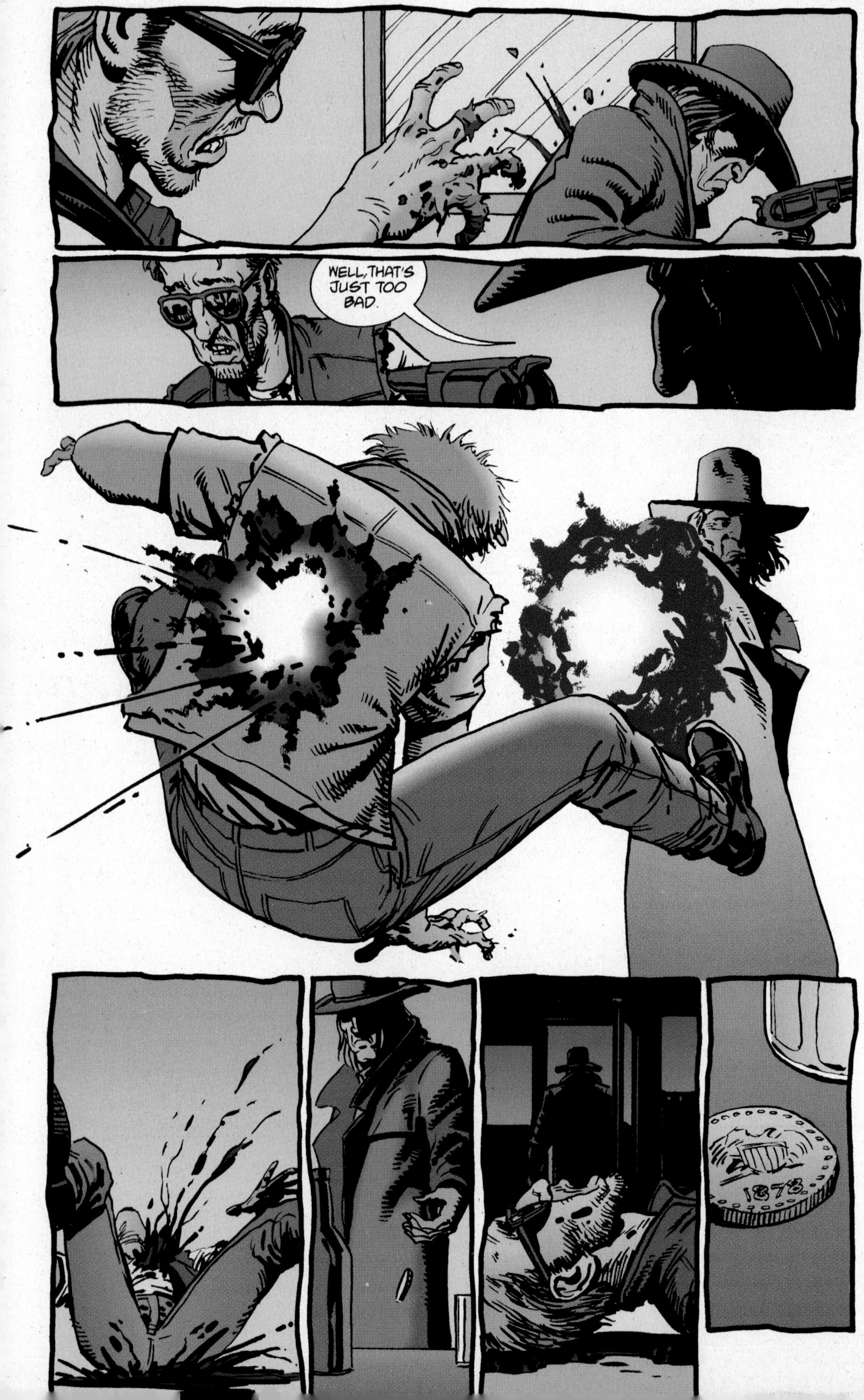
WELL, THAT'S JUST TOO BAD.
1878

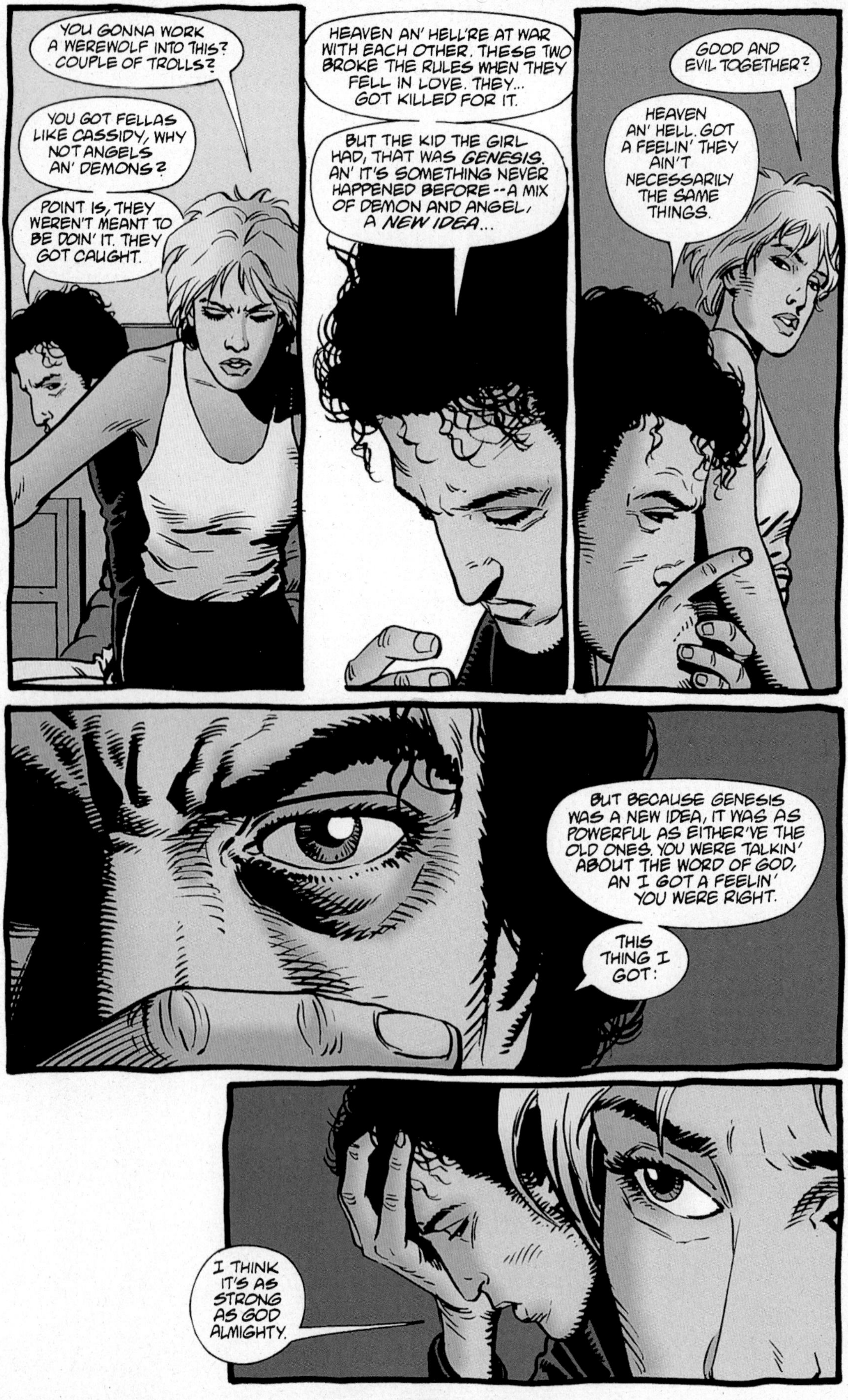

YOU GONNA WORK A WEREWOLF INTO THIS? COUPLE OF TROLLS?
YOU GOT FELLAS LIKE CASSIDY, WHY NOT ANGELS AN' DEMONS?
POINT IS, THEY WEREN'T MEANT TO BE DOIN' IT. THEY GOT CAUGHT.
HEAVEN AN' HELL'RE AT WAR WITH EACH OTHER. THESE TWO BROKE THE RULES WHEN THEY FELL IN LOVE. THEY... GOT KILLED FOR IT.
BUT THE KID THE GIRL HAD, THAT WAS *GENESIS*. AN' IT'S SOMETHING NEVER HAPPENED BEFORE--A MIX OF DEMON AND ANGEL, A *NEW IDEA*...
GOOD AND EVIL TOGETHER?
HEAVEN AN' HELL. GOT A FEELIN' THEY AIN'T NECESSARILY THE SAME THINGS.
BUT BECAUSE GENESIS WAS A NEW IDEA, IT WAS AS POWERFUL AS EITHER'VE THE OLD ONES. YOU WERE TALKIN' ABOUT THE WORD OF GOD, AN I GOT A FEELIN' YOU WERE RIGHT.
THIS THING I GOT:
I THINK IT'S AS STRONG AS GOD ALMIGHTY.

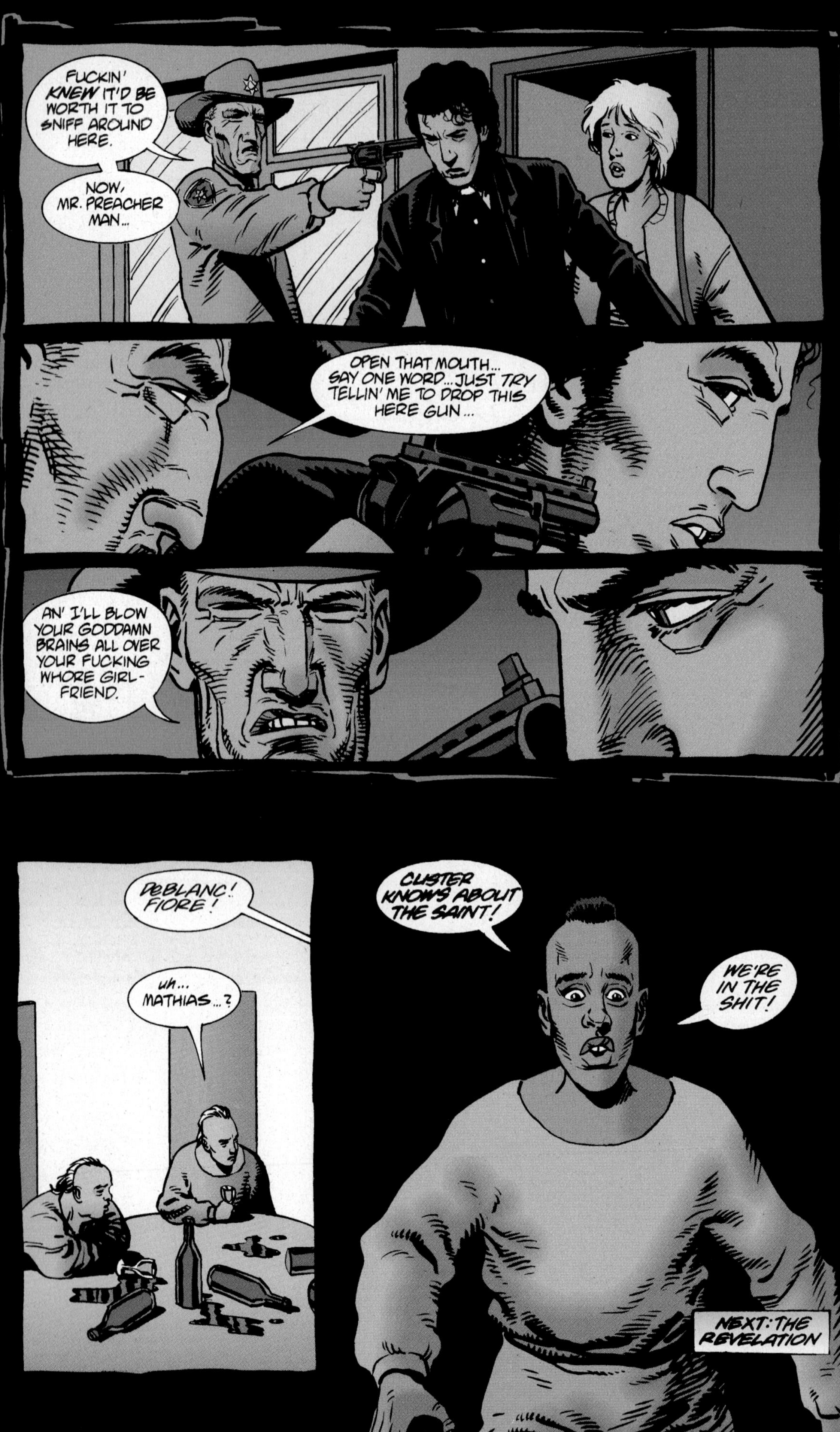
FUCKIN' KNEW IT'D BE WORTH IT TO SNIFF AROUND HERE.
NOW, MR. PREACHER MAN...
OPEN THAT MOUTH... SAY ONE WORD... JUST TRY TELLIN' ME TO DROP THIS HERE GUN...
AN' I'LL BLOW YOUR GODDAMN BRAINS ALL OVER YOUR FUCKING WHORE GIRL-FRIEND.
DeBLANC! FIORE!
uh... MATHIAS...?
CUSTER KNOWS ABOUT THE SAINT!
WE'RE IN THE SHIT!
NEXT: THE REVELATION

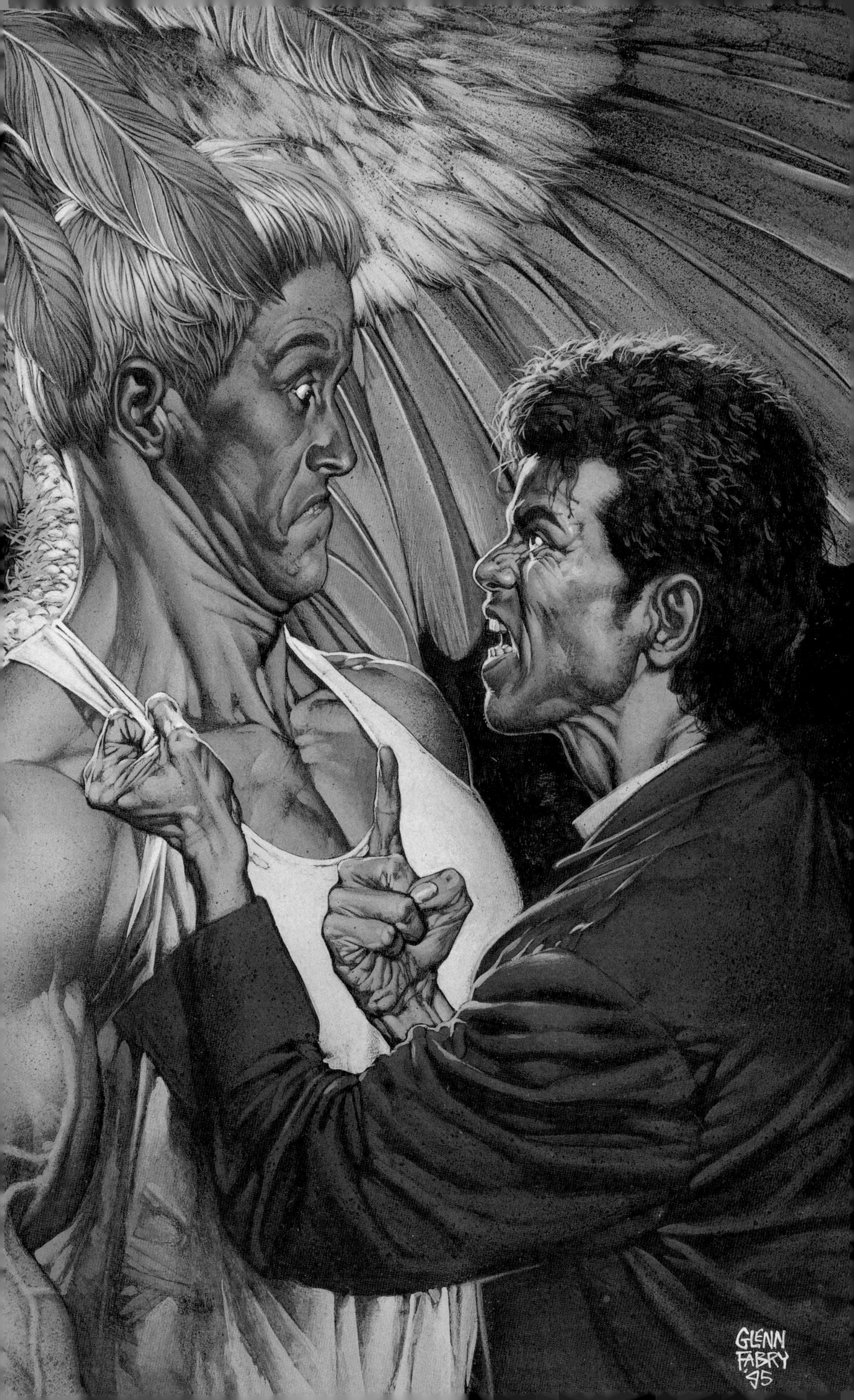
GLENN
FABRY
'95

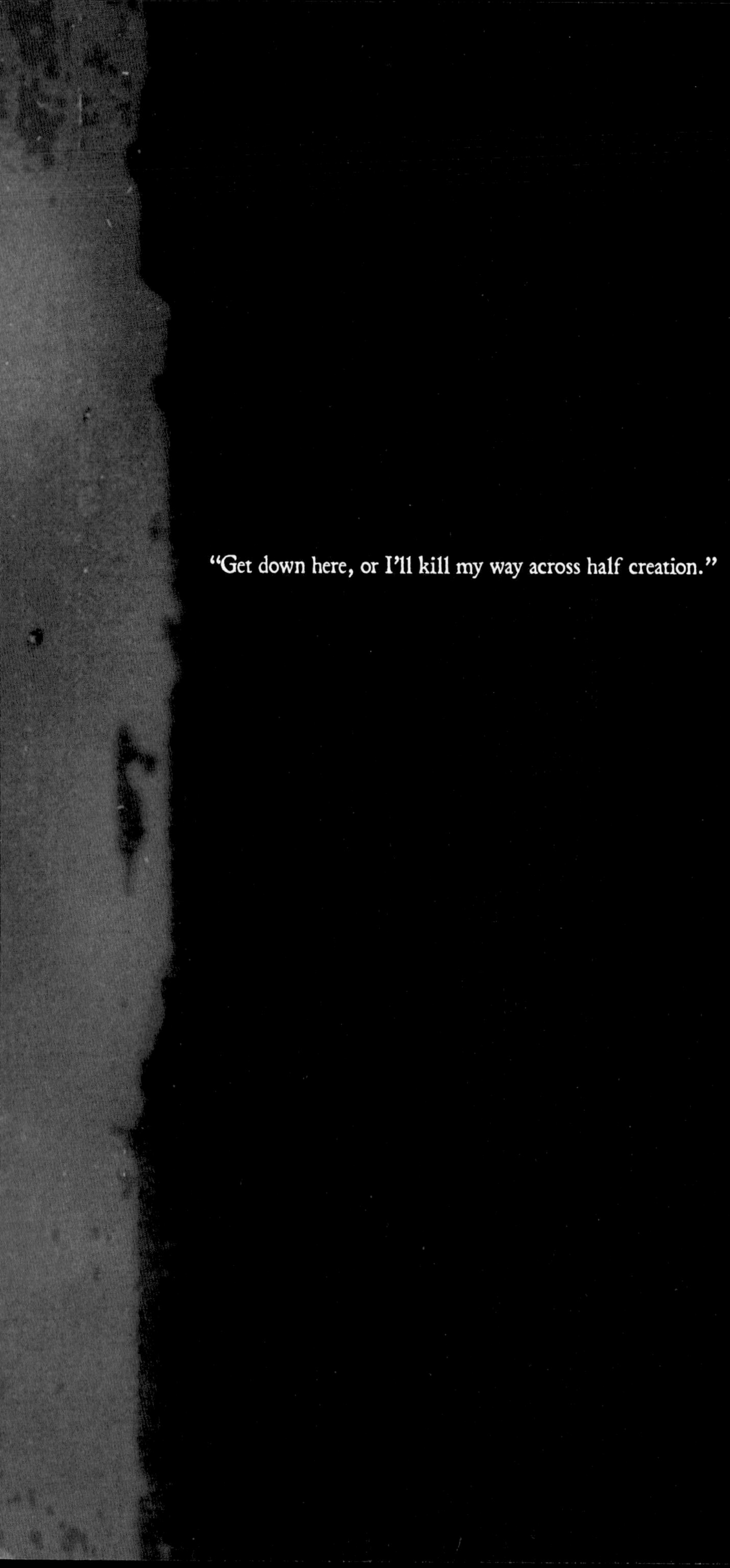
"Get down here, or I'll kill my way across half creation."

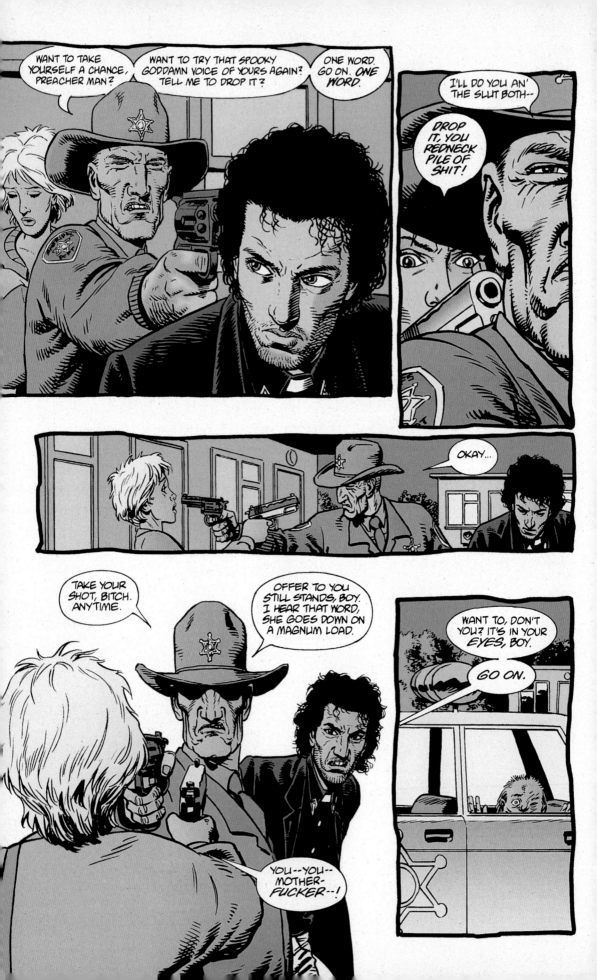

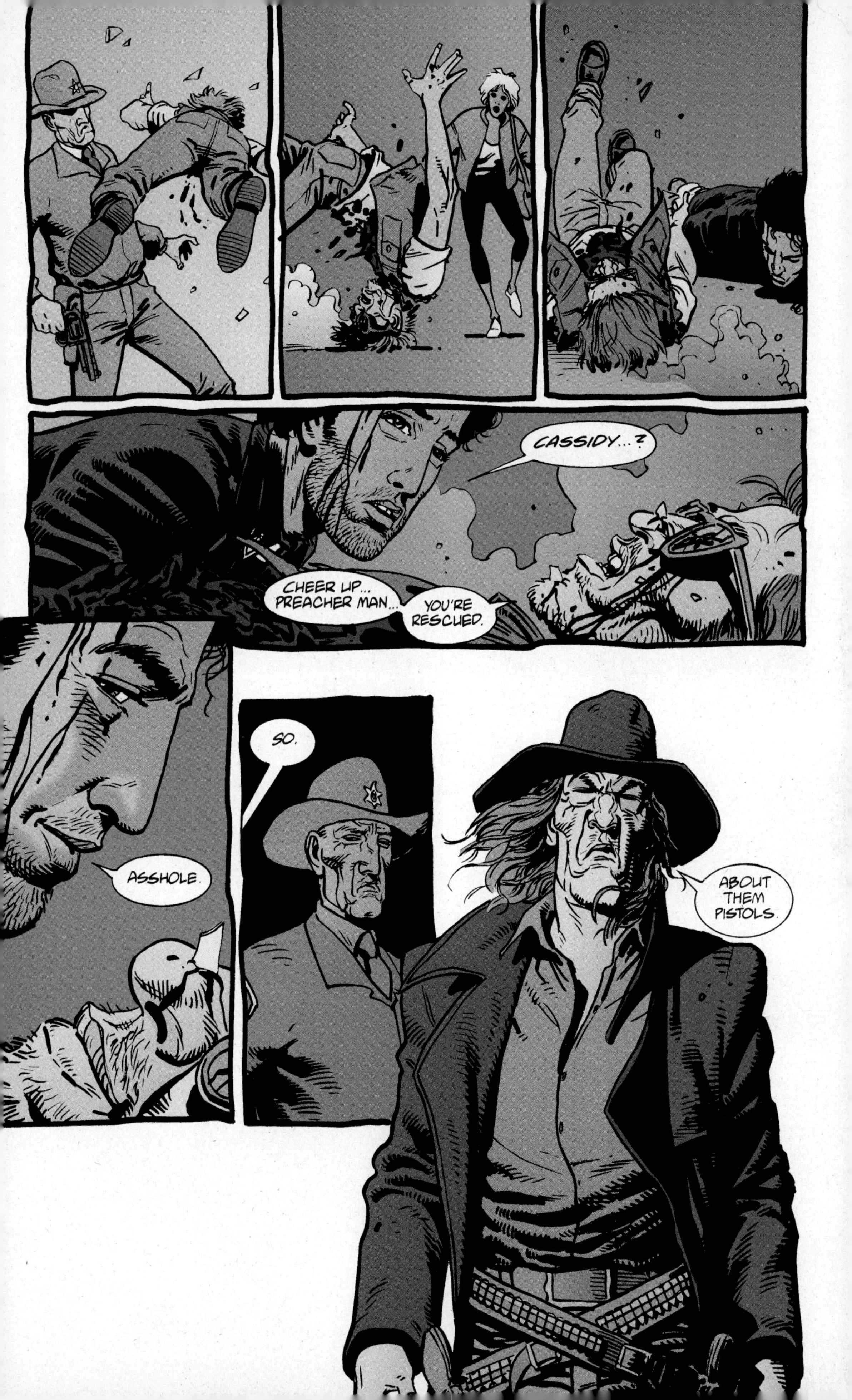
CASSIDY...?
CHEER UP... PREACHER MAN...
YOU'RE RESCUED.
ASSHOLE.
SO.
ABOUT THEM PISTOLS.

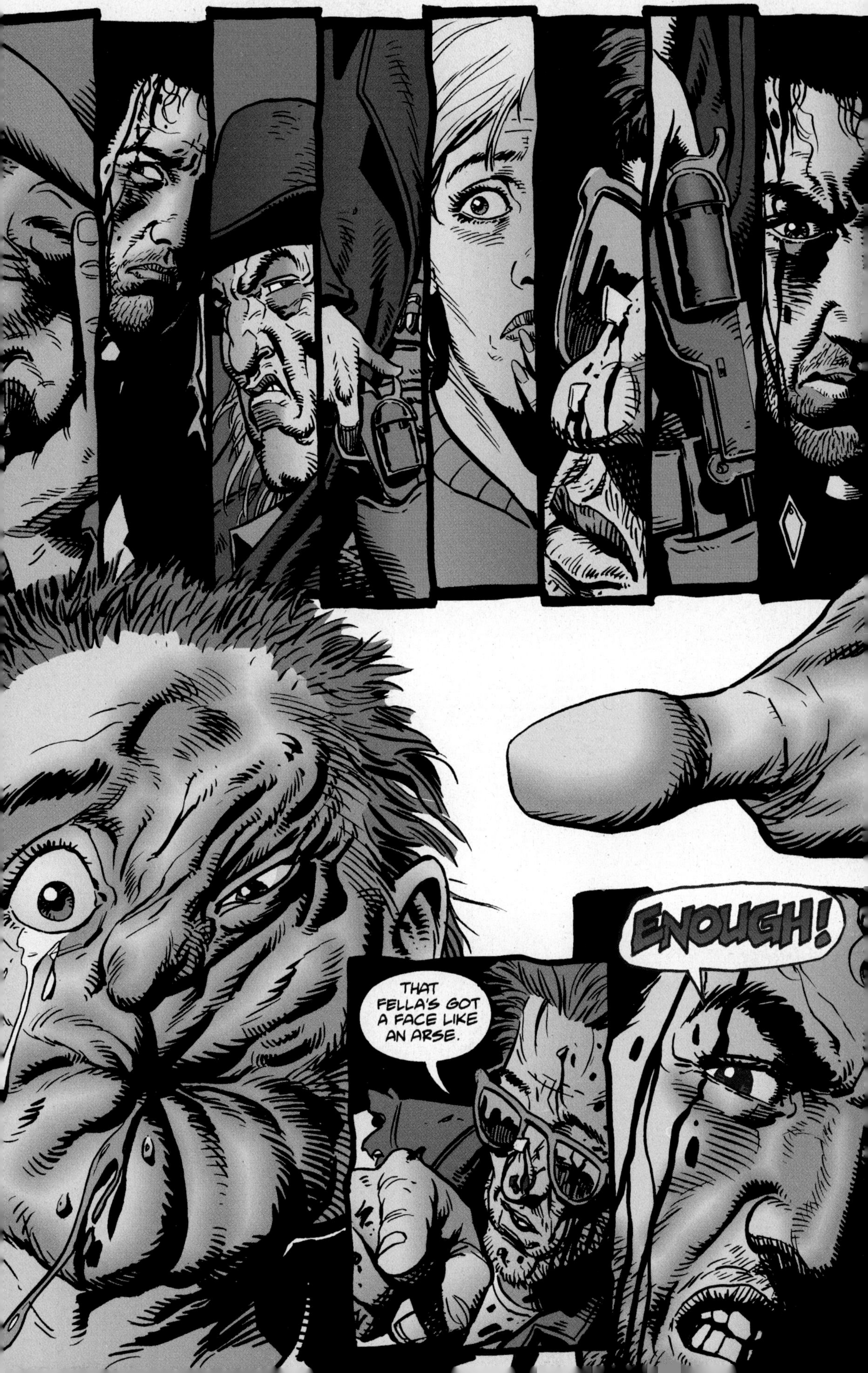
THAT FELLA'S GOT A FACE LIKE AN ARSE.
ENOUGH!

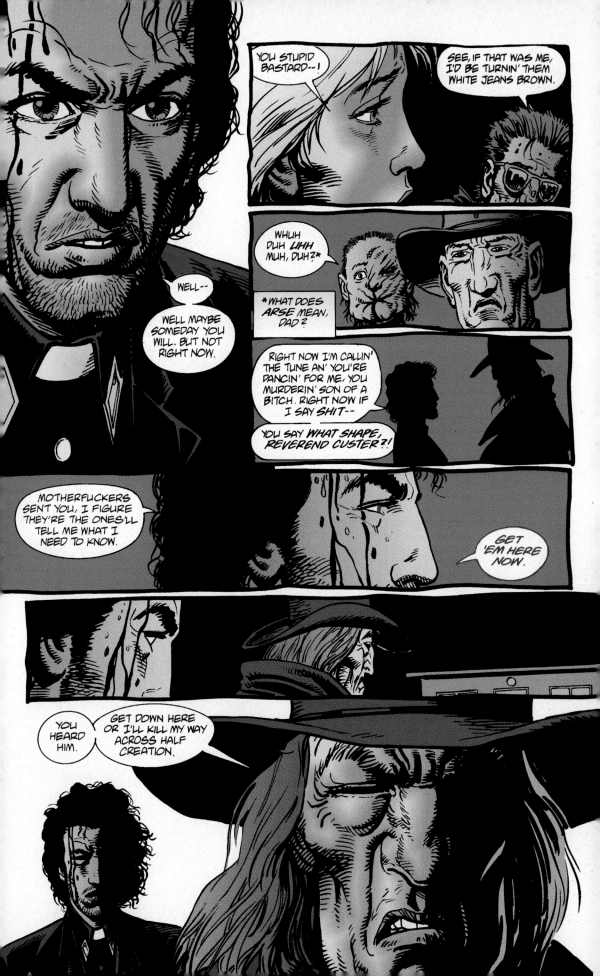

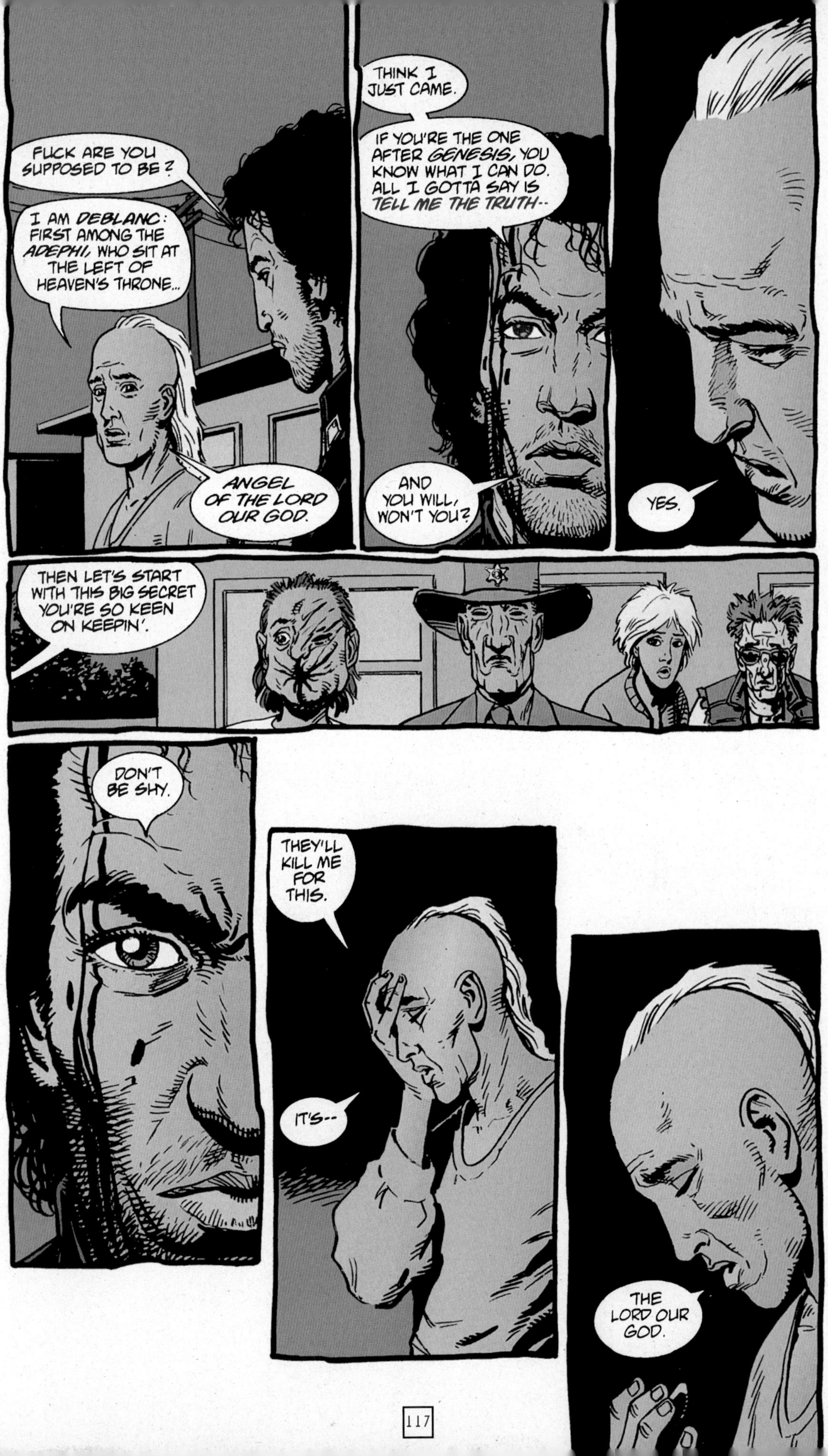
FUCK ARE YOU SUPPOSED TO BE?
I AM DEBLANC: FIRST AMONG THE ADEPHI, WHO SIT AT THE LEFT OF HEAVEN'S THRONE...
ANGEL OF THE LORD OUR GOD.
THINK I JUST CAME.
IF YOU'RE THE ONE AFTER GENESIS, YOU KNOW WHAT I CAN DO. ALL I GOTTA SAY IS TELL ME THE TRUTH--
AND YOU WILL, WON'T YOU?
YES.
THEN LET'S START WITH THIS BIG SECRET YOU'RE SO KEEN ON KEEPIN'.
DON'T BE SHY.
THEY'LL KILL ME FOR THIS.
IT'S--
THE LORD OUR GOD.

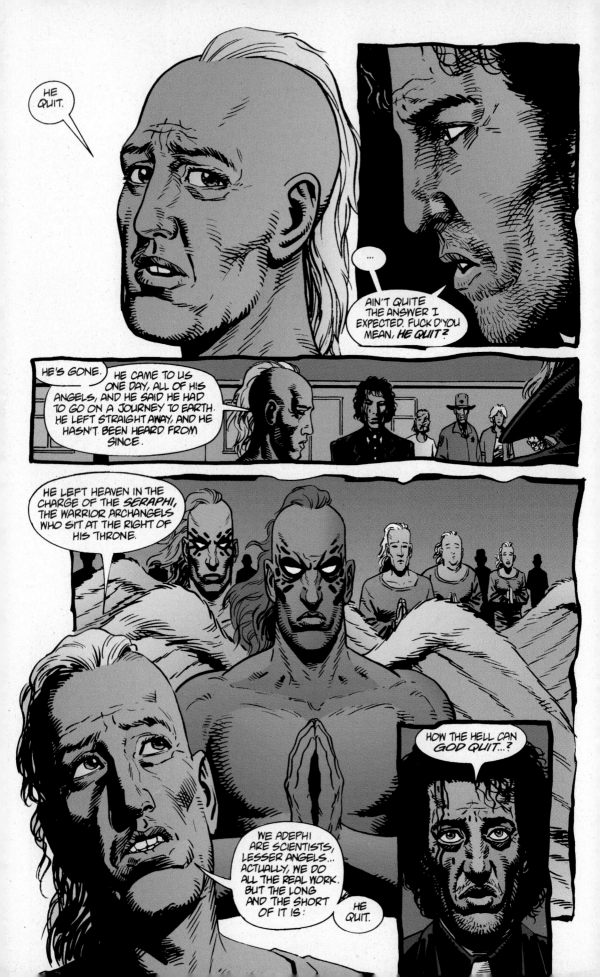

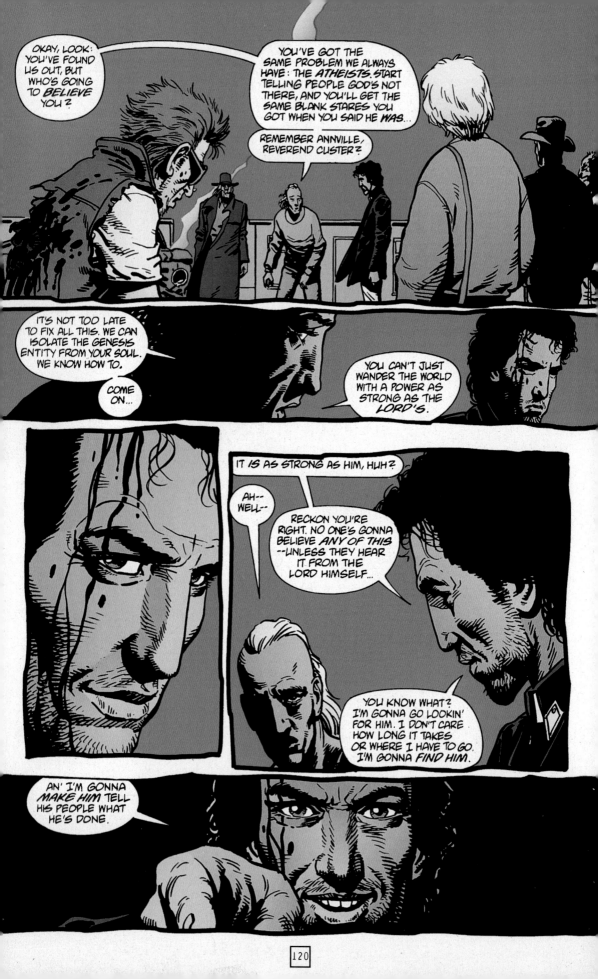

OKAY, LOOK: YOU'VE FOUND US OUT, BUT WHO'S GOING TO *BELIEVE* YOU?

YOU'VE GOT THE SAME PROBLEM WE ALWAYS HAVE: THE *ATHEISTS* START TELLING PEOPLE GOD'S NOT THERE, AND YOU'LL GET THE SAME BLANK STARES YOU GOT WHEN YOU SAID HE *WAS*...

REMEMBER ANNVILLE, REVEREND CUSTER?

IT'S NOT TOO LATE TO FIX ALL THIS. WE CAN ISOLATE THE GENESIS ENTITY FROM YOUR SOUL. WE KNOW HOW TO.

COME ON...

YOU CAN'T JUST WANDER THE WORLD WITH A POWER AS STRONG AS THE *LORD'S*.

IT *IS* AS STRONG AS HIM, HUH?

AH-- WELL--

RECKON YOU'RE RIGHT. NO ONE'S GONNA BELIEVE *ANY OF THIS* --UNLESS THEY HEAR IT FROM THE LORD HIMSELF...

YOU KNOW WHAT? I'M GONNA GO LOOKIN' FOR HIM. I DON'T CARE HOW LONG IT TAKES OR WHERE I HAVE TO GO. I'M GONNA *FIND HIM*.

AN' I'M GONNA *MAKE HIM* TELL HIS PEOPLE WHAT HE'S DONE.

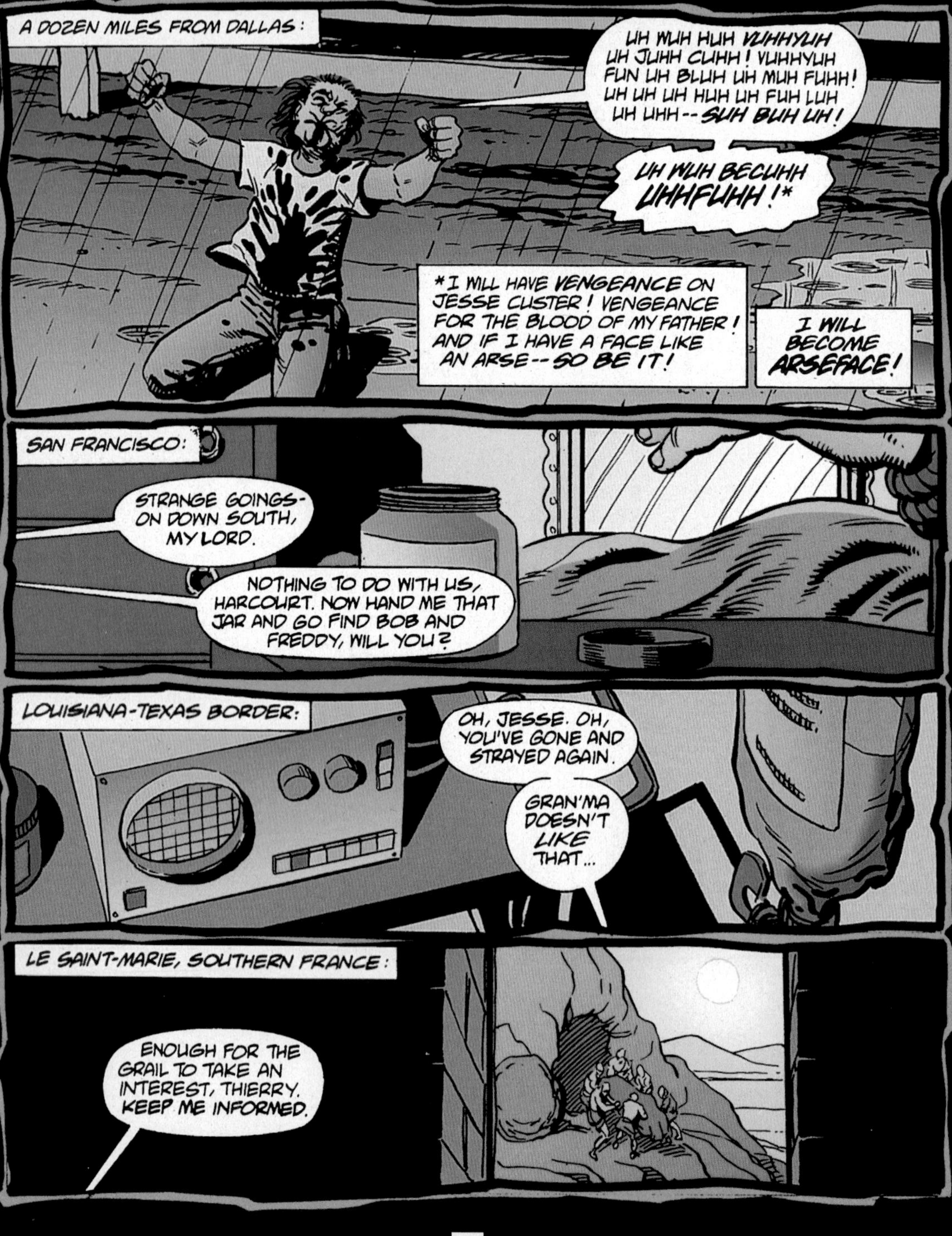
A DOZEN MILES FROM DALLAS:
UH WUH HUH VUHHYUH UH JUHH CUHH! VUHHYUH FUN UH BLUH UH MUH FUHH! UH UH UH HUH UH FUH LUH UH UHH-- SUH BUH UH!
UH WUH BECUHH UHHFUHH!*
*I WILL HAVE VENGEANCE ON JESSE CUSTER! VENGEANCE FOR THE BLOOD OF MY FATHER! AND IF I HAVE A FACE LIKE AN ARSE-- SO BE IT!
I WILL BECOME ARSEFACE!
SAN FRANCISCO:
STRANGE GOINGS-ON DOWN SOUTH, MY LORD.
NOTHING TO DO WITH US, HARCOURT. NOW HAND ME THAT JAR AND GO FIND BOB AND FREDDY, WILL YOU?
LOUISIANA-TEXAS BORDER:
OH, JESSE. OH, YOU'VE GONE AND STRAYED AGAIN.
GRAN'MA DOESN'T LIKE THAT...
LE SAINT-MARIE, SOUTHERN FRANCE:
ENOUGH FOR THE GRAIL TO TAKE AN INTEREST, THIERRY. KEEP ME INFORMED.

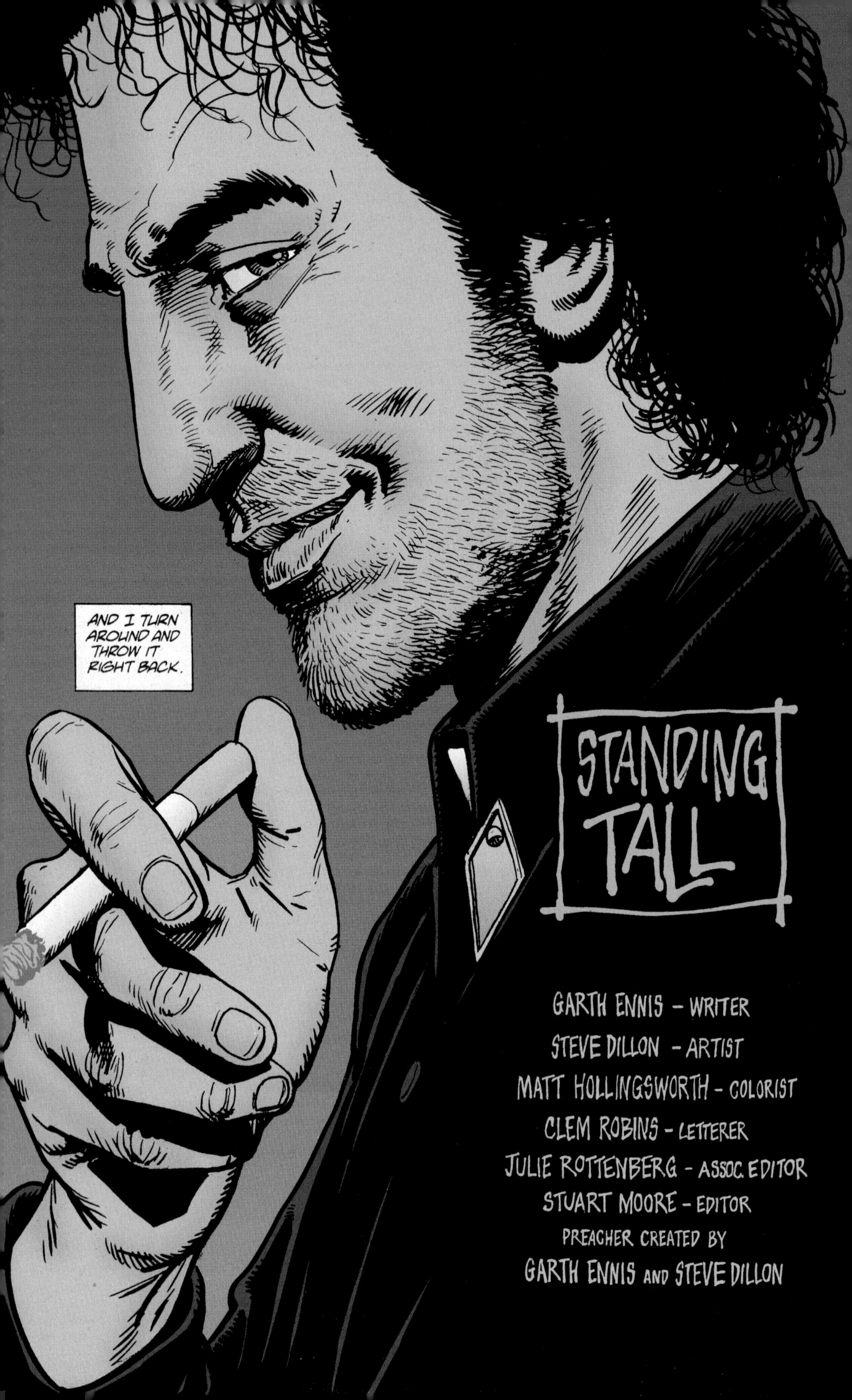
AND I TURN AROUND AND THROW IT RIGHT BACK.
STANDING TALL
GARTH ENNIS – WRITER
STEVE DILLON – ARTIST
MATT HOLLINGSWORTH – COLORIST
CLEM ROBINS – LETTERER
JULIE ROTTENBERG – ASSOC. EDITOR
STUART MOORE – EDITOR
PREACHER CREATED BY
GARTH ENNIS AND STEVE DILLON

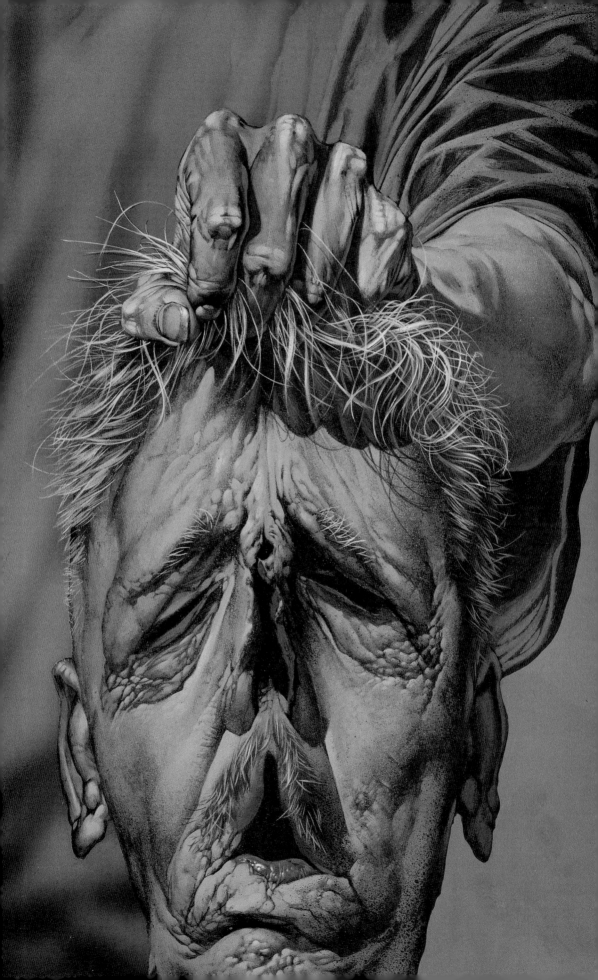

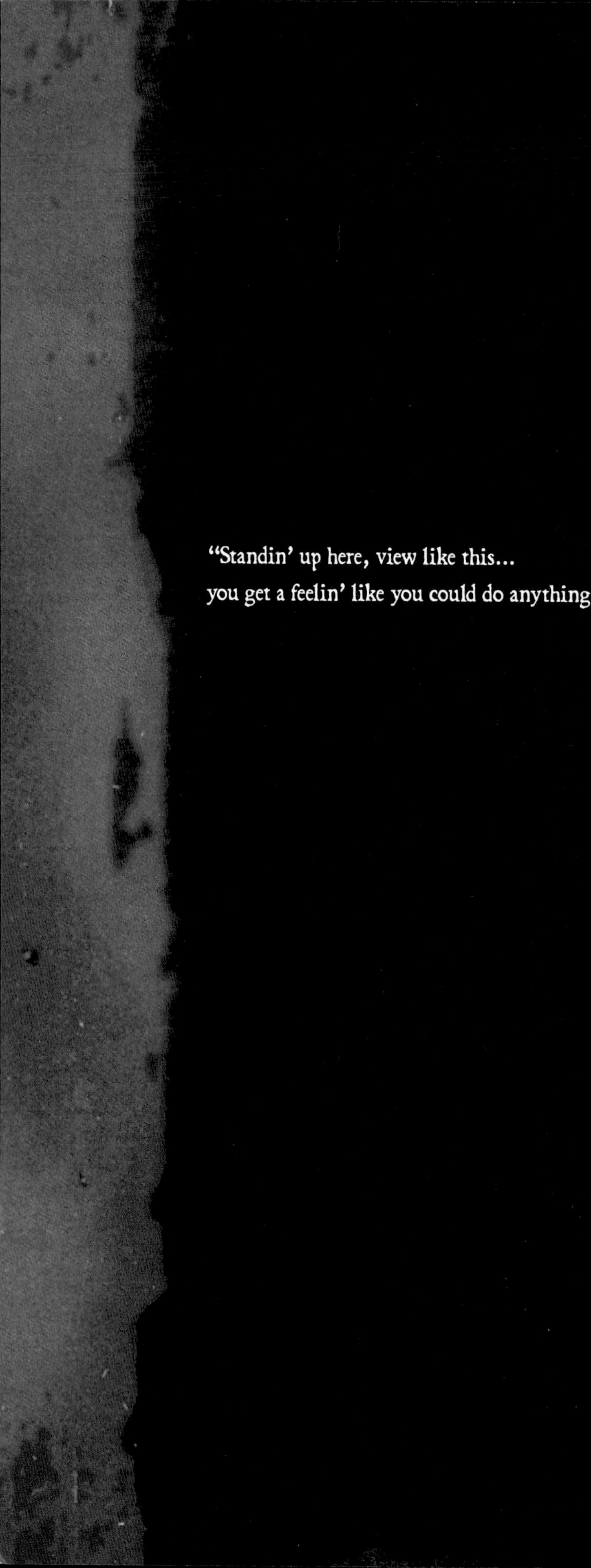
"Standin' up here, view like this...
you get a feelin' like you could do anything

A COPY OF ANAL RAMPAGE, PLEASE.

HMH?

A COPY OF ANAL RAMPAGE. PLEASE.

ONNA RACK. NEXT TO ANIMAL HEAT.

RIGHT.

FOUR FIFTY.

THERE YOU ARE. KEEP THE CHANGE. AND YOU HAVE YOURSELF A NICE DAY.

BOOKS
TOYS
MAGAZINES
VIDEOS
NOVELTIES
PRIVATE BOOTHS

'BYE NOW!

CURIOUS MOTHER-FUCKER.

EXPLODING CHICKEN

131

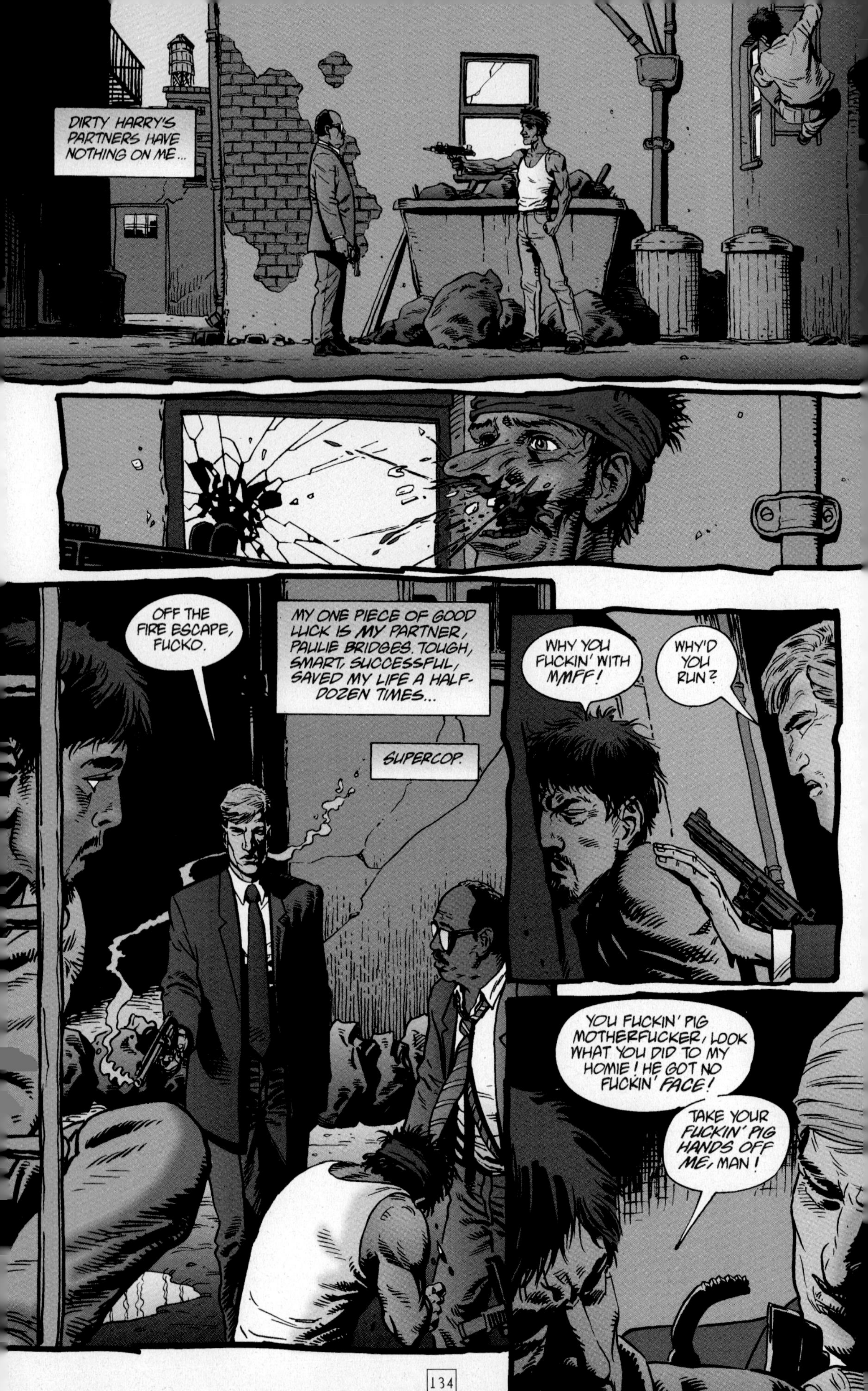
DIRTY HARRY'S PARTNERS HAVE NOTHING ON ME...
OFF THE FIRE ESCAPE, FUCKO.
MY ONE PIECE OF GOOD LUCK IS MY PARTNER, PAULIE BRIDGES. TOUGH, SMART, SUCCESSFUL, SAVED MY LIFE A HALF-DOZEN TIMES...
SUPERCOP.
WHY YOU FUCKIN' WITH MMFF!
WHY'D YOU RUN?
YOU FUCKIN' PIG MOTHERFUCKER, LOOK WHAT YOU DID TO MY HOMIE! HE GOT NO FUCKIN' FACE!
TAKE YOUR FUCKIN' PIG HANDS OFF ME, MAN!

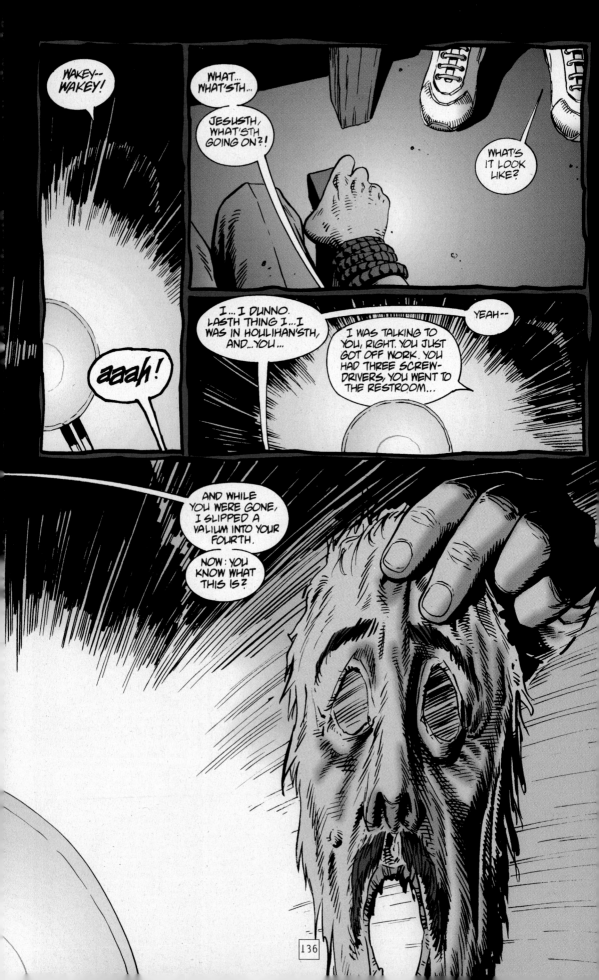

WAKEY-- WAKEY!

WHAT... WHAT'STH...

JESUSTH, WHAT'STH GOING ON?!

WHAT'S IT LOOK LIKE?

aaah!

I... I DUNNO. LASTH THING I...I WAS IN HOULIHAN'STH, AND...YOU...

YEAH--

I WAS TALKING TO YOU, RIGHT. YOU JUST GOT OFF WORK. YOU HAD THREE SCREW-DRIVERS, YOU WENT TO THE RESTROOM...

AND WHILE YOU WERE GONE, I SLIPPED A VALIUM INTO YOUR FOURTH.

NOW: YOU KNOW WHAT THIS IS?

SO ARE YOU NOT A WEE BIT WORRIED THEY'RE GONNA TWIG YOU DIDN'T GO UP IN FLAMES WITH THE REST OF YER FLOCK? THERE'S MORE'N LIKELY AN A.P.B. OUT ON YOU BY NOW.

BUT YOU WERE KIND OF INDISCREET FOR A DEAD MAN, WEREN'T YOU? MUST'VE BEEN A DOZEN PEOPLE SAW YOU BEFORE WE LEFT THE STATE. YOU WERE ON FIRST-NAME TERMS WITH THAT TRUCKER BEFORE WE HIT THE MISSISSIPPI...

WHOLE LOT OF JESSES IN THE SOUTH. 'SIDES, HE WAS SO FUCKIN' STONED HE'S FORGOTTEN EVER SEEIN' US, NEVER MIND GIVIN' US A RIDE.

HOW? JUST BONES LEFT.

FIGURE I'LL BE OKAY.

BULLSHIT. YOU'RE ACTING WAY TOO BLASÉ ABOUT THIS, YOU KNOW. YOU'RE PRACTICALLY A FUGITIVE.

TURNIP'S RIGHT--

TULIP.

WHAT YOU SHOULD'VE DONE WAS TO GRAB A FED BEFORE WE LEFT AN' PUT THE WORD ON HIM. END OF A.P.B.

FOR ONCE WE AGREE.

MAYBE. JUST WANTED TO GET OUTTA TEXAS.

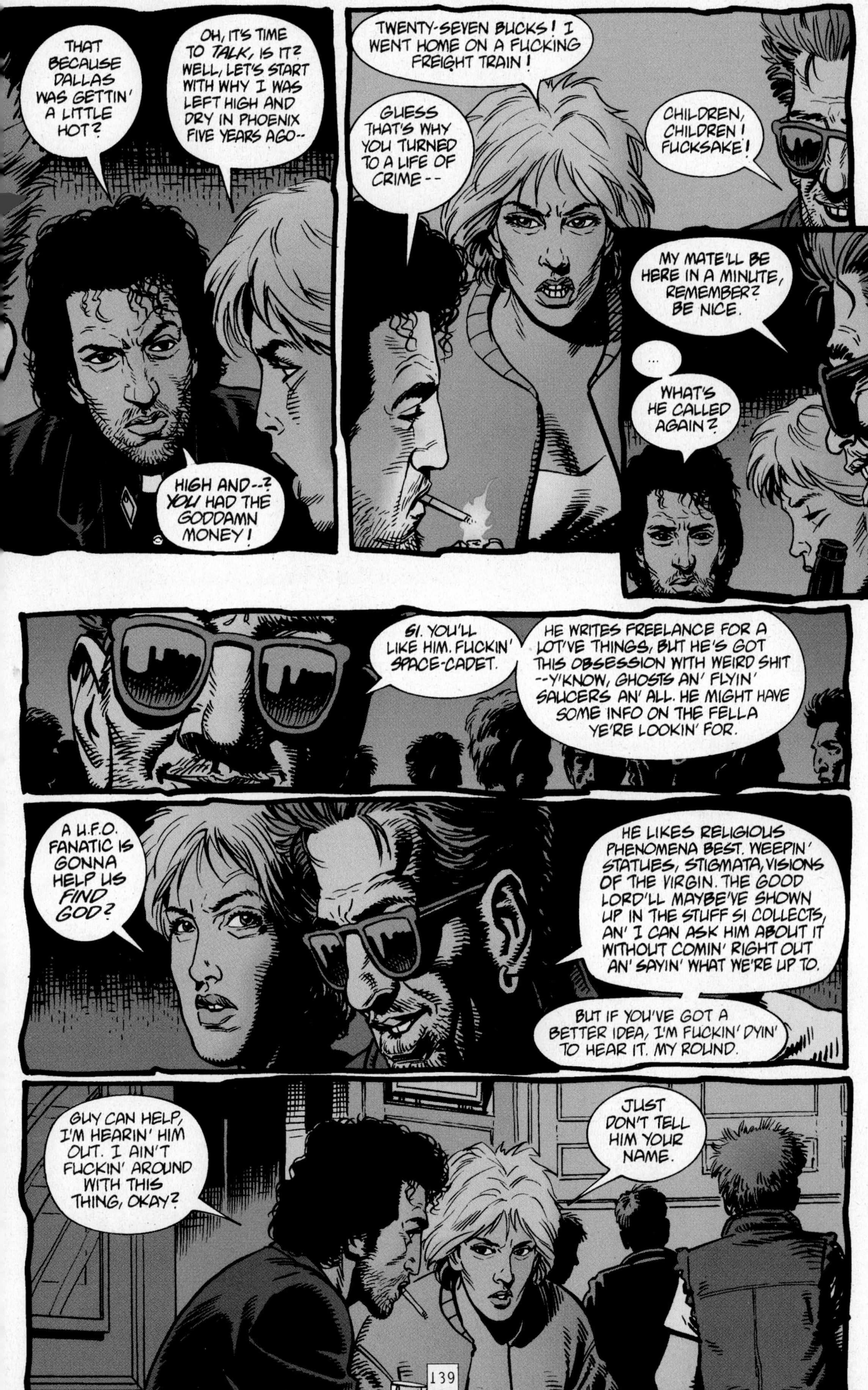

THAT BECAUSE DALLAS WAS GETTIN' A LITTLE HOT?
OH, IT'S TIME TO TALK, IS IT? WELL, LET'S START WITH WHY I WAS LEFT HIGH AND DRY IN PHOENIX FIVE YEARS AGO--
HIGH AND--? YOU HAD THE GODDAMN MONEY!
TWENTY-SEVEN BUCKS! I WENT HOME ON A FUCKING FREIGHT TRAIN!
GUESS THAT'S WHY YOU TURNED TO A LIFE OF CRIME--
CHILDREN, CHILDREN! FUCKSAKE!
MY MATE'LL BE HERE IN A MINUTE, REMEMBER? BE NICE.
...
WHAT'S HE CALLED AGAIN?
SI. YOU'LL LIKE HIM. FUCKIN' SPACE-CADET.
HE WRITES FREELANCE FOR A LOT'VE THINGS, BUT HE'S GOT THIS OBSESSION WITH WEIRD SHIT --Y'KNOW, GHOSTS AN' FLYIN' SAUCERS AN' ALL. HE MIGHT HAVE SOME INFO ON THE FELLA YE'RE LOOKIN' FOR.
A U.F.O. FANATIC IS GONNA HELP US FIND GOD?
HE LIKES RELIGIOUS PHENOMENA BEST. WEEPIN' STATUES, STIGMATA, VISIONS OF THE VIRGIN. THE GOOD LORD'LL MAYBE'VE SHOWN UP IN THE STUFF SI COLLECTS, AN' I CAN ASK HIM ABOUT IT WITHOUT COMIN' RIGHT OUT AN' SAYIN' WHAT WE'RE UP TO.
BUT IF YOU'VE GOT A BETTER IDEA, I'M FUCKIN' DYIN' TO HEAR IT. MY ROUND.
GUY CAN HELP, I'M HEARIN' HIM OUT. I AIN'T FUCKIN' AROUND WITH THIS THING, OKAY?
JUST DON'T TELL HIM YOUR NAME.

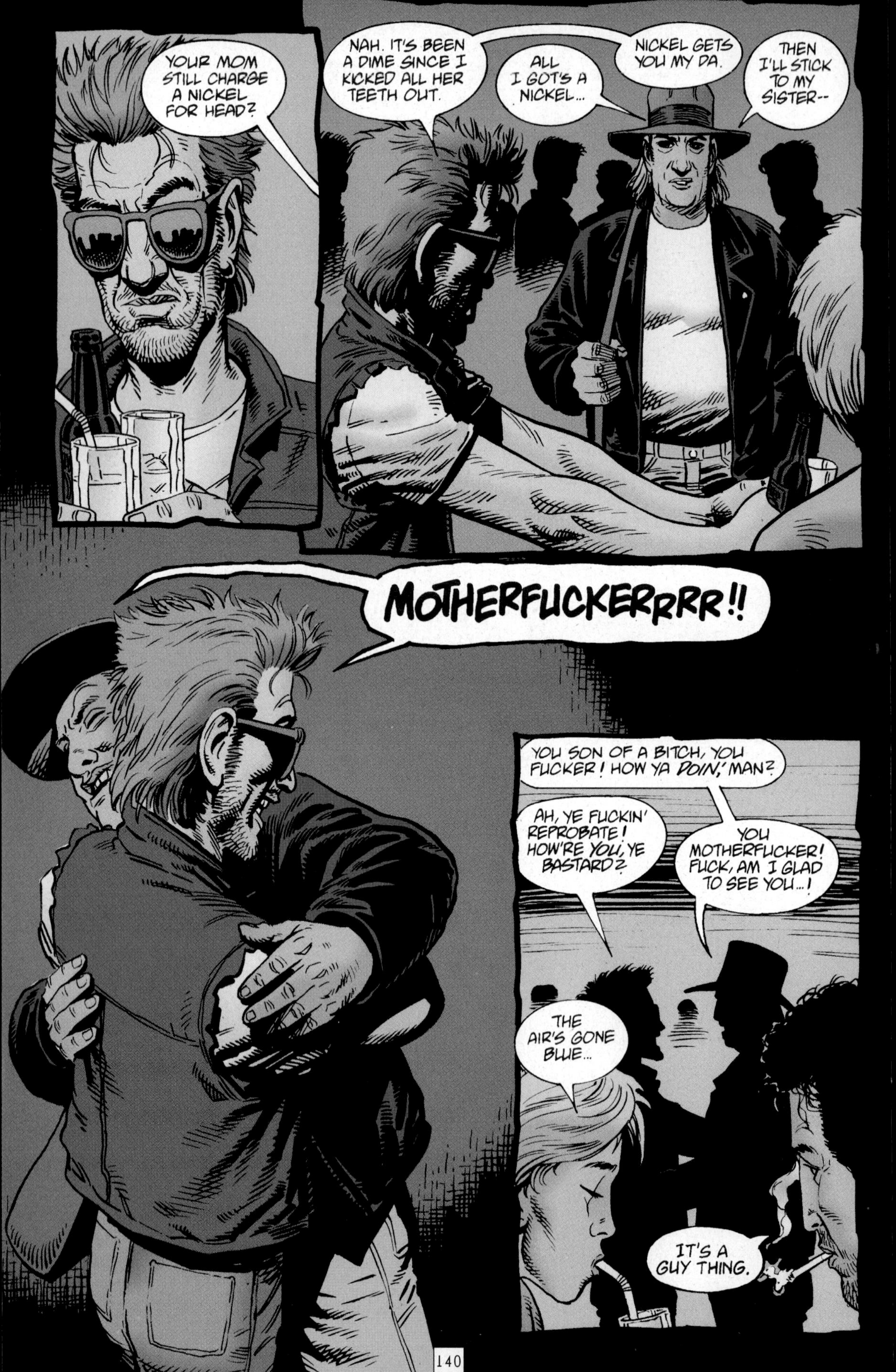
YOUR MOM STILL CHARGE A NICKEL FOR HEAD?
NAH. IT'S BEEN A DIME SINCE I KICKED ALL HER TEETH OUT.
ALL I GOT'S A NICKEL...
NICKEL GETS YOU MY DA.
THEN I'LL STICK TO MY SISTER--
MOTHERFUCKERRRR!!
YOU SON OF A BITCH, YOU FUCKER! HOW YA DOIN,' MAN?
AH, YE FUCKIN' REPROBATE! HOW'RE YOU, YE BASTARD?
YOU MOTHERFUCKER! FUCK, AM I GLAD TO SEE YOU...!
THE AIR'S GONE BLUE...
IT'S A GUY THING.

LISTEN, I'M SORRY ABOUT EARLIER--

WHAT'RE THOSE TWO TALKING ABOUT?

SI LOOKIN' FOR GOD FOR US. HE FIGURES IT'S A PRIVATE FAVOR TO CASS, HE WON'T ASK ANY QUESTIONS.

YOU THINK HE WOULD ANYWAY?

WOULDN'T LIKE TO TRY LYIN' TO HIM. HE'S A SMART GUY, YOU CAN SEE IT IN HIS EYES.

SO LIKE I SAY--

WELL... SURE. WE GOT THE SAME SENSE OF HUMOR--

YEP. CHILDISH AND SICK.

YOU AND "CASS" GOT AWFULLY FRIENDLY AWFULLY QUICK, DIDN'T YOU?

LOOK, I'M TRYNNA APOLOGIZE HERE. YOU AIN'T MAKIN' IT TOO EASY ON ME, Y'KNOW?

I DIDN'T MEAN TO START UP ABOUT WHAT YOU WERE DOIN' IN DALLAS. AN' I *WILL* EXPLAIN WHY I LEFT YOU BEFORE, SOON, BUT IT'S KIND OF HARD 'CAUSE IT HAS TO DO WITH SHIT I DON'T LIKE TO TALK ABOUT...

OKAY?

OKAY, SURE. THAT'S REASONABLE.

HEY, LISTEN: WHEN WE GET BACK TO THE HOTEL? LET'S CHECK OUT OF THE SINGLE ROOMS AND GET A DOUBLE INSTEAD. WE'VE... GOT SOME CATCHING UP TO DO.

YEAH?

IN YOUR DREAMS.

HEY, LISTEN, I'M SORRY I GOTTA LEAVE RIGHT NOW BUT I GOT A TON OF SHIT I GOTTA DO. I'LL SEE YOU GUYS AGAIN, OKAY? WHEN I GET CASS'S STUFF OFF THE INTERNET.

SURE. YOU TAKE CARE, SI.

IT WAS NICE MEETING YOU.

uh... INTERNET?

COMPUTER WHIZ KID, TOO. TALENTED BOY WE'VE GOT HERE.

YOUR MOM THINKS SO TOO.

I'LL SEE YOU.

WHAT D'YEZ WANNA DO NOW THEN?

YOU TWO ARE DESPERATE, SO YEZ ARE.

HERE, IT'S ONLY HALF TEN. D'YOU WANT TO COME ON AN' I'LL SHOW YOU ROUND A BIT, AYE?

YEAH...LISTEN, THIS IS GONNA SOUND KINDA STUPID:

YOU KNOW THE WAY TO THE EMPIRE STATE BUILDING?

FUCKIN' TOURIST!

WELL, I'M GONNA GO TURN IN.

HAVE FUN.

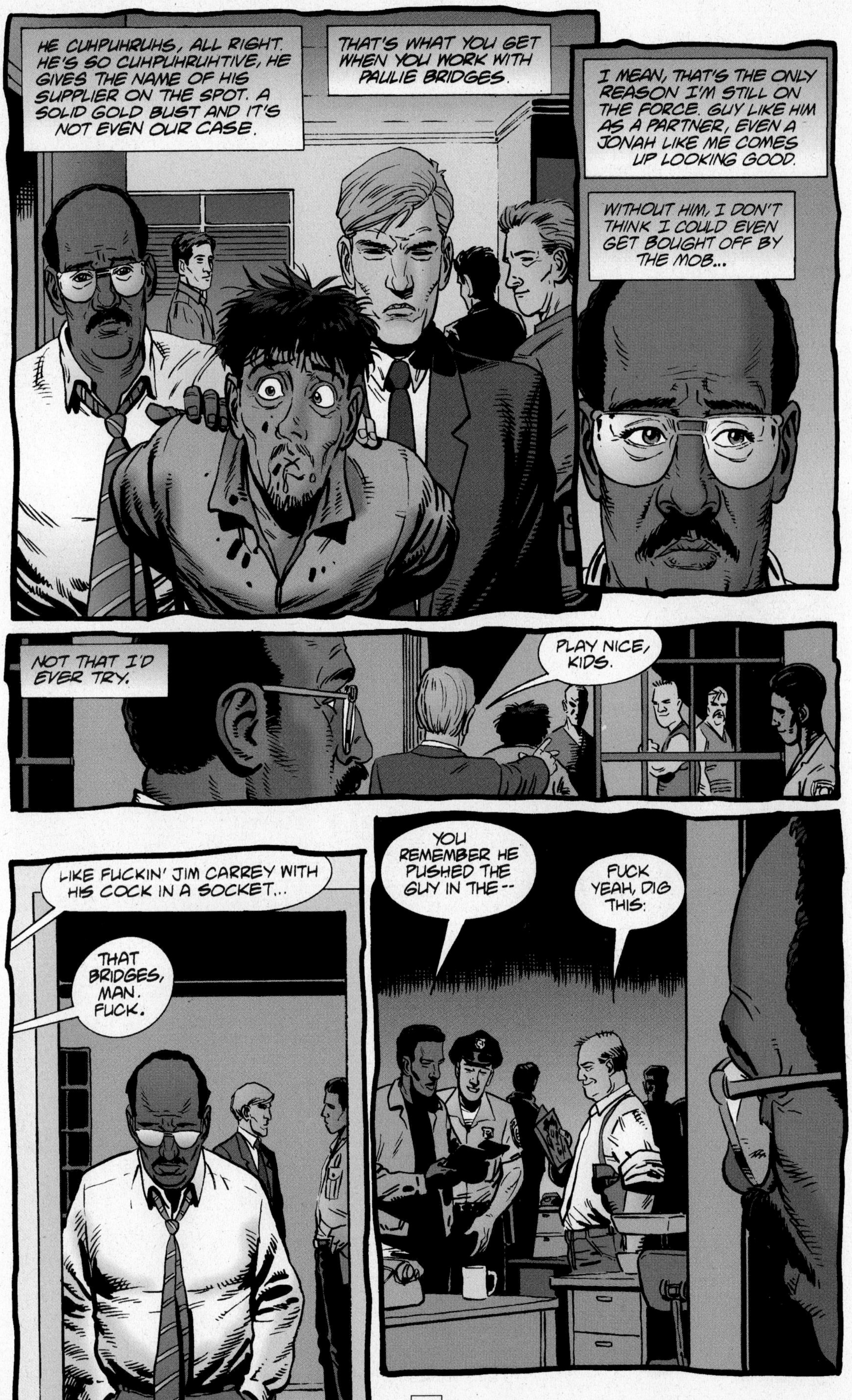
HE CUHPUHRUHS, ALL RIGHT. HE'S SO CUHPUHRUHTIVE, HE GIVES THE NAME OF HIS SUPPLIER ON THE SPOT. A SOLID GOLD BUST AND IT'S NOT EVEN OUR CASE.
THAT'S WHAT YOU GET WHEN YOU WORK WITH PAULIE BRIDGES.
I MEAN, THAT'S THE ONLY REASON I'M STILL ON THE FORCE. GUY LIKE HIM AS A PARTNER, EVEN A JONAH LIKE ME COMES UP LOOKING GOOD.
WITHOUT HIM, I DON'T THINK I COULD EVEN GET BOUGHT OFF BY THE MOB...
NOT THAT I'D EVER TRY.
PLAY NICE, KIDS.
LIKE FUCKIN' JIM CARREY WITH HIS COCK IN A SOCKET...
THAT BRIDGES, MAN. FUCK.
YOU REMEMBER HE PUSHED THE GUY IN THE--
FUCK YEAH, DIG THIS:

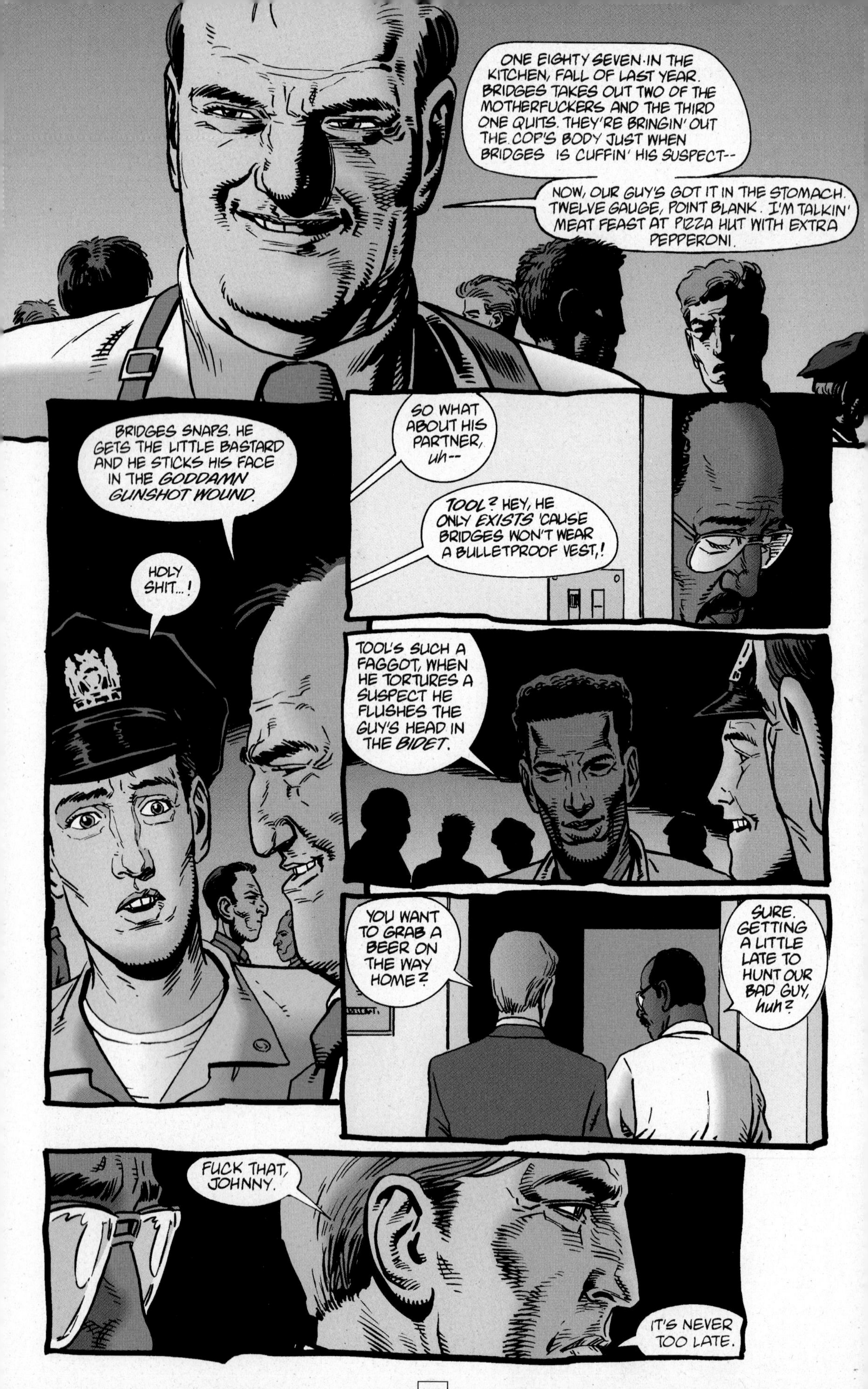

ONE EIGHTY SEVEN IN THE KITCHEN, FALL OF LAST YEAR. BRIDGES TAKES OUT TWO OF THE MOTHERFUCKERS AND THE THIRD ONE QUITS. THEY'RE BRINGIN' OUT THE COP'S BODY JUST WHEN BRIDGES IS CUFFIN' HIS SUSPECT--
NOW, OUR GUY'S GOT IT IN THE STOMACH. TWELVE GAUGE, POINT BLANK. I'M TALKIN' MEAT FEAST AT PIZZA HUT WITH EXTRA PEPPERONI.
BRIDGES SNAPS. HE GETS THE LITTLE BASTARD AND HE STICKS HIS FACE IN THE *GODDAMN GUNSHOT WOUND*.
HOLY SHIT...!
SO WHAT ABOUT HIS PARTNER, *uh*--
TOOL? HEY, HE ONLY *EXISTS* 'CAUSE BRIDGES WON'T WEAR A BULLETPROOF VEST!
TOOL'S SUCH A FAGGOT, WHEN HE TORTURES A SUSPECT HE FLUSHES THE GUY'S HEAD IN THE *BIDET*.
YOU WANT TO GRAB A BEER ON THE WAY HOME?
SURE. GETTING A LITTLE LATE TO HUNT OUR BAD GUY, *huh*?
FUCK THAT, JOHNNY.
IT'S NEVER TOO LATE.

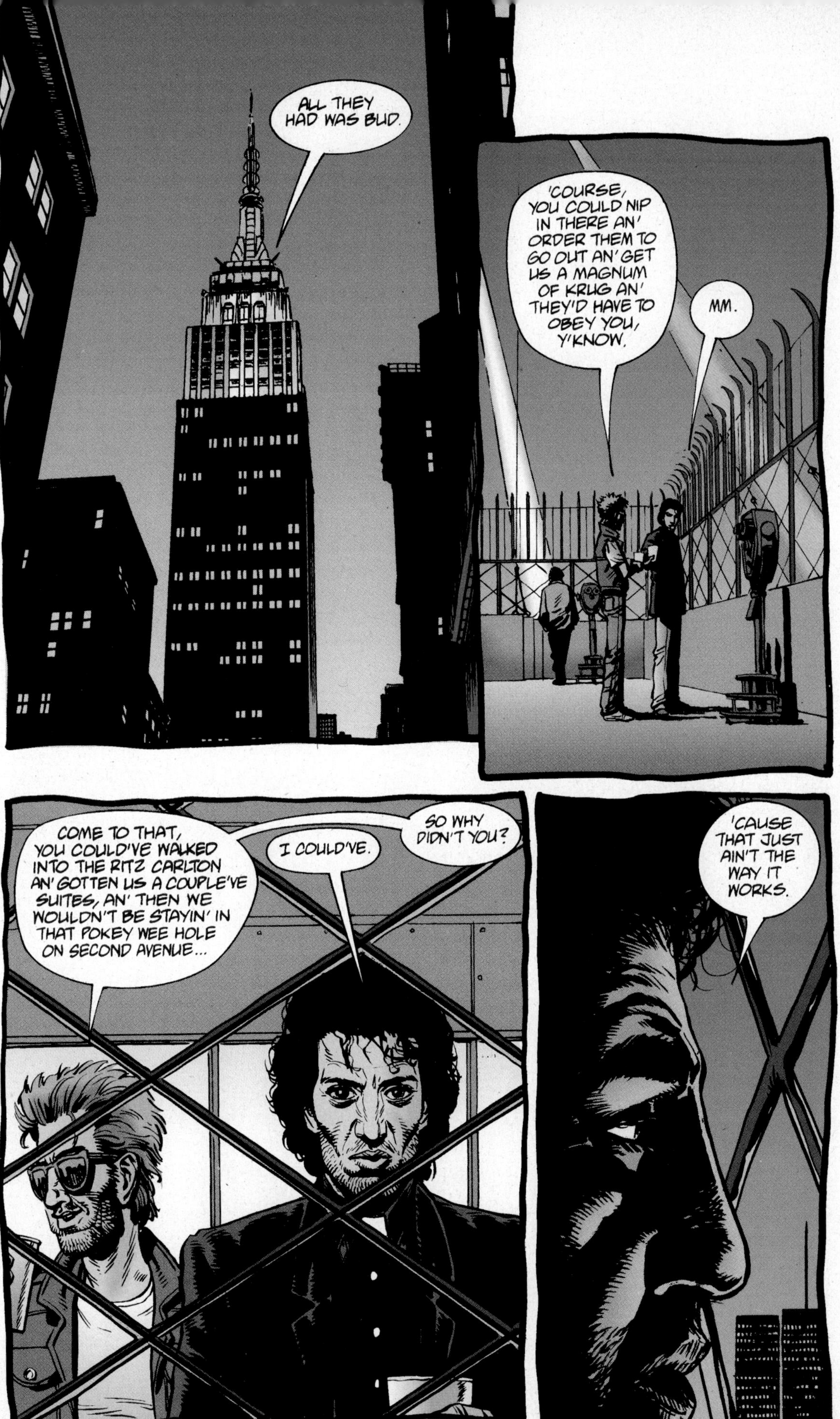
ALL THEY HAD WAS BUD.
'COURSE, YOU COULD NIP IN THERE AN' ORDER THEM TO GO OUT AN' GET US A MAGNUM OF KRUG AN' THEY'D HAVE TO OBEY YOU, Y'KNOW.
MM.
COME TO THAT, YOU COULD'VE WALKED INTO THE RITZ CARLTON AN' GOTTEN US A COUPLE'VE SUITES, AN' THEN WE WOULDN'T BE STAYIN' IN THAT POKEY WEE HOLE ON SECOND AVENUE...
I COULD'VE.
SO WHY DIDN'T YOU?
'CAUSE THAT JUST AIN'T THE WAY IT WORKS.

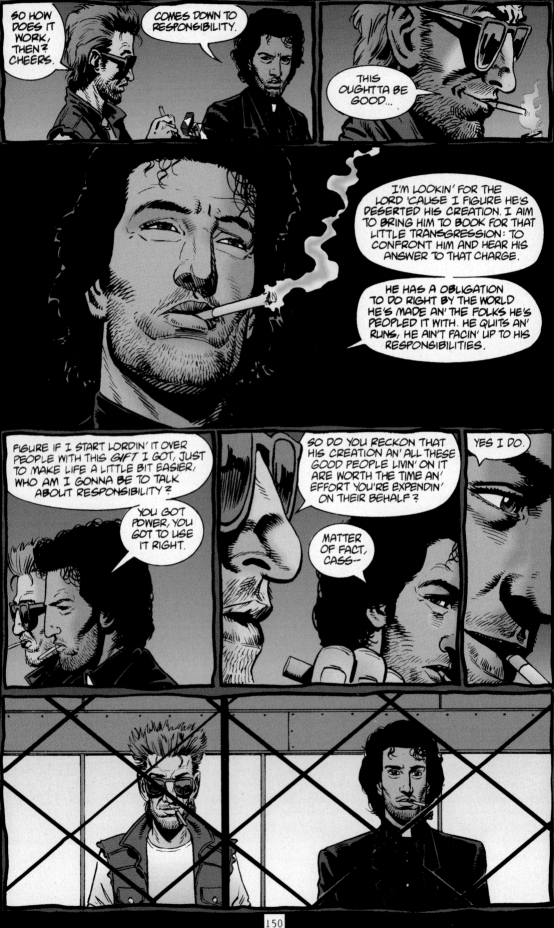

SO HOW DOES IT WORK, THEN? CHEERS.

COMES DOWN TO RESPONSIBILITY.

THIS OUGHTTA BE GOOD...

I'M LOOKIN' FOR THE LORD 'CAUSE I FIGURE HE'S DESERTED HIS CREATION. I AIM TO BRING HIM TO BOOK FOR THAT LITTLE TRANSGRESSION: TO CONFRONT HIM AND HEAR HIS ANSWER TO THAT CHARGE.

HE HAS A OBLIGATION TO DO RIGHT BY THE WORLD HE'S MADE AN' THE FOLKS HE'S PEOPLED IT WITH. HE QUITS AN' RUNS, HE AIN'T FACIN' UP TO HIS RESPONSIBILITIES.

FIGURE IF I START LORDIN' IT OVER PEOPLE WITH THIS GIFT I GOT, JUST TO MAKE LIFE A LITTLE BIT EASIER, WHO AM I GONNA BE TO TALK ABOUT RESPONSIBILITY?

YOU GOT POWER, YOU GOT TO USE IT RIGHT.

SO DO YOU RECKON THAT HIS CREATION AN' ALL THESE GOOD PEOPLE LIVIN' ON IT ARE WORTH THE TIME AN' EFFORT YOU'RE EXPENDIN' ON THEIR BEHALF?

MATTER OF FACT, CASS--

YES I DO.

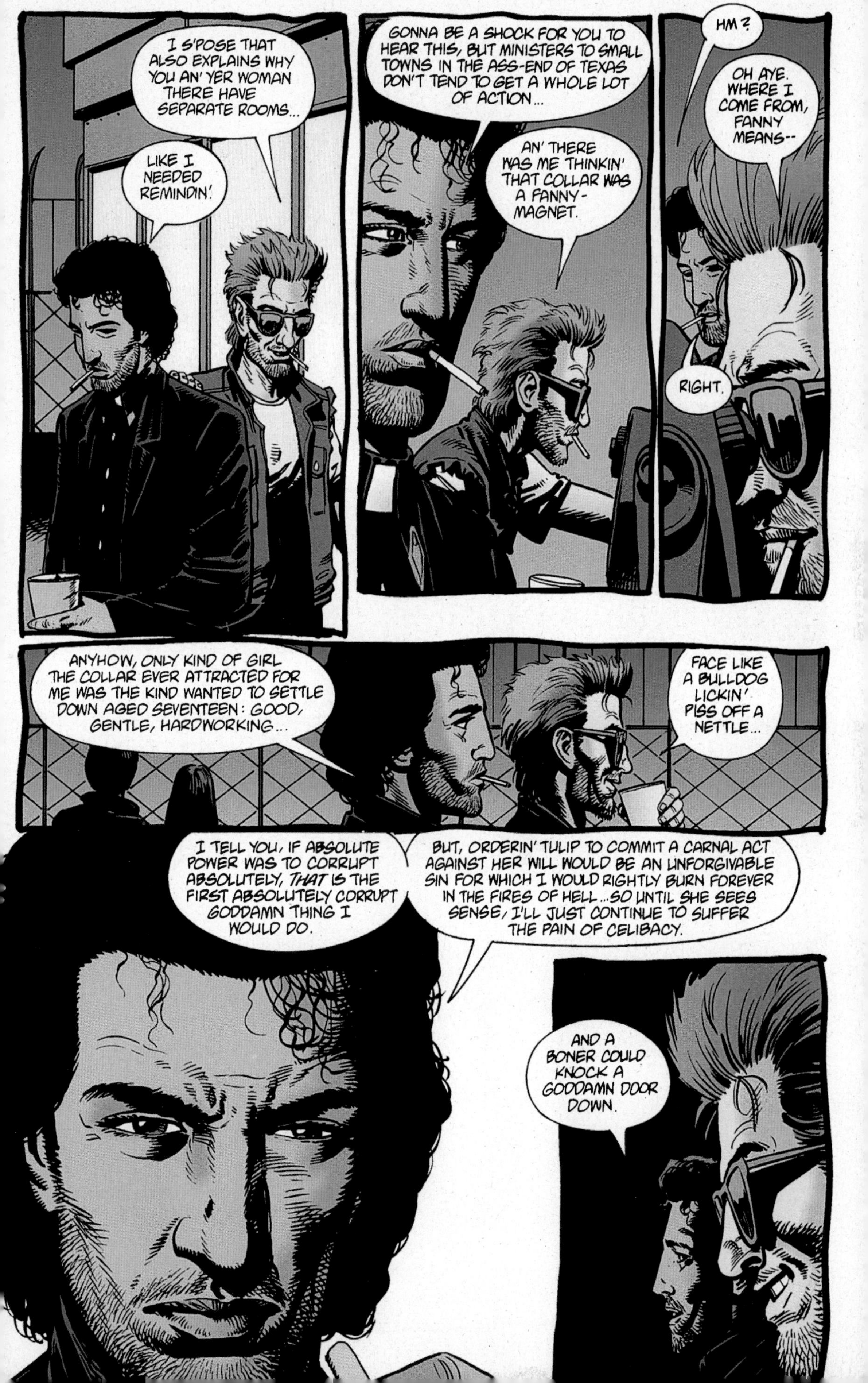
I S'POSE THAT ALSO EXPLAINS WHY YOU AN' YER WOMAN THERE HAVE SEPARATE ROOMS...
LIKE I NEEDED REMINDIN'.
GONNA BE A SHOCK FOR YOU TO HEAR THIS, BUT MINISTERS TO SMALL TOWNS IN THE ASS-END OF TEXAS DON'T TEND TO GET A WHOLE LOT OF ACTION...
AN' THERE WAS ME THINKIN' THAT COLLAR WAS A FANNY-MAGNET.
HM?
OH AYE. WHERE I COME FROM, FANNY MEANS--
RIGHT.
ANYHOW, ONLY KIND OF GIRL THE COLLAR EVER ATTRACTED FOR ME WAS THE KIND WANTED TO SETTLE DOWN AGED SEVENTEEN: GOOD, GENTLE, HARDWORKING...
FACE LIKE A BULLDOG LICKIN' PISS OFF A NETTLE...
I TELL YOU, IF ABSOLUTE POWER WAS TO CORRUPT ABSOLUTELY, THAT IS THE FIRST ABSOLUTELY CORRUPT GODDAMN THING I WOULD DO.
BUT, ORDERIN' TULIP TO COMMIT A CARNAL ACT AGAINST HER WILL WOULD BE AN UNFORGIVABLE SIN FOR WHICH I WOULD RIGHTLY BURN FOREVER IN THE FIRES OF HELL...SO UNTIL SHE SEES SENSE, I'LL JUST CONTINUE TO SUFFER THE PAIN OF CELIBACY.
AND A BONER COULD KNOCK A GODDAMN DOOR DOWN.

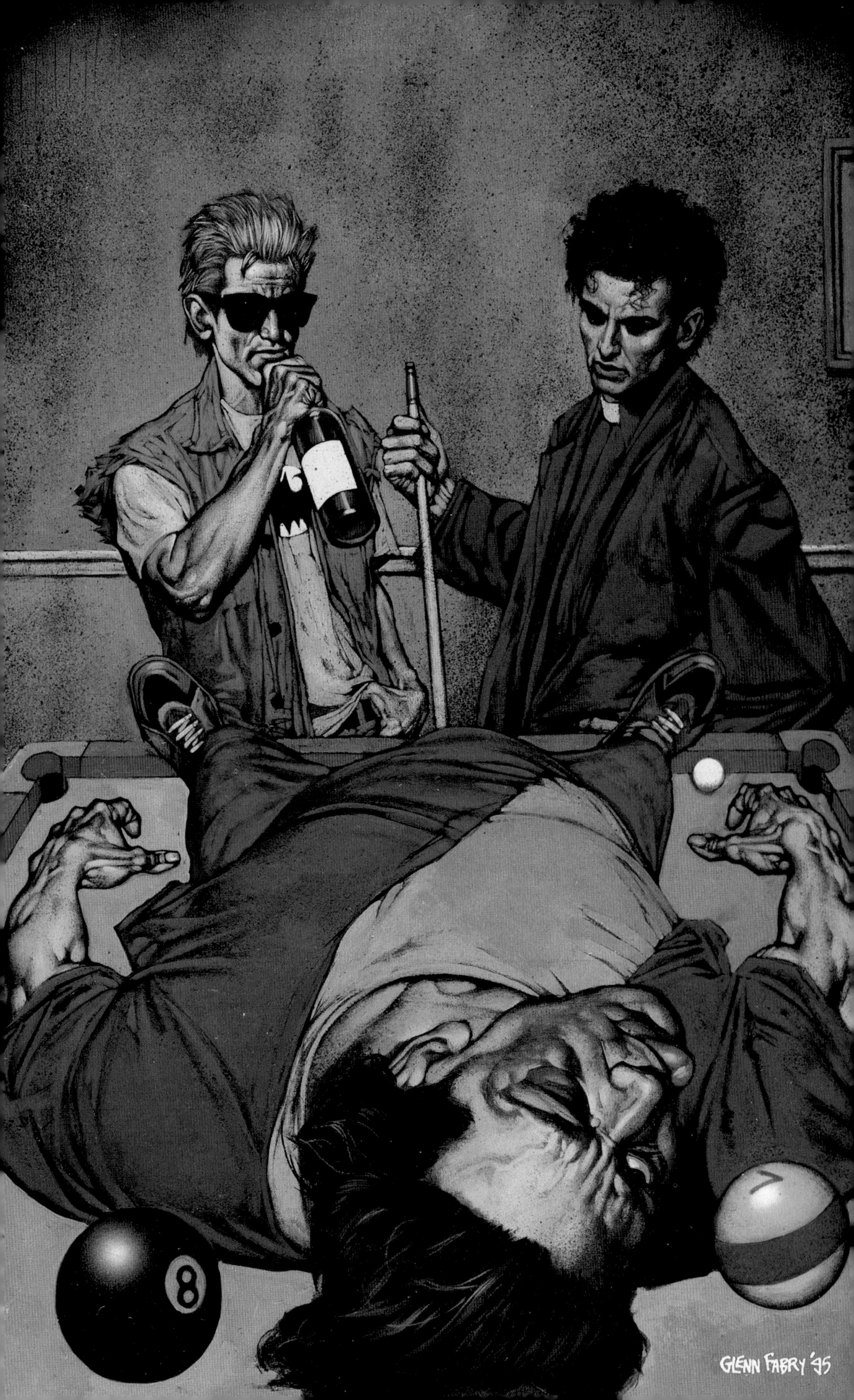
GLENN FABRY '95

"You're lookin' for God —
where the hell're you supposed to start?"

GETTIN' BACK TO THE QUESTION OF YOUR RESPONSIBILITY TO YOUR FELLOW MAN...

FIGURE WE'VE ABOUT COVERED IT. LET'S MOVE ON TO THE QUESTION OF YOU MEETIN' UP WITH TULIP, HUH?

YOU'RE FLOGGIN' A DEAD HORSE, MATE. I'VE TOLD YOU EVERYTHING I KNOW.

I'M DRIVIN' OUTTA DALLAS, SHE'S GETTIN' SHOT AT, SHE JUMPS IN-- FUCK, WOULD YOU STOP DOIN' THAT?

UMM...

THINK I DRUNK MYSELF SOBER-- THAT'S OUR TAB, CASS. SCOREBOARD'S ON YOUR LEFT.

JESSE CASS

BEATS ME WHY YOU'RE RUNNIN' A TAB. I DON'T SEE FUCKWIT OVER THERE TRYNNA STOP US LEAVIN', DO YOU?

JESSE CASS

AIN'T FAIR. FELLA'S PASSED OUT.

THERE'S YOUR RESPONSIBILITY TO YOUR FELLOW MAN RIGHT THERE...

CORRECT ME IF I'M WRONG, BUT WEREN'T YOU THE BLOKE THAT HIT HIM?

MAKIN' ME THE ONE RESPONSIBLE FOR HIM.

IS THIS THE KIND OF SOUND MORAL JUDGMENT YOU USED TO TEACH YOUR FLOCK?

HELL WITH MY FLOCK--

YOU TOOK CARE OF THAT EARLIER.

I DIDN'T HIT THE SON OF A BITCH SO WE COULD STEAL HIS BEER. I HIT HIM 'CAUSE HE CALLED ME A RED-NECK MOTHERFUCKER. GOTTA BE A MORE POLITE WAY TO ASK A FELLA TO DRINK UP AT CLOSIN' TIME, AIN'T THERE?

WHAT WE OWE HIM FOR?

TEN PITCHERS... EIGHTY BUCKS.

hh-hmm.

AH, I TAKE IT THAT EMBARRASSED COUGH MEANS YOUR HALF GOES ON THE I.O.U. YOU GAVE ME?

I'LL GET SOME CASH SOON AS I CAN--

RELAX.

HONESTLY, MATE, THAT'S THE LOT. WHATEVER IT IS SHE'S HIDING, YOU'LL HAVE TO GET IT FROM HER.

LOOK, THE SUN'LL NEARLY BE UP OUT THERE. I'LL HAVE TO STAY AN' KIP UNDER ONE'VE THE TABLES. THIS IS SI'S ADDRESS --I'LL SEE YOU THERE AT TEN TONIGHT, OKAY?

TONIGHT AT TEN.

I'LL TELL YOU, THIS DOESN'T HALF GO AGAINST THE GRAIN...

DON'T FORGET THE TIP.

YOU SURE THAT'S ALL YOU REMEMBER ABOUT TULIP...?

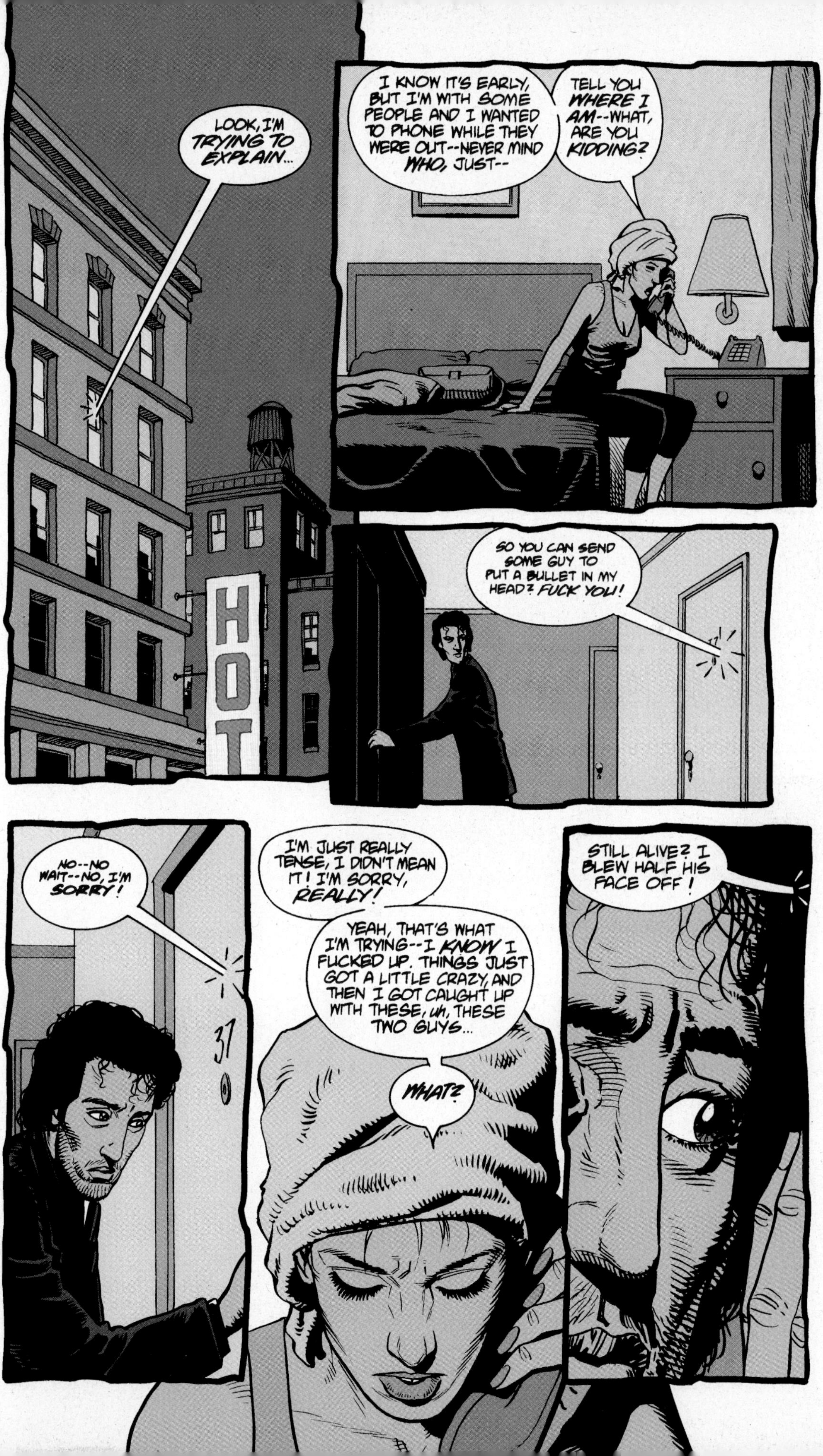
LOOK, I'M TRYING TO EXPLAIN...
I KNOW IT'S EARLY, BUT I'M WITH SOME PEOPLE AND I WANTED TO PHONE WHILE THEY WERE OUT--NEVER MIND WHO, JUST--
TELL YOU WHERE I AM--WHAT, ARE YOU KIDDING?
HOT
SO YOU CAN SEND SOME GUY TO PUT A BULLET IN MY HEAD? FUCK YOU!
NO--NO WAIT--NO, I'M SORRY!
37
I'M JUST REALLY TENSE, I DIDN'T MEAN IT! I'M SORRY, REALLY!
YEAH, THAT'S WHAT I'M TRYING--I KNOW I FUCKED UP. THINGS JUST GOT A LITTLE CRAZY, AND THEN I GOT CAUGHT UP WITH THESE, uh, THESE TWO GUYS...
WHAT?
STILL ALIVE? I BLEW HALF HIS FACE OFF!

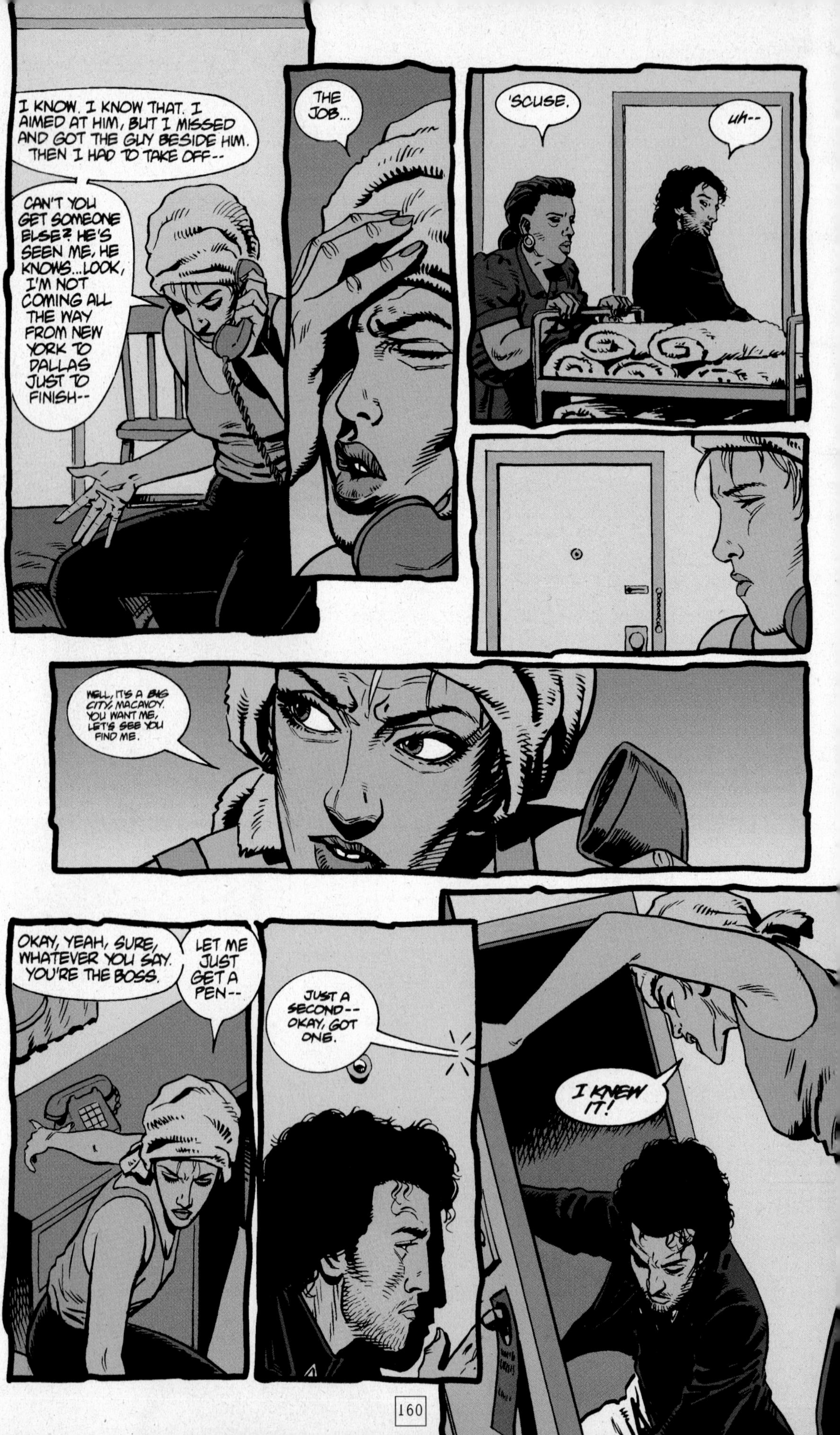

I KNOW. I KNOW THAT. I AIMED AT HIM, BUT I MISSED AND GOT THE GUY BESIDE HIM. THEN I HAD TO TAKE OFF--
CAN'T YOU GET SOMEONE ELSE? HE'S SEEN ME, HE KNOWS...LOOK, I'M NOT COMING ALL THE WAY FROM NEW YORK TO DALLAS JUST TO FINISH--
THE JOB...
'SCUSE.
uh--
WELL, IT'S A BIG CITY, MACAVOY. YOU WANT ME, LET'S SEE YOU FIND ME.
OKAY, YEAH, SURE, WHATEVER YOU SAY. YOU'RE THE BOSS.
LET ME JUST GET A PEN--
JUST A SECOND--OKAY, GOT ONE.
I KNEW IT!

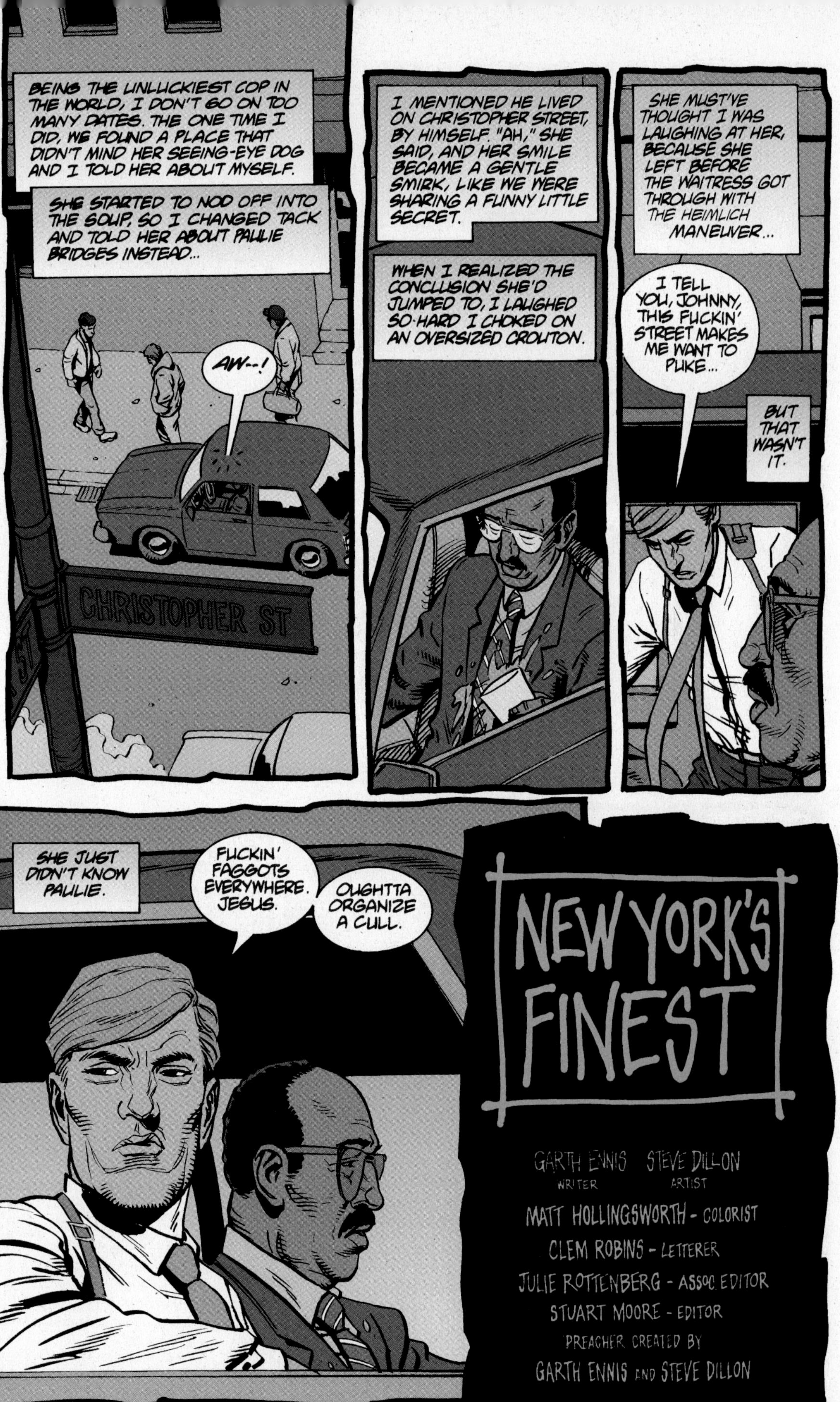
BEING THE UNLUCKIEST COP IN THE WORLD, I DON'T GO ON TOO MANY DATES. THE ONE TIME I DID, WE FOUND A PLACE THAT DIDN'T MIND HER SEEING-EYE DOG AND I TOLD HER ABOUT MYSELF.
SHE STARTED TO NOD OFF INTO THE SOUP, SO I CHANGED TACK AND TOLD HER ABOUT PAULIE BRIDGES INSTEAD...
AW--!
CHRISTOPHER ST
I MENTIONED HE LIVED ON CHRISTOPHER STREET, BY HIMSELF. "AH," SHE SAID, AND HER SMILE BECAME A GENTLE SMIRK, LIKE WE WERE SHARING A FUNNY LITTLE SECRET.
WHEN I REALIZED THE CONCLUSION SHE'D JUMPED TO, I LAUGHED SO HARD I CHOKED ON AN OVERSIZED CROUTON.
SHE MUST'VE THOUGHT I WAS LAUGHING AT HER, BECAUSE SHE LEFT BEFORE THE WAITRESS GOT THROUGH WITH THE HEIMLICH MANEUVER...
I TELL YOU, JOHNNY, THIS FUCKIN' STREET MAKES ME WANT TO PUKE...
BUT THAT WASN'T IT.
SHE JUST DIDN'T KNOW PAULIE.
FUCKIN' FAGGOTS EVERYWHERE. JESUS.
OUGHTTA ORGANIZE A CULL.
NEW YORK'S FINEST
GARTH ENNIS WRITER
STEVE DILLON ARTIST
MATT HOLLINGSWORTH - COLORIST
CLEM ROBINS - LETTERER
JULIE ROTTENBERG - ASSOC. EDITOR
STUART MOORE - EDITOR
PREACHER CREATED BY
GARTH ENNIS AND STEVE DILLON

THEY'RE NOT HURTING ANY-BODY, PAULIE--

WHAT'S THE ADDRESS?

EIGHTY-FIRST AND LEX.

DID A YUPPIE AT LAST, HUH?

MAYBE NOW WE'LL RATE SOME BACKUP.

HEARD A HALF HOUR AGO. LADY CALLS IN--HUSBAND'S BEEN GONE TWO NIGHTS RUNNING, THEN THIS PACKAGE SHOWS UP IN THE MAIL. SHE STARTS TO OPEN IT WHEN SHE REALIZES IT'S *LEAKING BLOOD.*

SHE'S READ ABOUT OUR BOY'S M.O. IN THE POST --

SO SHE SHITS HER LITTLE PANTIES AND DIALS NINE-ELEVEN.

...

I HAD TO BREAK INTO MY APARTMENT LAST NIGHT. LOST MY KEYS. BOY, THE TROUBLE I HAD --

PAULIE? WHAT'D YOU SAY?

WAKE ME WHEN YOU GET THERE.

MOW YOU ALL DOWN...

APARTMENT FOUR-TWELVE, DETECTIVE BRIDGES.

HEY, YOU KNOW WHAT? I'M GOING FOR DETECTIVE MYSELF, AND I'VE GOT SOME FREE TIME TOMORROW...

MAYBE YOU COULD LIKE GIVE ME A FEW POINTERS ON THE EXAM? IF WE COULD MEET...?

I'M BUSY TOMORROW. MY PARTNER MIGHT BE FREE.

TT.

MAYBE I'LL TRY FOR TRAFFIC.

...DON'T GET IT, PAULIE. YOU WOULD'VE HAD HER, NO PROBLEM--

FOUR-EIGHT ...FOUR-TEN...

HEY, BRIDGES. HER NAME'S CONROY. SHE'S ALREADY SCARED, SO YOU BETTER TAKE IT EASY--

HOW SCARED?

AAHHHHHH

MEAT-
BALLS?

SPECIAL
AT THE
DELI.

TOOL.

HELLO,
DETECTIVE.

IS THAT A FACT?
LOOK, THIS MAY
BE VERY FUNNY
FOR YOU--

IT CERTAINLY
IS. IF YOU CAN'T
LAUGH AT SEVERED TES-
TICLES IN THE
MAIL, WHAT
CAN YOU
LAUGH AT?

BRRRNNG

I'M THE
KILLER.

NOW SEEING AS THAT
JUICY LITTLE DETAIL
HASN'T YET BEEN
MADE PUBLIC, I
FIGURE YOU'RE
CONVINCED I'M
ON THE LEVEL.

I JUST WANTED
TO ESTABLISH
THAT FOR WHEN
I CALL AGAIN...

IT'S HIM! VENUCCI,
I'VE GOT HIM ON THE
LINE! TAP IT!

HUH?

HOW THE FUCK
CAN I? YOUR PHONE
ISN'T HOOKED UP!
AND DON'T FUCKING
SHOUT AT ME, TOOL!

BUT--
BUT--

'BYE FOR
NOW.

...GOD'STH
STHAKE,
KILL ME...

AH, YOU FOUND IT!

NICE NEIGHBOR-HOOD SI LIVES IN.

AYE, BUT LOOK AT HIS LITTLE ISLAND OF ELEGANCE AND TASTE IN THE MIDDLE OF IT. HE'S AWAY OUT FOR MORE BEER.

SO WHAT'VE YEZ BEEN UP TO?

SEEIN' THE TOWN.

HAVE WE EVER. HE IS SUCH A GODDAMN TOURIST...

AIN'T ASHAMED OF IT, NEITHER. TIMES SQUARE, BATTERY PARK, STATUE OF LIBERTY--SHE WAS SOMETHIN', OUT THERE IN THE WATER WITH THE SUN GOIN' DOWN BEHIND HER...

LOVELY ARSE ON HER, TOO.

KINDA LIPPY FOR TEMPEST-TOSS'D WRETCHED REFUSE OF A FORBIGN SHORE, AIN'T YOU?

YOU'RE RIGHT. I'M JUST A HUMBLE WEE HUDDLED MASS YEARNIN' TO BREATHE FREE.

LISTEN: SI WAS ASKIN' IF THIS STUFF ABOUT SIGHTINGS OF GOD WAS FOR YOU AN' NOT ME, SO I JUST WENT AHEAD AND OWNED UP.

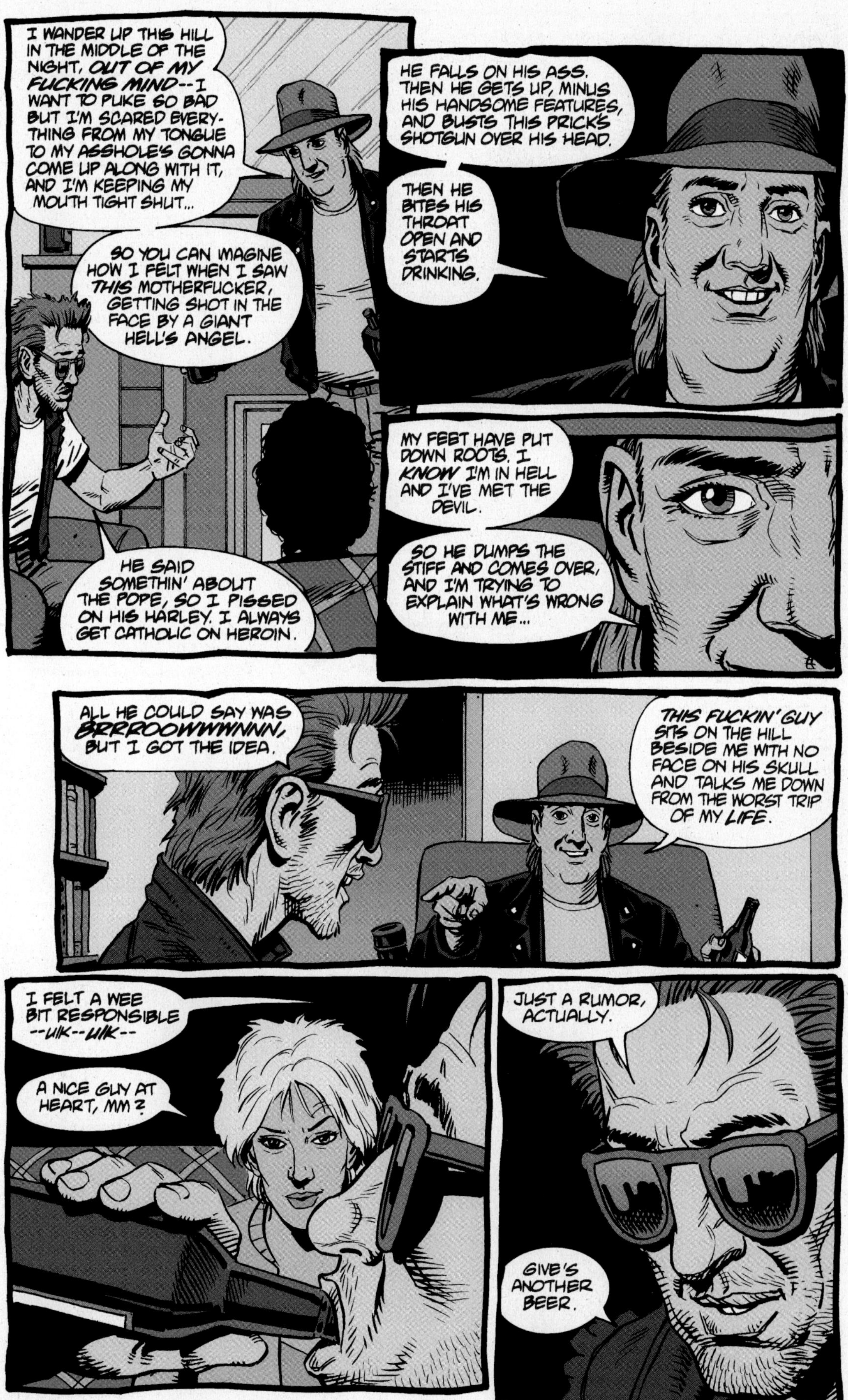
I WANDER UP THIS HILL IN THE MIDDLE OF THE NIGHT, OUT OF MY FUCKING MIND--I WANT TO PUKE SO BAD BUT I'M SCARED EVERY-THING FROM MY TONGUE TO MY ASSHOLE'S GONNA COME UP ALONG WITH IT, AND I'M KEEPING MY MOUTH TIGHT SHUT...
SO YOU CAN IMAGINE HOW I FELT WHEN I SAW THIS MOTHERFUCKER, GETTING SHOT IN THE FACE BY A GIANT HELL'S ANGEL.
HE SAID SOMETHIN' ABOUT THE POPE, SO I PISSED ON HIS HARLEY. I ALWAYS GET CATHOLIC ON HEROIN.
HE FALLS ON HIS ASS. THEN HE GETS UP, MINUS HIS HANDSOME FEATURES, AND BUSTS THIS PRICK'S SHOTGUN OVER HIS HEAD.
THEN HE BITES HIS THROAT OPEN AND STARTS DRINKING.
MY FEET HAVE PUT DOWN ROOTS. I KNOW I'M IN HELL AND I'VE MET THE DEVIL.
SO HE DUMPS THE STIFF AND COMES OVER, AND I'M TRYING TO EXPLAIN WHAT'S WRONG WITH ME...
ALL HE COULD SAY WAS BRRROOWWWNNN, BUT I GOT THE IDEA.
THIS FUCKIN' GUY SITS ON THE HILL BESIDE ME WITH NO FACE ON HIS SKULL AND TALKS ME DOWN FROM THE WORST TRIP OF MY LIFE.
I FELT A WEE BIT RESPONSIBLE --UK--UK--
A NICE GUY AT HEART, MM?
JUST A RUMOR, ACTUALLY.
GIVE'S ANOTHER BEER.

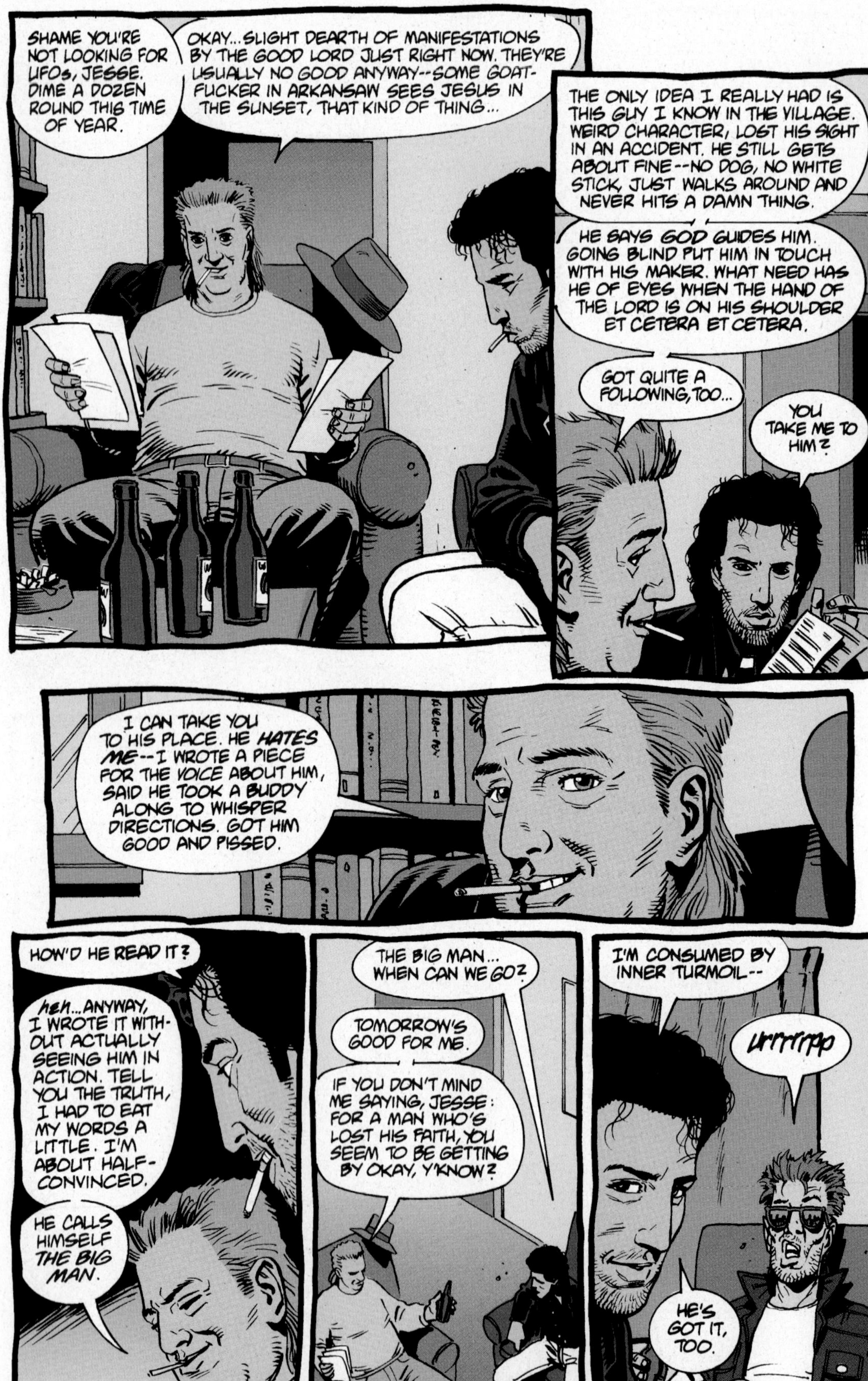
SHAME YOU'RE NOT LOOKING FOR UFOs, JESSE. DIME A DOZEN ROUND THIS TIME OF YEAR.
OKAY... SLIGHT DEARTH OF MANIFESTATIONS BY THE GOOD LORD JUST RIGHT NOW. THEY'RE USUALLY NO GOOD ANYWAY--SOME GOAT-FUCKER IN ARKANSAW SEES JESUS IN THE SUNSET, THAT KIND OF THING...
THE ONLY IDEA I REALLY HAD IS THIS GUY I KNOW IN THE VILLAGE. WEIRD CHARACTER, LOST HIS SIGHT IN AN ACCIDENT. HE STILL GETS ABOUT FINE--NO DOG, NO WHITE STICK, JUST WALKS AROUND AND NEVER HITS A DAMN THING.
HE SAYS GOD GUIDES HIM. GOING BLIND PUT HIM IN TOUCH WITH HIS MAKER. WHAT NEED HAS HE OF EYES WHEN THE HAND OF THE LORD IS ON HIS SHOULDER ET CETERA ET CETERA.
GOT QUITE A FOLLOWING, TOO...
YOU TAKE ME TO HIM?
I CAN TAKE YOU TO HIS PLACE. HE HATES ME--I WROTE A PIECE FOR THE VOICE ABOUT HIM, SAID HE TOOK A BUDDY ALONG TO WHISPER DIRECTIONS. GOT HIM GOOD AND PISSED.
HOW'D HE READ IT?
heh... ANYWAY, I WROTE IT WITHOUT ACTUALLY SEEING HIM IN ACTION. TELL YOU THE TRUTH, I HAD TO EAT MY WORDS A LITTLE. I'M ABOUT HALF-CONVINCED.
HE CALLS HIMSELF THE BIG MAN.
THE BIG MAN... WHEN CAN WE GO?
TOMORROW'S GOOD FOR ME.
IF YOU DON'T MIND ME SAYING, JESSE: FOR A MAN WHO'S LOST HIS FAITH, YOU SEEM TO BE GETTING BY OKAY, Y'KNOW?
I'M CONSUMED BY INNER TURMOIL--
Urrrrrpp
HE'S GOT IT, TOO.

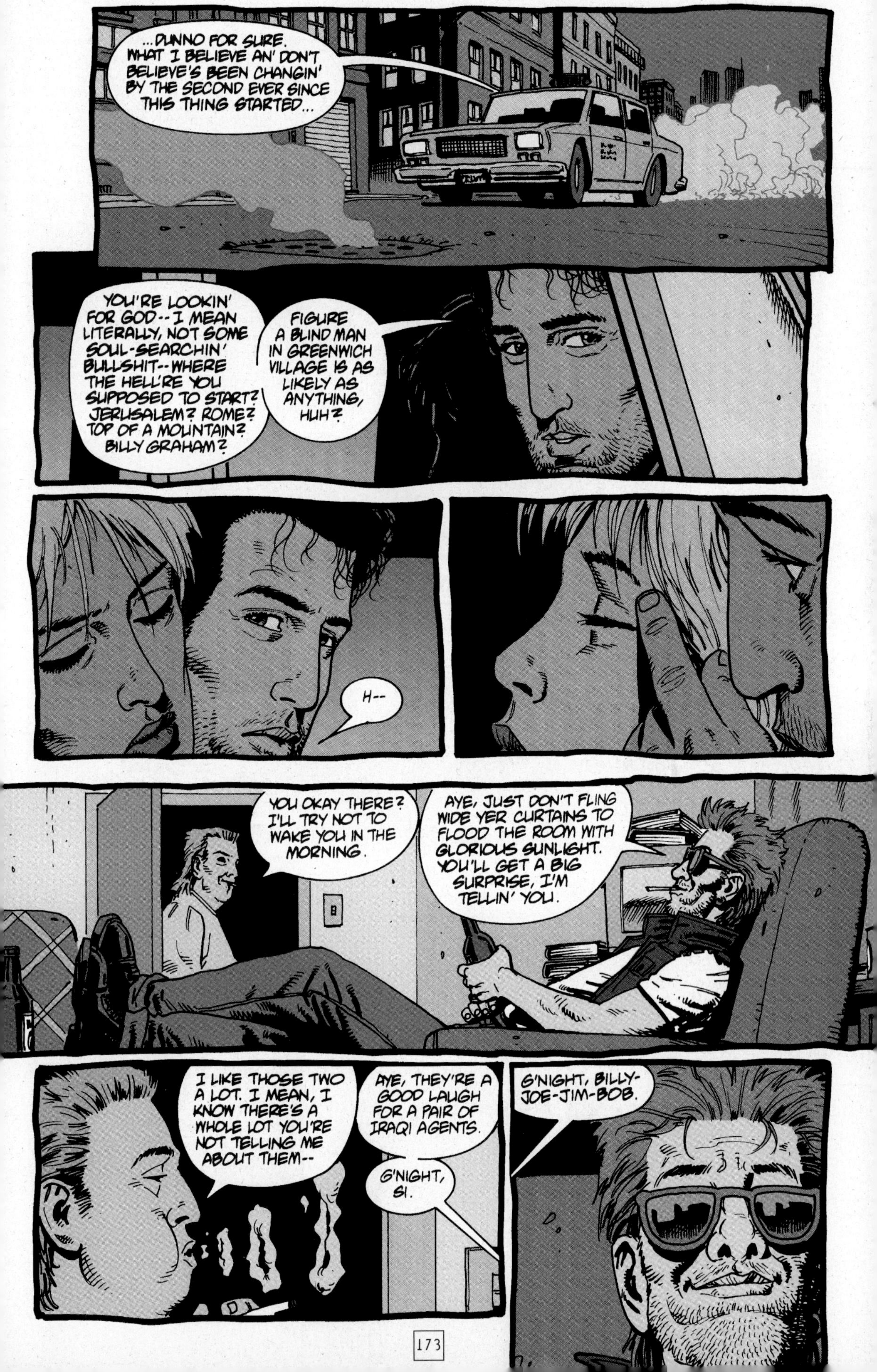
...DUNNO FOR SURE. WHAT I BELIEVE AN' DON'T BELIEVE'S BEEN CHANGIN' BY THE SECOND EVER SINCE THIS THING STARTED...
YOU'RE LOOKIN' FOR GOD--I MEAN LITERALLY, NOT SOME SOUL-SEARCHIN' BULLSHIT--WHERE THE HELL'RE YOU SUPPOSED TO START? JERUSALEM? ROME? TOP OF A MOUNTAIN? BILLY GRAHAM?
FIGURE A BLIND MAN IN GREENWICH VILLAGE IS AS LIKELY AS ANYTHING, HUH?
H--
YOU OKAY THERE? I'LL TRY NOT TO WAKE YOU IN THE MORNING.
AYE, JUST DON'T FLING WIDE YER CURTAINS TO FLOOD THE ROOM WITH GLORIOUS SUNLIGHT. YOU'LL GET A BIG SURPRISE, I'M TELLIN' YOU.
I LIKE THOSE TWO A LOT. I MEAN, I KNOW THERE'S A WHOLE LOT YOU'RE NOT TELLING ME ABOUT THEM--
AYE, THEY'RE A GOOD LAUGH FOR A PAIR OF IRAQI AGENTS.
G'NIGHT, SI.
G'NIGHT, BILLY-JOE-JIM-BOB.

YOU BEEN TALKING TO A GUY CALLED COLTRANE, TOOL? *SI* COLTRANE?

UH, NO, LIEUTENANT. NOT THAT I KNOW OF.

NOT THAT YOU KNOW OF.

HE'S A REPORTER. NAME'S ON THIS ARTICLE IN *NEWS-WEEK* RIGHT HERE. HE SEEMS TO KNOW YOU, BRIDGES AND YOUR LATEST CASE INSIDE-OUT. *NOW WHAT HAVE I TOLD YOU ABOUT TALK-ING TO THE PRESS?*

BUT I--

HE'S GOT THE CONROY KILLING IN HERE, TOOL! WE RELEASED IT FOUR O'CLOCK YESTERDAY, TOO LATE FOR THEM GOING TO PRESS *BUT HE'S GOT IT IN!*

I--I--NO, WAIT, COLTRANE-- I THINK MAY-BE HE DID TRY TO ASK US SOME QUESTIONS BUT WE WOULDN'T HAVE SAID A *WORD,* I SWEAR! HE'S GOT TO HAVE FOLLOWED US--

IF BRIDGES HAD MET HIM EVEN BRIEFLY HE'D'VE NOTICED THE SON OF A BITCH TRAILING YOU A MILE OFF. *YOU* MISSING HIM I COULD BELIEVE, BUT NOT BRIDGES.

WHO, I CAN'T HELP BUT NOTICE, ISN'T HERE...

HE CALLED IN SICK, MA'AM. HE'S BEEN, WELL, ACTING KIND OF TWITCHY JUST LATELY. NOT REALLY HIMSELF.

I GUESS HE MIGHT'VE MISSED THIS REPORTER CHARACTER, FEELING LIKE THAT.

THAT'S SWELL.

GET OUT, TOOL.

174

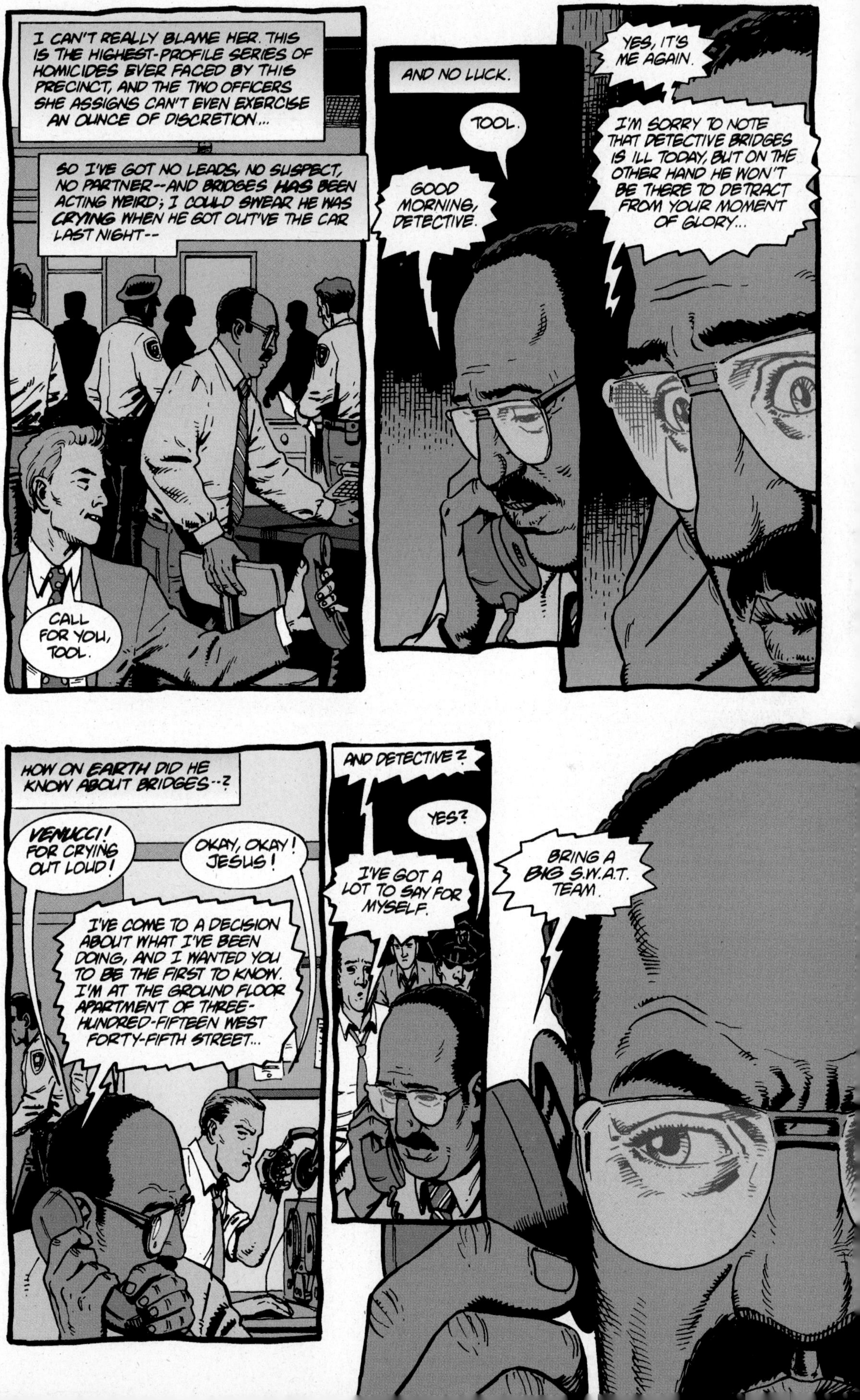
I CAN'T REALLY BLAME HER. THIS IS THE HIGHEST-PROFILE SERIES OF HOMICIDES EVER FACED BY THIS PRECINCT, AND THE TWO OFFICERS SHE ASSIGNS CAN'T EVEN EXERCISE AN OUNCE OF DISCRETION...
SO I'VE GOT NO LEADS, NO SUSPECT, NO PARTNER--AND BRIDGES HAS BEEN ACTING WEIRD; I COULD SWEAR HE WAS CRYING WHEN HE GOT OUT'VE THE CAR LAST NIGHT--
CALL FOR YOU, TOOL.
AND NO LUCK.
TOOL.
GOOD MORNING, DETECTIVE.
YES, IT'S ME AGAIN.
I'M SORRY TO NOTE THAT DETECTIVE BRIDGES IS ILL TODAY, BUT ON THE OTHER HAND HE WON'T BE THERE TO DETRACT FROM YOUR MOMENT OF GLORY...
HOW ON EARTH DID HE KNOW ABOUT BRIDGES--?
VENUCCI! FOR CRYING OUT LOUD!
OKAY, OKAY! JESUS!
I'VE COME TO A DECISION ABOUT WHAT I'VE BEEN DOING, AND I WANTED YOU TO BE THE FIRST TO KNOW. I'M AT THE GROUND FLOOR APARTMENT OF THREE-HUNDRED-FIFTEEN WEST FORTY-FIFTH STREET...
AND DETECTIVE?
YES?
I'VE GOT A LOT TO SAY FOR MYSELF.
BRING A BIG S.W.A.T. TEAM.

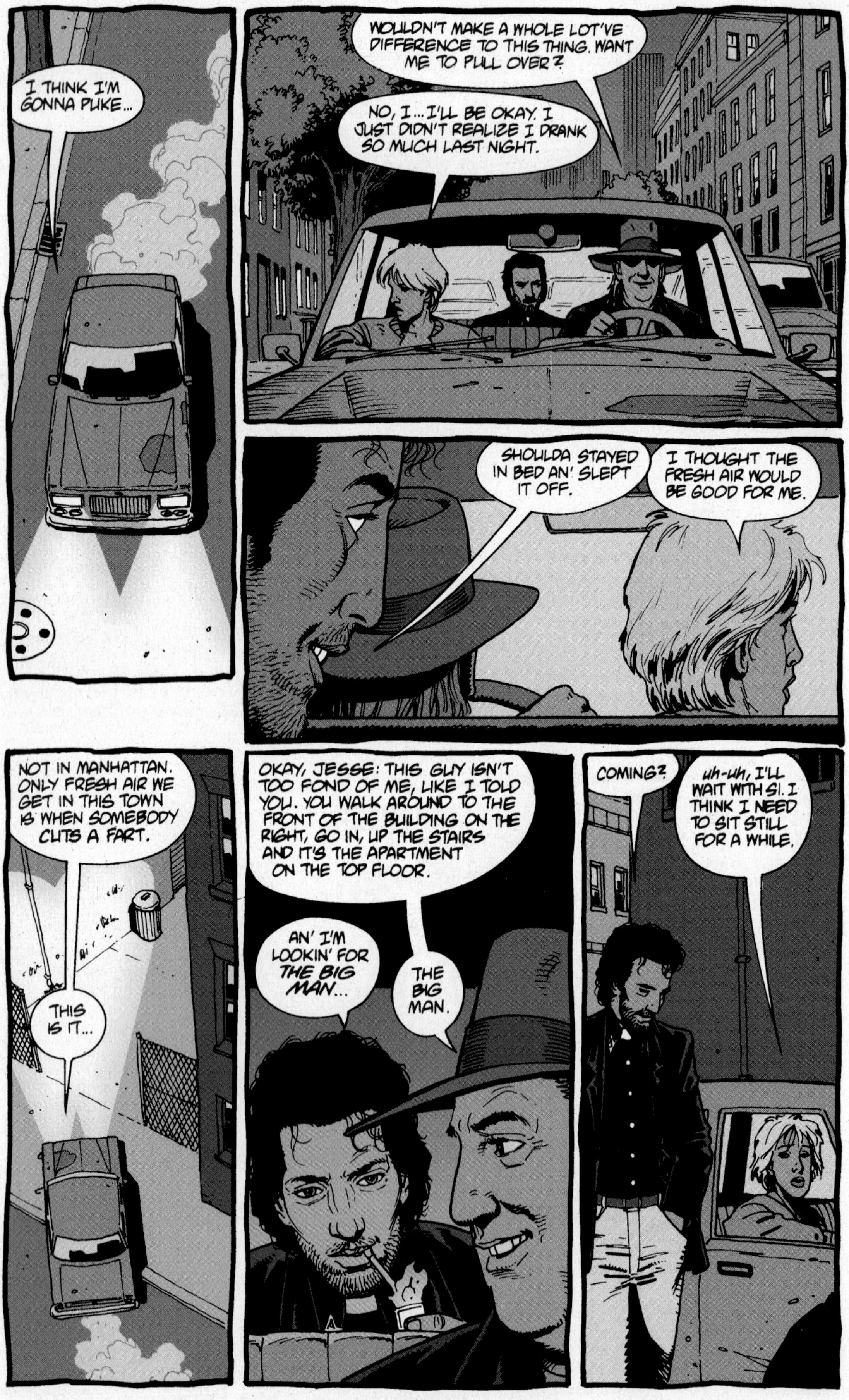
I THINK I'M GONNA PUKE...
WOULDN'T MAKE A WHOLE LOT'VE DIFFERENCE TO THIS THING. WANT ME TO PULL OVER?
NO, I... I'LL BE OKAY. I JUST DIDN'T REALIZE I DRANK SO MUCH LAST NIGHT.
SHOULDA STAYED IN BED AN' SLEPT IT OFF.
I THOUGHT THE FRESH AIR WOULD BE GOOD FOR ME.
NOT IN MANHATTAN. ONLY FRESH AIR WE GET IN THIS TOWN IS WHEN SOMEBODY CUTS A FART.
THIS IS IT...
OKAY, JESSE: THIS GUY ISN'T TOO FOND OF ME, LIKE I TOLD YOU. YOU WALK AROUND TO THE FRONT OF THE BUILDING ON THE RIGHT, GO IN, UP THE STAIRS AND IT'S THE APARTMENT ON THE TOP FLOOR.
AN' I'M LOOKIN' FOR THE BIG MAN...
THE BIG MAN.
COMING?
UH-UH, I'LL WAIT WITH SI. I THINK I NEED TO SIT STILL FOR A WHILE.

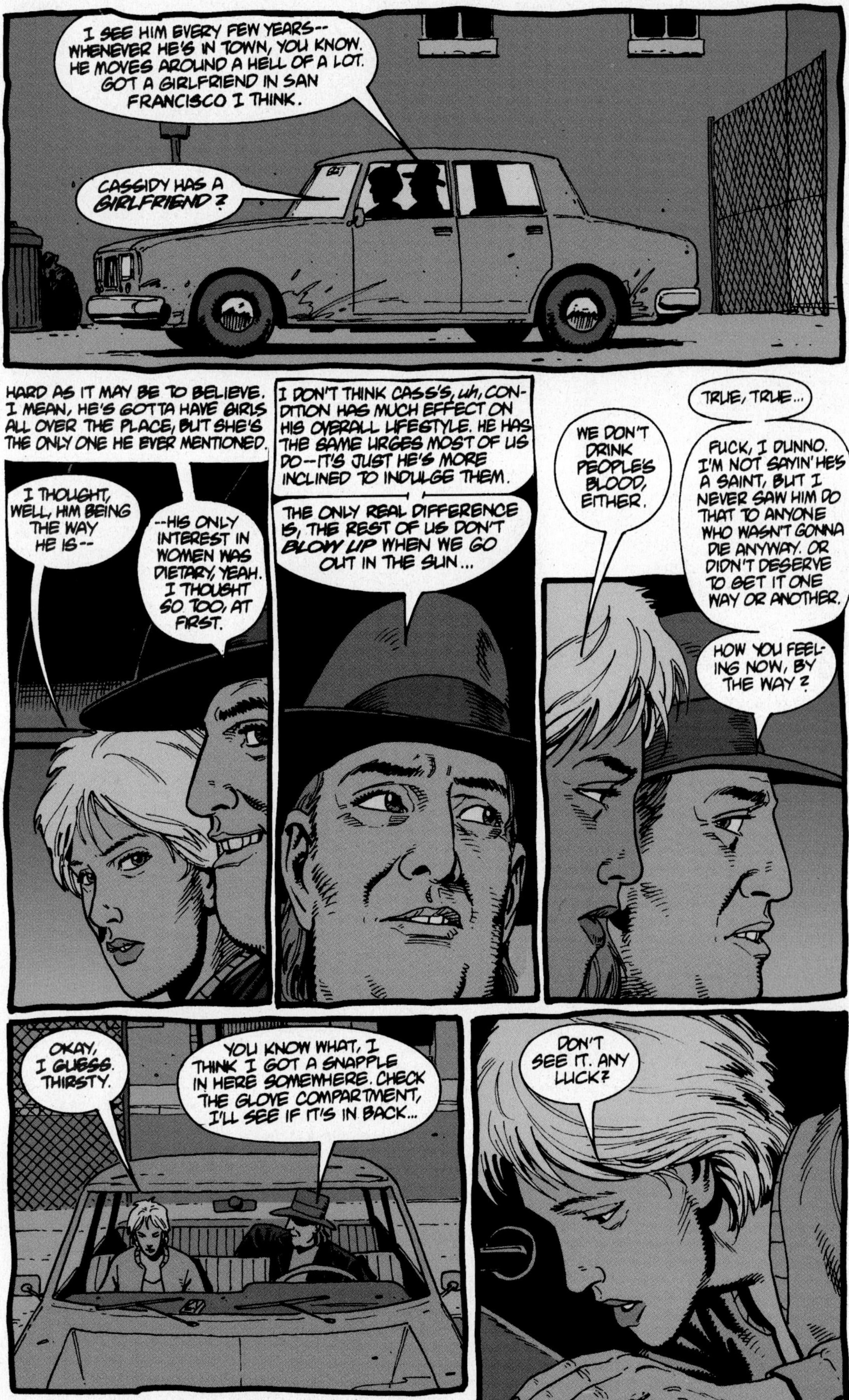
I SEE HIM EVERY FEW YEARS-- WHENEVER HE'S IN TOWN, YOU KNOW. HE MOVES AROUND A HELL OF A LOT. GOT A GIRLFRIEND IN SAN FRANCISCO I THINK.
CASSIDY HAS A *GIRLFRIEND?*
HARD AS IT MAY BE TO BELIEVE. I MEAN, HE'S GOTTA HAVE GIRLS ALL OVER THE PLACE, BUT SHE'S THE ONLY ONE HE EVER MENTIONED.
I THOUGHT, WELL, HIM BEING THE WAY HE IS--
--HIS ONLY INTEREST IN WOMEN WAS DIETARY, YEAH. I THOUGHT SO TOO, AT FIRST.
I DON'T THINK CASS'S, *uh,* CONDITION HAS MUCH EFFECT ON HIS OVERALL LIFESTYLE. HE HAS THE SAME URGES MOST OF US DO--IT'S JUST HE'S MORE INCLINED TO INDULGE THEM.
THE ONLY REAL DIFFERENCE IS, THE REST OF US DON'T *BLOW UP* WHEN WE GO OUT IN THE SUN...
WE DON'T DRINK PEOPLE'S BLOOD, EITHER.
TRUE, TRUE...
FUCK, I DUNNO. I'M NOT SAYIN' HE'S A SAINT, BUT I NEVER SAW HIM DO THAT TO ANYONE WHO WASN'T GONNA DIE ANYWAY. OR DIDN'T DESERVE TO GET IT ONE WAY OR ANOTHER.
HOW YOU FEELING NOW, BY THE WAY?
OKAY, I GUESS. THIRSTY.
YOU KNOW WHAT, I THINK I GOT A SNAPPLE IN HERE SOMEWHERE. CHECK THE GLOVE COMPARTMENT, I'LL SEE IF IT'S IN BACK...
DON'T SEE IT. ANY LUCK?

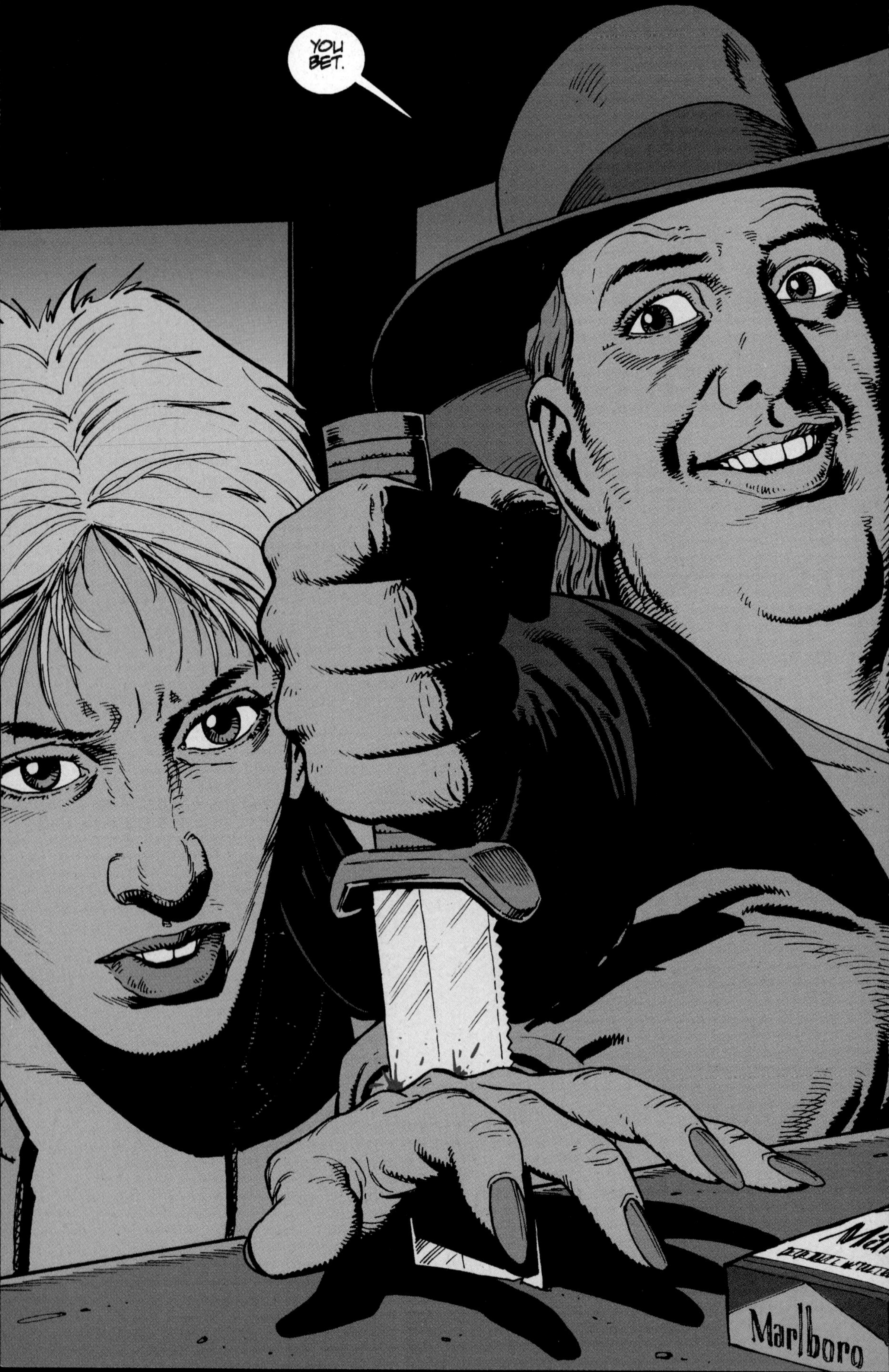
YOU BET.
Marlboro

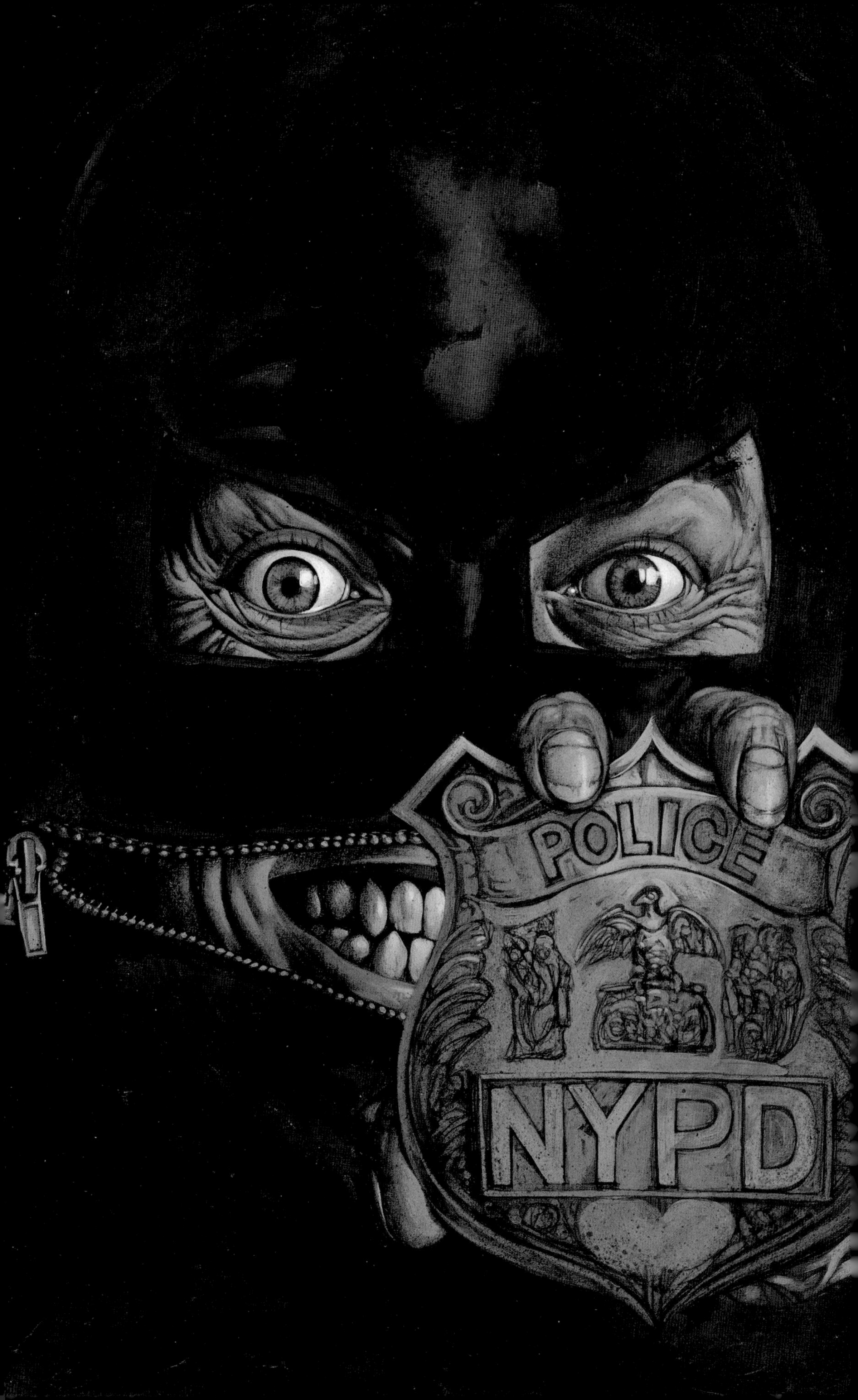
POLICE
NYPD

"There's worse to come, I'm afraid."

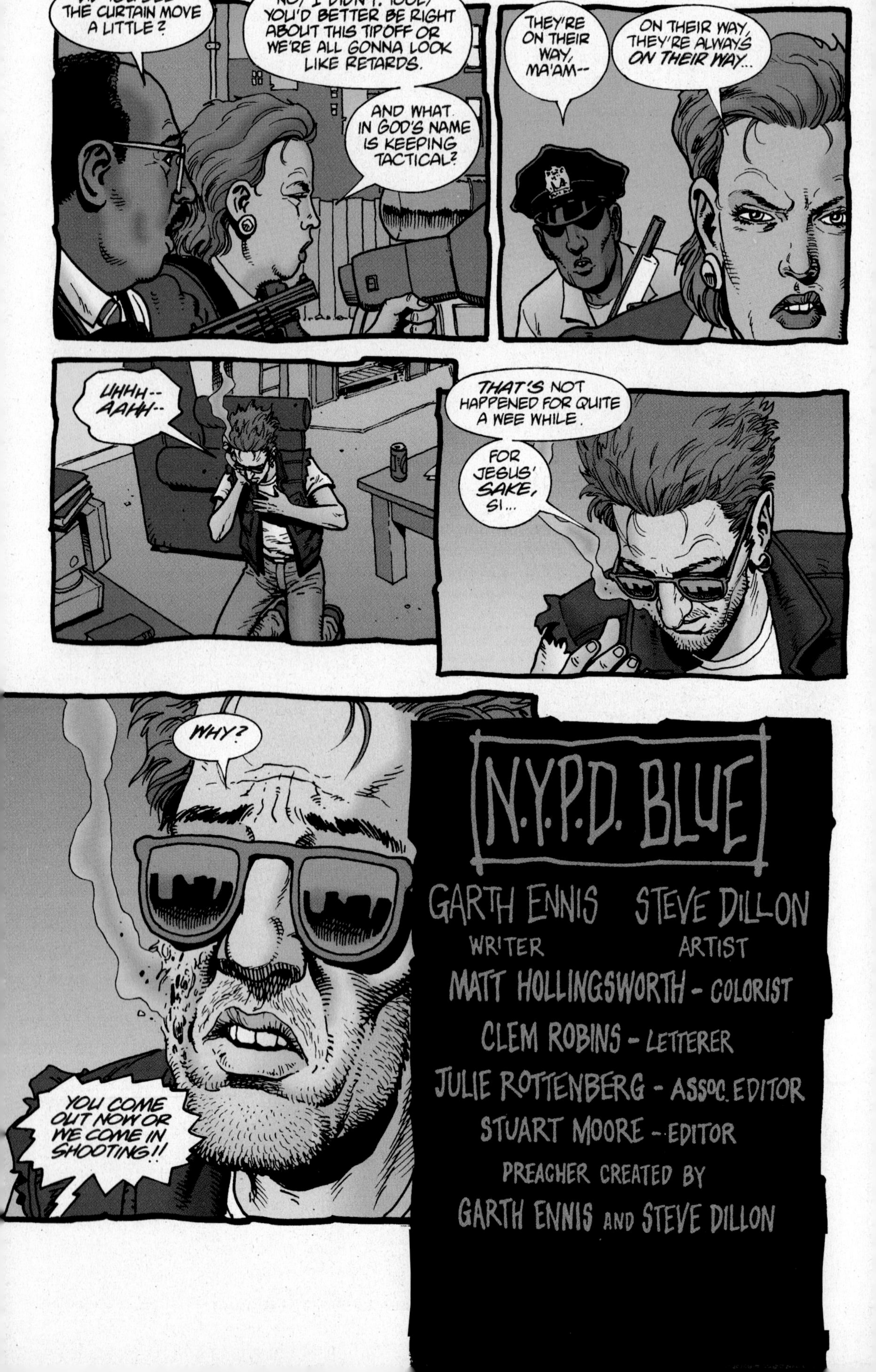
DID YOU SEE THE CURTAIN MOVE A LITTLE?
NO, I DIDN'T. TOOL, YOU'D BETTER BE RIGHT ABOUT THIS TIPOFF OR WE'RE ALL GONNA LOOK LIKE RETARDS.
AND WHAT IN GOD'S NAME IS KEEPING TACTICAL?
THEY'RE ON THEIR WAY, MA'AM--
ON THEIR WAY, THEY'RE ALWAYS ON THEIR WAY...
UHHH-- AAHH--
THAT'S NOT HAPPENED FOR QUITE A WEE WHILE.
FOR JESUS' SAKE, SI...
WHY?
YOU COME OUT NOW OR WE COME IN SHOOTING!!
N.Y.P.D. BLUE
GARTH ENNIS WRITER
STEVE DILLON ARTIST
MATT HOLLINGSWORTH - COLORIST
CLEM ROBINS - LETTERER
JULIE ROTTENBERG - ASSOC. EDITOR
STUART MOORE - EDITOR
PREACHER CREATED BY GARTH ENNIS AND STEVE DILLON

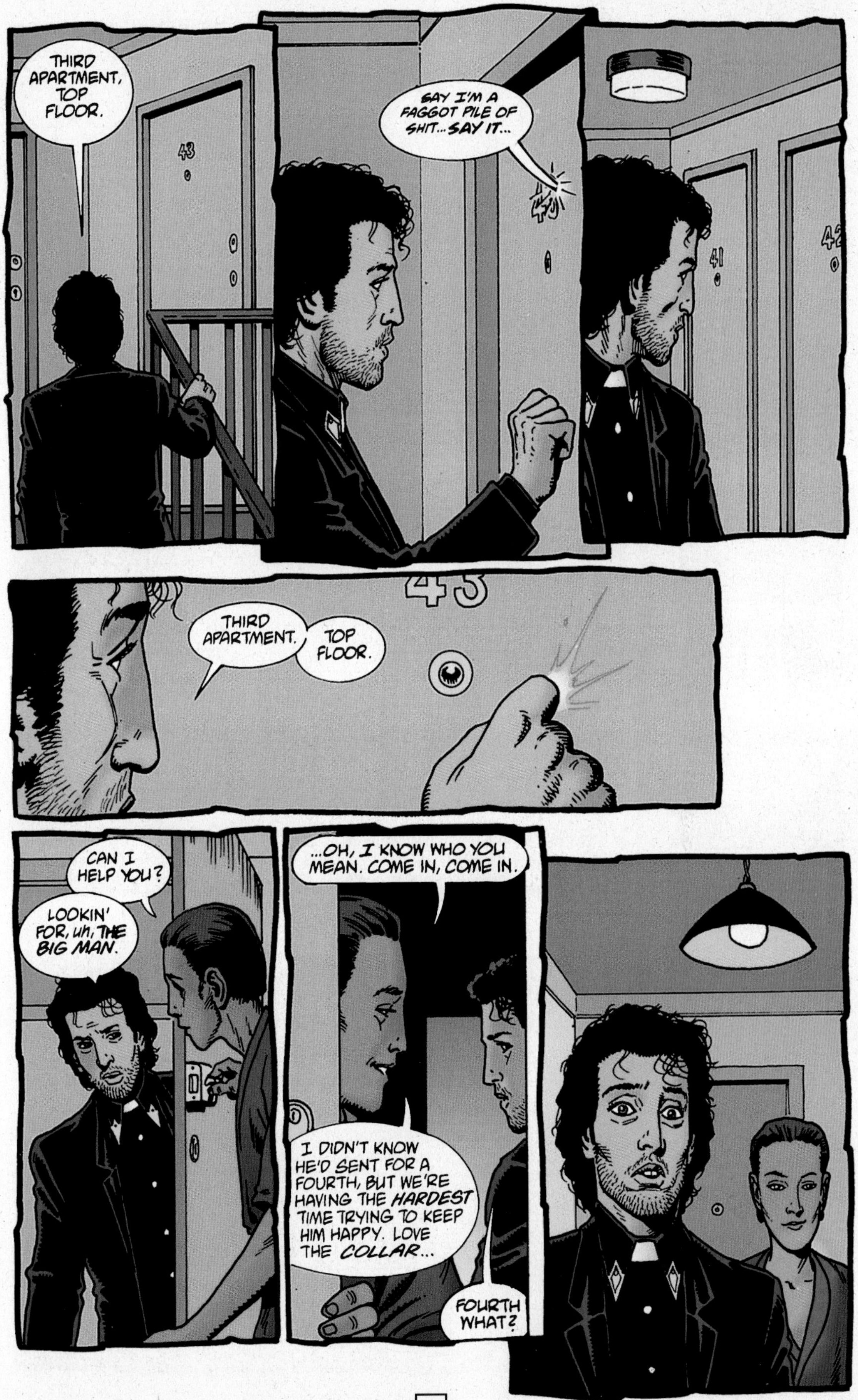
THIRD APARTMENT, TOP FLOOR.
SAY I'M A FAGGOT PILE OF SHIT... SAY IT...
THIRD APARTMENT.
TOP FLOOR.
CAN I HELP YOU?
LOOKIN' FOR, uh, THE BIG MAN.
...OH, I KNOW WHO YOU MEAN. COME IN, COME IN.
I DIDN'T KNOW HE'D SENT FOR A FOURTH, BUT WE'RE HAVING THE HARDEST TIME TRYING TO KEEP HIM HAPPY. LOVE THE COLLAR...
FOURTH WHAT?

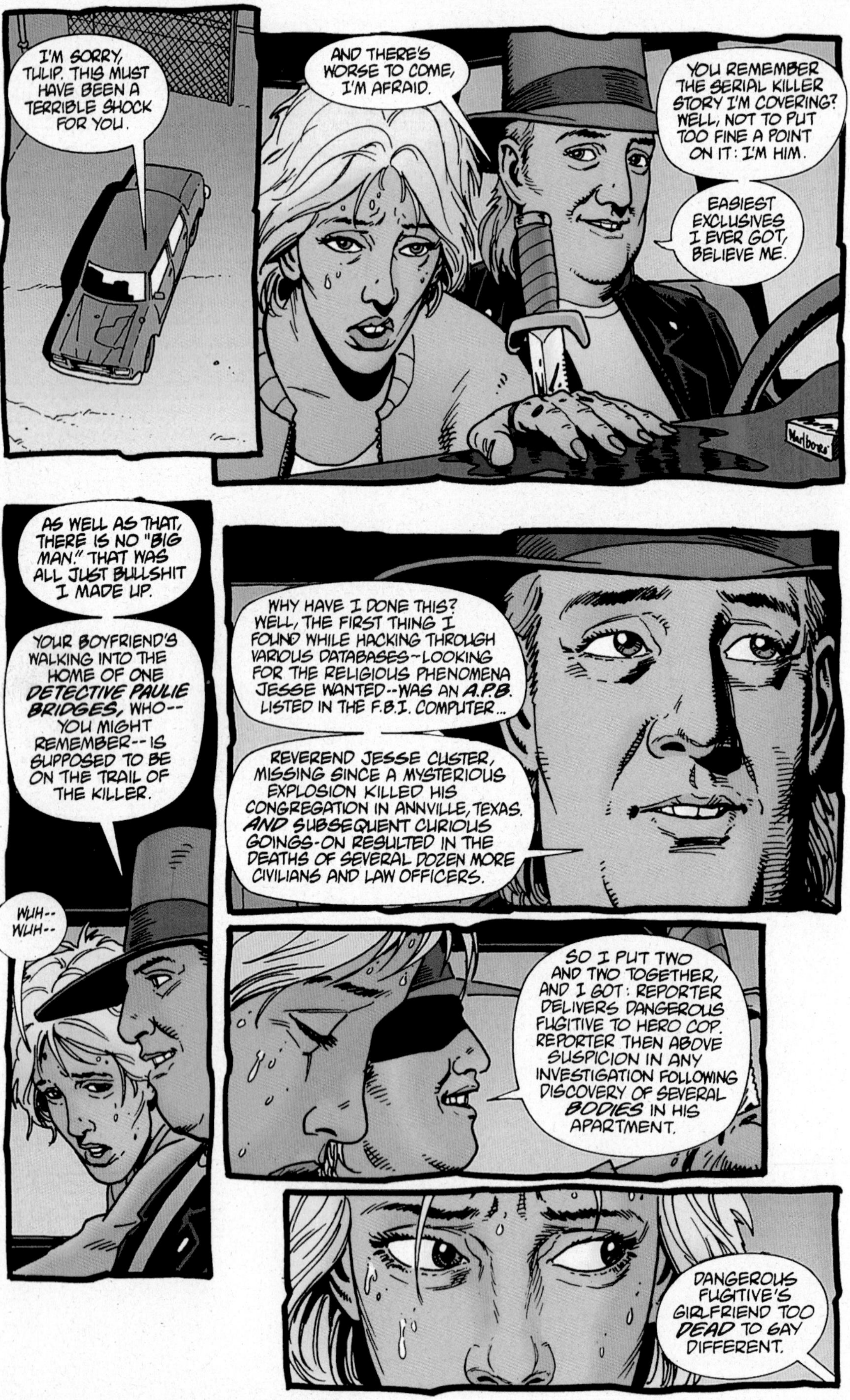
I'M SORRY, TULIP. THIS MUST HAVE BEEN A TERRIBLE SHOCK FOR YOU.
AND THERE'S WORSE TO COME, I'M AFRAID.
YOU REMEMBER THE SERIAL KILLER STORY I'M COVERING? WELL, NOT TO PUT TOO FINE A POINT ON IT: I'M HIM.
EASIEST EXCLUSIVES I EVER GOT, BELIEVE ME.
Marlboro
AS WELL AS THAT, THERE IS NO "BIG MAN." THAT WAS ALL JUST BULLSHIT I MADE UP.
YOUR BOYFRIEND'S WALKING INTO THE HOME OF ONE DETECTIVE PAULIE BRIDGES, WHO-- YOU MIGHT REMEMBER--IS SUPPOSED TO BE ON THE TRAIL OF THE KILLER.
WUH-- WUH--
WHY HAVE I DONE THIS? WELL, THE FIRST THING I FOUND WHILE HACKING THROUGH VARIOUS DATABASES--LOOKING FOR THE RELIGIOUS PHENOMENA JESSE WANTED--WAS AN A.P.B. LISTED IN THE F.B.I. COMPUTER...
REVEREND JESSE CUSTER, MISSING SINCE A MYSTERIOUS EXPLOSION KILLED HIS CONGREGATION IN ANNVILLE, TEXAS. AND SUBSEQUENT CURIOUS GOINGS-ON RESULTED IN THE DEATHS OF SEVERAL DOZEN MORE CIVILIANS AND LAW OFFICERS.
SO I PUT TWO AND TWO TOGETHER, AND I GOT: REPORTER DELIVERS DANGEROUS FUGITIVE TO HERO COP. REPORTER THEN ABOVE SUSPICION IN ANY INVESTIGATION FOLLOWING DISCOVERY OF SEVERAL BODIES IN HIS APARTMENT.
DANGEROUS FUGITIVE'S GIRLFRIEND TOO DEAD TO SAY DIFFERENT.

CAH... SUH...

CASSIDY IS THE ICING ON THE CAKE.

BODIES IN RE-PORTER'S HOME PUT DOWN TO UNIDENTIFIED KILLER, WHO BURST INTO FLAMES WHILE RESISTING ARREST THERE. "I'VE BEEN STAYING WITH MY FOLKS IN THE BRONX," SAID REPORTER. "LITTLE DID I KNOW THIS MADMAN WAS TURNING MY HOME INTO AN ABATTOIR IN MY ABSENCE."

WHYYY...?

BECAUSE IT'S FUN.

TWO YEARS BACK I WAS DRIVING HOME DRUNK WHEN I RAN A GUY OVER. I GOT OUT TO HELP, SAW I'D KILLED HIM. IT WAS FOUR A.M.: NO ONE AROUND. I GOT BACK IN THE CAR AND DROVE LIKE HELL, AND IT WAS FIVE MINUTES BEFORE I REALIZED I WAS LAUGHING FIT TO BUST--

SO I BEGAN SEEING WHAT ELSE I COULD GET AWAY WITH, AND IT JUST GOT FUNNIER EACH TIME.

WHY? YOU EXPECTING SOME CRAP ABOUT GETTING RAPED BY MY DAD? OR BEING A WOLF THAT PREYS ON SHEEPLIKE HUMANITY, BLAH-BLAH-BLAH?

'CAUSE I'D GOTTEN CLEAN AWAY WITH IT.

AND THEN I'LL SHOW YOU JUST HOW MUCH FUN SERIAL KILLING CAN BE.

ANYWAY, DON'T SCREAM, OR THE COPS'LL COME AND THEY'LL GET JESSE ANYWAY. I'M GONNA GO TELL BRIDGES ABOUT HIS LUCKY BREAK.

THEN WE'LL HEAD UP TO MY FOLKS' PLACE, AND I'LL GET 'EM OUT OF THE FREEZER...

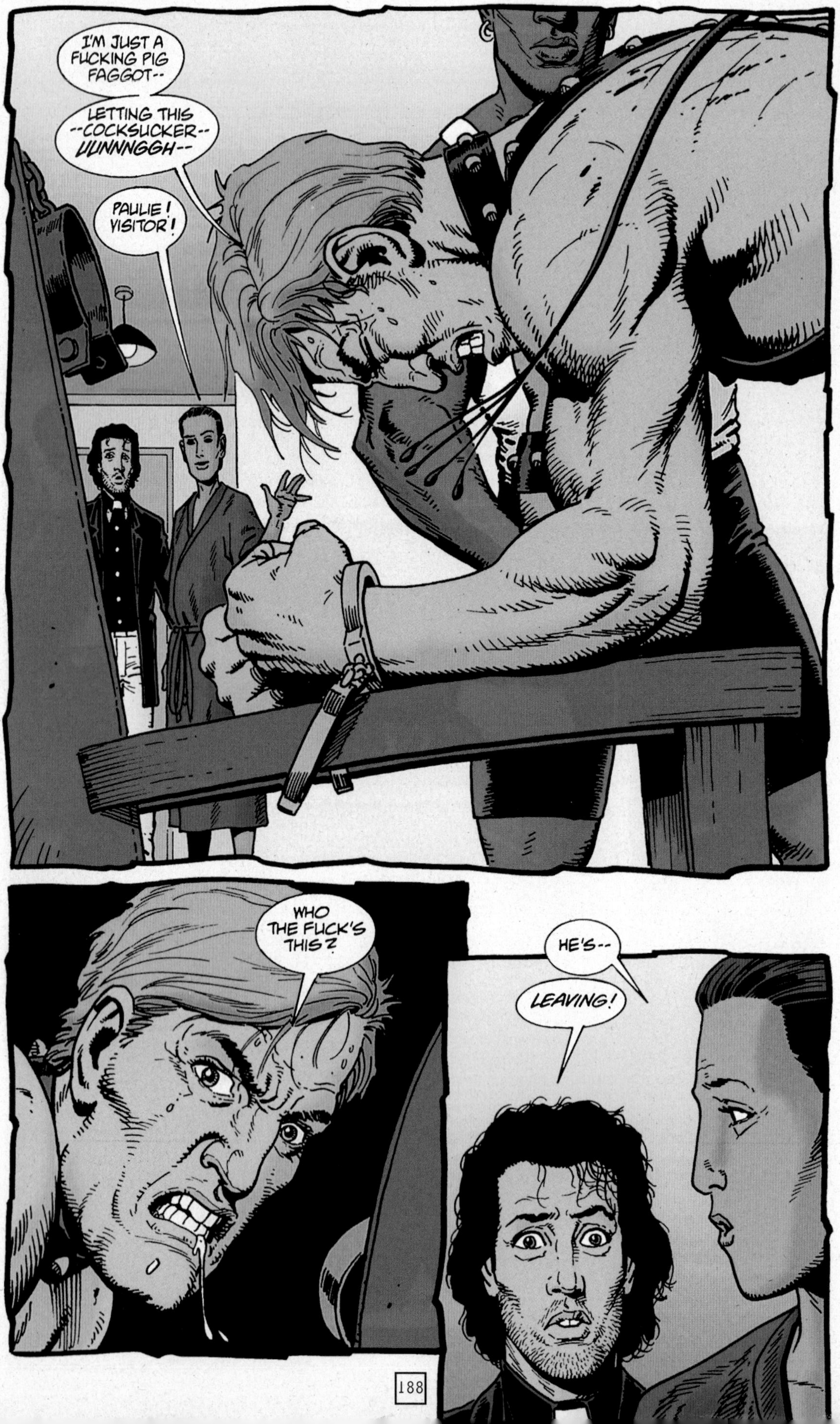
I'M JUST A FUCKING PIG FAGGOT--
LETTING THIS --COCKSUCKER-- UUNNNGGH--
PAULIE! VISITOR!
WHO THE FUCK'S THIS?
HE'S--
LEAVING!

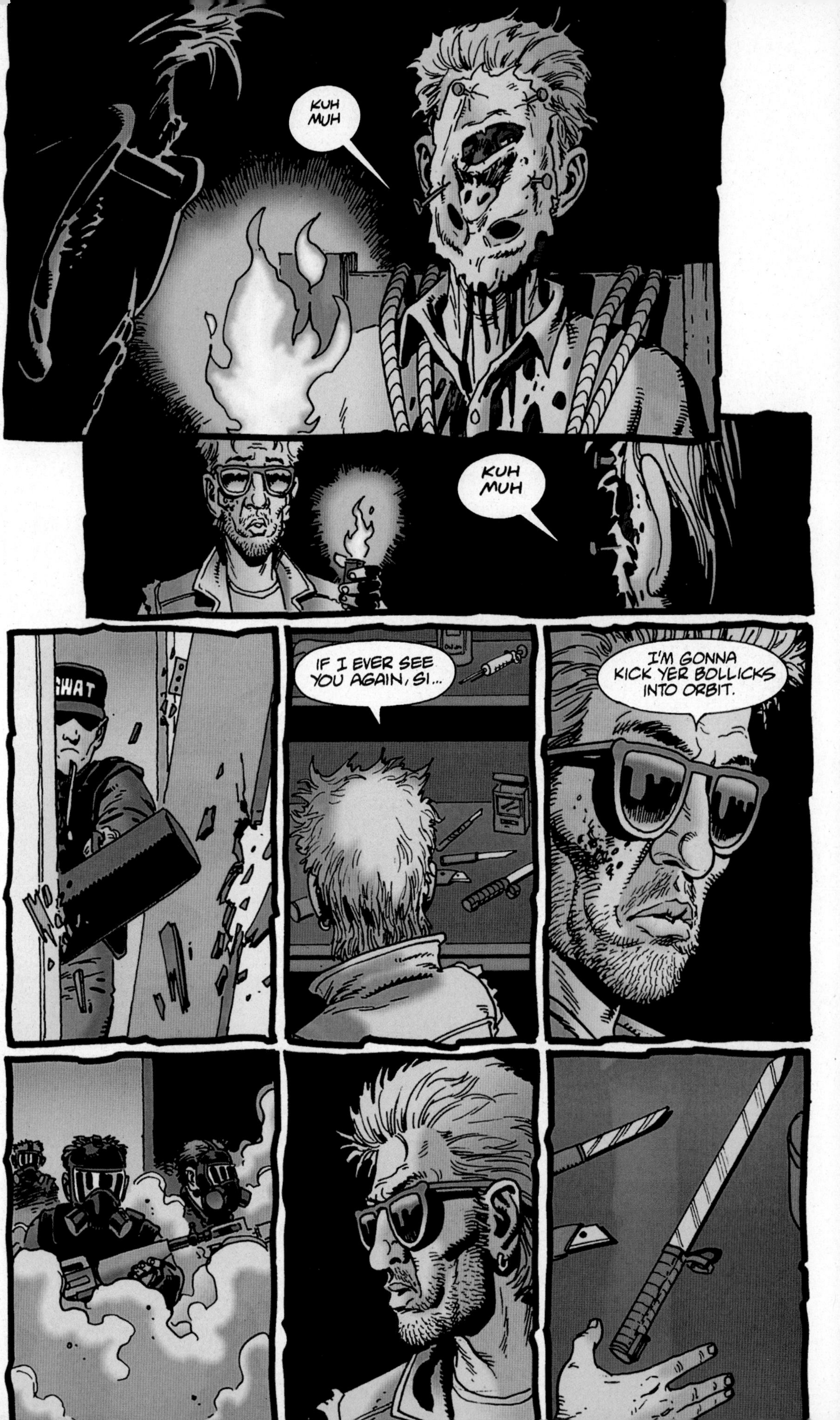
KUH MUH
KUH MUH
IF I EVER SEE YOU AGAIN, SI...
I'M GONNA KICK YER BOLLICKS INTO ORBIT.

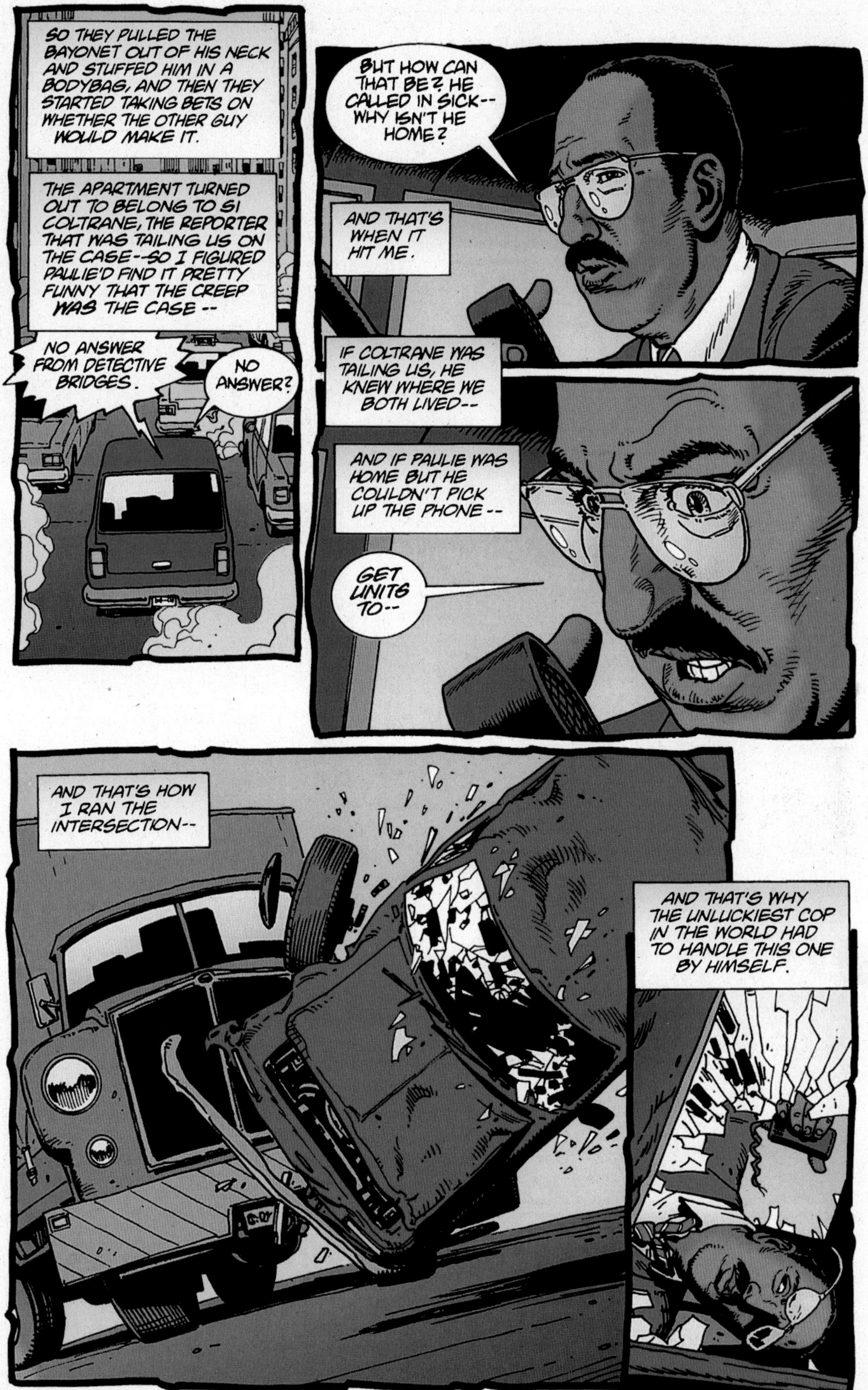
SO THEY PULLED THE BAYONET OUT OF HIS NECK AND STUFFED HIM IN A BODYBAG, AND THEN THEY STARTED TAKING BETS ON WHETHER THE OTHER GUY WOULD MAKE IT.
THE APARTMENT TURNED OUT TO BELONG TO SI COLTRANE, THE REPORTER THAT WAS TAILING US ON THE CASE--SO I FIGURED PAULIE'D FIND IT PRETTY FUNNY THAT THE CREEP WAS THE CASE --
NO ANSWER FROM DETECTIVE BRIDGES.
NO ANSWER?
BUT HOW CAN THAT BE? HE CALLED IN SICK-- WHY ISN'T HE HOME?
AND THAT'S WHEN IT HIT ME.
IF COLTRANE WAS TAILING US, HE KNEW WHERE WE BOTH LIVED--
AND IF PAULIE WAS HOME BUT HE COULDN'T PICK UP THE PHONE --
GET UNITS TO--
AND THAT'S HOW I RAN THE INTERSECTION--
AND THAT'S WHY THE UNLUCKIEST COP IN THE WORLD HAD TO HANDLE THIS ONE BY HIMSELF.

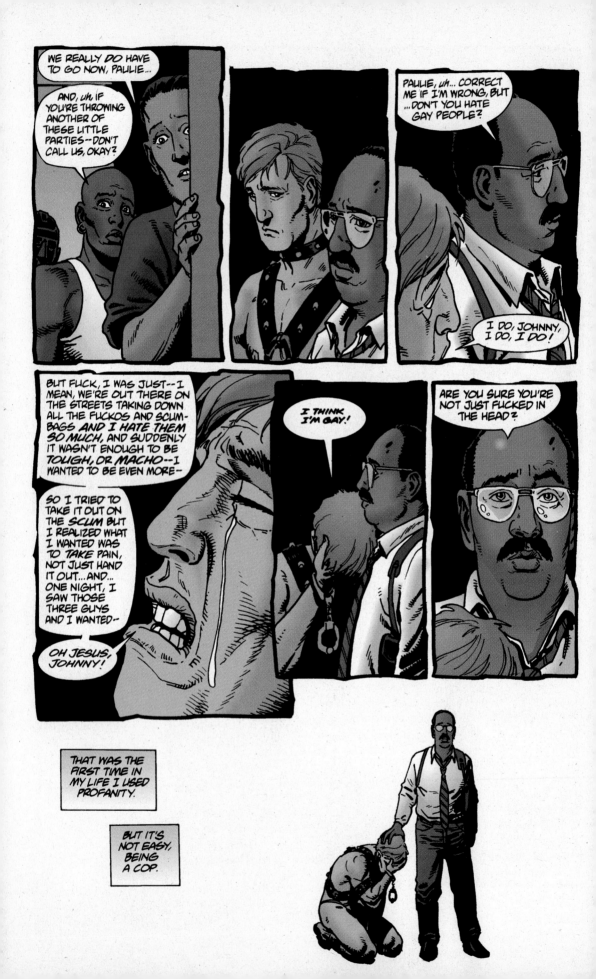

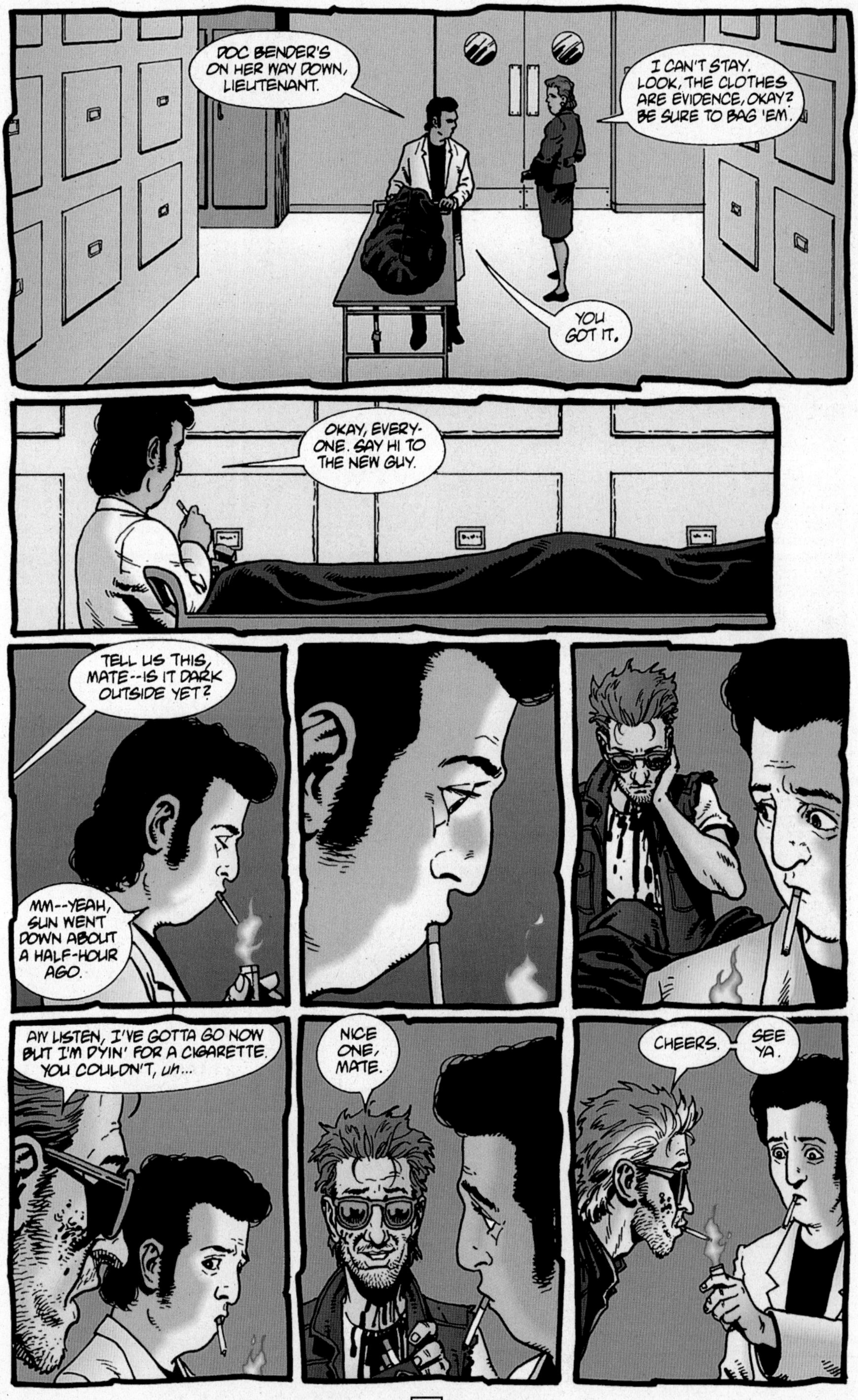
DOC BENDER'S ON HER WAY DOWN, LIEUTENANT.
I CAN'T STAY. LOOK, THE CLOTHES ARE EVIDENCE, OKAY? BE SURE TO BAG 'EM.
YOU GOT IT.
OKAY, EVERY-ONE. SAY HI TO THE NEW GUY.
TELL US THIS, MATE--IS IT DARK OUTSIDE YET?
MM--YEAH, SUN WENT DOWN ABOUT A HALF-HOUR AGO.
AW LISTEN, I'VE GOTTA GO NOW BUT I'M DYIN' FOR A CIGARETTE. YOU COULDN'T, uh...
NICE ONE, MATE.
CHEERS.
SEE YA.

FOR SINGLE-HANDEDLY TAKING DOWN MASS MURDERER SIMON "SERIAL SI" COLTRANE, JOHN TOOL MADE SERGEANT A MONTH LATER, AND LIEUTENANT THE FOLLOWING YEAR.

COPS COPS KILLER SOLO

DETECTIVE JOHN TOOL NYPD HERO

THE YEAR AFTER THAT HE LOST BOTH ARMS IN A HORRIFIC GLAZING ACCIDENT.

PAUL BRIDGES LEFT THE FORCE, BUT MADE A POINT OF KEEPING IN TOUCH WITH HIS FORMER PARTNER...

WHO IS THIS?

CASSIDY WENT WEST, BUT NOT BEFORE STOPPING FOR A SNACK IN HIS FAVORITE BROOKLYN NEIGHBORHOOD--

WHO YOU CALLIN' GUINEA, YOU MOTHER-FUCKIN' MICK?

OF THE REVEREND JESSE CUSTER AND MS. TULIP O'HARE, THERE HAS SO FAR BEEN NO NEWS.

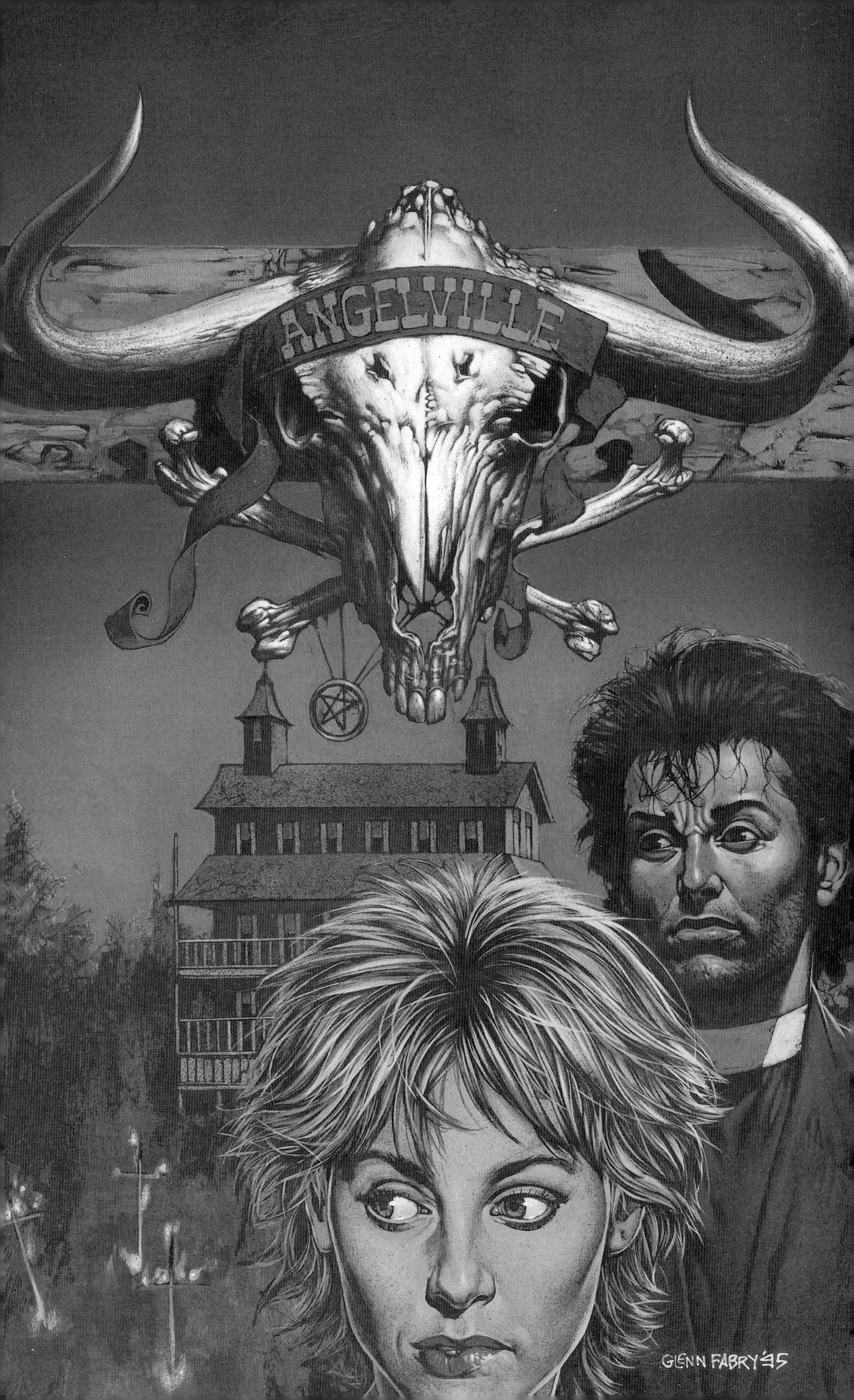
ANGELVILLE
GLENN FABRY '95

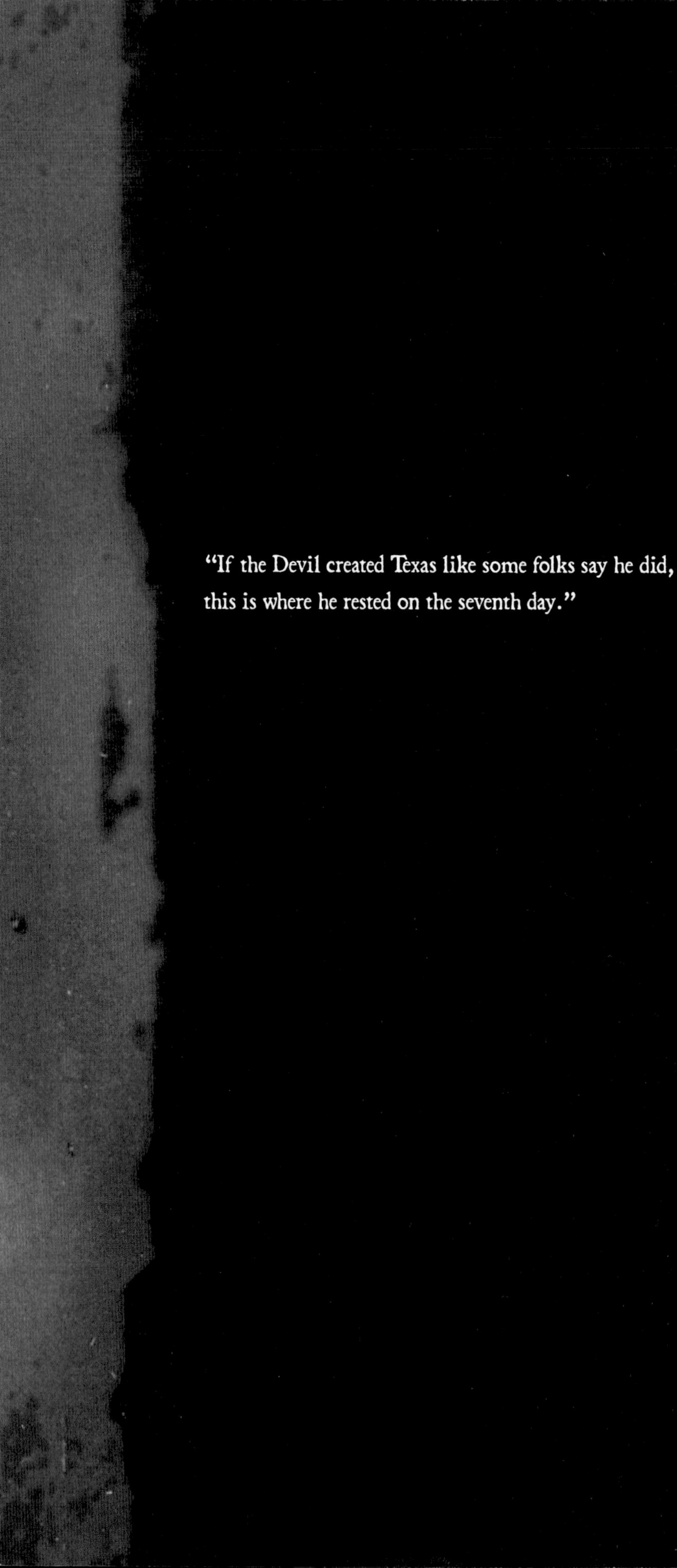
"If the Devil created Texas like some folks say he did,
this is where he rested on the seventh day."

SORRY.

C'MON, TULIP, YOU AIN'T SAID A WORD IN TWO HOURS. WE'RE NEARLY IN DALLAS NOW.

I'M SORRY, OKAY? REALLY.

YEAH, WELL. US ASSHOLES GOT NERVE TO SPARE.

I DRIFTED AROUND FOR A COUPLE OF YEARS, FINALLY ENDED UP IN DALLAS. I GUESS I WASN'T TOO NICE A PERSON TO BE WITH.

I JUST CAN'T BELIEVE YOU'VE GOT THE NERVE TO SAY IT TO ME.

THE JOBS I HAD WERE ALWAYS LOUSY, AND I COULDN'T HOLD ONTO FRIENDS FOR TOO LONG. BEGAN DRINKING QUITE A BIT.

IT'S HORRIBLE HOW ATTRACTIVE IT CAN GET TO KEEP YOURSELF MISERABLE THAT WAY, YOU KNOW? JUST POURING THE SELF-PITY DOWN ALONG WITH THE VODKA, STARTING AGAIN IN THE MORNING 'CAUSE YOU'VE GOT A PERFECT RIGHT TO, IT'S ALL SOME-BODY ELSE'S FAULT...

IT WAS.

uh-uh. I USED YOU UP AS AN EXCUSE PRETTY EARLY ON.

EVENTUALLY I HAD MY LITTLE SCARE: EVERY DRINKER GETS THEM, IT'S WHETHER YOU'RE SMART ENOUGH TO NOTICE THAT COUNTS.

I PEED BLOOD.

214

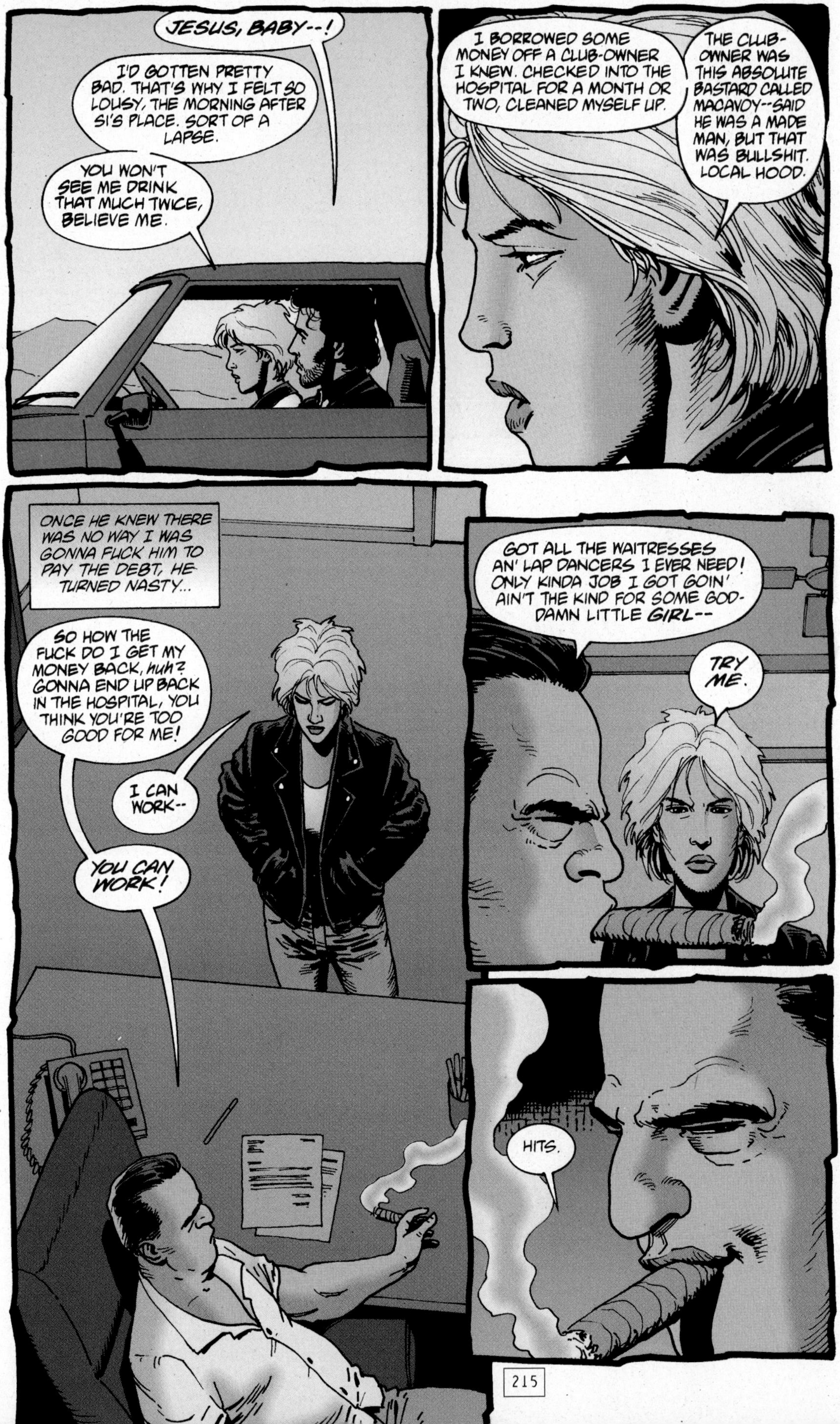
JESUS, BABY--!
I'D GOTTEN PRETTY BAD. THAT'S WHY I FELT SO LOUSY, THE MORNING AFTER SI'S PLACE. SORT OF A LAPSE.
YOU WON'T SEE ME DRINK THAT MUCH TWICE, BELIEVE ME.
I BORROWED SOME MONEY OFF A CLUB-OWNER I KNEW. CHECKED INTO THE HOSPITAL FOR A MONTH OR TWO, CLEANED MYSELF UP.
THE CLUB-OWNER WAS THIS ABSOLUTE BASTARD CALLED MACAVOY--SAID HE WAS A MADE MAN, BUT THAT WAS BULLSHIT. LOCAL HOOD.
ONCE HE KNEW THERE WAS NO WAY I WAS GONNA FUCK HIM TO PAY THE DEBT, HE TURNED NASTY...
SO HOW THE FUCK DO I GET MY MONEY BACK, huh? GONNA END UP BACK IN THE HOSPITAL, YOU THINK YOU'RE TOO GOOD FOR ME!
I CAN WORK--
YOU CAN WORK!
GOT ALL THE WAITRESSES AN' LAP DANCERS I EVER NEED! ONLY KINDA JOB I GOT GOIN' AIN'T THE KIND FOR SOME GOD-DAMN LITTLE GIRL--
TRY ME.
HITS.

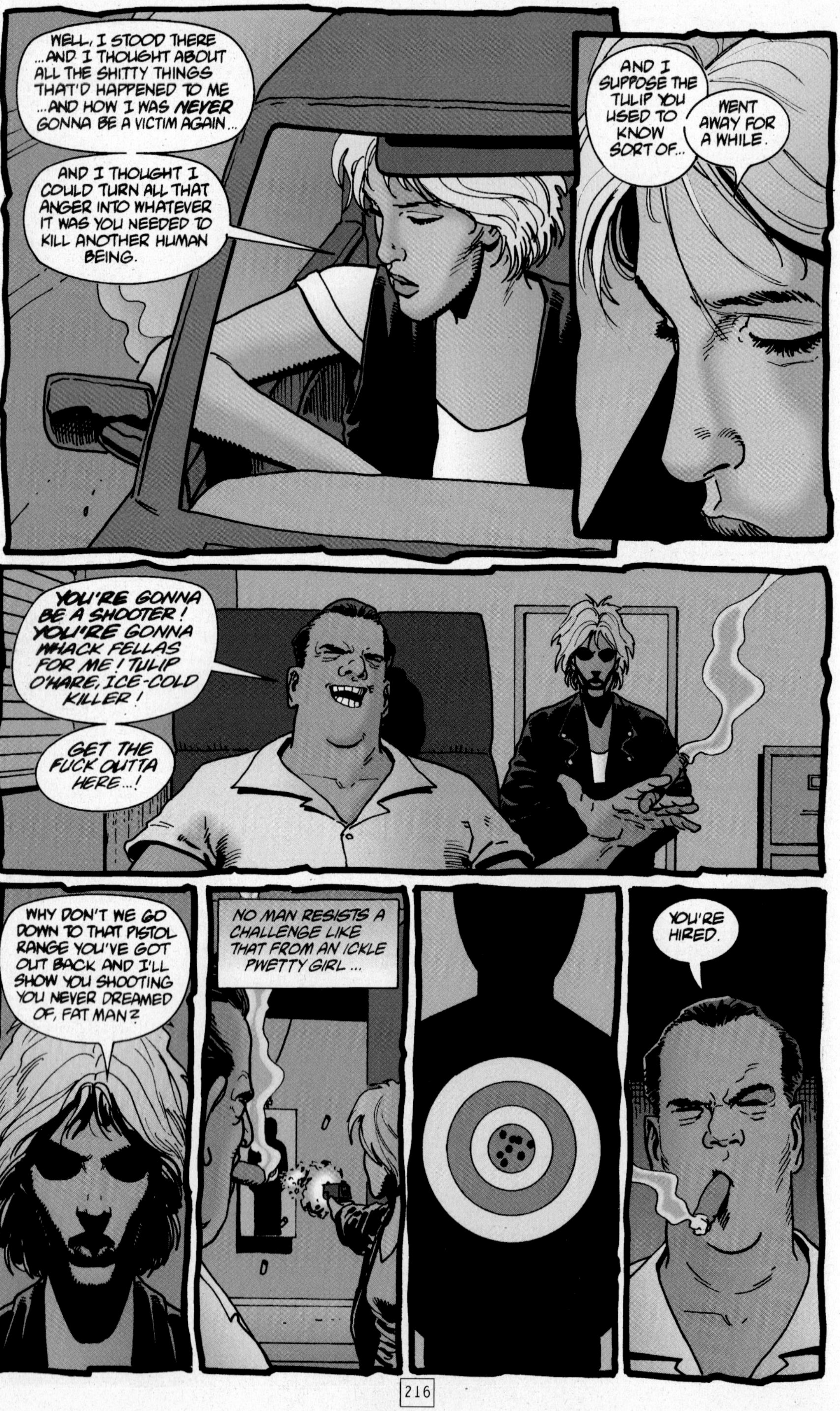
WELL, I STOOD THERE ...AND I THOUGHT ABOUT ALL THE SHITTY THINGS THAT'D HAPPENED TO ME ...AND HOW I WAS NEVER GONNA BE A VICTIM AGAIN...
AND I THOUGHT I COULD TURN ALL THAT ANGER INTO WHATEVER IT WAS YOU NEEDED TO KILL ANOTHER HUMAN BEING.
AND I SUPPOSE THE TULIP YOU USED TO KNOW SORT OF...
WENT AWAY FOR A WHILE.
YOU'RE GONNA BE A SHOOTER! YOU'RE GONNA WHACK FELLAS FOR ME! TULIP O'HARE, ICE-COLD KILLER!
GET THE FUCK OUTTA HERE...!
WHY DON'T WE GO DOWN TO THAT PISTOL RANGE YOU'VE GOT OUT BACK AND I'LL SHOW YOU SHOOTING YOU NEVER DREAMED OF, FAT MAN?
NO MAN RESISTS A CHALLENGE LIKE THAT FROM AN ICKLE PWETTY GIRL...
YOU'RE HIRED.

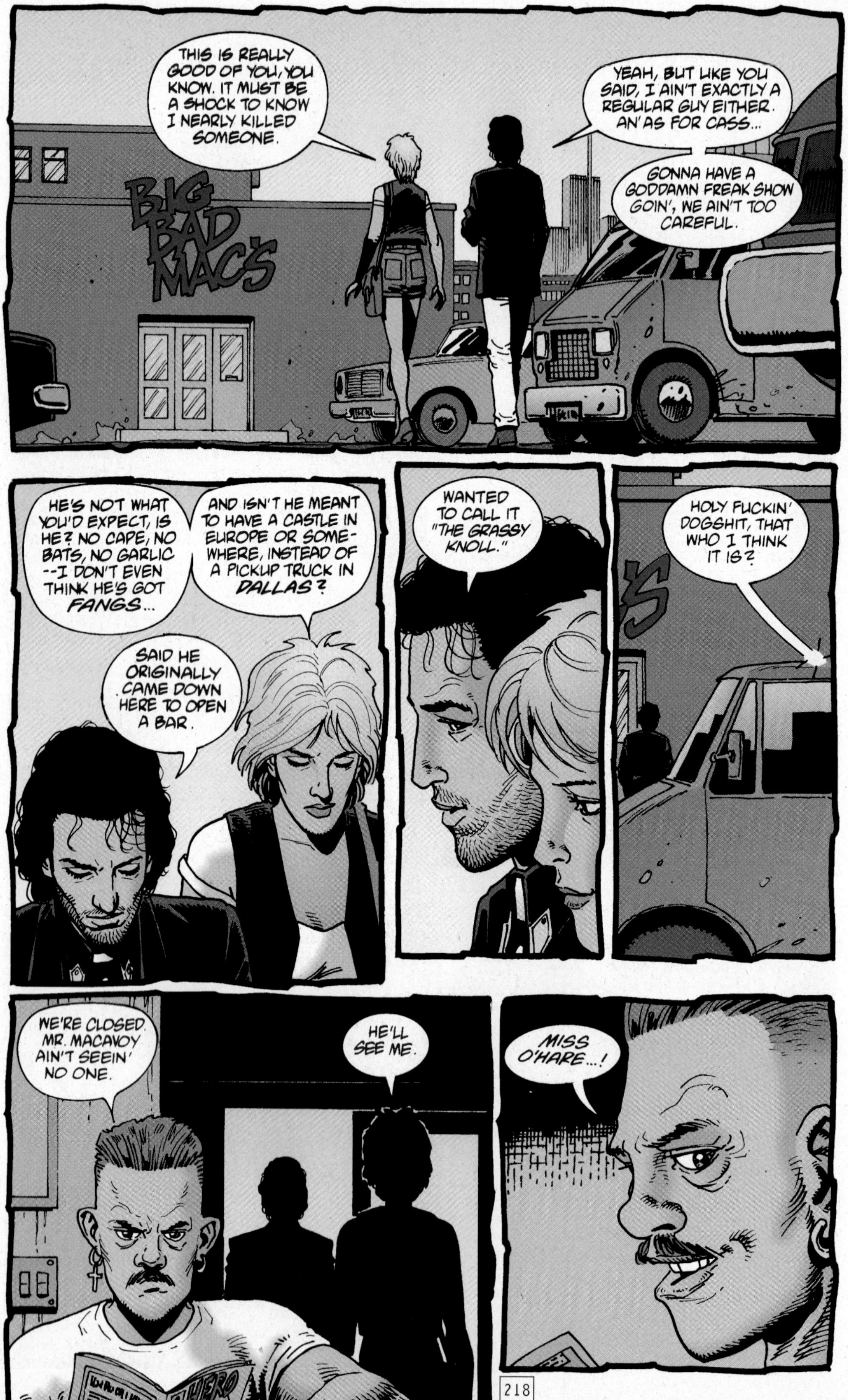
THIS IS REALLY GOOD OF YOU, YOU KNOW. IT MUST BE A SHOCK TO KNOW I NEARLY KILLED SOMEONE.
YEAH, BUT LIKE YOU SAID, I AIN'T EXACTLY A REGULAR GUY EITHER. AN' AS FOR CASS...
GONNA HAVE A GODDAMN FREAK SHOW GOIN', WE AIN'T TOO CAREFUL.
BIG BAD MAC'S
HE'S NOT WHAT YOU'D EXPECT, IS HE? NO CAPE, NO BATS, NO GARLIC --I DON'T EVEN THINK HE'S GOT FANGS...
AND ISN'T HE MEANT TO HAVE A CASTLE IN EUROPE OR SOMEWHERE, INSTEAD OF A PICKUP TRUCK IN DALLAS?
SAID HE ORIGINALLY CAME DOWN HERE TO OPEN A BAR.
WANTED TO CALL IT "THE GRASSY KNOLL."
HOLY FUCKIN' DOGSHIT, THAT WHO I THINK IT IS?
WE'RE CLOSED. MR. MACAVOY AIN'T SEEIN' NO ONE.
HE'LL SEE ME.
MISS O'HARE...!

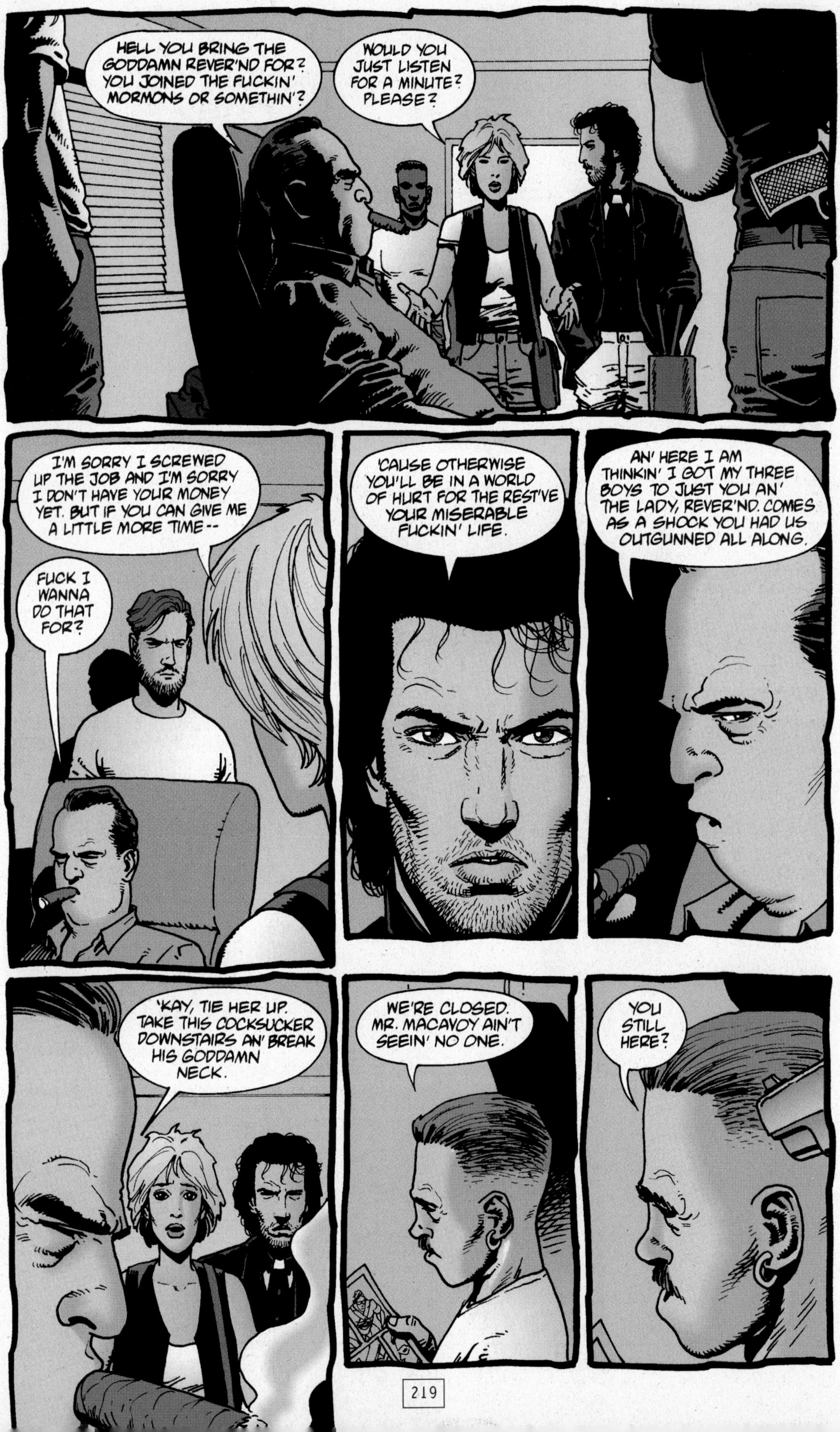
HELL YOU BRING THE GODDAMN REVER'ND FOR? YOU JOINED THE FUCKIN' MORMONS OR SOMETHIN'?
WOULD YOU JUST LISTEN FOR A MINUTE? PLEASE?
I'M SORRY I SCREWED UP THE JOB AND I'M SORRY I DON'T HAVE YOUR MONEY YET. BUT IF YOU CAN GIVE ME A LITTLE MORE TIME--
FUCK I WANNA DO THAT FOR?
'CAUSE OTHERWISE YOU'LL BE IN A WORLD OF HURT FOR THE REST'VE YOUR MISERABLE FUCKIN' LIFE.
AN' HERE I AM THINKIN' I GOT MY THREE BOYS TO JUST YOU AN' THE LADY, REVER'ND. COMES AS A SHOCK YOU HAD US OUTGUNNED ALL ALONG.
'KAY, TIE HER UP. TAKE THIS COCKSUCKER DOWNSTAIRS AN' BREAK HIS GODDAMN NECK.
WE'RE CLOSED. MR. MACAVOY AIN'T SEEIN' NO ONE.
YOU STILL HERE?

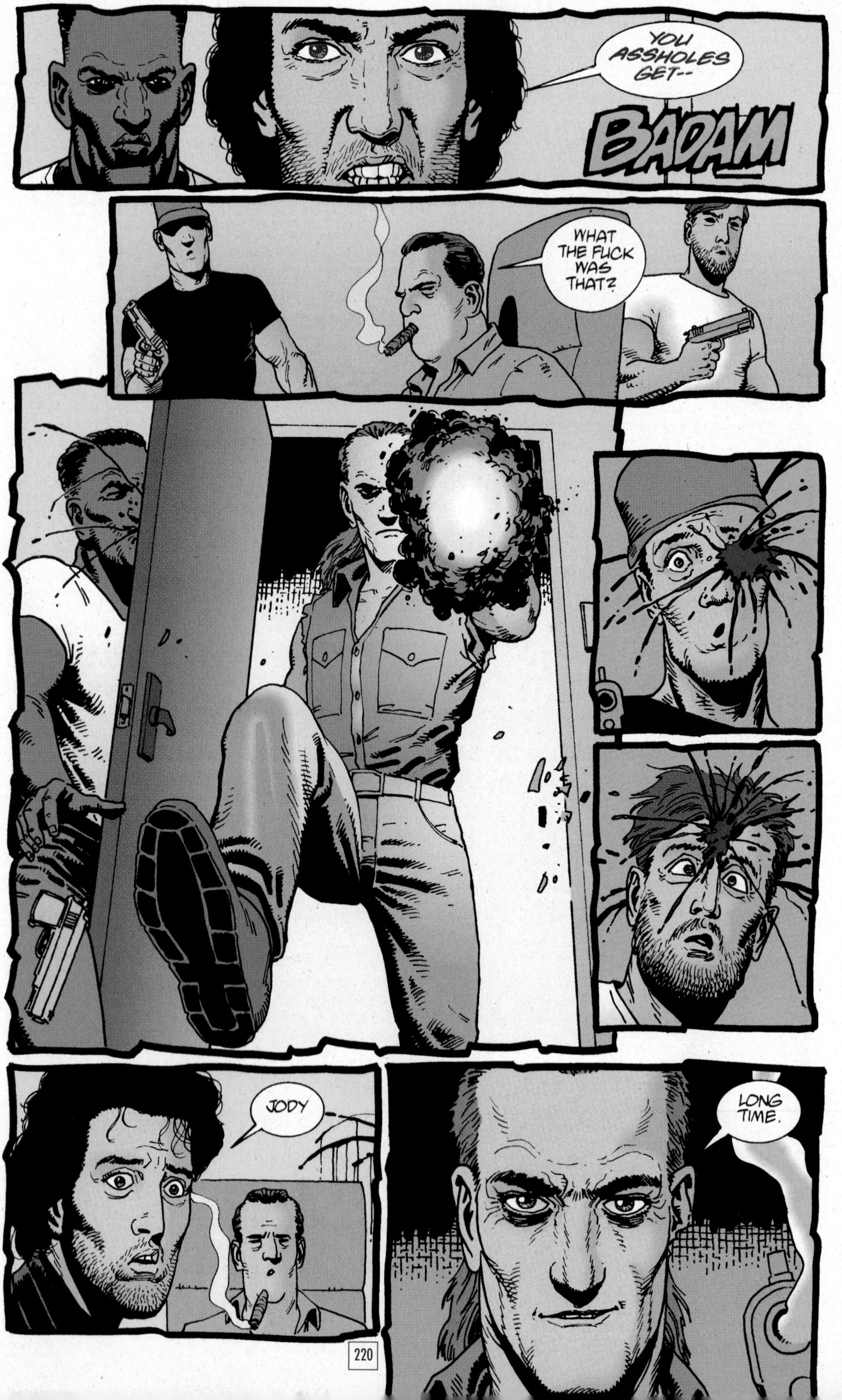
YOU ASSHOLES GET--
BADAM
WHAT THE FUCK WAS THAT?
JODY
LONG TIME.

JESUS CHRIST...

WANNA TRY THAT AGAIN, BOYZ

YOU--

GODDAMN YOU, JODY. YOU DROP THAT FUCKIN' GUN.

'KAY, NOW WE GOT THAT SETTLED.

GONNA TAKE US A WALK OUTSIDE. T.C.'S GOT THE VAN READY. ANY BULLSHIT, I SHOOT YOU IN THE LEGS AN' HER IN THE FACE. MAYBE LET T.C. PUT THE DICK TO HER FIRST, SO JUST BEHAVE YOUR FUCKIN' SELF.

LET'S GO.

DO LIKE HE SAYS.

er...

YOU CAN GO TAKE A BIG OL' SUCK ON THE DEVIL'S PECKER, FAT BOY.

LITTLE JESSE!

I KNEW IT WAS YOU!

WE'RE SITTIN' HERE GETTIN' STONED FOR THE TRIP HOME, I SEE YOU GO PAST, I SAY TO JODY *GODDAMN* IF IT AIN'T LITTLE JESSE! AN' US ABOUT GIVEN UP LOOKIN' FOR YOU!

COOZE GOT A NAME?

YOU--

JESSE, WHO *ARE* THEY?

SHE'S NOBODY. SHE WAS HITCHIN' OUTTA DEERFORTH, I GAVE HER A RIDE. MAY AS WELL JUST LET HER GO, huh?

MAY AS WELL DO HER NOW, T.C. HER BEIN' NOTHIN' TO HIM...

FIGURES!

NAH, JODY'S JUST FUCKIN' WITH YOU. WE KNOW WHO SHE IS! WE 'MEMBER HER WITH YOU IN PHOENIX, ALL THEM YEARS BACK!

PHOENIX? JESSE?

JESUS, TULIP.

I'M SO SORRY.

223

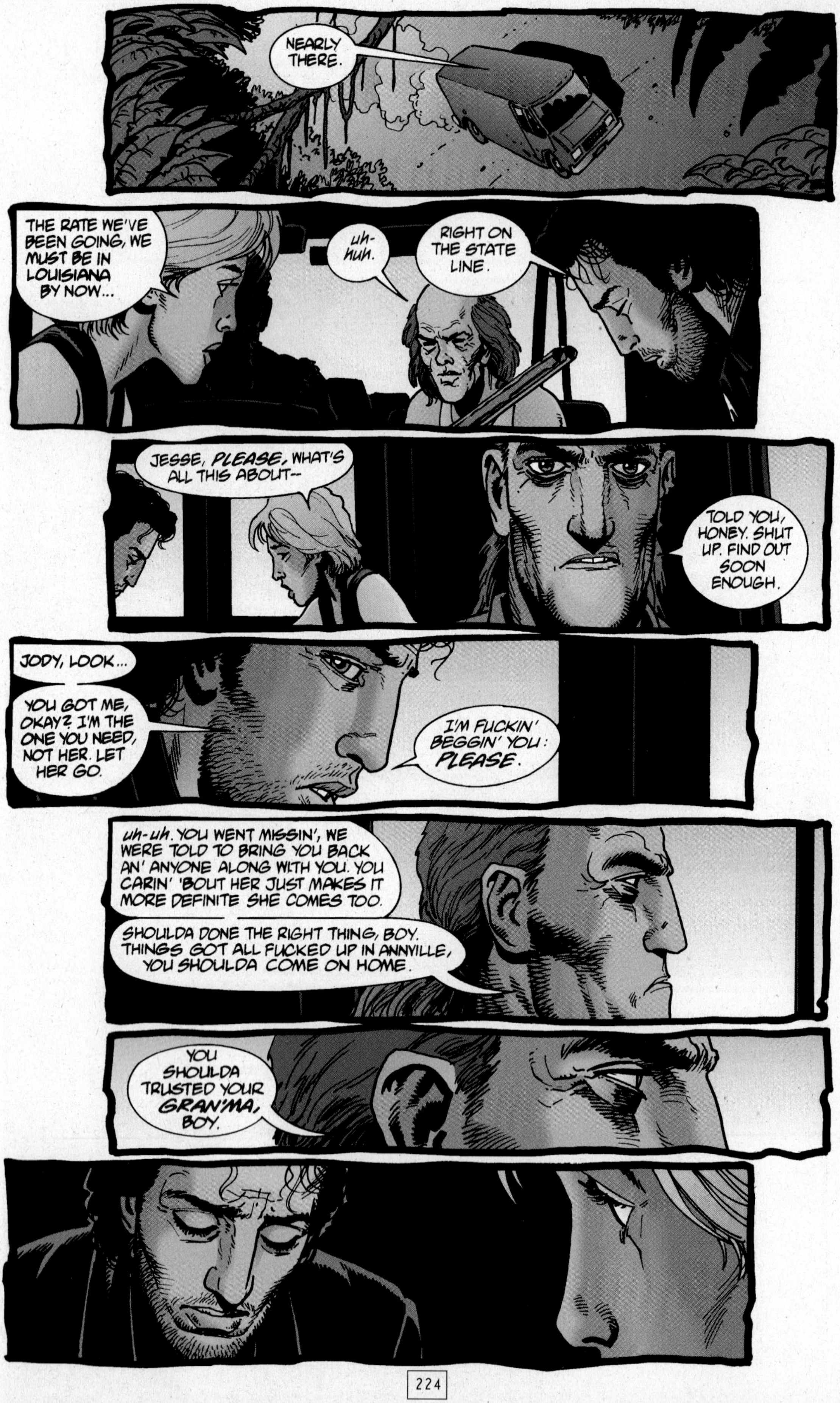
NEARLY THERE.
THE RATE WE'VE BEEN GOING, WE MUST BE IN LOUISIANA BY NOW...
uh-huh.
RIGHT ON THE STATE LINE.
JESSE, PLEASE, WHAT'S ALL THIS ABOUT--
TOLD YOU, HONEY. SHUT UP. FIND OUT SOON ENOUGH.
JODY, LOOK...
YOU GOT ME, OKAY? I'M THE ONE YOU NEED, NOT HER. LET HER GO.
I'M FUCKIN' BEGGIN' YOU: PLEASE.
uh-uh. YOU WENT MISSIN', WE WERE TOLD TO BRING YOU BACK AN' ANYONE ALONG WITH YOU. YOU CARIN' 'BOUT HER JUST MAKES IT MORE DEFINITE SHE COMES TOO.
SHOULDA DONE THE RIGHT THING, BOY. THINGS GOT ALL FUCKED UP IN ANNVILLE, YOU SHOULDA COME ON HOME.
YOU SHOULDA TRUSTED YOUR GRAN'MA, BOY.

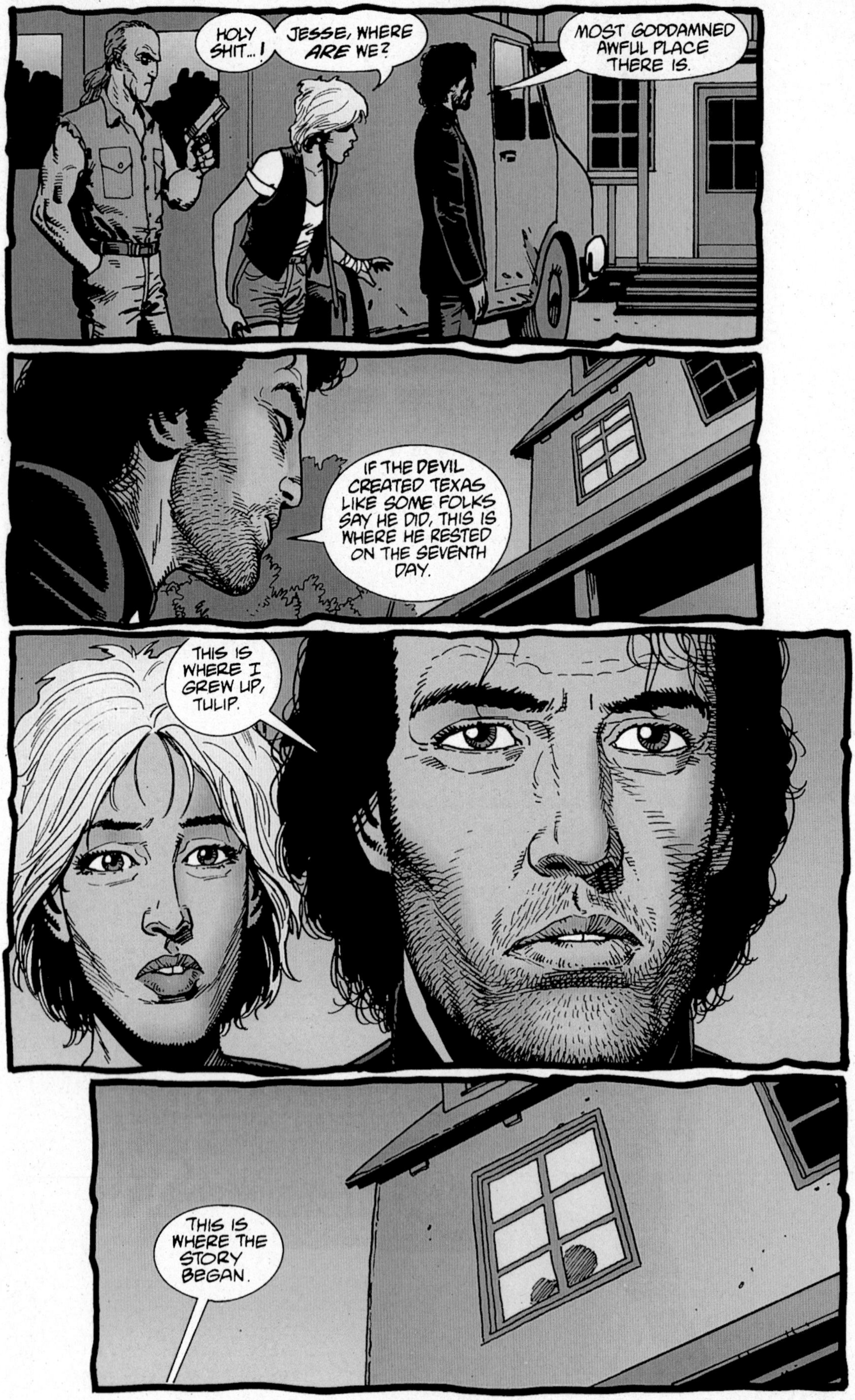
HOLY SHIT...!
JESSE, WHERE ARE WE?
MOST GODDAMNED AWFUL PLACE THERE IS.
IF THE DEVIL CREATED TEXAS LIKE SOME FOLKS SAY HE DID, THIS IS WHERE HE RESTED ON THE SEVENTH DAY.
THIS IS WHERE I GREW UP, TULIP.
THIS IS WHERE THE STORY BEGAN.

ANKLES IN BEHIND THEM CHAIRLEGS. DON'T WANT 'EM MOVIN' 'ROUND THE ROOM.

TIGHT, NOW.

FOR CHRIST'S SAKE--!

TULIP, LISTEN TO ME NOW: I KNOW YOU GOT ABOUT A HUNDRED QUESTIONS YOU WANNA ASK, BUT YOU GOTTA STAY QUIET.

NO MATTER WHAT HAPPENS, NO MATTER WHAT YOU SEE HERE: ONLY CHANCE YOU GOT IS NOT TO SAY A GODDAMN WORD.

BUT... BUT WHAT ABOUT YOU...?

WANNA SMOKE, BOYZ?

FUCK YOUR-SELF.

CHANGE YOUR MIND, YOU LEMME KNOW.

SONUVABITCH--!

SHE'S HERE, JODY.

GOOD EVENING, BOYS...

227

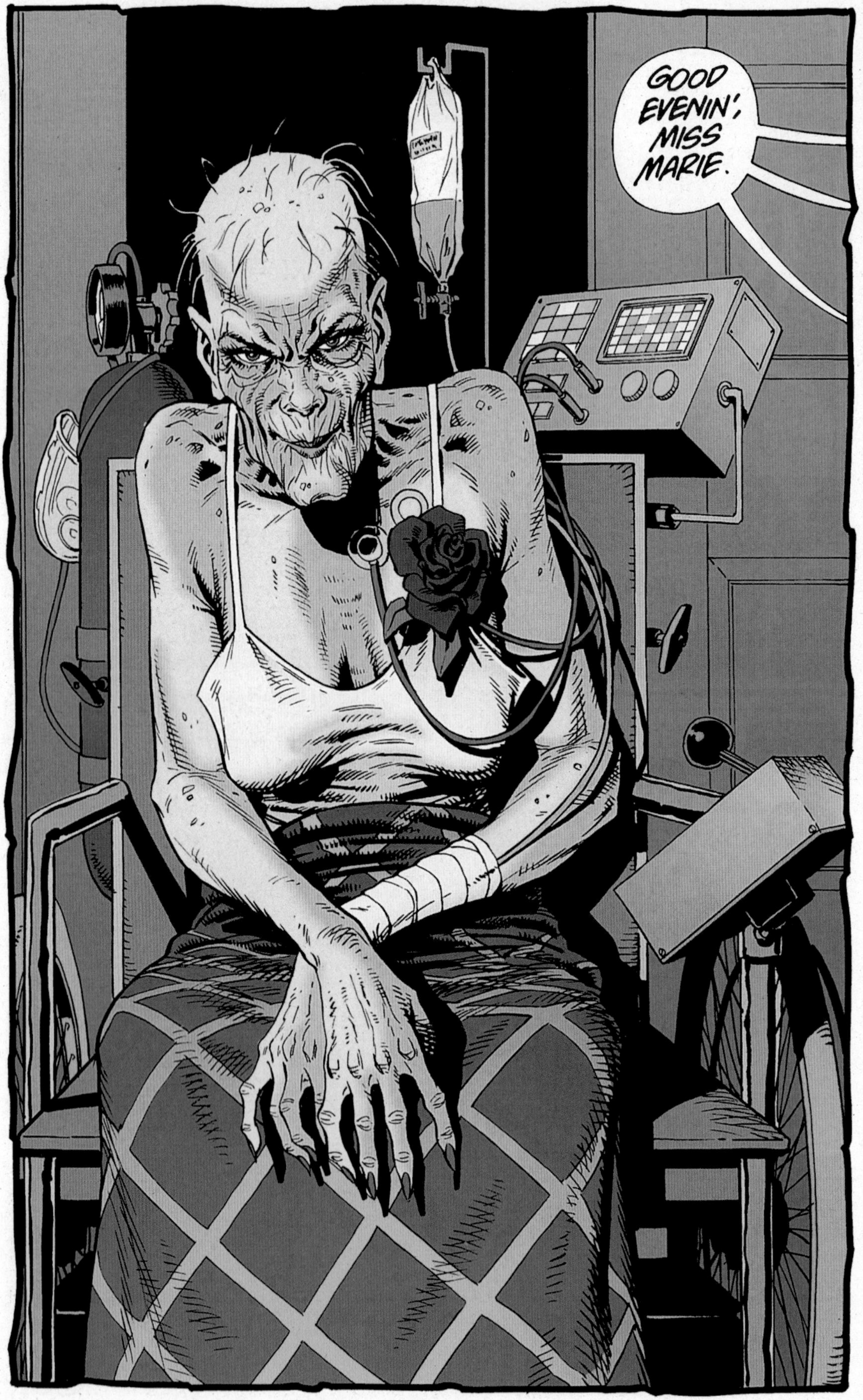
GOOD EVENIN', MISS MARIE.

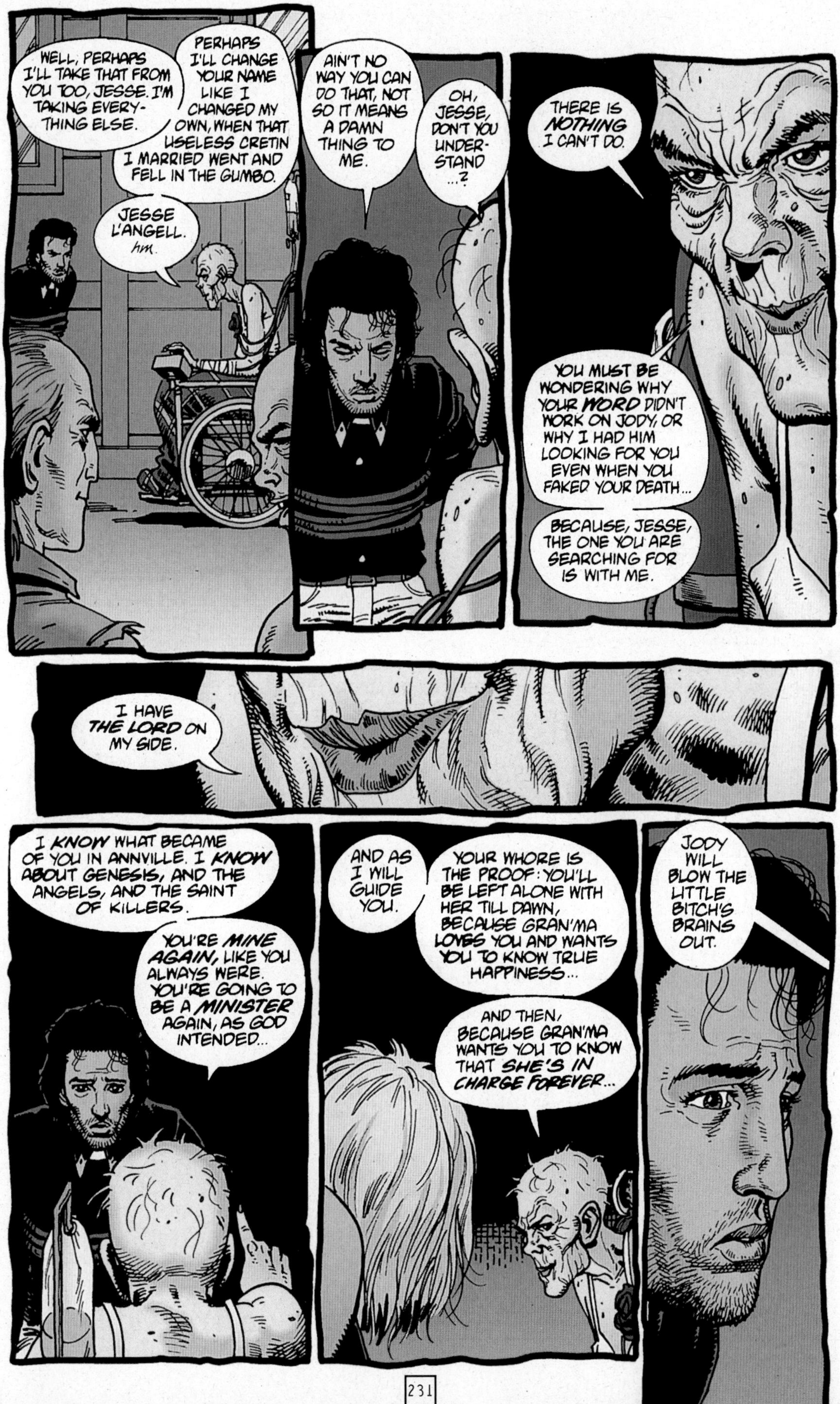

WELL, PERHAPS I'LL TAKE THAT FROM YOU TOO, JESSE. I'M TAKING EVERYTHING ELSE.
PERHAPS I'LL CHANGE YOUR NAME LIKE I CHANGED MY OWN, WHEN THAT USELESS CRETIN I MARRIED WENT AND FELL IN THE GUMBO.
JESSE L'ANGELL. hm.
AIN'T NO WAY YOU CAN DO THAT, NOT SO IT MEANS A DAMN THING TO ME.
OH, JESSE, DON'T YOU UNDERSTAND ...?
THERE IS NOTHING I CAN'T DO.
YOU MUST BE WONDERING WHY YOUR WORD DIDN'T WORK ON JODY, OR WHY I HAD HIM LOOKING FOR YOU EVEN WHEN YOU FAKED YOUR DEATH...
BECAUSE, JESSE, THE ONE YOU ARE SEARCHING FOR IS WITH ME.
I HAVE THE LORD ON MY SIDE.
I KNOW WHAT BECAME OF YOU IN ANNVILLE. I KNOW ABOUT GENESIS, AND THE ANGELS, AND THE SAINT OF KILLERS.
YOU'RE MINE AGAIN, LIKE YOU ALWAYS WERE. YOU'RE GOING TO BE A MINISTER AGAIN, AS GOD INTENDED...
AND AS I WILL GUIDE YOU.
YOUR WHORE IS THE PROOF: YOU'LL BE LEFT ALONE WITH HER TILL DAWN, BECAUSE GRAN'MA LOVES YOU AND WANTS YOU TO KNOW TRUE HAPPINESS...
AND THEN, BECAUSE GRAN'MA WANTS YOU TO KNOW THAT SHE'S IN CHARGE FOREVER...
JODY WILL BLOW THE LITTLE BITCH'S BRAINS OUT.

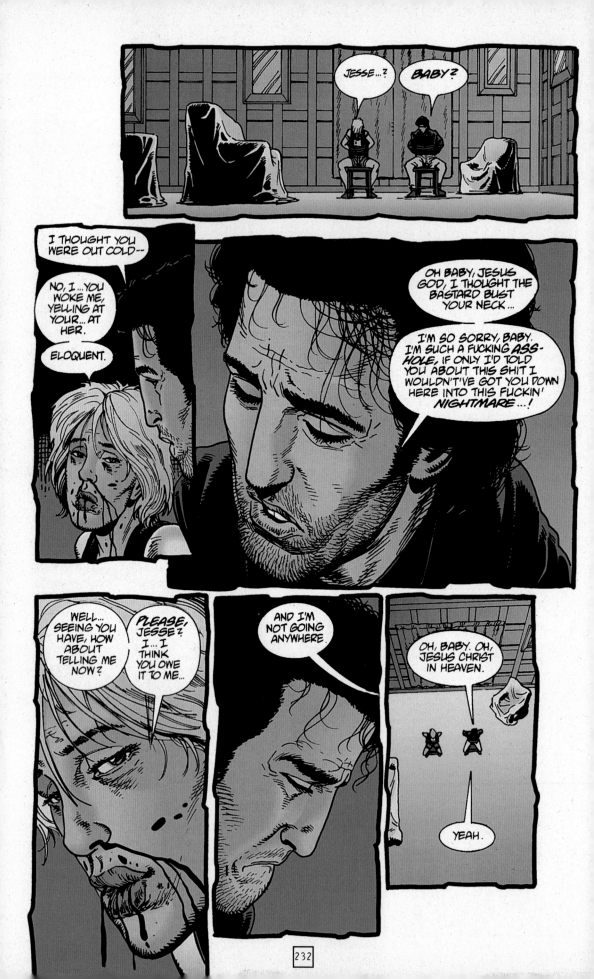

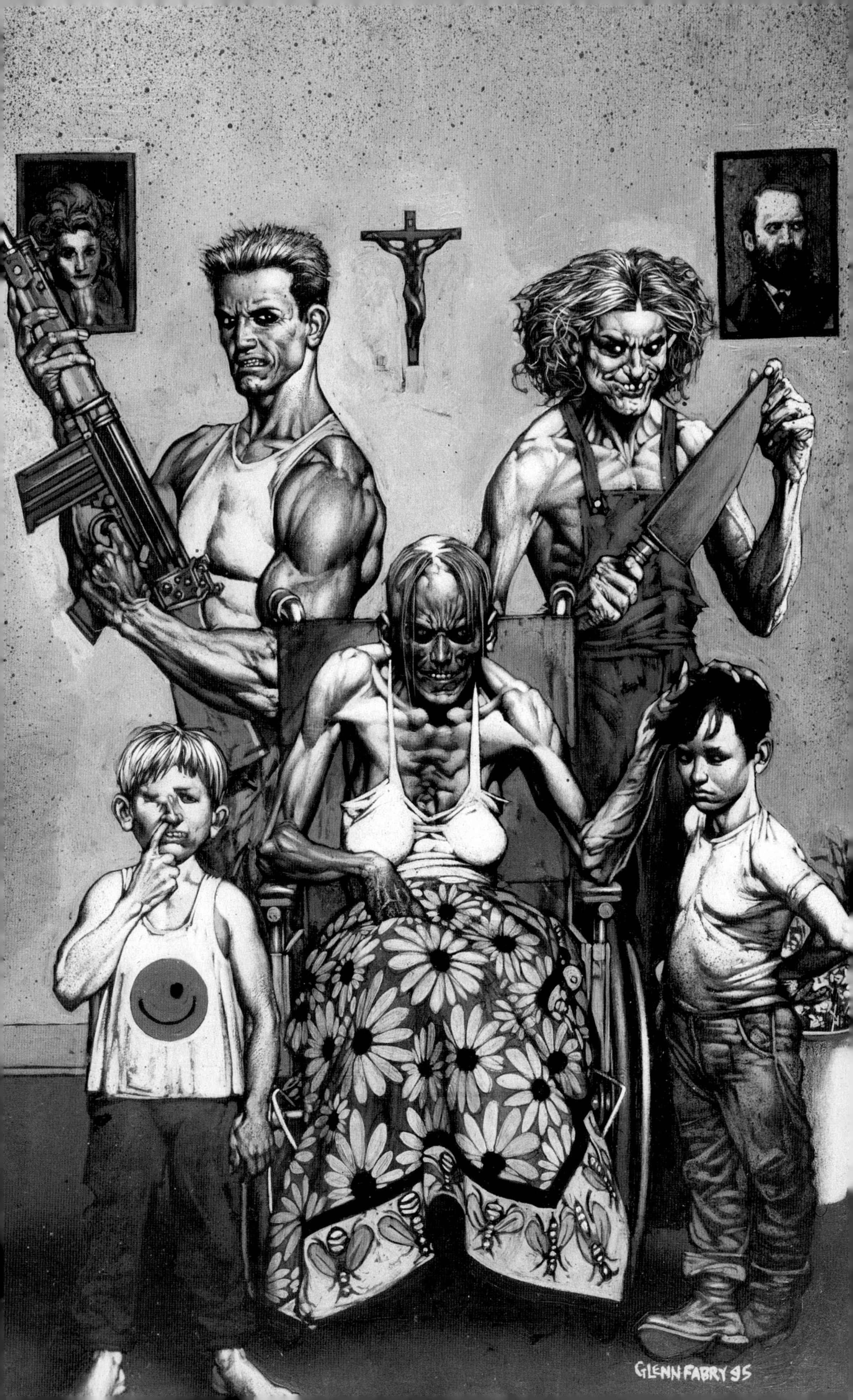
GLENN FABRY 95

"You gotta be one of the good guys, son.
'Cause there's way too many of the bad."

PPTT!

BABYKILLER!!

AND THAT'S ABOUT HOW MY MOM AN' DAD MET UP.

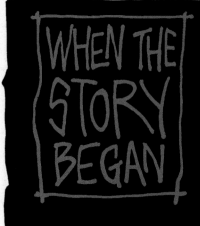

WHEN THE STORY BEGAN

GARTH ENNIS — WRITER   STEVE DILLON — ARTIST

MATT HOLLINGSWORTH — COLORIST

CLEM ROBINS — LETTERER

JULIE ROTTENBERG — ASS'T EDITOR

STUART MOORE — EDITOR

PREACHER CREATED BY

GARTH ENNIS AND STEVE DILLON

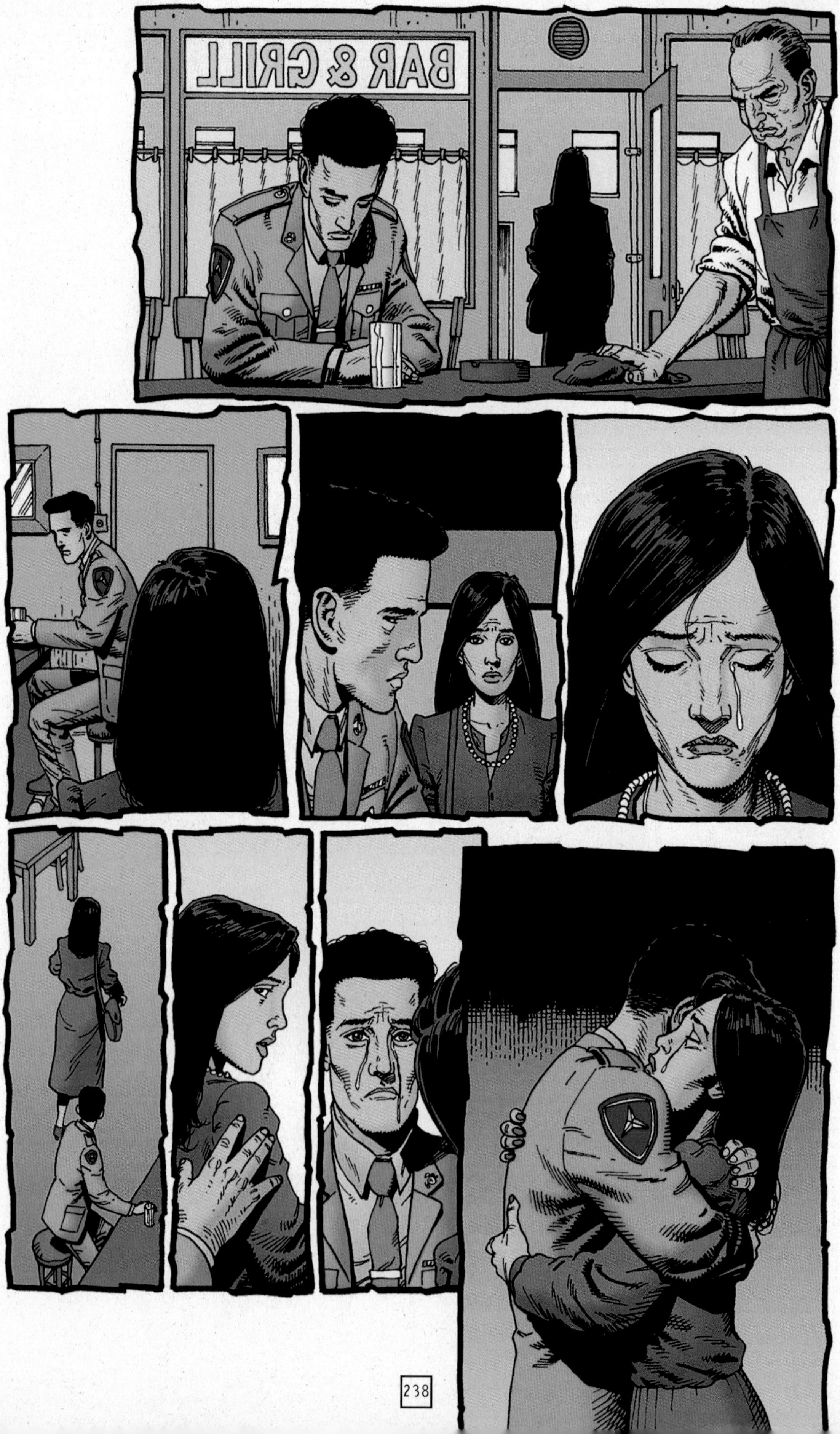
BAR & GRILL

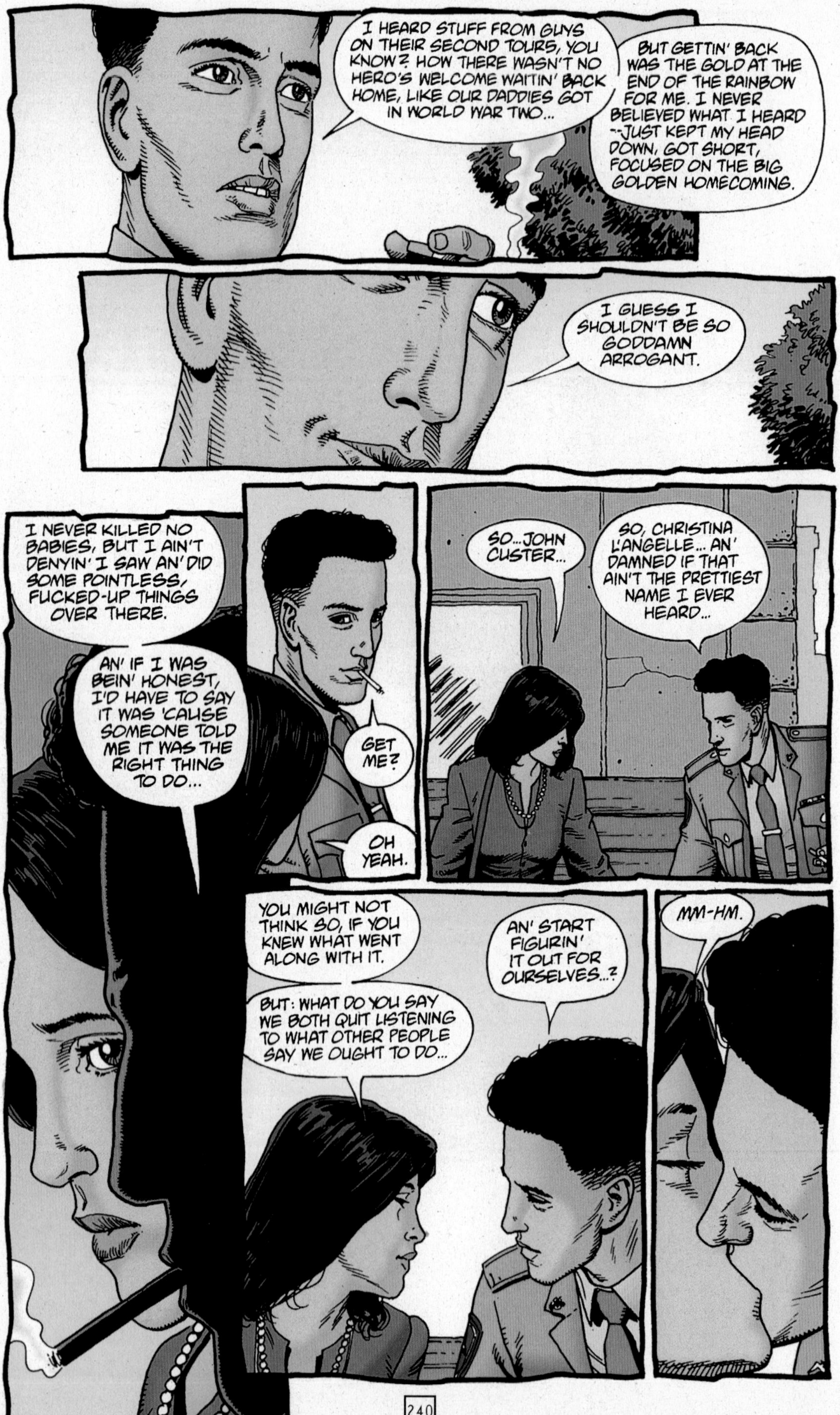
I HEARD STUFF FROM GUYS ON THEIR SECOND TOURS, YOU KNOW? HOW THERE WASN'T NO HERO'S WELCOME WAITIN' BACK HOME, LIKE OUR DADDIES GOT IN WORLD WAR TWO...
BUT GETTIN' BACK WAS THE GOLD AT THE END OF THE RAINBOW FOR ME. I NEVER BELIEVED WHAT I HEARD --JUST KEPT MY HEAD DOWN, GOT SHORT, FOCUSED ON THE BIG GOLDEN HOMECOMING.
I GUESS I SHOULDN'T BE SO GODDAMN ARROGANT.
I NEVER KILLED NO BABIES, BUT I AIN'T DENYIN' I SAW AN' DID SOME POINTLESS, FUCKED-UP THINGS OVER THERE.
AN' IF I WAS BEIN' HONEST, I'D HAVE TO SAY IT WAS 'CAUSE SOMEONE TOLD ME IT WAS THE RIGHT THING TO DO...
GET ME?
OH YEAH.
SO...JOHN CUSTER...
SO, CHRISTINA L'ANGELLE... AN' DAMNED IF THAT AIN'T THE PRETTIEST NAME I EVER HEARD...
YOU MIGHT NOT THINK SO, IF YOU KNEW WHAT WENT ALONG WITH IT.
BUT: WHAT DO YOU SAY WE BOTH QUIT LISTENING TO WHAT OTHER PEOPLE SAY WE OUGHT TO DO...
AN' START FIGURIN' IT OUT FOR OURSELVES...?
MM-HM.

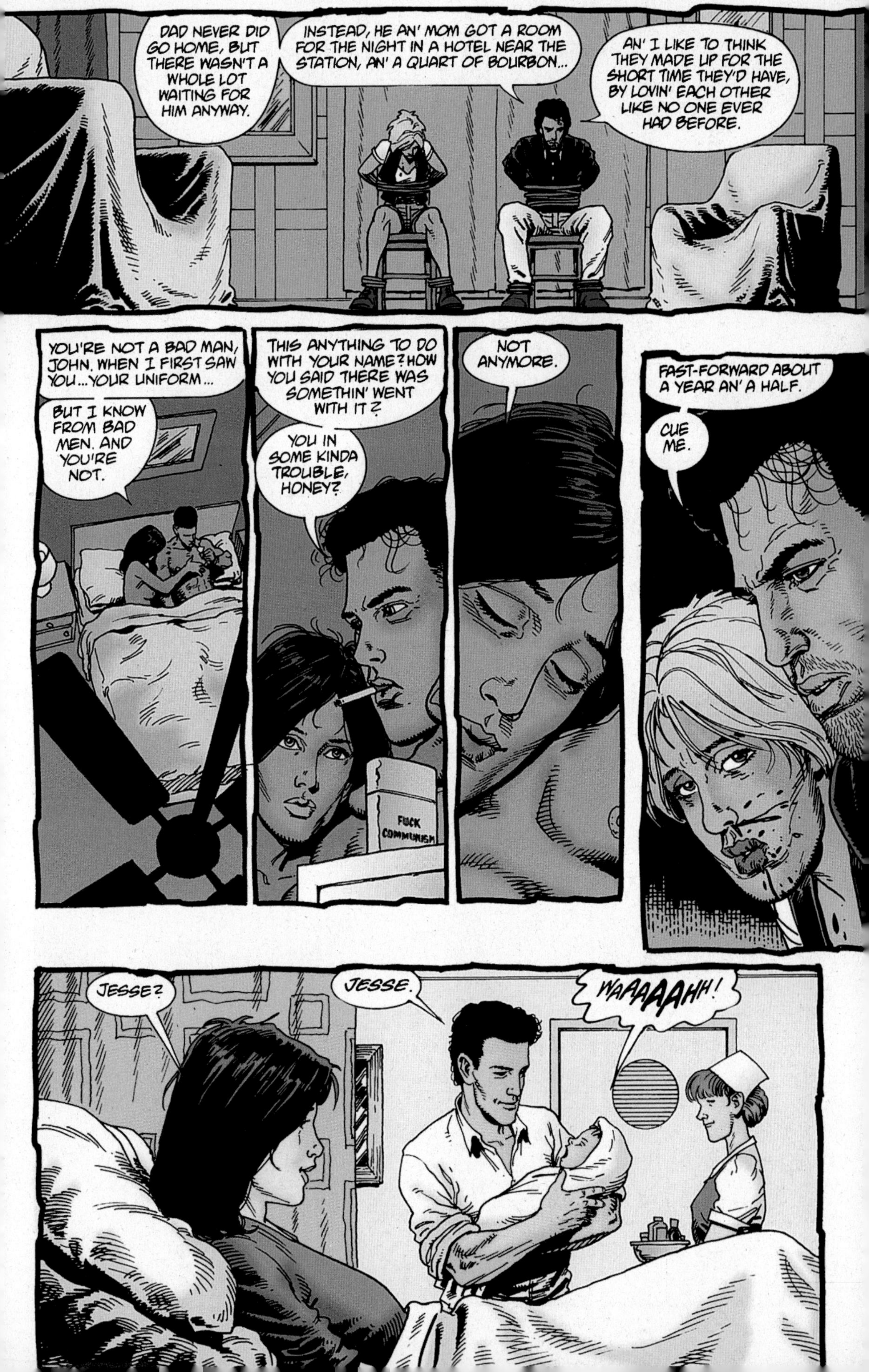
DAD NEVER DID GO HOME, BUT THERE WASN'T A WHOLE LOT WAITING FOR HIM ANYWAY.
INSTEAD, HE AN' MOM GOT A ROOM FOR THE NIGHT IN A HOTEL NEAR THE STATION, AN' A QUART OF BOURBON...
AN' I LIKE TO THINK THEY MADE UP FOR THE SHORT TIME THEY'D HAVE, BY LOVIN' EACH OTHER LIKE NO ONE EVER HAD BEFORE.
YOU'RE NOT A BAD MAN, JOHN. WHEN I FIRST SAW YOU...YOUR UNIFORM...
BUT I KNOW FROM BAD MEN. AND YOU'RE NOT.
THIS ANYTHING TO DO WITH YOUR NAME? HOW YOU SAID THERE WAS SOMETHIN' WENT WITH IT?
YOU IN SOME KINDA TROUBLE, HONEY?
FUCK COMMUNISM
NOT ANYMORE.
FAST-FORWARD ABOUT A YEAR AN' A HALF.
CUE ME.
JESSE?
JESSE.
WAAAAAHH!

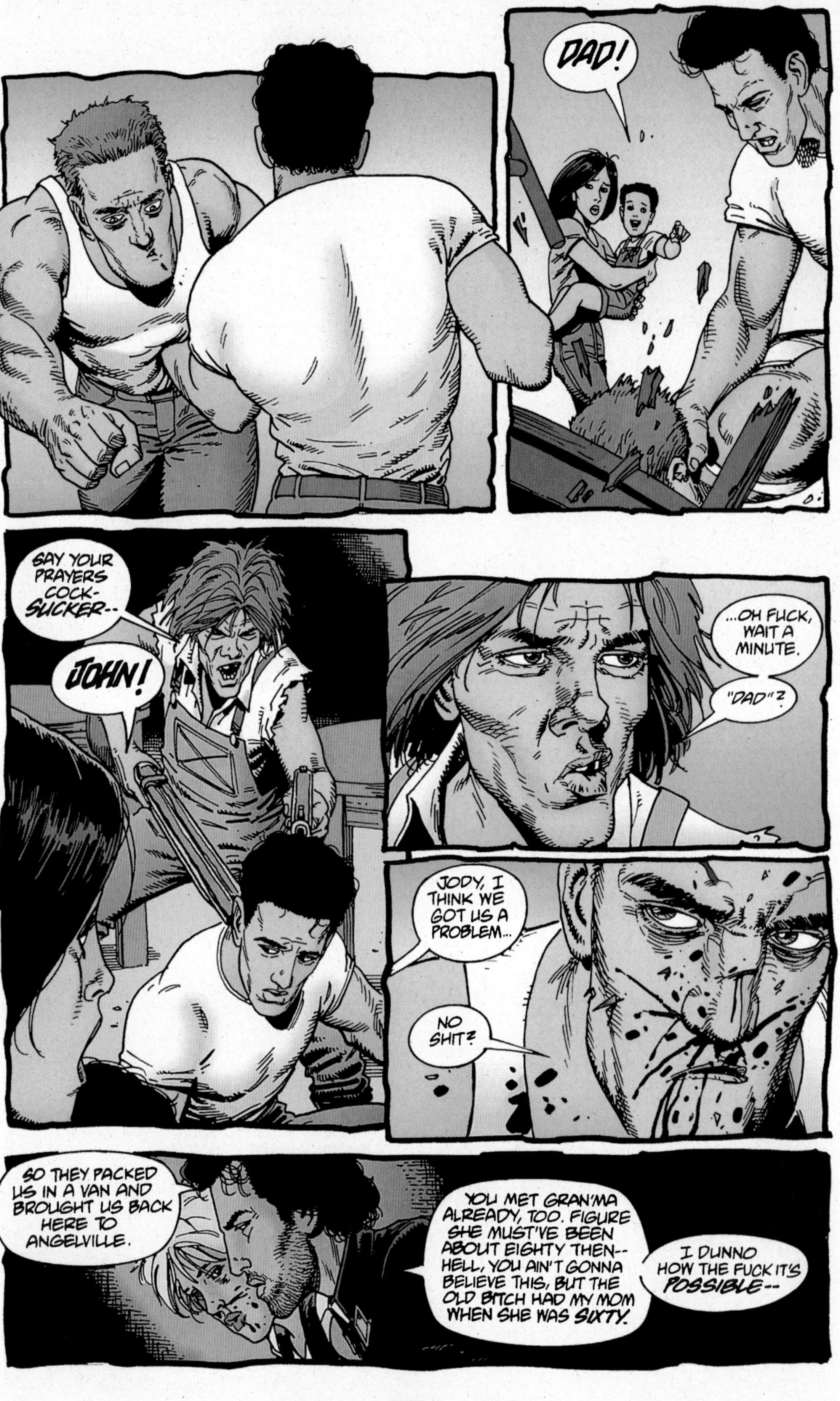
DAD!
SAY YOUR PRAYERS COCK-SUCKER--
JOHN!
...OH FUCK, WAIT A MINUTE.
"DAD"?
JODY, I THINK WE GOT US A PROBLEM...
NO SHIT?
SO THEY PACKED US IN A VAN AND BROUGHT US BACK HERE TO ANGELVILLE.
YOU MET GRAN'MA ALREADY, TOO. FIGURE SHE MUST'VE BEEN ABOUT EIGHTY THEN-- HELL, YOU AIN'T GONNA BELIEVE THIS, BUT THE OLD BITCH HAD MY MOM WHEN SHE WAS *SIXTY*.
I DUNNO HOW THE FUCK IT'S *POSSIBLE*--

UNLESS THE L'ANGELLES GOT MORE'N JUST BLOOD IN THEIR VEINS.

DEVIL'S OWN PISS, IS WHAT I FIGURE.

THEY'RE A FRENCH PURITAN FAMILY, SETTLED HERE AROUND THE TIME OF NAPOLEON. CONVERTED THE LOCAL INDIANS TO CORPSES--CHEAPER'N CHRISTIANITY --AN' SET ABOUT SPREADIN' THE WORD TO ANY SETTLERS DUMB ENOUGH TO SHOW UP.

ALL THE MEN WERE PREACHERS 'CEPT IN TIME OF WAR. THE WOMEN WERE MEANT FOR NOTHIN' MORE'N BREEDIN' THE NEXT GENERATION, WHICH THEY TOOK TO REAL WELL. FAMILY GOES *WAY BACK*. BLOOD IS *EVERYTHING*.

GRAN'MA'S KEEPIN' UP THE TRADITION WITH A VENGEANCE, BELIEVE ME. COULDN'T FIND ANY-ONE TO MARRY HER TILL SHE WAS OVER FIFTY--

PROBABLY 'CAUSE SHE WAS BORN WITH A FACE LIKE *DRIED-UP SHIT*.

AN' A SOUL TO MATCH.

JOHN CUSTER, YOU WILL MARRY MY DAUGHTER.

YOU WILL BOTH LIVE *HERE* WITH YOUR SON JESSE, AS A PROPER FAMILY IN THE EYES OF THE LORD. YOU WILL CARE FOR THEM AS A HUSBAND AND FATHER. YOU WILL GROOM YOUR SON FOR HIS DESTINY AS A MAN OF GOD. YOU WILL *NEVER* LEAVE THIS PLACE.

IF A DAY COMES ON WHICH YOU ARE FOOLISH ENOUGH TO *TRY:*

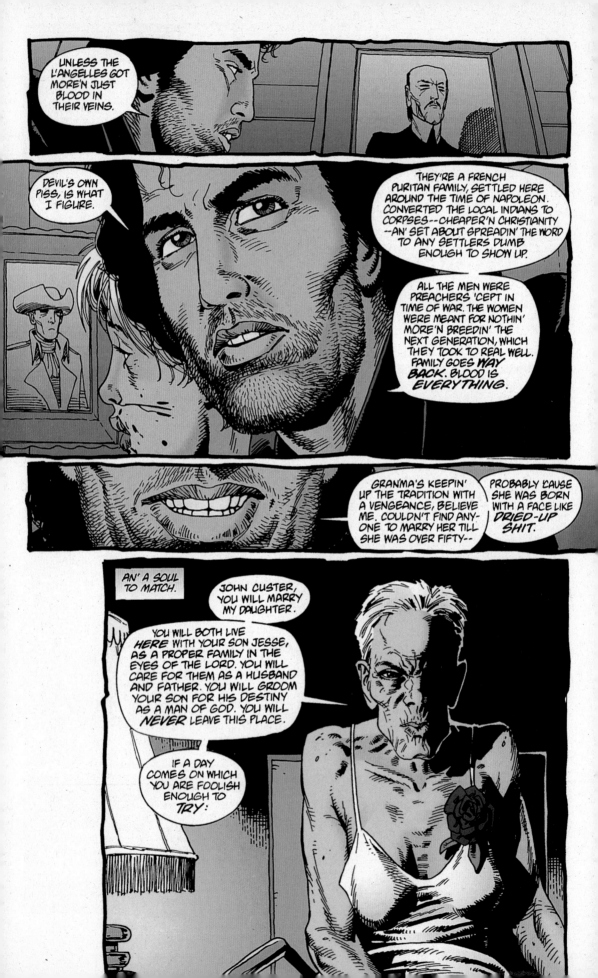

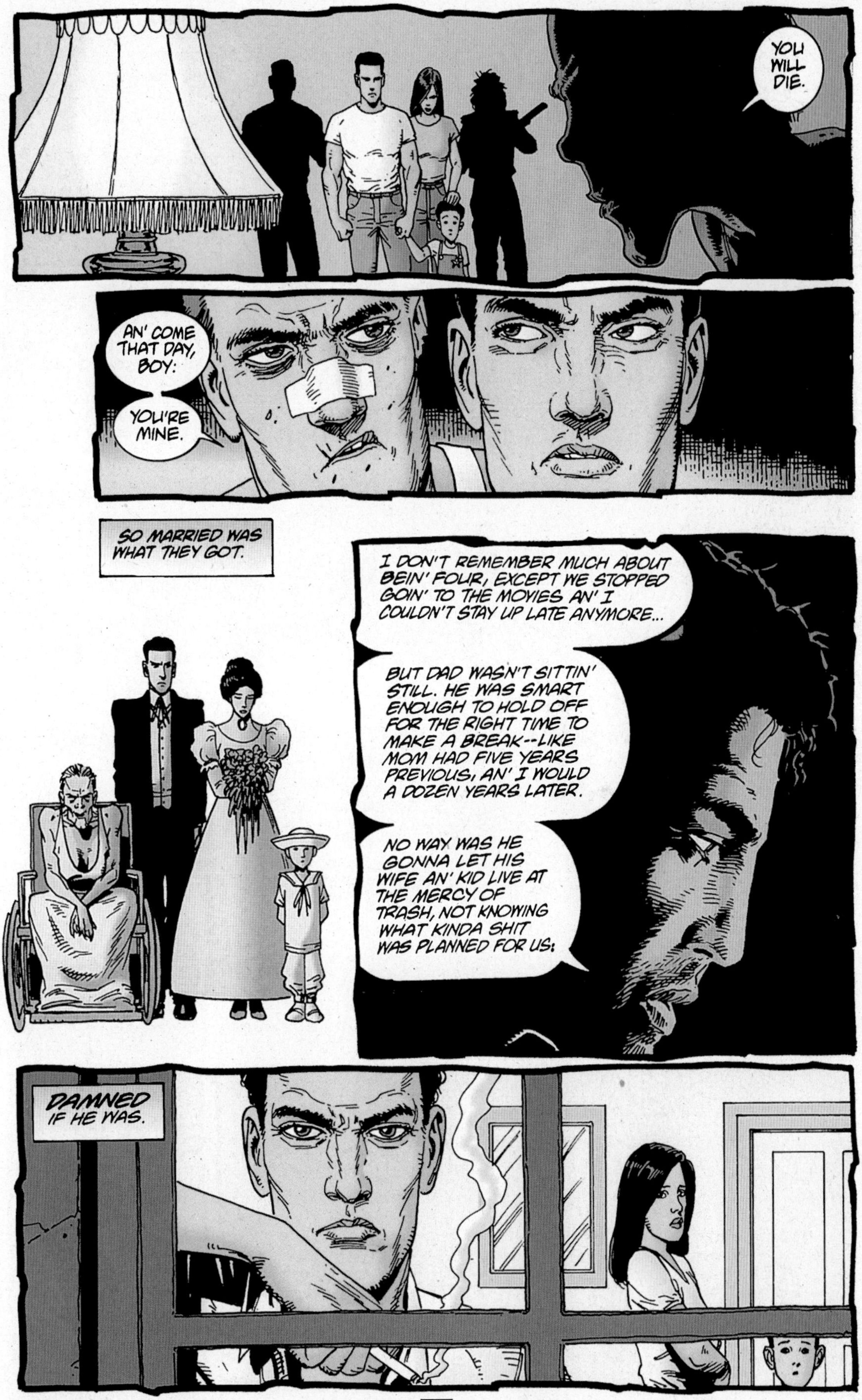
YOU WILL DIE.
AN' COME THAT DAY, BOY:
YOU'RE MINE.
SO MARRIED WAS WHAT THEY GOT.
I DON'T REMEMBER MUCH ABOUT BEIN' FOUR, EXCEPT WE STOPPED GOIN' TO THE MOVIES AN' I COULDN'T STAY UP LATE ANYMORE...
BUT DAD WASN'T SITTIN' STILL. HE WAS SMART ENOUGH TO HOLD OFF FOR THE RIGHT TIME TO MAKE A BREAK--LIKE MOM HAD FIVE YEARS PREVIOUS, AN' I WOULD A DOZEN YEARS LATER.
NO WAY WAS HE GONNA LET HIS WIFE AN' KID LIVE AT THE MERCY OF TRASH, NOT KNOWING WHAT KINDA SHIT WAS PLANNED FOR US:
DAMNED IF HE WAS.

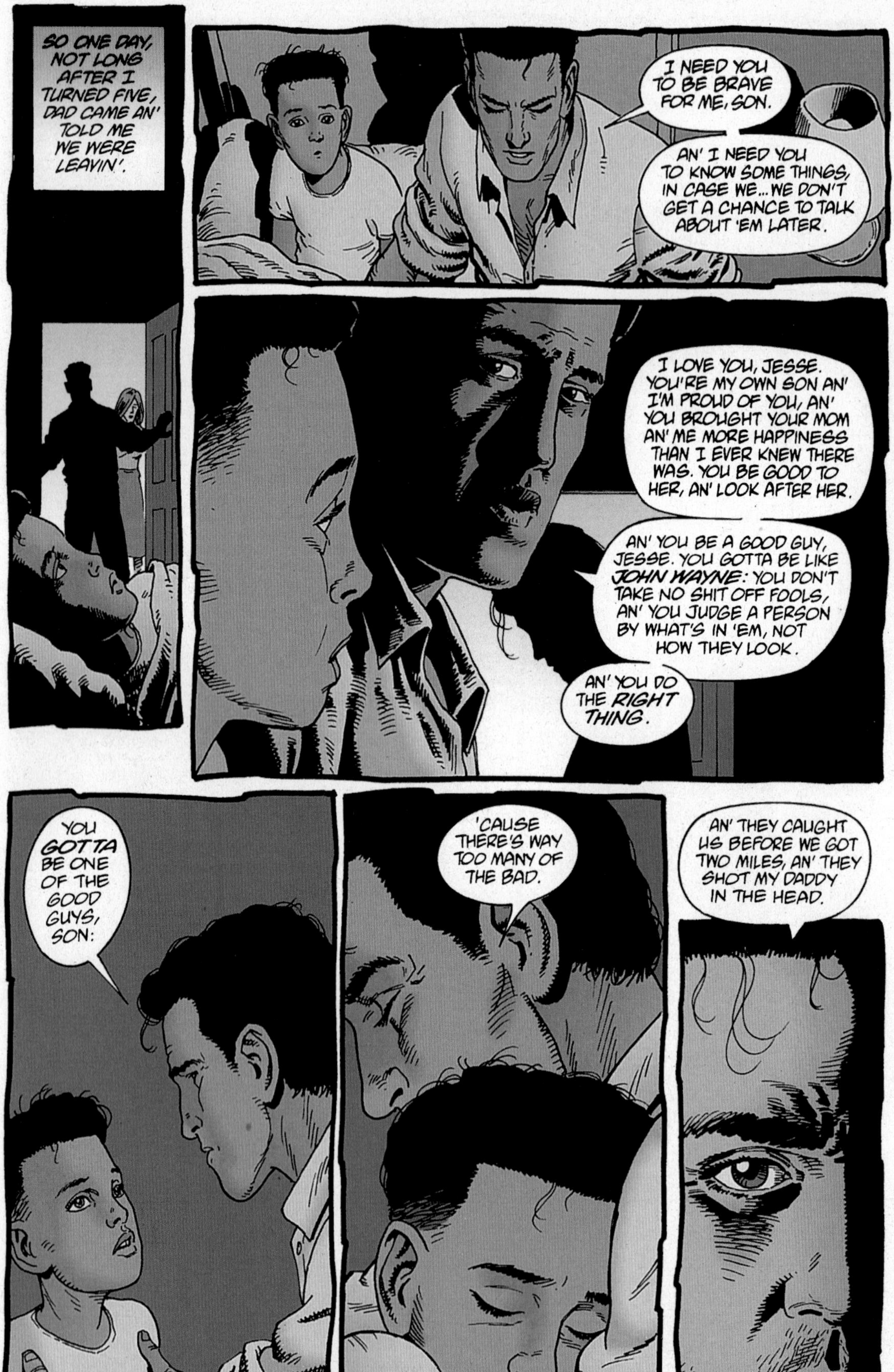
SO ONE DAY, NOT LONG AFTER I TURNED FIVE, DAD CAME AN' TOLD ME WE WERE LEAVIN'.
I NEED YOU TO BE BRAVE FOR ME, SON.
AN' I NEED YOU TO KNOW SOME THINGS, IN CASE WE... WE DON'T GET A CHANCE TO TALK ABOUT 'EM LATER.
I LOVE YOU, JESSE. YOU'RE MY OWN SON AN' I'M PROUD OF YOU, AN' YOU BROUGHT YOUR MOM AN' ME MORE HAPPINESS THAN I EVER KNEW THERE WAS. YOU BE GOOD TO HER, AN' LOOK AFTER HER.
AN' YOU BE A GOOD GUY, JESSE. YOU GOTTA BE LIKE JOHN WAYNE: YOU DON'T TAKE NO SHIT OFF FOOLS, AN' YOU JUDGE A PERSON BY WHAT'S IN 'EM, NOT HOW THEY LOOK.
AN' YOU DO THE RIGHT THING.
YOU GOTTA BE ONE OF THE GOOD GUYS, SON:
'CAUSE THERE'S WAY TOO MANY OF THE BAD.
AN' THEY CAUGHT US BEFORE WE GOT TWO MILES, AN' THEY SHOT MY DADDY IN THE HEAD.

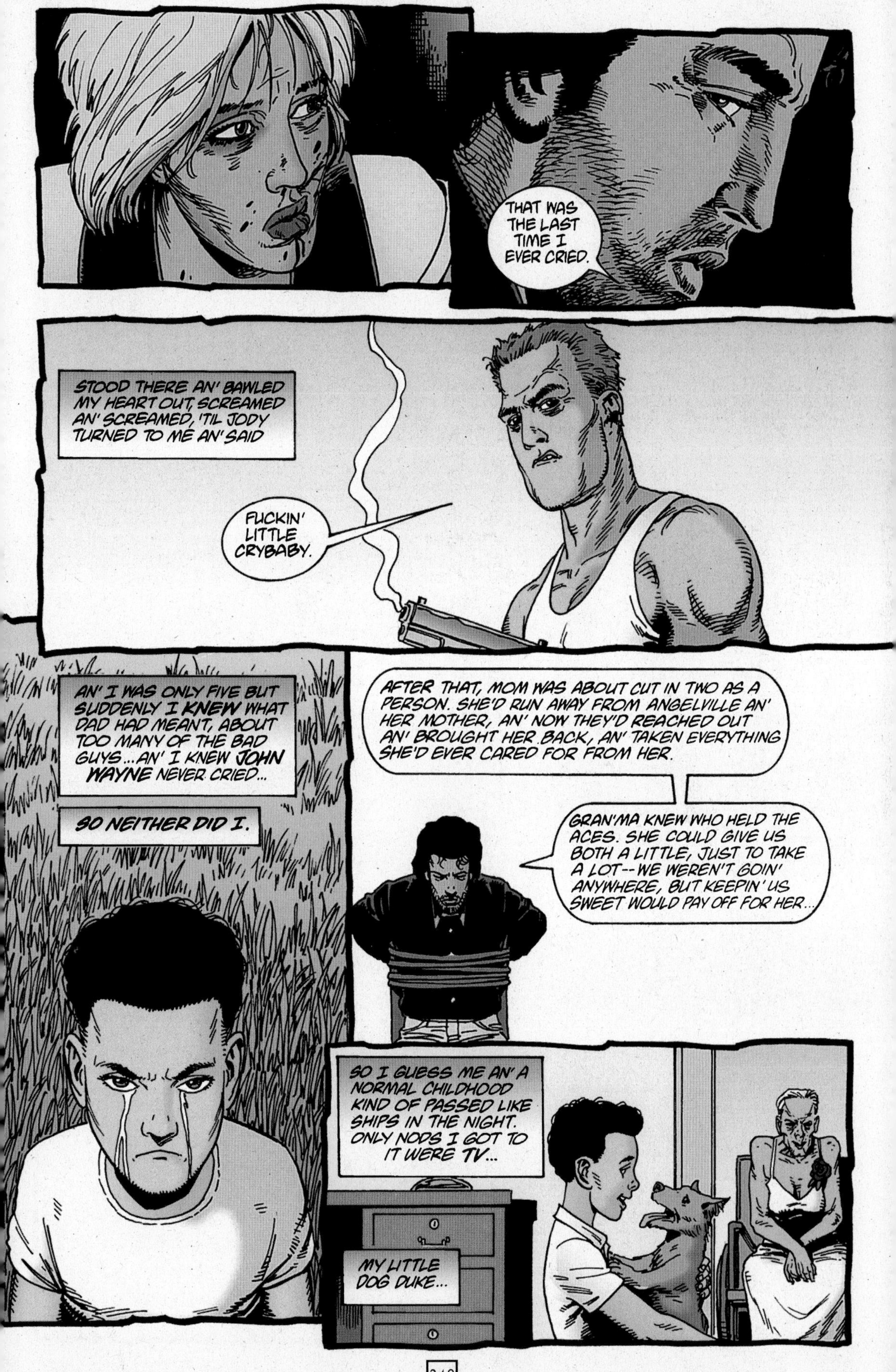
THAT WAS THE LAST TIME I EVER CRIED.
STOOD THERE AN' BAWLED MY HEART OUT, SCREAMED AN' SCREAMED, 'TIL JODY TURNED TO ME AN' SAID
FUCKIN' LITTLE CRYBABY.
AN' I WAS ONLY FIVE BUT SUDDENLY I KNEW WHAT DAD HAD MEANT, ABOUT TOO MANY OF THE BAD GUYS... AN' I KNEW JOHN WAYNE NEVER CRIED...
SO NEITHER DID I.
AFTER THAT, MOM WAS ABOUT CUT IN TWO AS A PERSON. SHE'D RUN AWAY FROM ANGELVILLE AN' HER MOTHER, AN' NOW THEY'D REACHED OUT AN' BROUGHT HER BACK, AN' TAKEN EVERYTHING SHE'D EVER CARED FOR FROM HER.
GRAN'MA KNEW WHO HELD THE ACES. SHE COULD GIVE US BOTH A LITTLE, JUST TO TAKE A LOT--WE WEREN'T GOIN' ANYWHERE, BUT KEEPIN' US SWEET WOULD PAY OFF FOR HER...
SO I GUESS ME AN' A NORMAL CHILDHOOD KIND OF PASSED LIKE SHIPS IN THE NIGHT. ONLY NODS I GOT TO IT WERE TV...
MY LITTLE DOG DUKE...

AND MY BEST FRIEND BILLY-BOB.

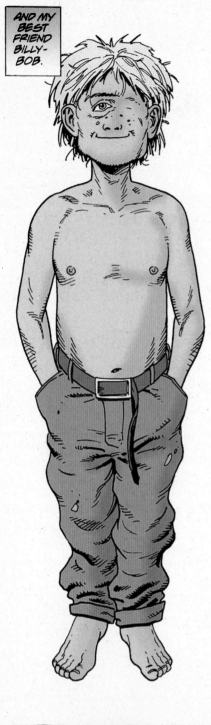

BILLY-BOB'S FOLKS LIVED WAY OUT IN THE BAYOU. I FIGURE HE LOOKED THE WAY HE DID 'CAUSE SOMEONE DUMPED CHEMICALS IN THE SWAMP, WAY IT HAPPENED IN THE CARTOONS.

TURNED OUT IT WASN'T THAT AT ALL...

YOU EVER WONDER WHO YOU'RE GONNA GROW UP TO MARRY, BILLY-BOB?

NOPE.

GONNA MARRY MY SISTER LORIE.

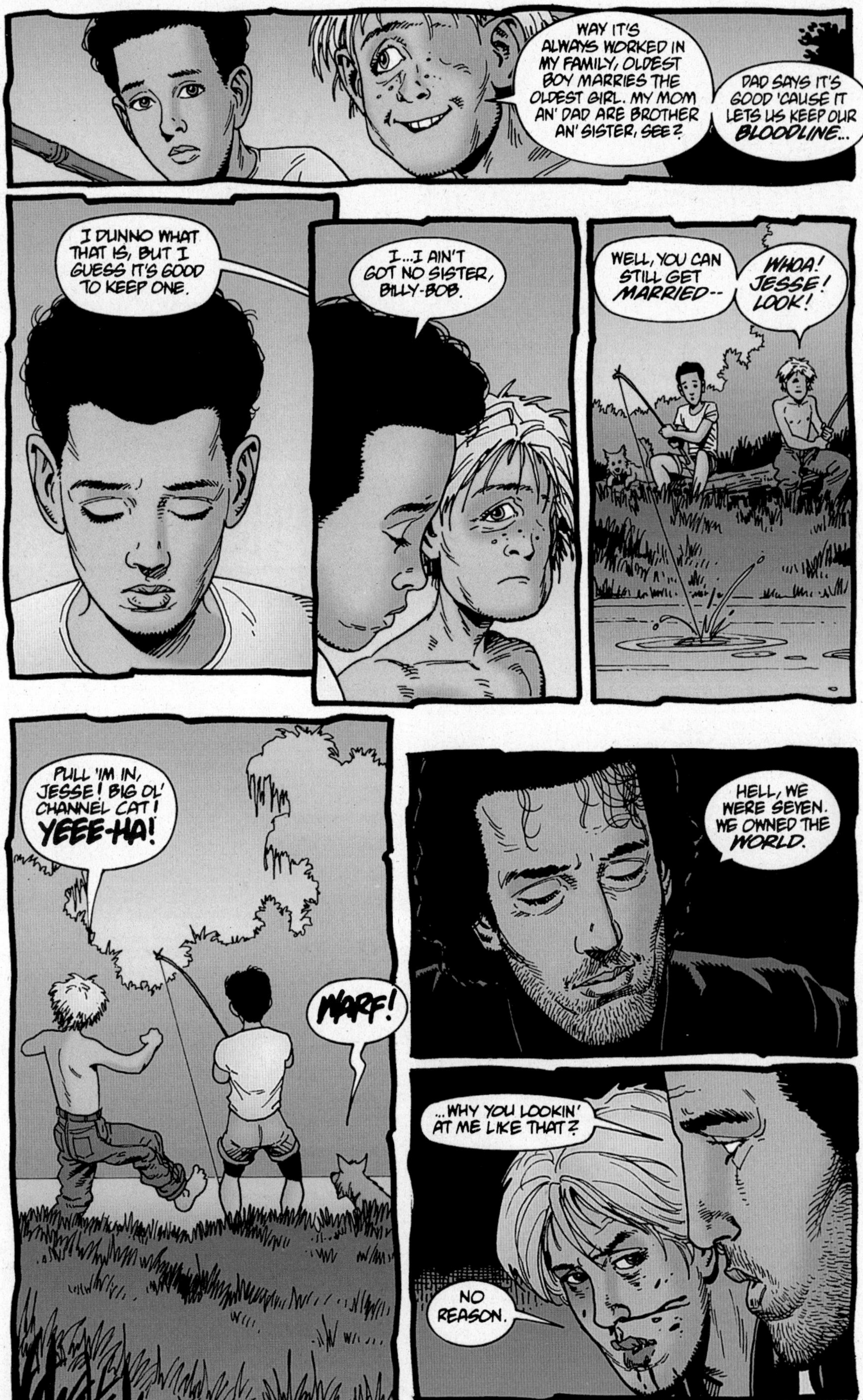
WAY IT'S ALWAYS WORKED IN MY FAMILY, OLDEST BOY MARRIES THE OLDEST GIRL. MY MOM AN' DAD ARE BROTHER AN' SISTER, SEE?
DAD SAYS IT'S GOOD 'CAUSE IT LETS US KEEP OUR BLOODLINE...
I DUNNO WHAT THAT IS, BUT I GUESS IT'S GOOD TO KEEP ONE.
I...I AIN'T GOT NO SISTER, BILLY-BOB.
WELL, YOU CAN STILL GET MARRIED--
WHOA! JESSE! LOOK!
PULL 'IM IN, JESSE! BIG OL' CHANNEL CAT! YEEE-HA!
WARF!
HELL, WE WERE SEVEN. WE OWNED THE WORLD.
...WHY YOU LOOKIN' AT ME LIKE THAT?
NO REASON.

SO EVEN THOUGH I WAS SCARED OF A GUY WHO SAW EVERYTHING I DID, AND I COULDN'T GET IT STRAIGHT HOW HE LIVED IN MY HEART, I PRETTY SOON REALIZED THE RIGHT ANSWER WAS

YES.

IT WAS NICE TO HAVE A FRIEND LIKE GOD.

I WAS SEVEN.

SO IT WENT. I HAD TO LEARN A PAGE OF THE BIBLE EVERY DAY, AN' MOM TAUGHT ME OTHER STUFF: ENGLISH, MATH, LITTLE BIT OF HISTORY. CLEVER LADY, MY MOM.

BUT LIKE I TOLD YOU, HER HEART LEFT HER WHEN DAD GOT SHOT. AN' EVEN THOUGH SHE LOVED ME, AN' SHE WANTED TO GET ME OUT'VE ANGELVILLE MORE'N *ANYTHING*--

YOU COULD SEE, MAYBE ONCE A DAY AT LEAST, ALL SHE WANTED WAS TO GO ON AN' BE WITH DAD.

I NEVER THOUGHT BAD OF HER FOR IT.

LAST DAY I SAW HER, I WAS ELEVEN. ME AN' BILLY-BOB WERE TOO BUSY WATCHIN' *WILE E. COYOTE* TO PLAY WITH DUKE...

HUH?

SAYS THAT'S WHAT HE'D DO.

WHAT YOU RECKON HE'S GONNA DO WITH THE ROADRUNNER, HE EVER CATCHES IT?

T.C. SAYS HE'S GONNA STICK HIS PECKER IN IT.

WARF.

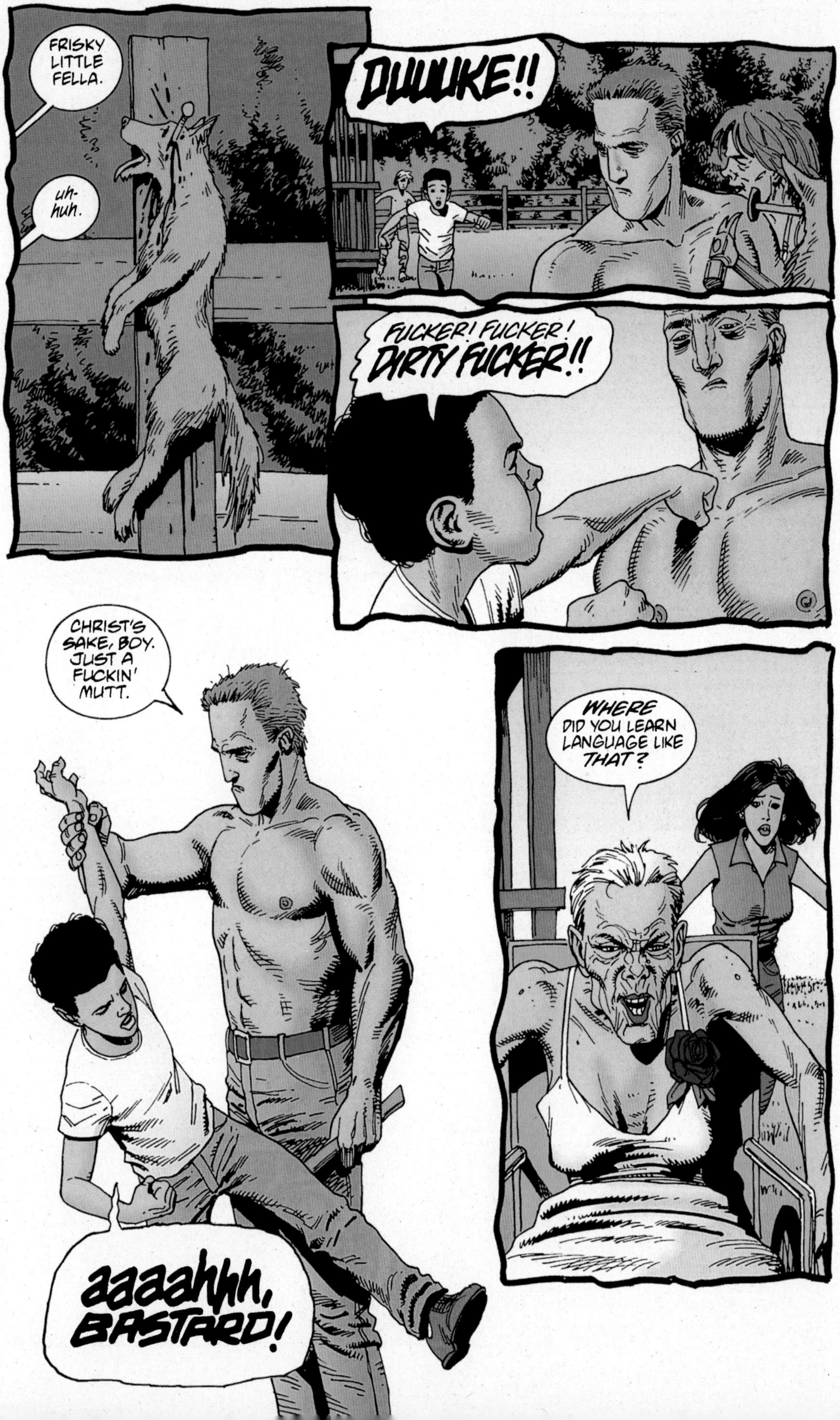
FRISKY LITTLE FELLA.
uh-huh.
DUUUKE!!
FUCKER! FUCKER! DIRTY FUCKER!!
CHRIST'S SAKE, BOY. JUST A FUCKIN' MUTT.
aaaahhh, BASTARD!
WHERE DID YOU LEARN LANGUAGE LIKE THAT?

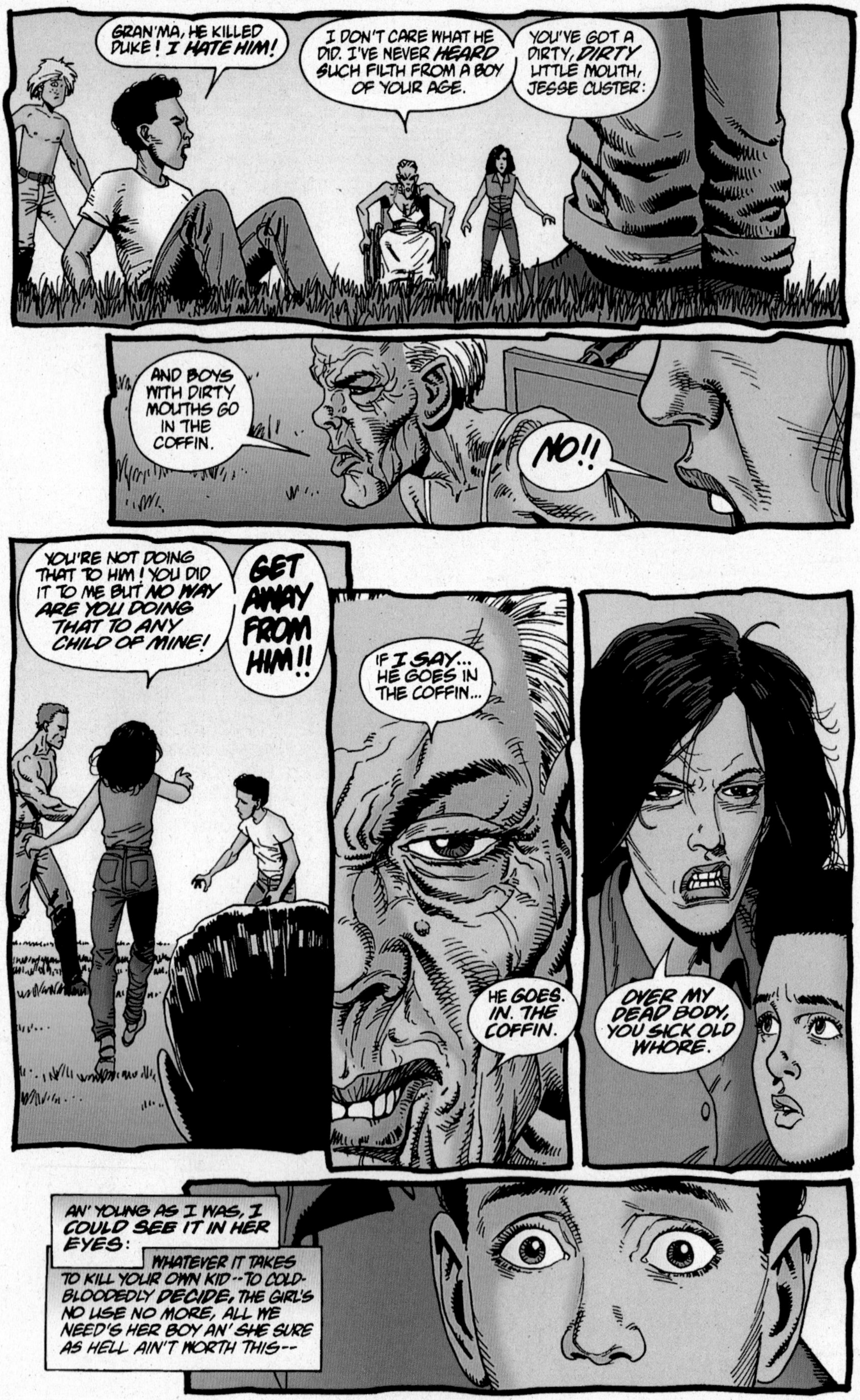
GRAN'MA, HE KILLED DUKE! I HATE HIM!
I DON'T CARE WHAT HE DID. I'VE NEVER HEARD SUCH FILTH FROM A BOY OF YOUR AGE.
YOU'VE GOT A DIRTY, DIRTY LITTLE MOUTH, JESSE CUSTER:
AND BOYS WITH DIRTY MOUTHS GO IN THE COFFIN.
NO!!
YOU'RE NOT DOING THAT TO HIM! YOU DID IT TO ME BUT NO WAY ARE YOU DOING THAT TO ANY CHILD OF MINE!
GET AWAY FROM HIM!!
IF I SAY... HE GOES IN THE COFFIN...
HE GOES. IN. THE COFFIN.
OVER MY DEAD BODY, YOU SICK OLD WHORE.
AN' YOUNG AS I WAS, I COULD SEE IT IN HER EYES:
WHATEVER IT TAKES TO KILL YOUR OWN KID--TO COLD-BLOODEDLY DECIDE, THE GIRL'S NO USE NO MORE, ALL WE NEED'S HER BOY AN' SHE SURE AS HELL AIN'T WORTH THIS--

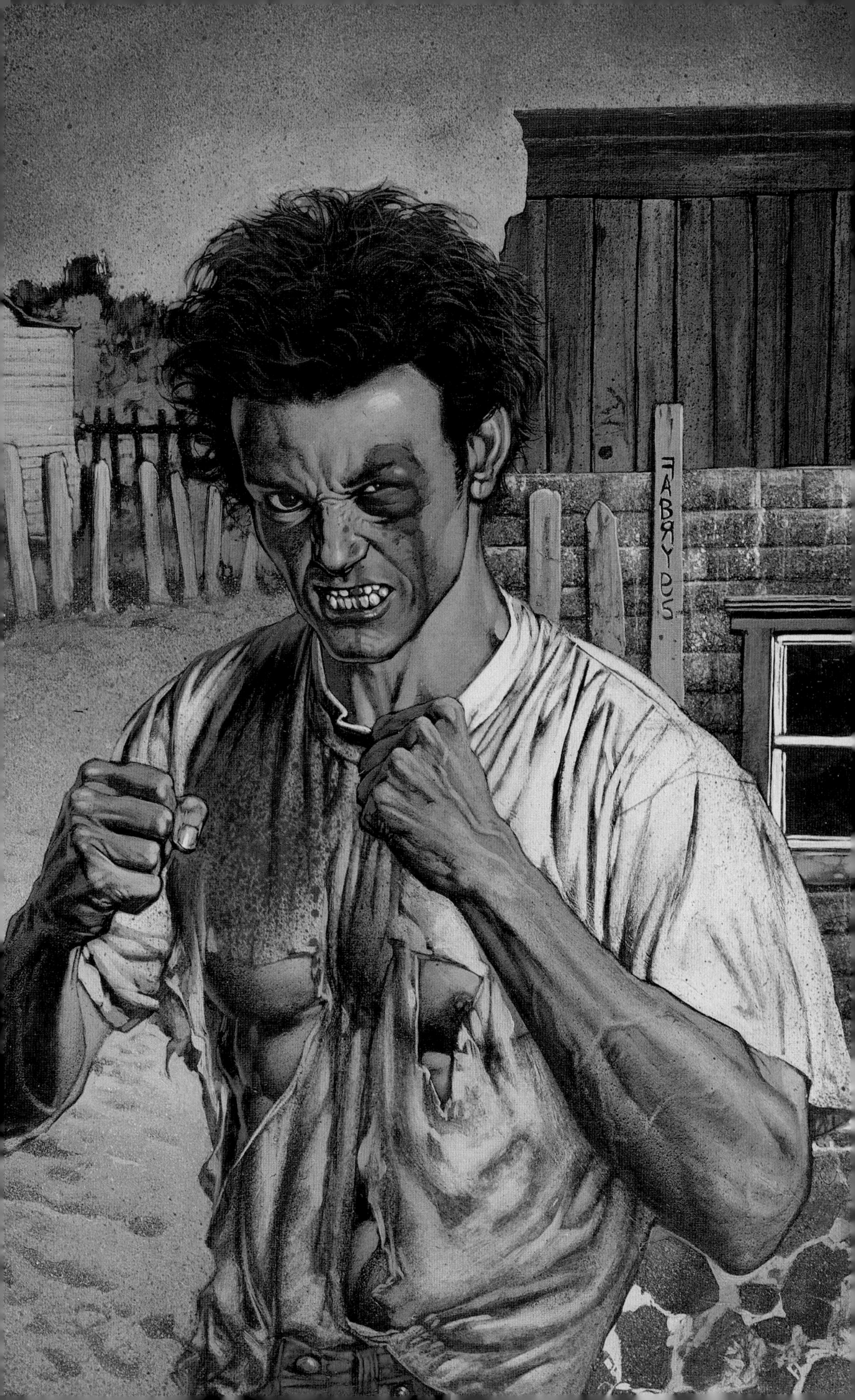
FABRY 05

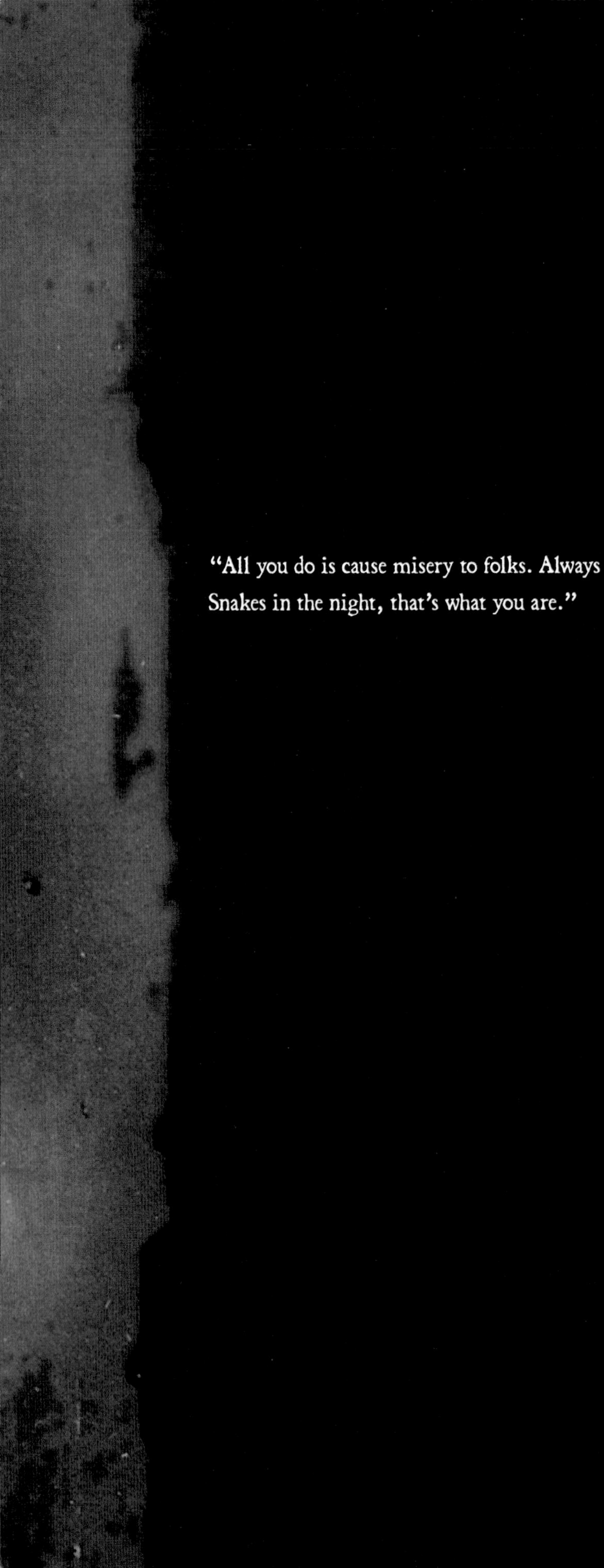
"All you do is cause misery to folks. Always
Snakes in the night, that's what you are."

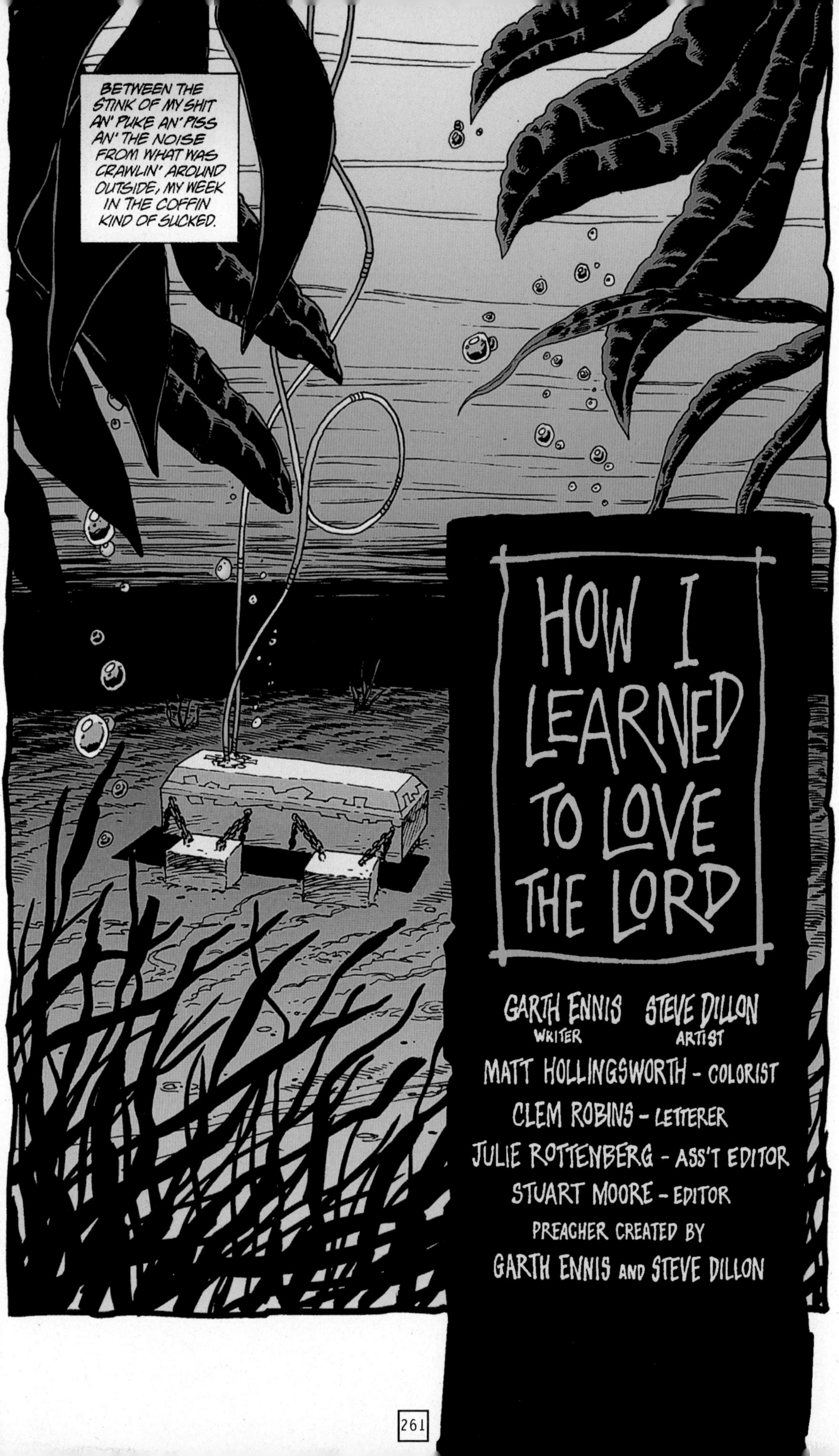
BETWEEN THE STINK OF MY SHIT AN' PUKE AN' PISS AN' THE NOISE FROM WHAT WAS CRAWLIN' AROUND OUTSIDE, MY WEEK IN THE COFFIN KIND OF SUCKED.
HOW I LEARNED TO LOVE THE LORD
GARTH ENNIS WRITER
STEVE DILLON ARTIST
MATT HOLLINGSWORTH - COLORIST
CLEM ROBINS - LETTERER
JULIE ROTTENBERG - ASS'T EDITOR
STUART MOORE - EDITOR
PREACHER CREATED BY GARTH ENNIS AND STEVE DILLON

YOU'RE GOING TO BE A GOOD LITTLE BOY FROM NOW ON, AREN'T YOU? NO MORE FILTHY WORDS? NO MORE DISOBEDIENCE?

BECAUSE OTHERWISE IT'S THE COFFIN AGAIN, JESSE. *BAD BOYS* ALWAYS GET THE COFFIN AROUND THESE PARTS.

UH... AA--

GOOD *BOYZ* MM? YES?

YUH--

YUH.

GOOD BOY.

I GUESS IT WAS ROUND THEN I GREW TO BELIEVE IN THE *LORD.* MOM WAS GONE, SO WAS DAD. GRAN'MA'S PAGE A DAY BEGAN TO TELL.

I KNEW *SHE* DIDN'T LOVE ME. JODY AN' T.C., I DOUBT THEY EVEN KNEW THE DAMN WORD. BUT EVERY DAY I'D HAVE THE BIBLE TELLIN' ME *GOD* LOVED ME...

WELL, I THOUGHT.

LONG AS SOMEBODY DID.

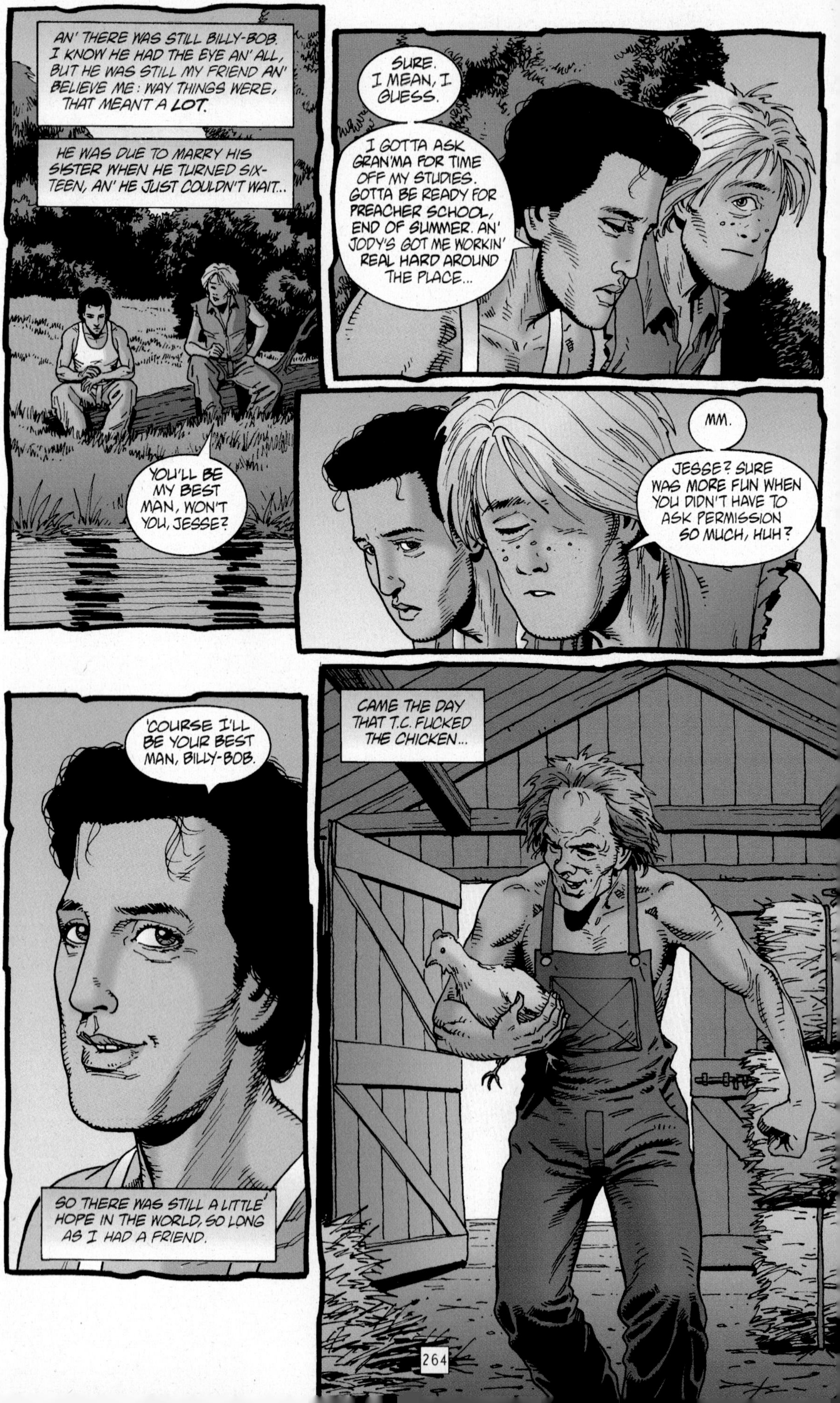

AN' THERE WAS STILL BILLY-BOB. I KNOW HE HAD THE EYE AN' ALL, BUT HE WAS STILL MY FRIEND AN' BELIEVE ME: WAY THINGS WERE, THAT MEANT A LOT.
HE WAS DUE TO MARRY HIS SISTER WHEN HE TURNED SIX-TEEN, AN' HE JUST COULDN'T WAIT...
YOU'LL BE MY BEST MAN, WON'T YOU, JESSE?
SURE. I MEAN, I GUESS.
I GOTTA ASK GRAN'MA FOR TIME OFF MY STUDIES. GOTTA BE READY FOR PREACHER SCHOOL, END OF SUMMER. AN' JODY'S GOT ME WORKIN' REAL HARD AROUND THE PLACE...
MM.
JESSE? SURE WAS MORE FUN WHEN YOU DIDN'T HAVE TO ASK PERMISSION SO MUCH, HUH?
'COURSE I'LL BE YOUR BEST MAN, BILLY-BOB.
SO THERE WAS STILL A LITTLE HOPE IN THE WORLD, SO LONG AS I HAD A FRIEND.
CAME THE DAY THAT T.C. FUCKED THE CHICKEN...

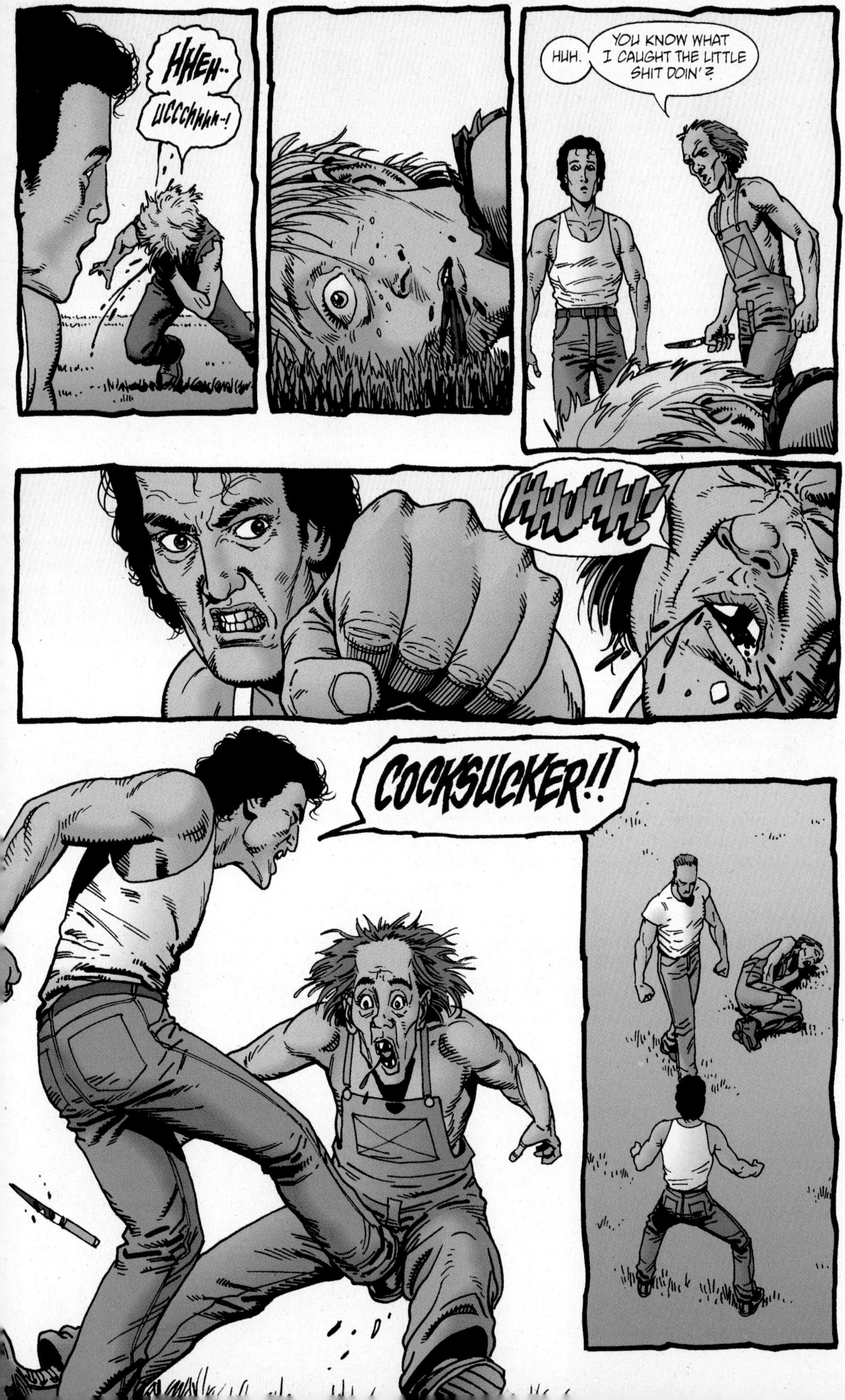
HHEH..
UCCChhhh--!
HUH.
YOU KNOW WHAT I CAUGHT THE LITTLE SHIT DOIN'?
HHUHH!
COCKSUCKER!!

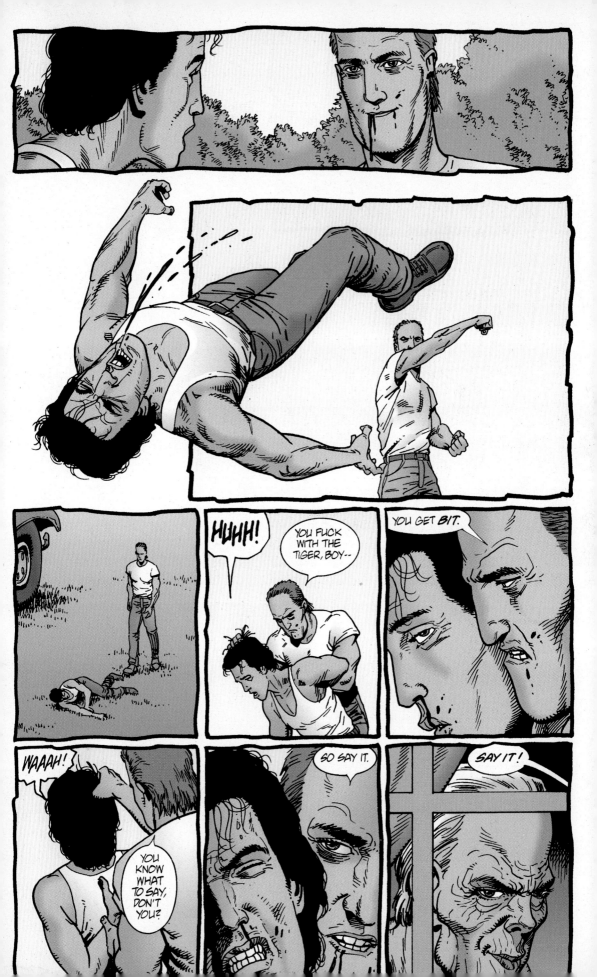

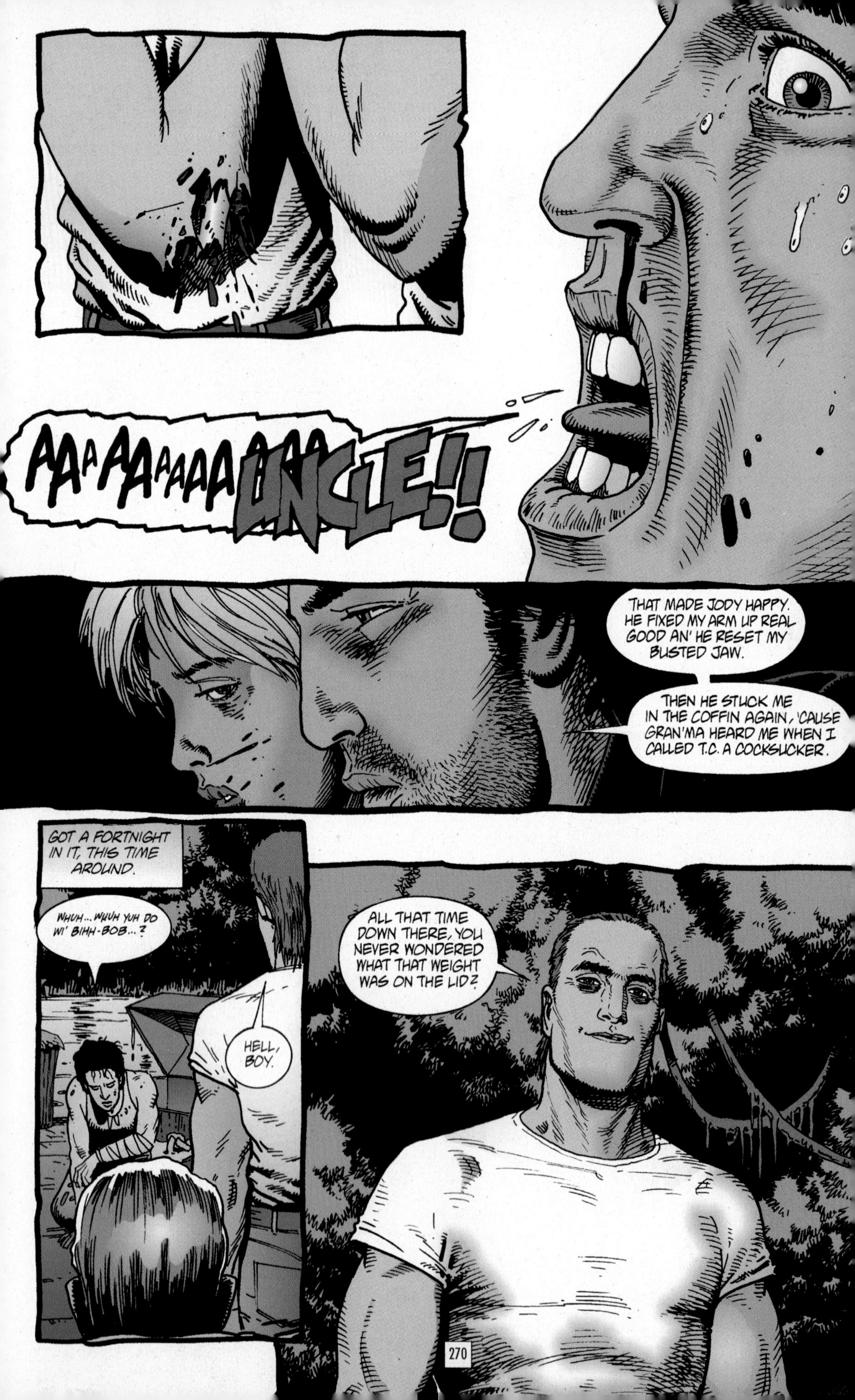
AAaAAaaaAUNCLE!!
THAT MADE JODY HAPPY. HE FIXED MY ARM UP REAL GOOD AN' HE RESET MY BUSTED JAW.
THEN HE STUCK ME IN THE COFFIN AGAIN, 'CAUSE GRAN'MA HEARD ME WHEN I CALLED T.C. A COCKSUCKER.
GOT A FORTNIGHT IN IT, THIS TIME AROUND.
WHUH... WHUH YUH DO WI' BIHH-BOB...?
HELL, BOY.
ALL THAT TIME DOWN THERE, YOU NEVER WONDERED WHAT THAT WEIGHT WAS ON THE LID?

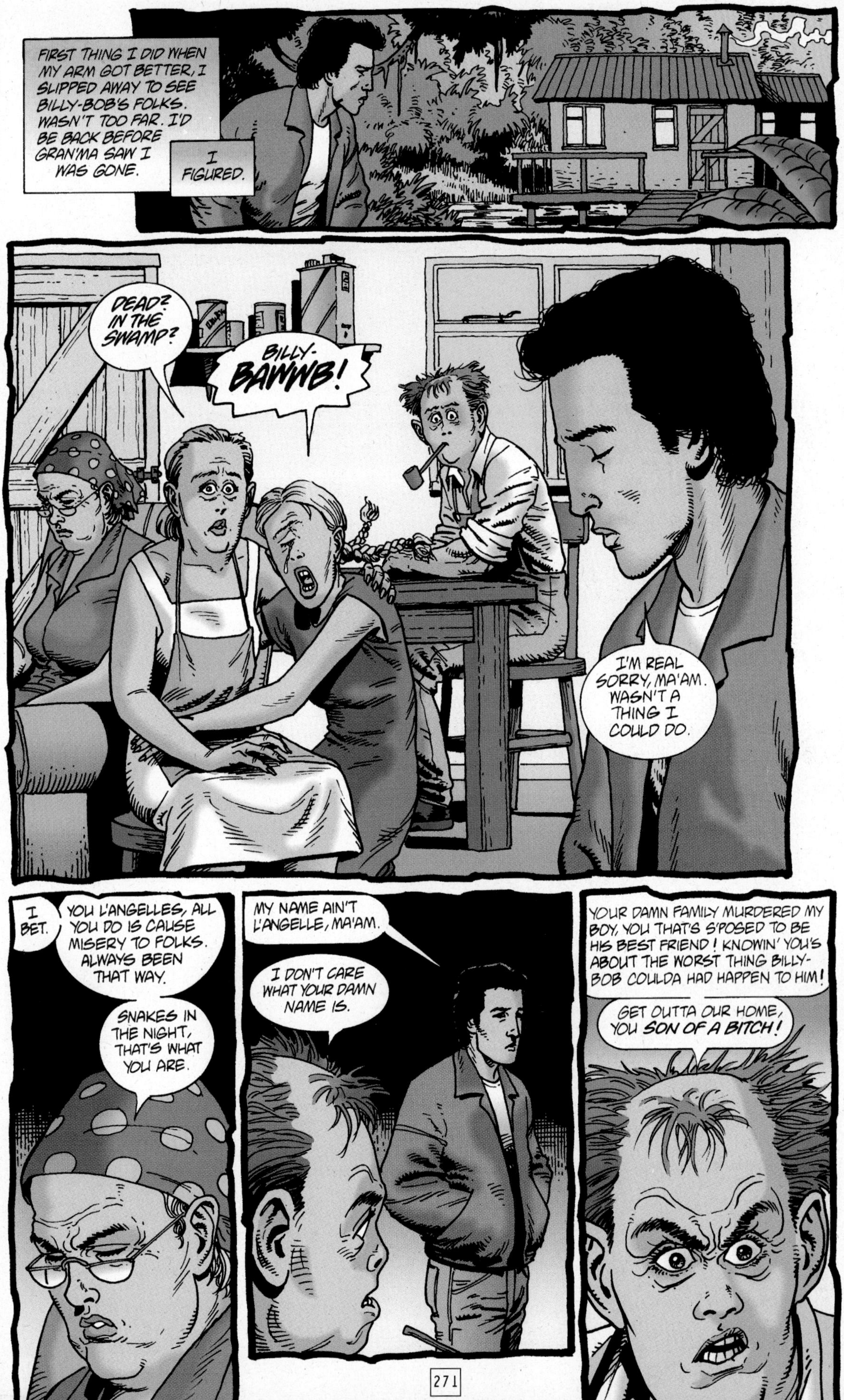
FIRST THING I DID WHEN MY ARM GOT BETTER, I SLIPPED AWAY TO SEE BILLY-BOB'S FOLKS. WASN'T TOO FAR. I'D BE BACK BEFORE GRAN'MA SAW I WAS GONE.
I FIGURED.
DEAD? IN THE SWAMP?
BILLY-BAWWB!
I'M REAL SORRY, MA'AM. WASN'T A THING I COULD DO.
I BET.
YOU L'ANGELLES, ALL YOU DO IS CAUSE MISERY TO FOLKS. ALWAYS BEEN THAT WAY.
SNAKES IN THE NIGHT, THAT'S WHAT YOU ARE.
MY NAME AIN'T L'ANGELLE, MA'AM.
I DON'T CARE WHAT YOUR DAMN NAME IS.
YOUR DAMN FAMILY MURDERED MY BOY, YOU THAT'S S'POSED TO BE HIS BEST FRIEND! KNOWIN' YOU'S ABOUT THE WORST THING BILLY-BOB COULDA HAD HAPPEN TO HIM!
GET OUTTA OUR HOME, YOU SON OF A BITCH!

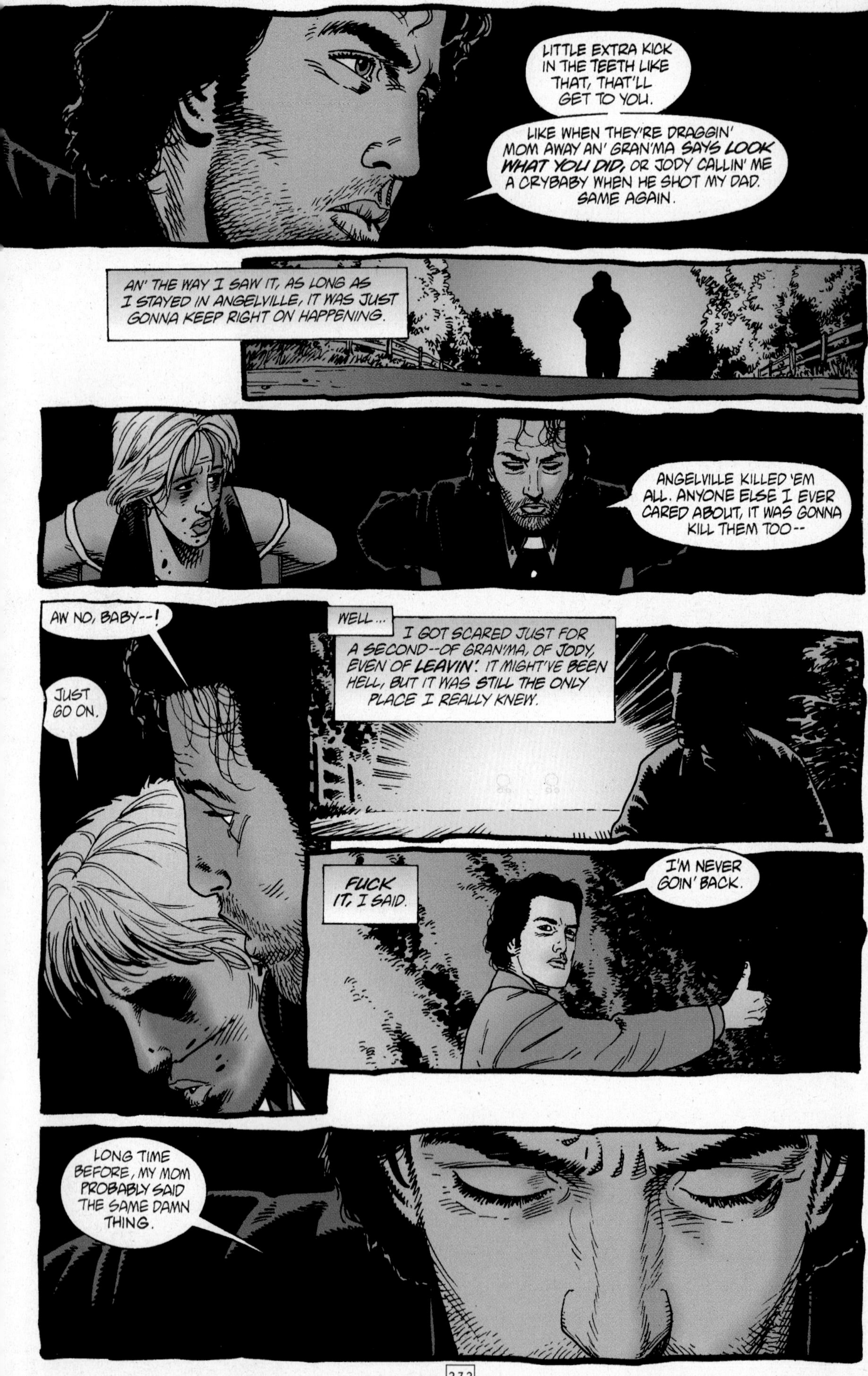
LITTLE EXTRA KICK IN THE TEETH LIKE THAT, THAT'LL GET TO YOU.
LIKE WHEN THEY'RE DRAGGIN' MOM AWAY AN' GRAN'MA SAYS LOOK WHAT YOU DID, OR JODY CALLIN' ME A CRYBABY WHEN HE SHOT MY DAD. SAME AGAIN.
AN' THE WAY I SAW IT, AS LONG AS I STAYED IN ANGELVILLE, IT WAS JUST GONNA KEEP RIGHT ON HAPPENING.
ANGELVILLE KILLED 'EM ALL. ANYONE ELSE I EVER CARED ABOUT, IT WAS GONNA KILL THEM TOO--
AW NO, BABY--!
JUST GO ON.
WELL...
I GOT SCARED JUST FOR A SECOND--OF GRAN'MA, OF JODY, EVEN OF LEAVIN'. IT MIGHT'VE BEEN HELL, BUT IT WAS STILL THE ONLY PLACE I REALLY KNEW.
FUCK IT, I SAID.
I'M NEVER GOIN' BACK.
LONG TIME BEFORE, MY MOM PROBABLY SAID THE SAME DAMN THING.

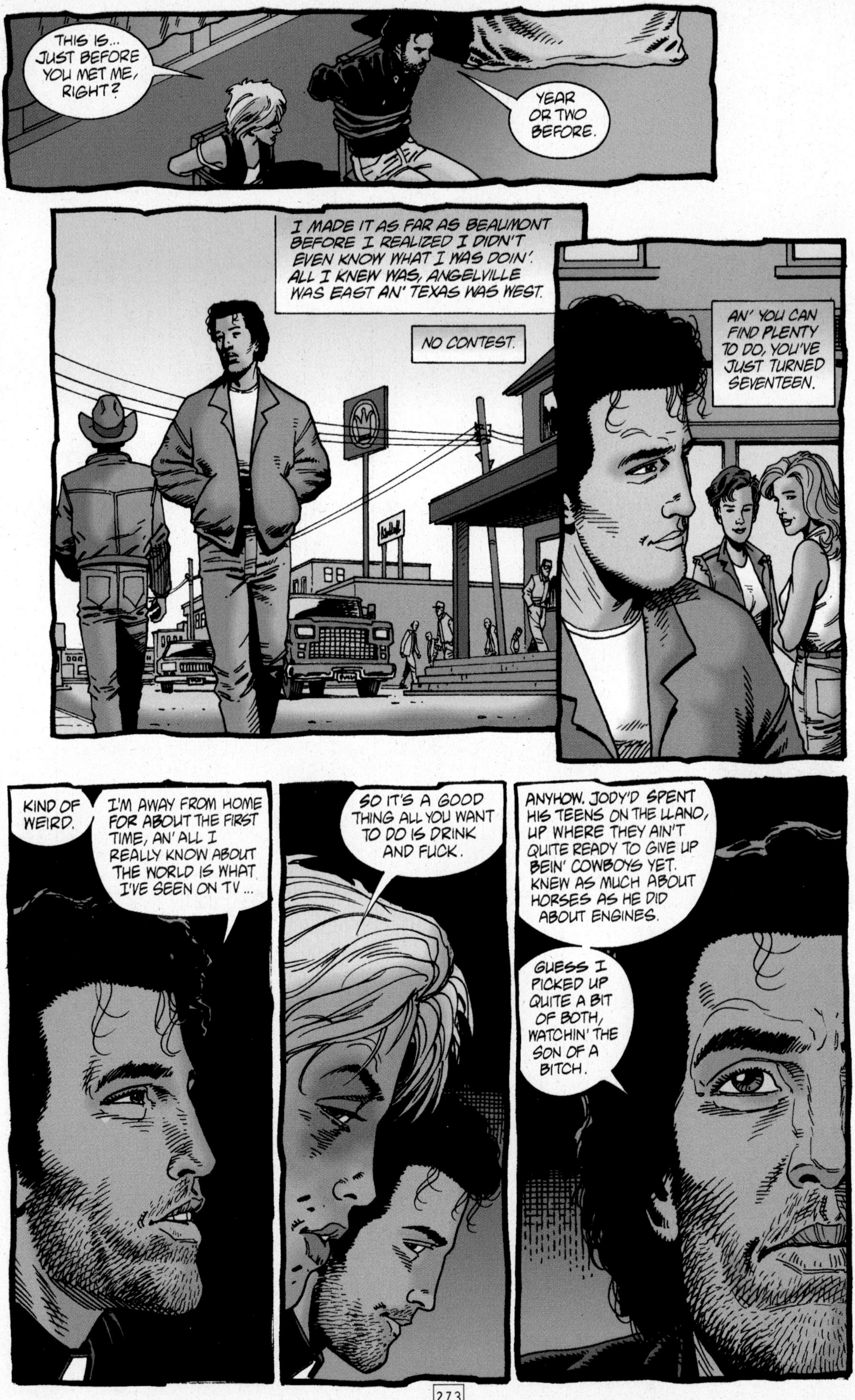
THIS IS... JUST BEFORE YOU MET ME, RIGHT?
YEAR OR TWO BEFORE.
I MADE IT AS FAR AS BEAUMONT BEFORE I REALIZED I DIDN'T EVEN KNOW WHAT I WAS DOIN'. ALL I KNEW WAS, ANGELVILLE WAS EAST AN' TEXAS WAS WEST.
NO CONTEST.
AN' YOU CAN FIND PLENTY TO DO, YOU'VE JUST TURNED SEVENTEEN.
KIND OF WEIRD.
I'M AWAY FROM HOME FOR ABOUT THE FIRST TIME, AN' ALL I REALLY KNOW ABOUT THE WORLD IS WHAT I'VE SEEN ON TV...
SO IT'S A GOOD THING ALL YOU WANT TO DO IS DRINK AND FUCK.
ANYHOW. JODY'D SPENT HIS TEENS ON THE LLANO, UP WHERE THEY AIN'T QUITE READY TO GIVE UP BEIN' COWBOYS YET. KNEW AS MUCH ABOUT HORSES AS HE DID ABOUT ENGINES.
GUESS I PICKED UP QUITE A BIT OF BOTH, WATCHIN' THE SON OF A BITCH.

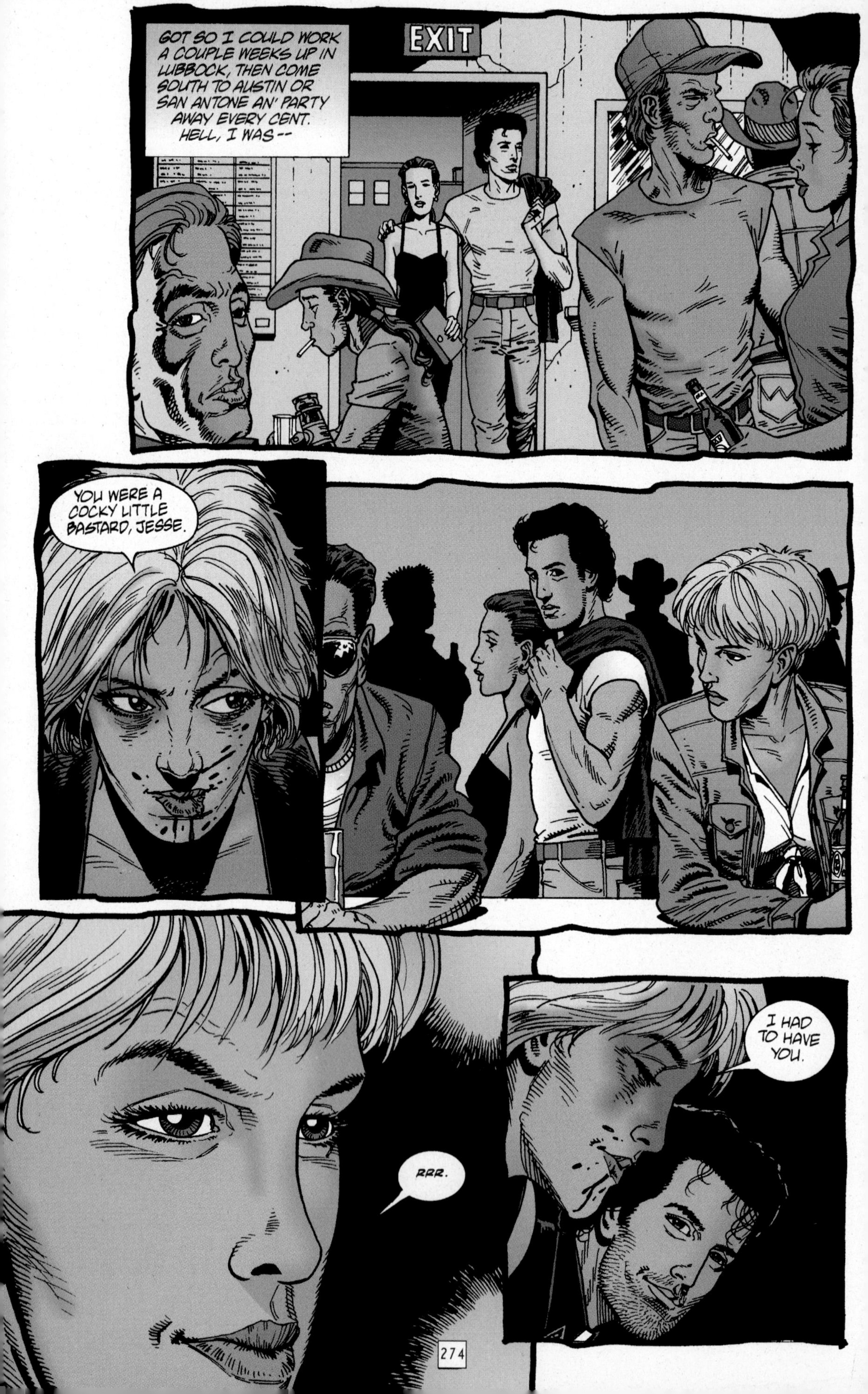
GOT SO I COULD WORK A COUPLE WEEKS UP IN LUBBOCK, THEN COME SOUTH TO AUSTIN OR SAN ANTONE AN' PARTY AWAY EVERY CENT. HELL, I WAS --
EXIT
YOU WERE A COCKY LITTLE BASTARD, JESSE.
RRR.
I HAD TO HAVE YOU.

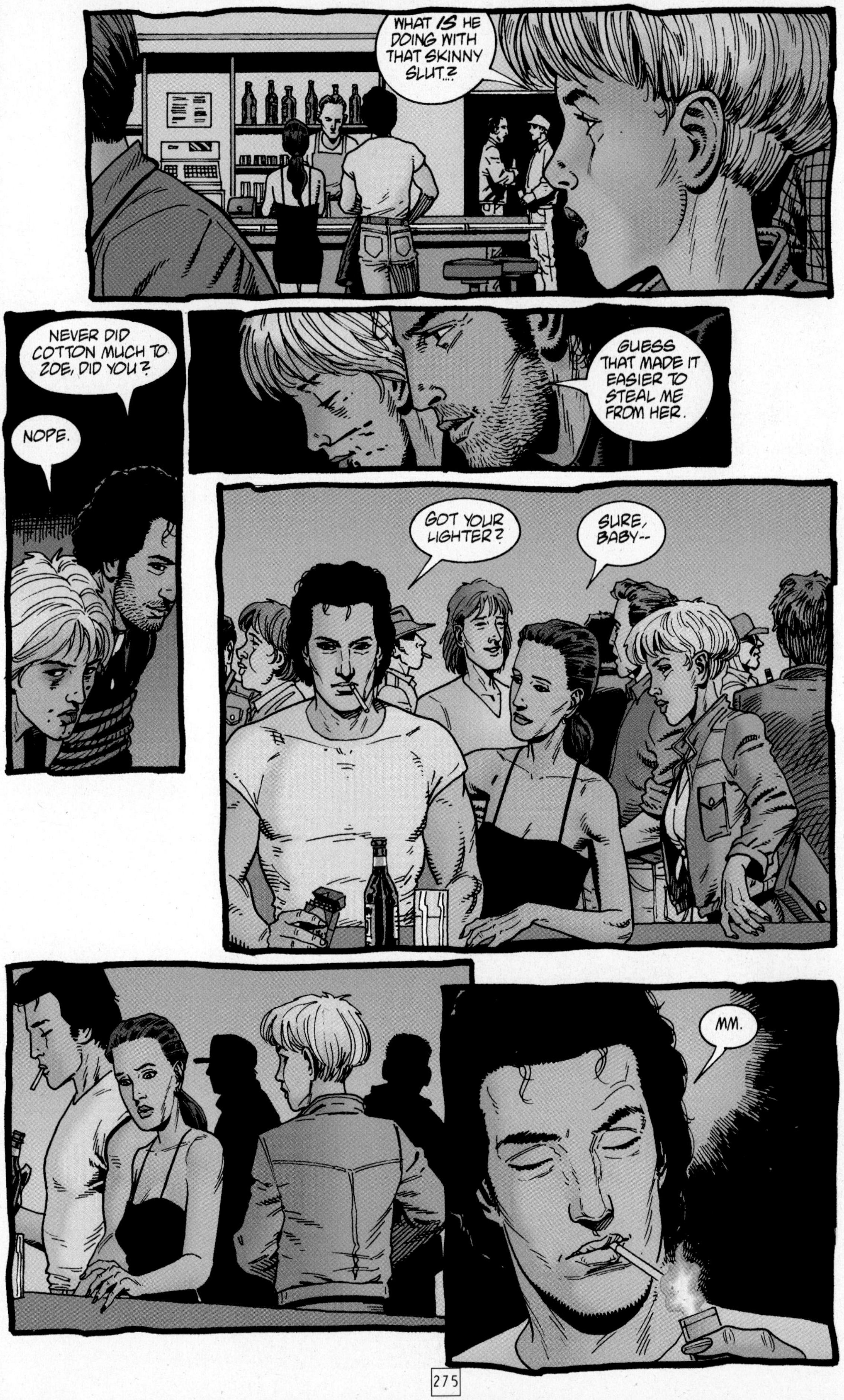
WHAT IS HE DOING WITH THAT SKINNY SLUT...?
NEVER DID COTTON MUCH TO ZOE, DID YOU?
NOPE.
GUESS THAT MADE IT EASIER TO STEAL ME FROM HER.
GOT YOUR LIGHTER?
SURE, BABY--
MM.

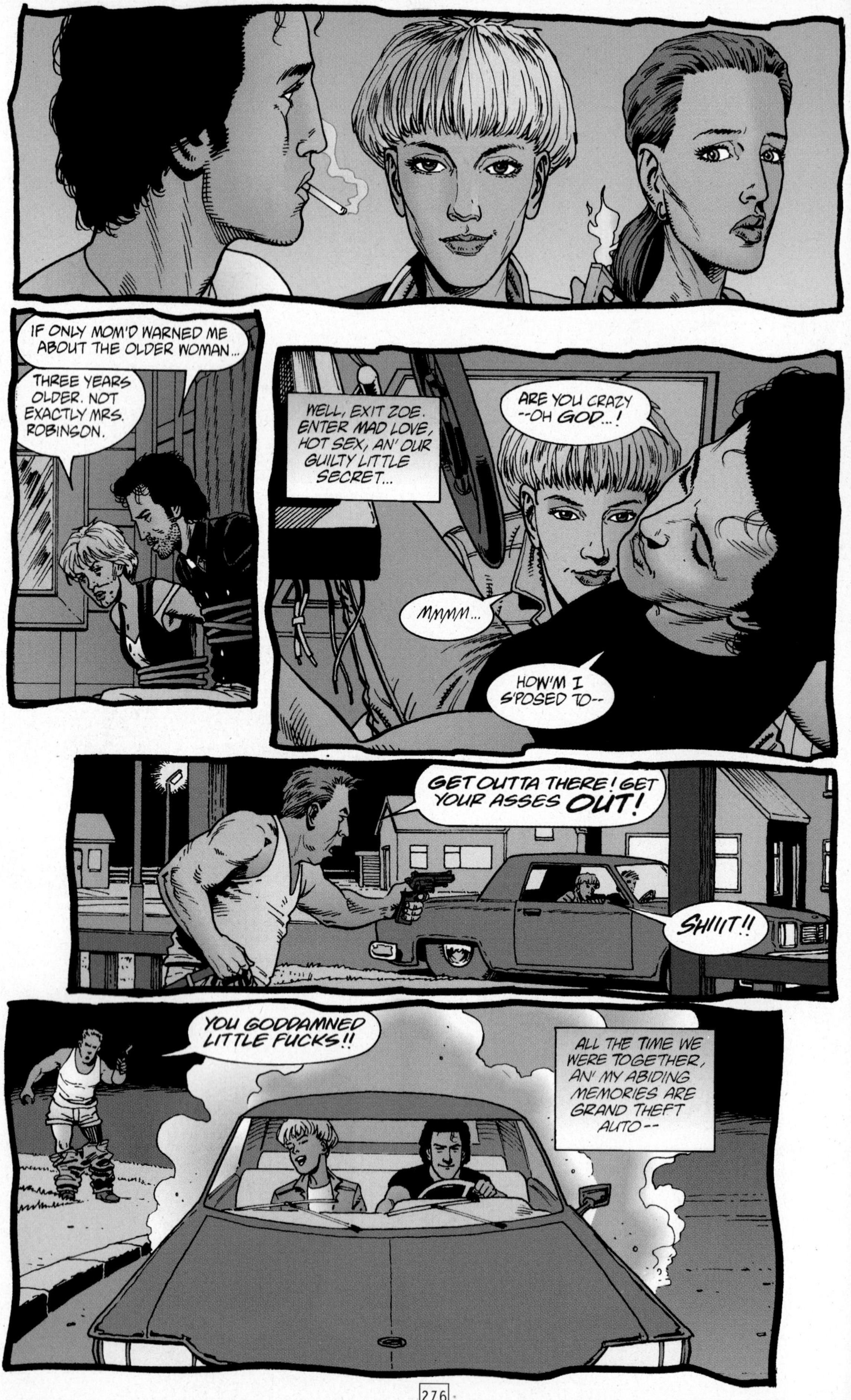
IF ONLY MOM'D WARNED ME ABOUT THE OLDER WOMAN...
THREE YEARS OLDER. NOT EXACTLY MRS. ROBINSON.
WELL, EXIT ZOE. ENTER MAD LOVE, HOT SEX, AN' OUR GUILTY LITTLE SECRET...
ARE YOU CRAZY --OH GOD...!
MMMM...
HOW'M I S'POSED TO--
GET OUTTA THERE! GET YOUR ASSES OUT!
SHIIIT!!
YOU GODDAMNED LITTLE FUCKS!!
ALL THE TIME WE WERE TOGETHER, AN' MY ABIDING MEMORIES ARE GRAND THEFT AUTO--

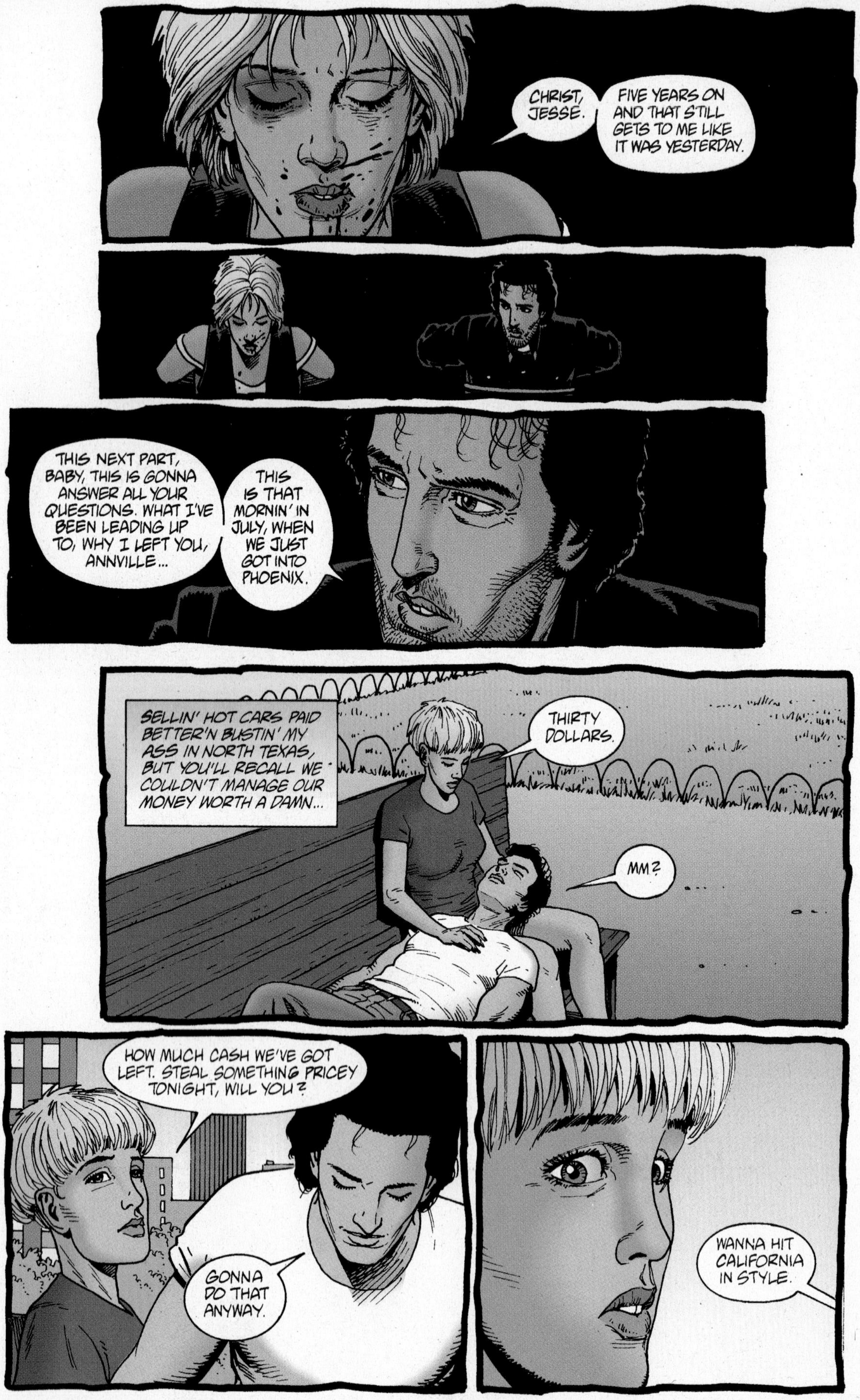

CHRIST, JESSE.
FIVE YEARS ON AND THAT STILL GETS TO ME LIKE IT WAS YESTERDAY.
THIS NEXT PART, BABY, THIS IS GONNA ANSWER ALL YOUR QUESTIONS. WHAT I'VE BEEN LEADING UP TO, WHY I LEFT YOU, ANNVILLE...
THIS IS THAT MORNIN' IN JULY, WHEN WE JUST GOT INTO PHOENIX.
SELLIN' HOT CARS PAID BETTER'N BUSTIN' MY ASS IN NORTH TEXAS, BUT YOU'LL RECALL WE COULDN'T MANAGE OUR MONEY WORTH A DAMN...
THIRTY DOLLARS.
MM?
HOW MUCH CASH WE'VE GOT LEFT. STEAL SOMETHING PRICEY TONIGHT, WILL YOU?
GONNA DO THAT ANYWAY.
WANNA HIT CALIFORNIA IN STYLE.

YOU TOOK SOME FINDIN', BOY.
I'LL MAKE THIS REAL SIMPLE. YOU COME WITH US NICE AN' QUIET AN' DON'T MAKE NO FUSS, OR I'LL SHOOT HER THROUGH THE FUCKIN' HEAD.
MY GIRLFRIENDS ASKED ME WHAT'S HE LIKE AN' I SAID, HE'S KIND OF SHY...
BUT THAT'S THE KINDA GIRL I AM HE'S MY KINDA GUY--
JESSE?

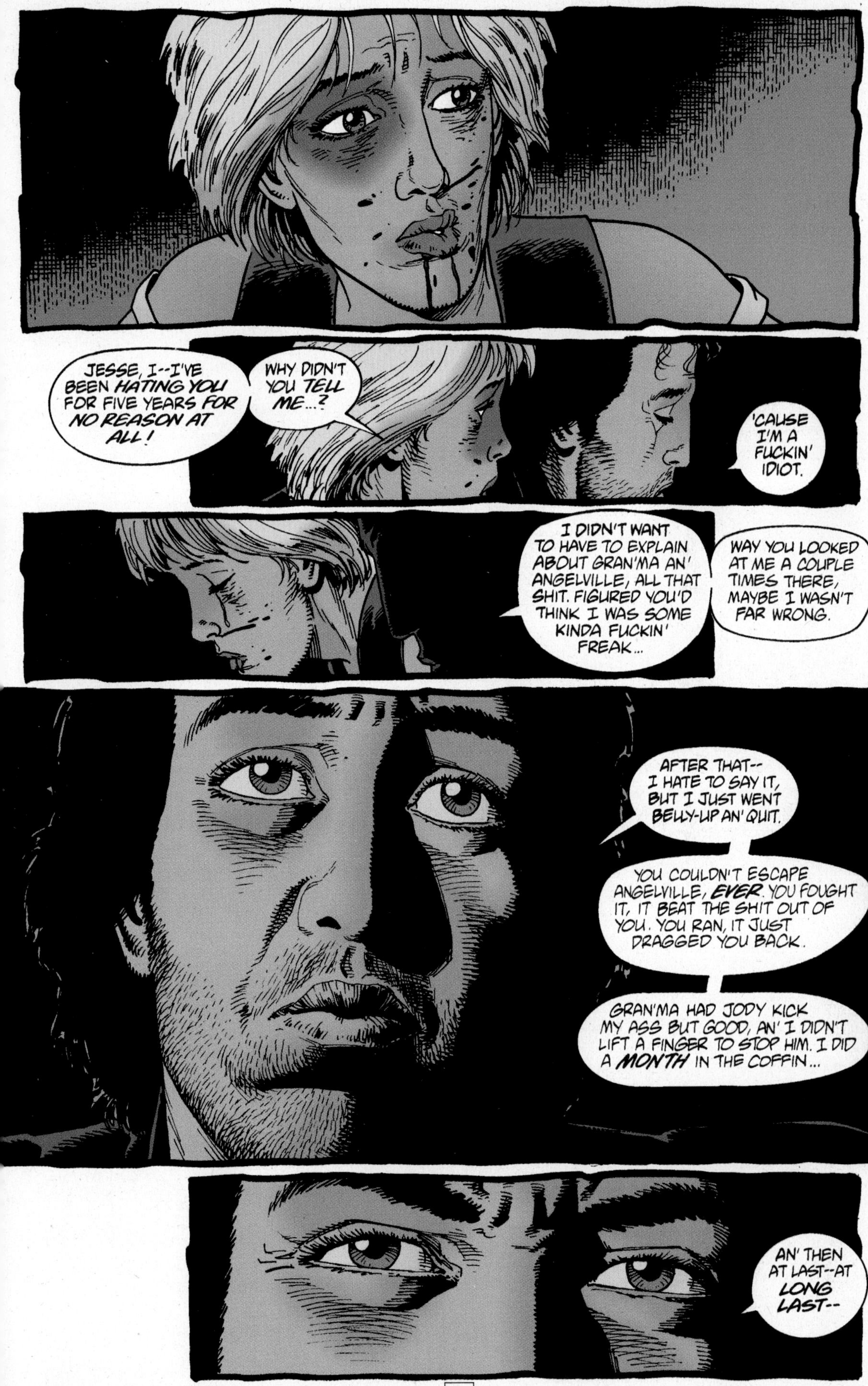
JESSE, I--I'VE BEEN HATING YOU FOR FIVE YEARS FOR NO REASON AT ALL!
WHY DIDN'T YOU TELL ME...?
'CAUSE I'M A FUCKIN' IDIOT.
I DIDN'T WANT TO HAVE TO EXPLAIN ABOUT GRAN'MA AN' ANGELVILLE, ALL THAT SHIT. FIGURED YOU'D THINK I WAS SOME KINDA FUCKIN' FREAK...
WAY YOU LOOKED AT ME A COUPLE TIMES THERE, MAYBE I WASN'T FAR WRONG.
AFTER THAT-- I HATE TO SAY IT, BUT I JUST WENT BELLY-UP AN' QUIT.
YOU COULDN'T ESCAPE ANGELVILLE, EVER. YOU FOUGHT IT, IT BEAT THE SHIT OUT OF YOU. YOU RAN, IT JUST DRAGGED YOU BACK.
GRAN'MA HAD JODY KICK MY ASS BUT GOOD, AN' I DIDN'T LIFT A FINGER TO STOP HIM. I DID A MONTH IN THE COFFIN...
AN' THEN AT LAST--AT LONG LAST--

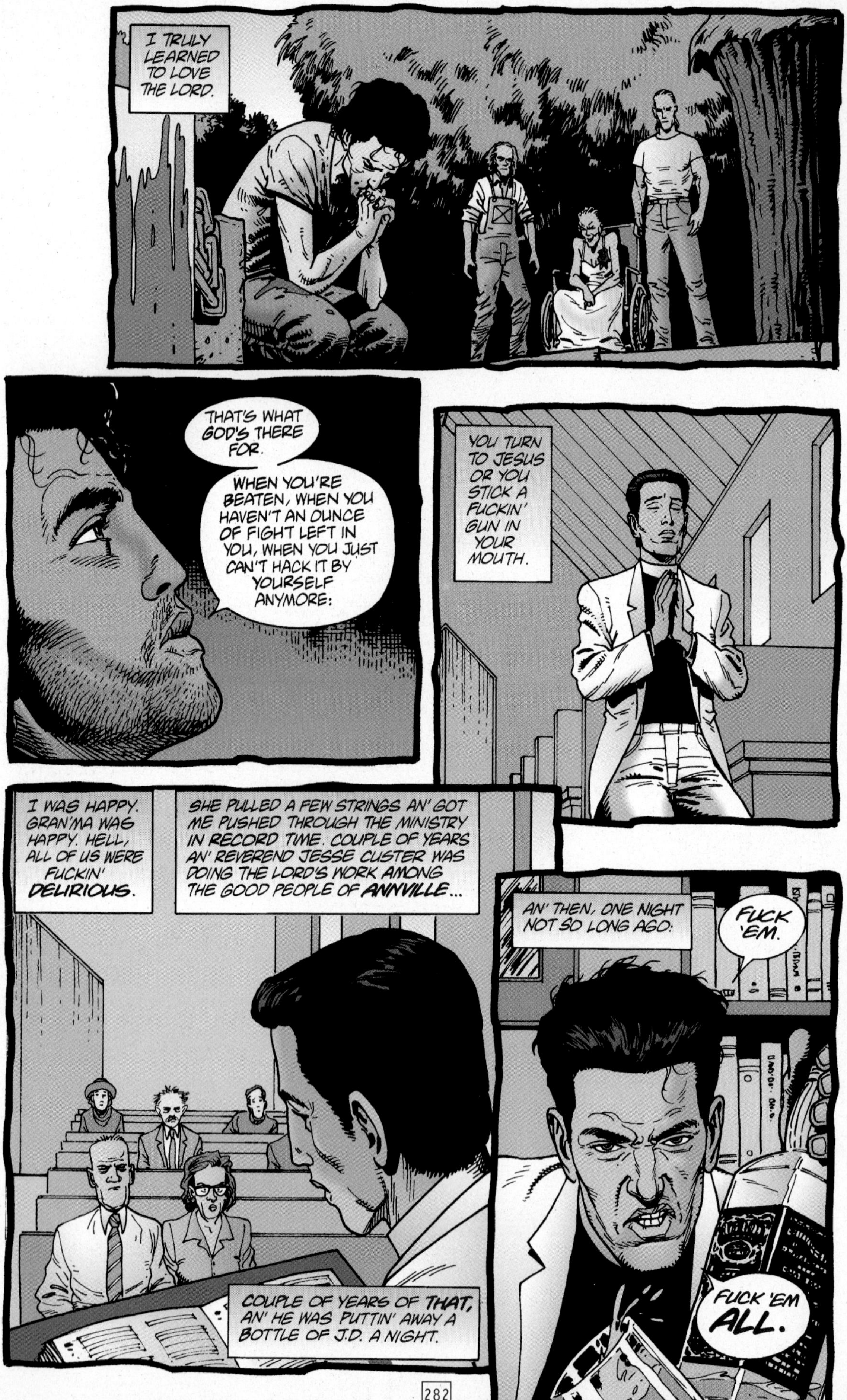
I TRULY LEARNED TO LOVE THE LORD.
THAT'S WHAT GOD'S THERE FOR.
WHEN YOU'RE BEATEN, WHEN YOU HAVEN'T AN OUNCE OF FIGHT LEFT IN YOU, WHEN YOU JUST CAN'T HACK IT BY YOURSELF ANYMORE:
YOU TURN TO JESUS OR YOU STICK A FUCKIN' GUN IN YOUR MOUTH.
I WAS HAPPY. GRAN'MA WAS HAPPY. HELL, ALL OF US WERE FUCKIN' DELIRIOUS.
SHE PULLED A FEW STRINGS AN' GOT ME PUSHED THROUGH THE MINISTRY IN RECORD TIME. COUPLE OF YEARS AN' REVEREND JESSE CUSTER WAS DOING THE LORD'S WORK AMONG THE GOOD PEOPLE OF ANNVILLE...
COUPLE OF YEARS OF THAT, AN' HE WAS PUTTIN' AWAY A BOTTLE OF J.D. A NIGHT.
AN' THEN, ONE NIGHT NOT SO LONG AGO:
FUCK 'EM.
FUCK 'EM ALL.

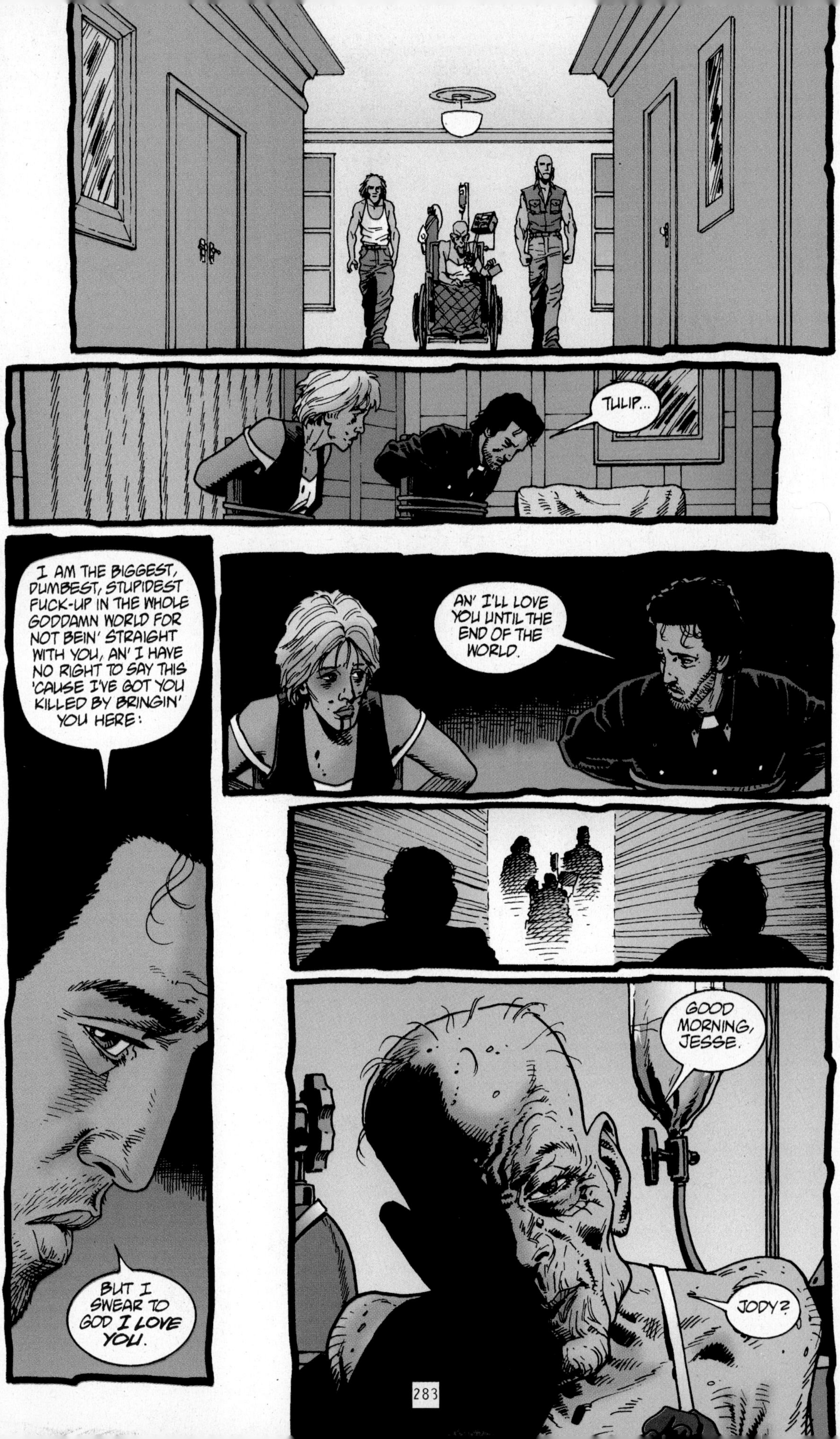
TULIP...
I AM THE BIGGEST, DUMBEST, STUPIDEST FUCK-UP IN THE WHOLE GODDAMN WORLD FOR NOT BEIN' STRAIGHT WITH YOU, AN' I HAVE NO RIGHT TO SAY THIS 'CAUSE I'VE GOT YOU KILLED BY BRINGIN' YOU HERE:
BUT I SWEAR TO GOD I LOVE YOU.
AN' I'LL LOVE YOU UNTIL THE END OF THE WORLD.
GOOD MORNING, JESSE.
JODY?

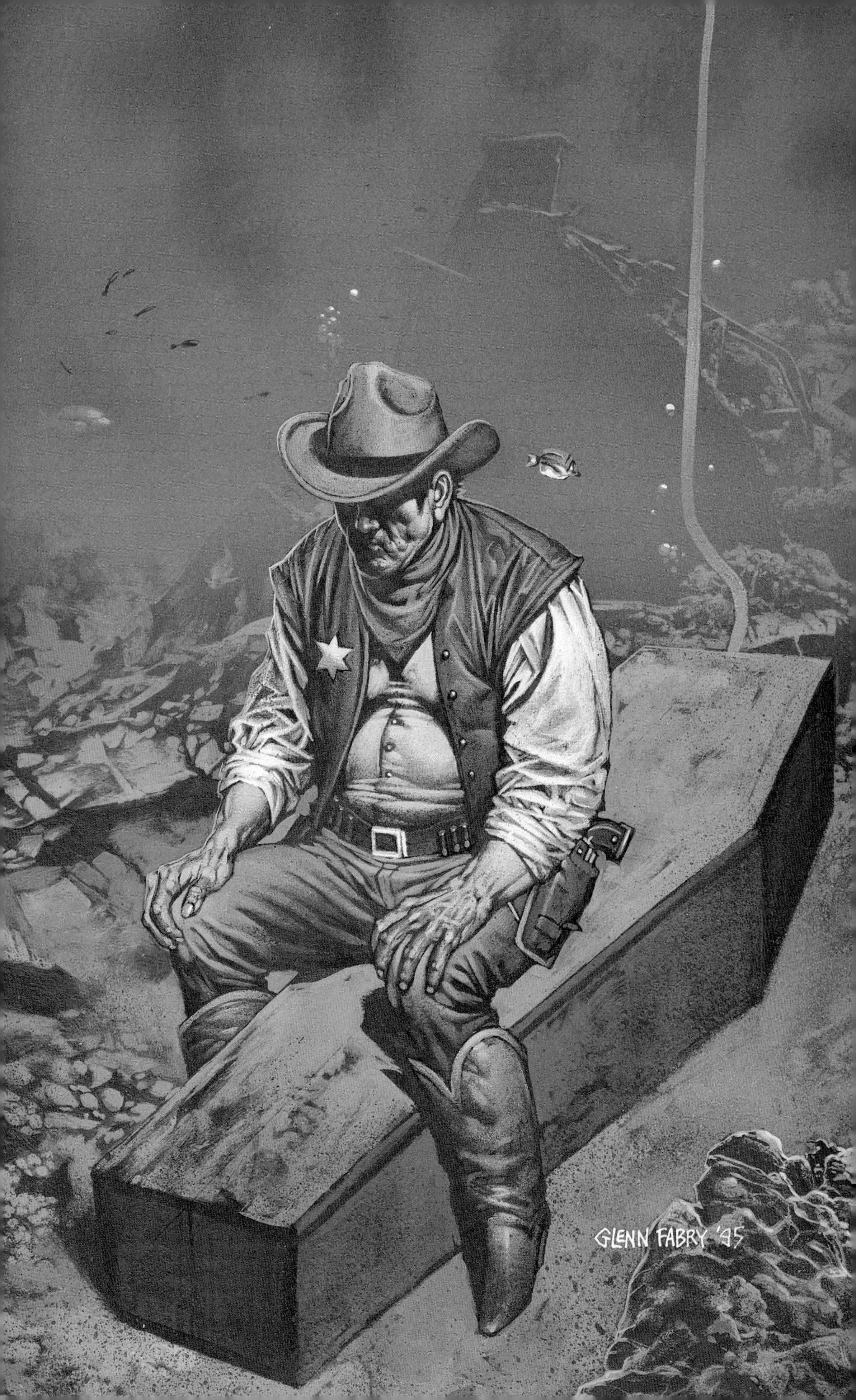
GLENN FABRY '95

"Christ, I think I'd grow old overnight if I lost you."

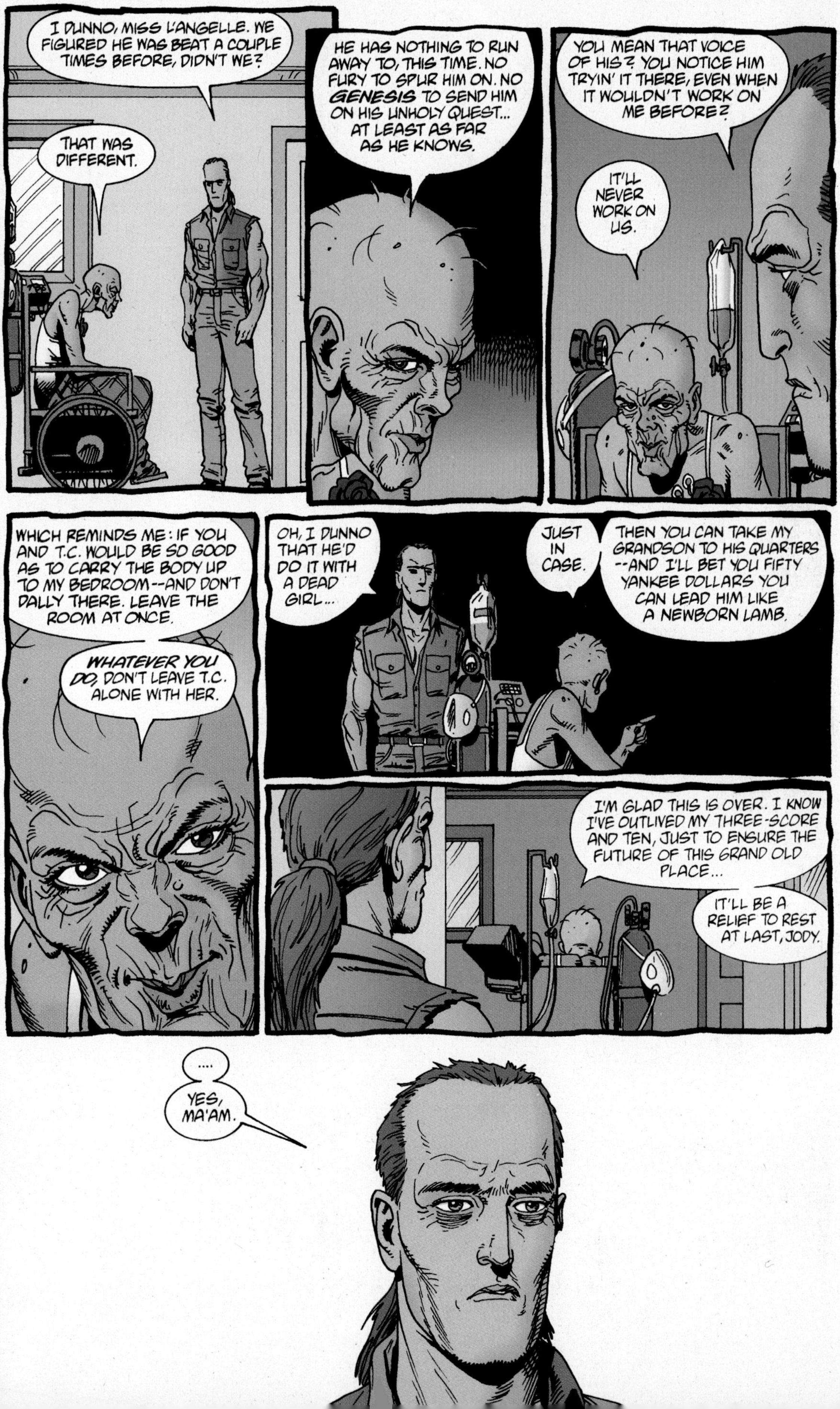
I DUNNO, MISS L'ANGELLE. WE FIGURED HE WAS BEAT A COUPLE TIMES BEFORE, DIDN'T WE?
THAT WAS DIFFERENT.
HE HAS NOTHING TO RUN AWAY TO, THIS TIME. NO FURY TO SPUR HIM ON. NO GENESIS TO SEND HIM ON HIS UNHOLY QUEST... AT LEAST AS FAR AS HE KNOWS.
YOU MEAN THAT VOICE OF HIS? YOU NOTICE HIM TRYIN' IT THERE, EVEN WHEN IT WOULDN'T WORK ON ME BEFORE?
IT'LL NEVER WORK ON US.
WHICH REMINDS ME: IF YOU AND T.C. WOULD BE SO GOOD AS TO CARRY THE BODY UP TO MY BEDROOM--AND DON'T DALLY THERE. LEAVE THE ROOM AT ONCE.
WHATEVER YOU DO, DON'T LEAVE T.C. ALONE WITH HER.
OH, I DUNNO THAT HE'D DO IT WITH A DEAD GIRL...
JUST IN CASE.
THEN YOU CAN TAKE MY GRANDSON TO HIS QUARTERS --AND I'LL BET YOU FIFTY YANKEE DOLLARS YOU CAN LEAD HIM LIKE A NEWBORN LAMB.
I'M GLAD THIS IS OVER. I KNOW I'VE OUTLIVED MY THREE-SCORE AND TEN, JUST TO ENSURE THE FUTURE OF THIS GRAND OLD PLACE...
IT'LL BE A RELIEF TO REST AT LAST, JODY.
....
YES, MA'AM.

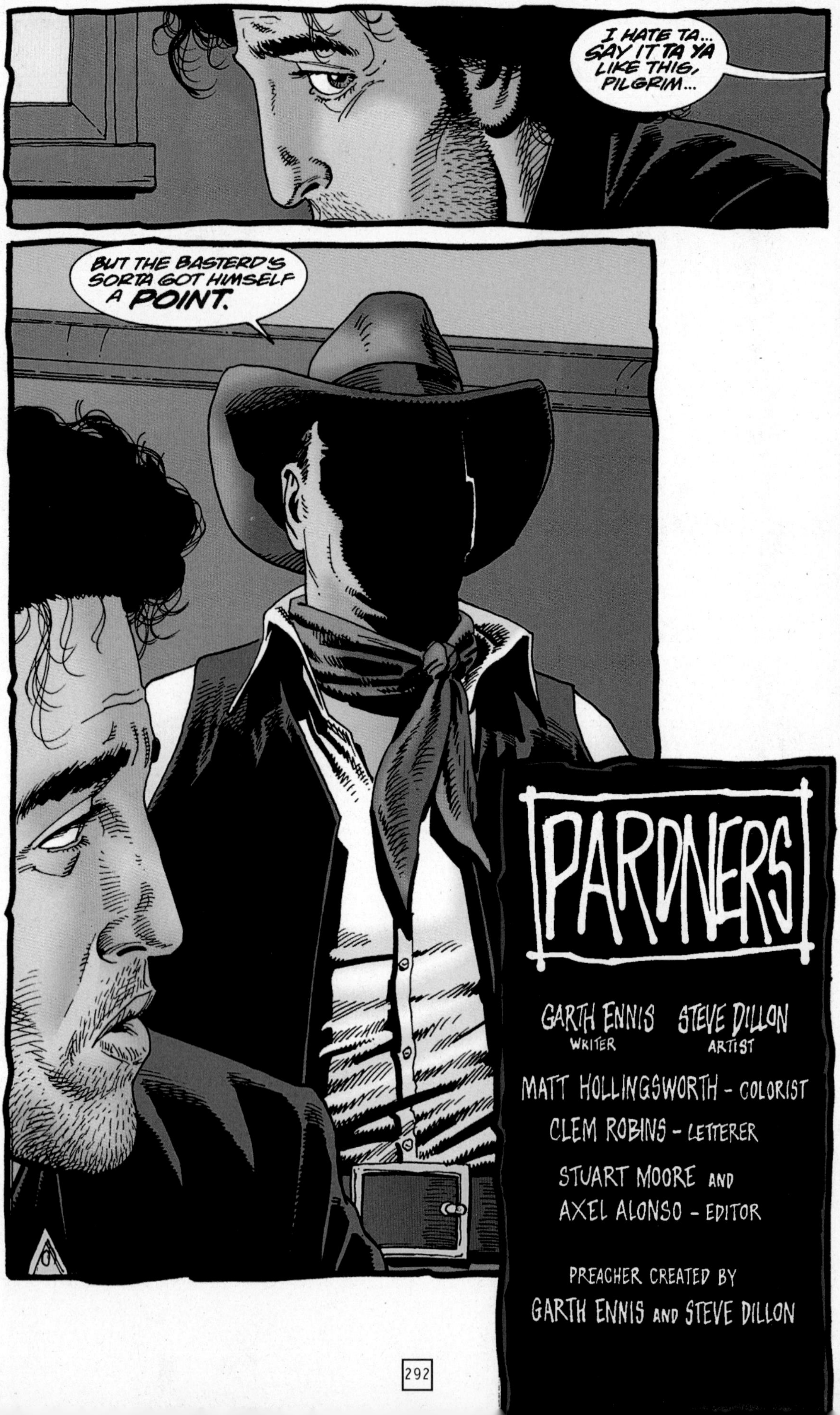
I HATE TA... SAY IT TA YA LIKE THIS, PILGRIM...
BUT THE BASTERD'S SORTA GOT HIMSELF A POINT.
PARDNERS
GARTH ENNIS WRITER
STEVE DILLON ARTIST
MATT HOLLINGSWORTH - COLORIST
CLEM ROBINS - LETTERER
STUART MOORE AND AXEL ALONSO - EDITOR
PREACHER CREATED BY GARTH ENNIS AND STEVE DILLON

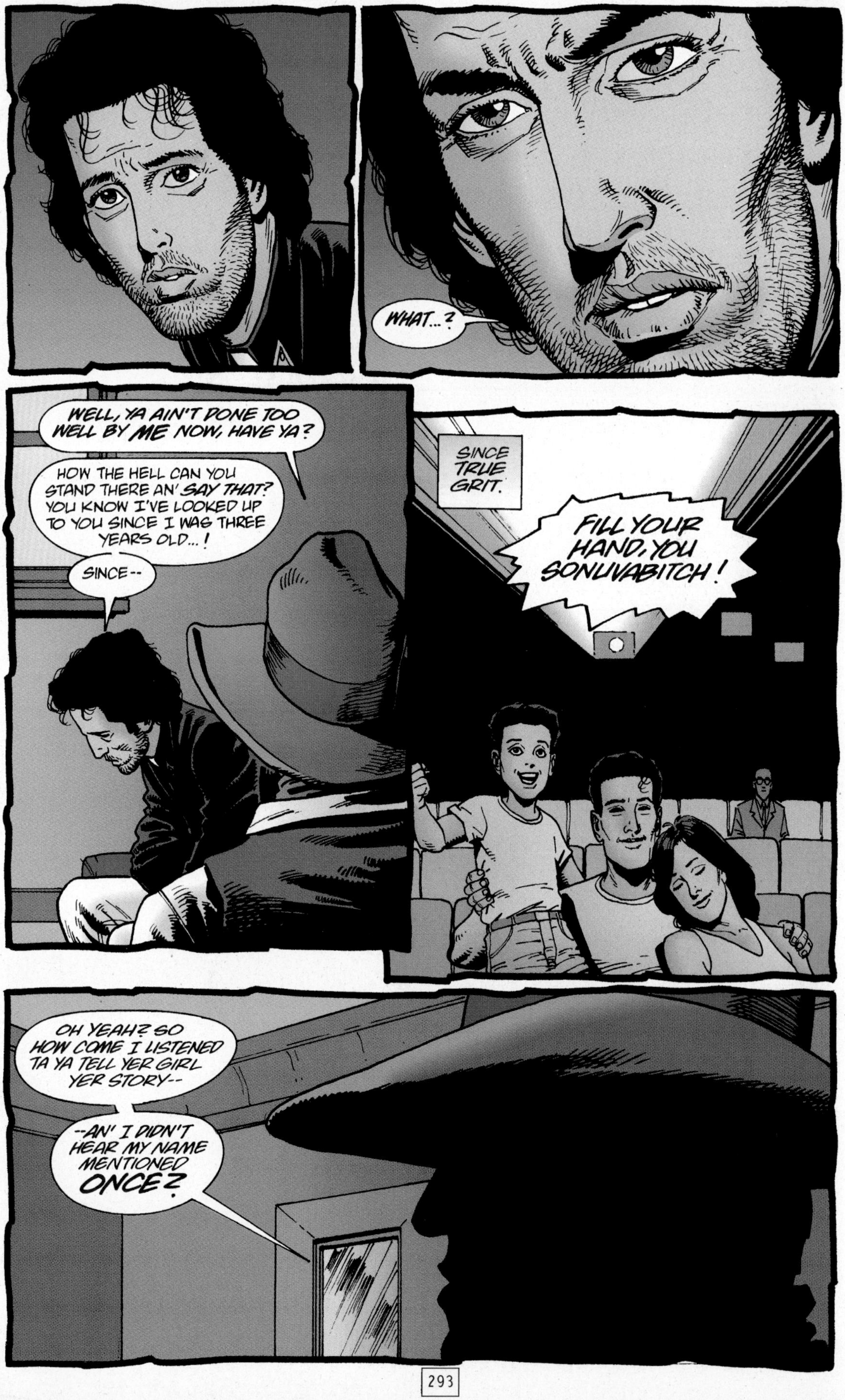
WHAT...?
WELL, YA AIN'T DONE TOO WELL BY ME NOW, HAVE YA?
HOW THE HELL CAN YOU STAND THERE AN' SAY THAT? YOU KNOW I'VE LOOKED UP TO YOU SINCE I WAS THREE YEARS OLD...!
SINCE--
SINCE TRUE GRIT.
FILL YOUR HAND, YOU SONUVABITCH!
OH YEAH? SO HOW COME I LISTENED TA YA TELL YER GIRL YER STORY--
--AN' I DIDN'T HEAR MY NAME MENTIONED ONCE?

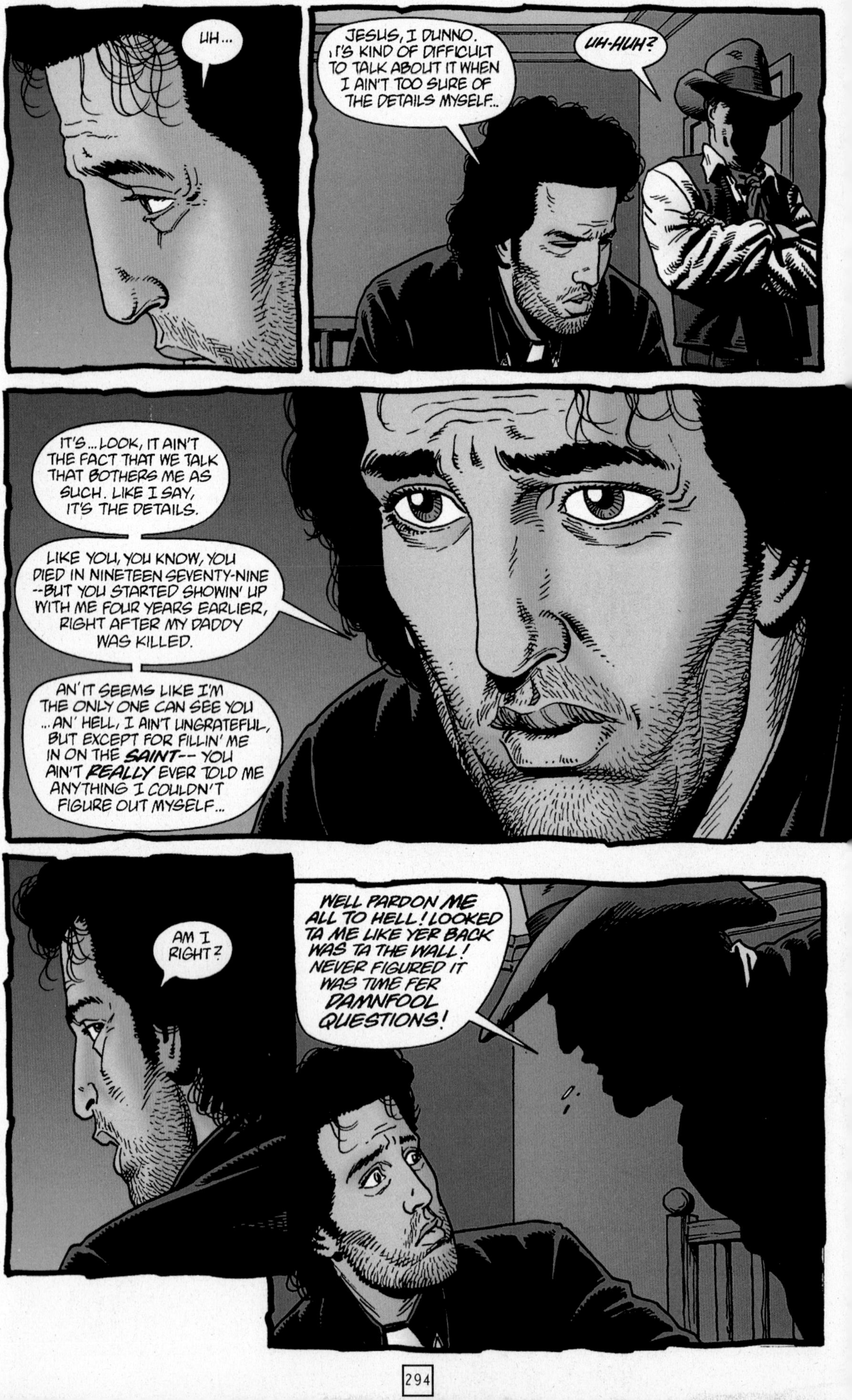
UH...
JESUS, I DUNNO. IT'S KIND OF DIFFICULT TO TALK ABOUT IT WHEN I AIN'T TOO SURE OF THE DETAILS MYSELF...
UH-HUH?
IT'S...LOOK, IT AIN'T THE FACT THAT WE TALK THAT BOTHERS ME AS SUCH. LIKE I SAY, IT'S THE DETAILS.
LIKE YOU, YOU KNOW, YOU DIED IN NINETEEN SEVENTY-NINE --BUT YOU STARTED SHOWIN' UP WITH ME FOUR YEARS EARLIER, RIGHT AFTER MY DADDY WAS KILLED.
AN' IT SEEMS LIKE I'M THE ONLY ONE CAN SEE YOU ...AN' HELL, I AIN'T UNGRATEFUL, BUT EXCEPT FOR FILLIN' ME IN ON THE SAINT-- YOU AIN'T REALLY EVER TOLD ME ANYTHING I COULDN'T FIGURE OUT MYSELF...
AM I RIGHT?
WELL PARDON ME ALL TO HELL! LOOKED TA ME LIKE YER BACK WAS TA THE WALL! NEVER FIGURED IT WAS TIME FER DAMNFOOL QUESTIONS!

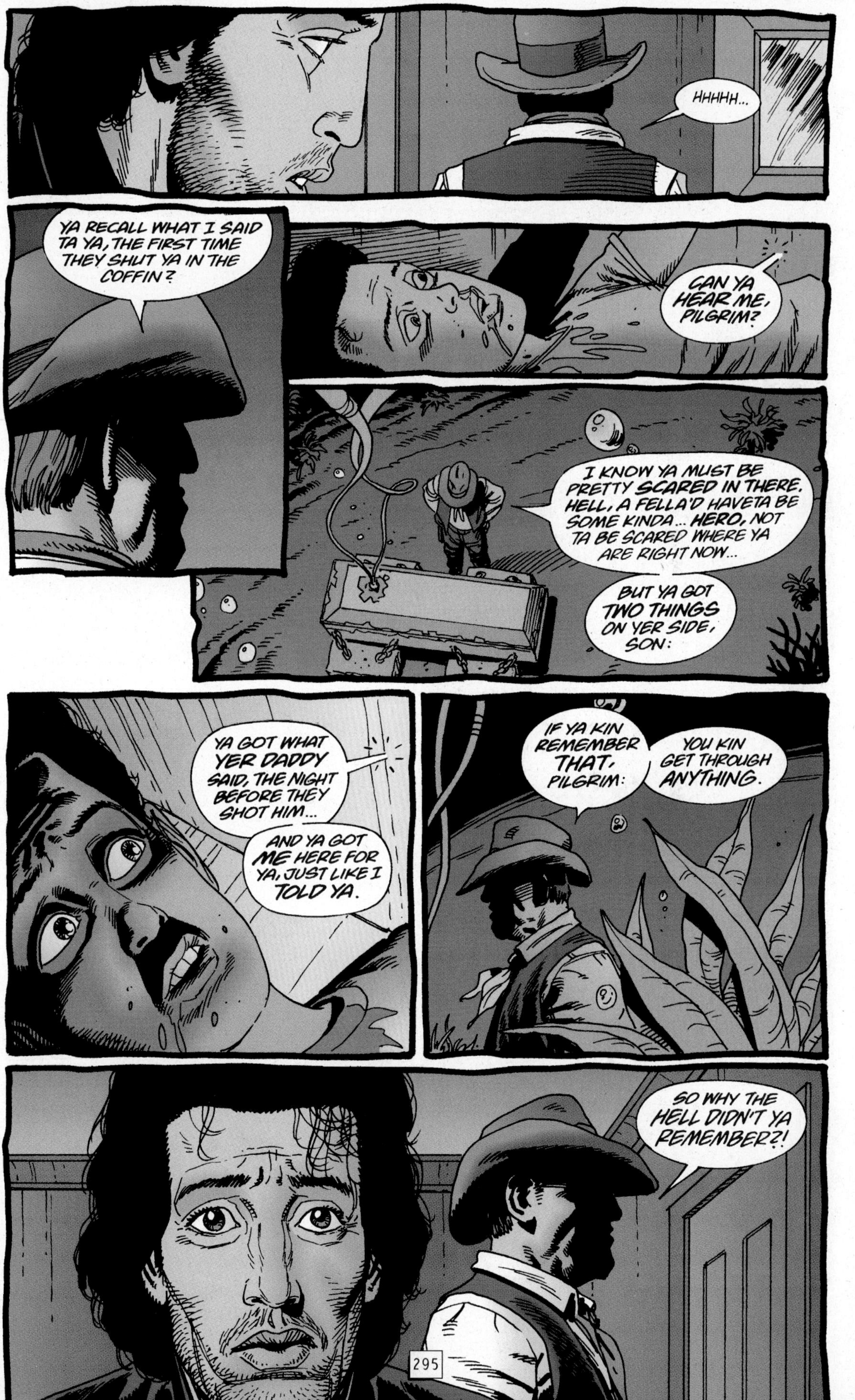
HHHHH...
YA RECALL WHAT I SAID TA YA, THE FIRST TIME THEY SHUT YA IN THE COFFIN?
CAN YA HEAR ME, PILGRIM?
I KNOW YA MUST BE PRETTY SCARED IN THERE. HELL, A FELLA'D HAVETA BE SOME KINDA... HERO, NOT TA BE SCARED WHERE YA ARE RIGHT NOW...
BUT YA GOT TWO THINGS ON YER SIDE, SON:
YA GOT WHAT YER DADDY SAID, THE NIGHT BEFORE THEY SHOT HIM...
AND YA GOT ME HERE FOR YA, JUST LIKE I TOLD YA.
IF YA KIN REMEMBER THAT, PILGRIM:
YOU KIN GET THROUGH ANYTHING.
SO WHY THE HELL DIDN'T YA REMEMBER?!

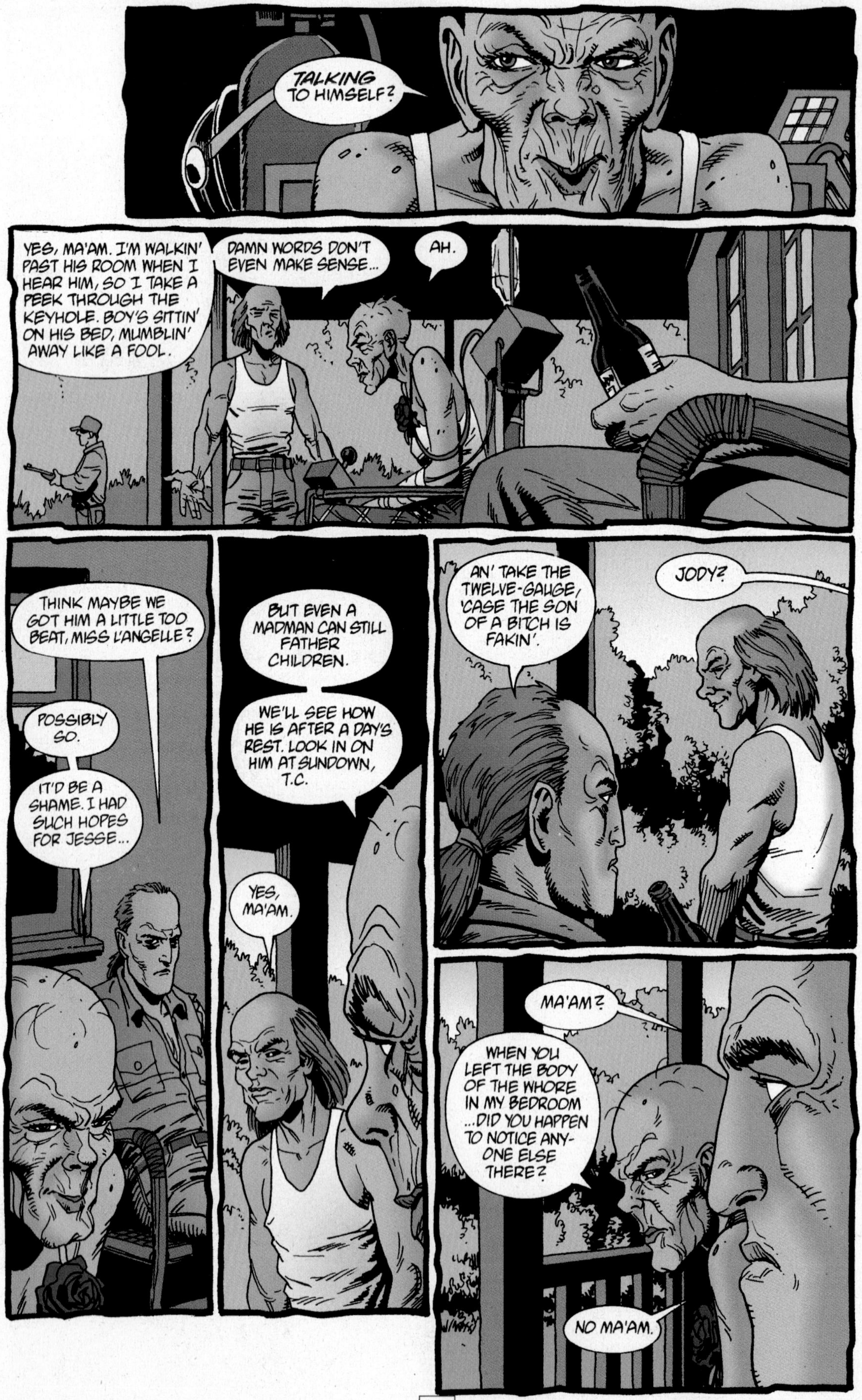
TALKING TO HIMSELF?
YES, MA'AM. I'M WALKIN' PAST HIS ROOM WHEN I HEAR HIM, SO I TAKE A PEEK THROUGH THE KEYHOLE. BOY'S SITTIN' ON HIS BED, MUMBLIN' AWAY LIKE A FOOL.
DAMN WORDS DON'T EVEN MAKE SENSE...
AH.
THINK MAYBE WE GOT HIM A LITTLE TOO BEAT, MISS L'ANGELLE?
POSSIBLY SO.
IT'D BE A SHAME. I HAD SUCH HOPES FOR JESSE...
BUT EVEN A MADMAN CAN STILL FATHER CHILDREN.
WE'LL SEE HOW HE IS AFTER A DAY'S REST. LOOK IN ON HIM AT SUNDOWN, T.C.
YES, MA'AM.
JODY?
AN' TAKE THE TWELVE-GAUGE, 'CASE THE SON OF A BITCH IS FAKIN'.
MA'AM?
WHEN YOU LEFT THE BODY OF THE WHORE IN MY BEDROOM ...DID YOU HAPPEN TO NOTICE ANY-ONE ELSE THERE?
NO MA'AM.

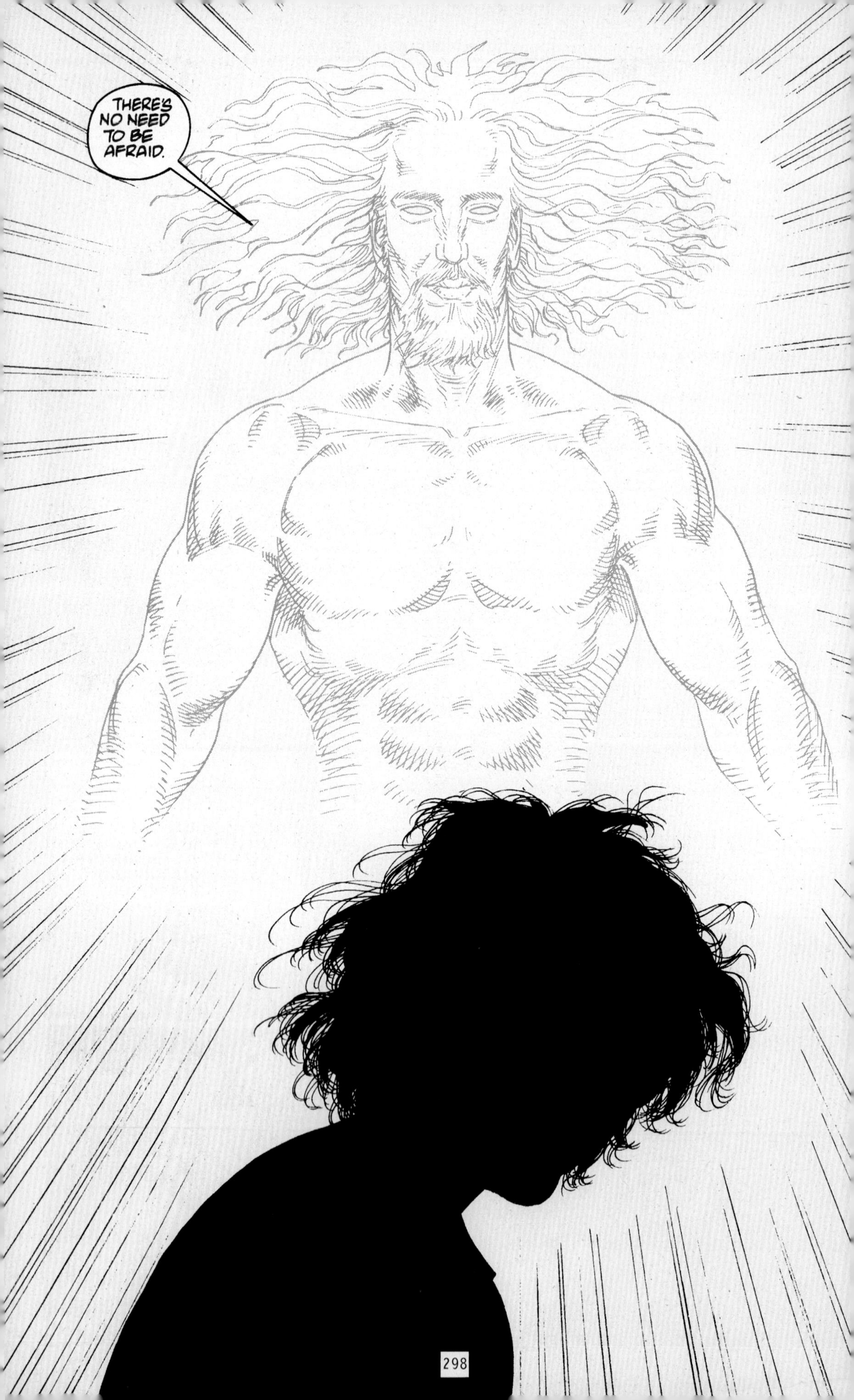
THERE'S NO NEED TO BE AFRAID.

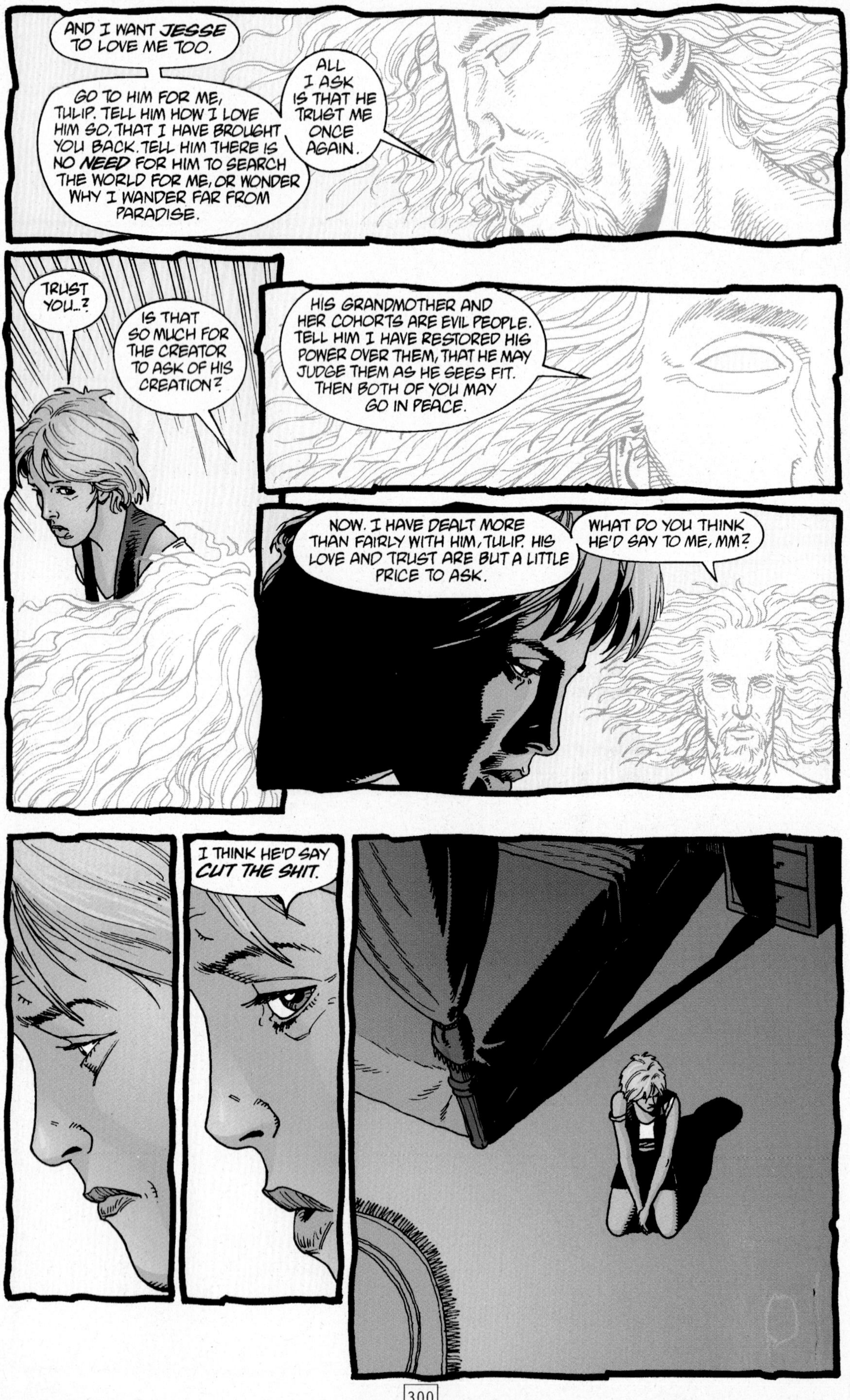

AND I WANT JESSE TO LOVE ME TOO.
GO TO HIM FOR ME, TULIP. TELL HIM HOW I LOVE HIM SO, THAT I HAVE BROUGHT YOU BACK. TELL HIM THERE IS NO NEED FOR HIM TO SEARCH THE WORLD FOR ME, OR WONDER WHY I WANDER FAR FROM PARADISE.
ALL I ASK IS THAT HE TRUST ME ONCE AGAIN.
TRUST YOU...?
IS THAT SO MUCH FOR THE CREATOR TO ASK OF HIS CREATION?
HIS GRANDMOTHER AND HER COHORTS ARE EVIL PEOPLE. TELL HIM I HAVE RESTORED HIS POWER OVER THEM, THAT HE MAY JUDGE THEM AS HE SEES FIT. THEN BOTH OF YOU MAY GO IN PEACE.
NOW. I HAVE DEALT MORE THAN FAIRLY WITH HIM, TULIP. HIS LOVE AND TRUST ARE BUT A LITTLE PRICE TO ASK.
WHAT DO YOU THINK HE'D SAY TO ME, MM?
I THINK HE'D SAY CUT THE SHIT.

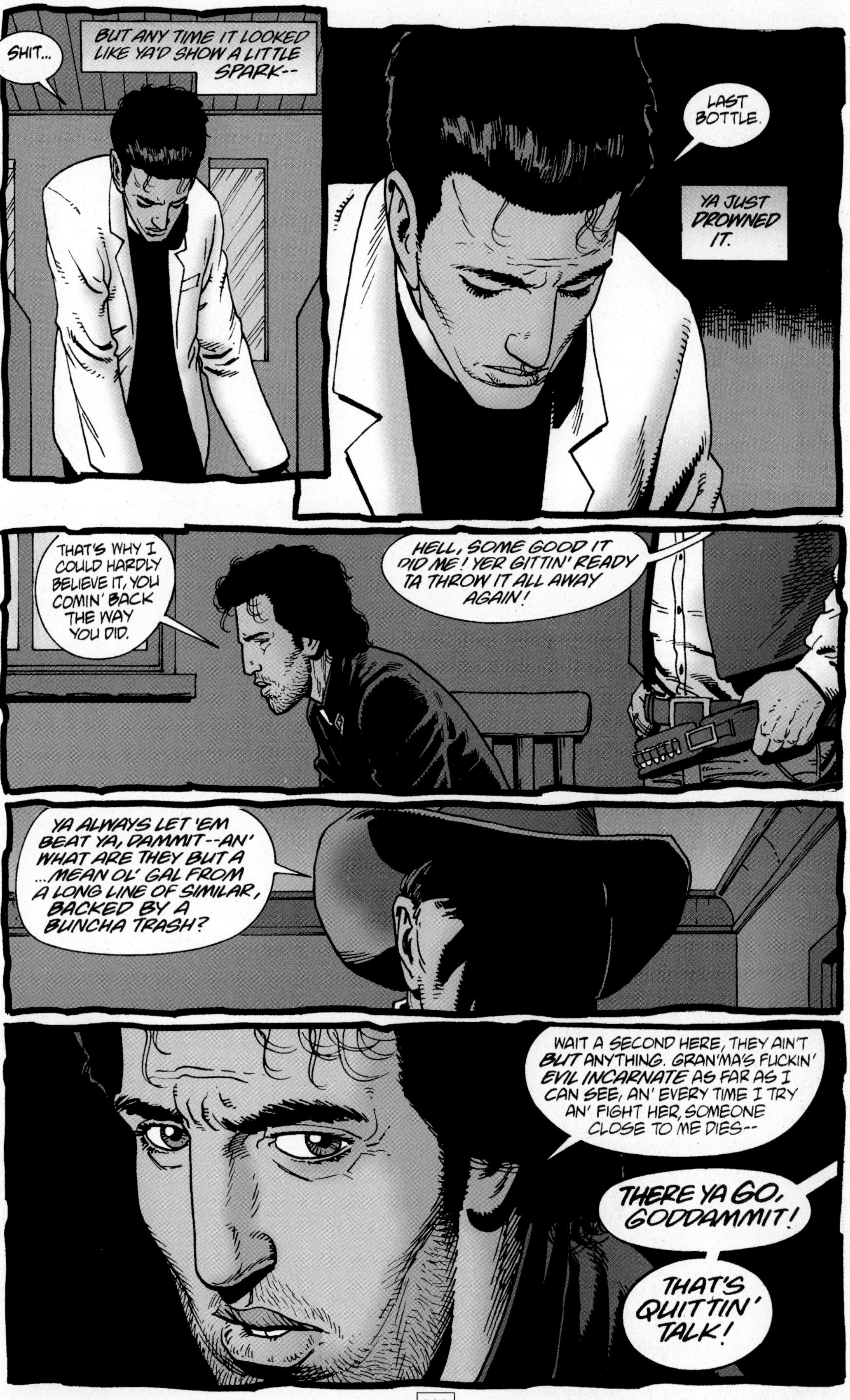
SHIT...
BUT ANY TIME IT LOOKED LIKE YA'D SHOW A LITTLE SPARK--
LAST BOTTLE.
YA JUST DROWNED IT.
THAT'S WHY I COULD HARDLY BELIEVE IT, YOU COMIN' BACK THE WAY YOU DID.
HELL, SOME GOOD IT DID ME! YER GITTIN' READY TA THROW IT ALL AWAY AGAIN!
YA ALWAYS LET 'EM BEAT YA, DAMMIT--AN' WHAT ARE THEY BUT A ...MEAN OL' GAL FROM A LONG LINE OF SIMILAR, BACKED BY A BUNCHA TRASH?
WAIT A SECOND HERE, THEY AIN'T BUT ANYTHING. GRAN'MA'S FUCKIN' EVIL INCARNATE AS FAR AS I CAN SEE, AN' EVERY TIME I TRY AN' FIGHT HER, SOMEONE CLOSE TO ME DIES--
THERE YA GO, GODDAMMIT!
THAT'S QUITTIN' TALK!

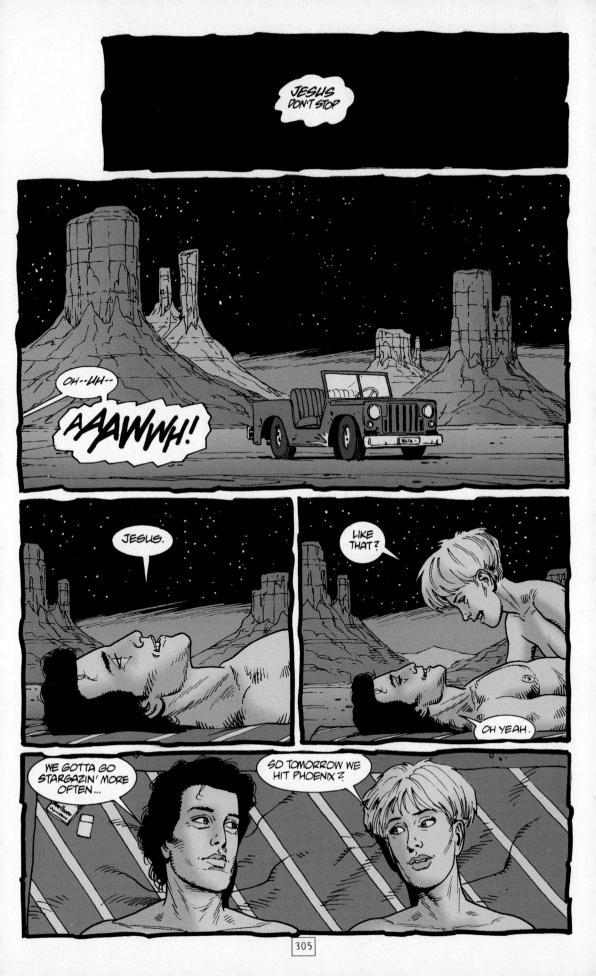

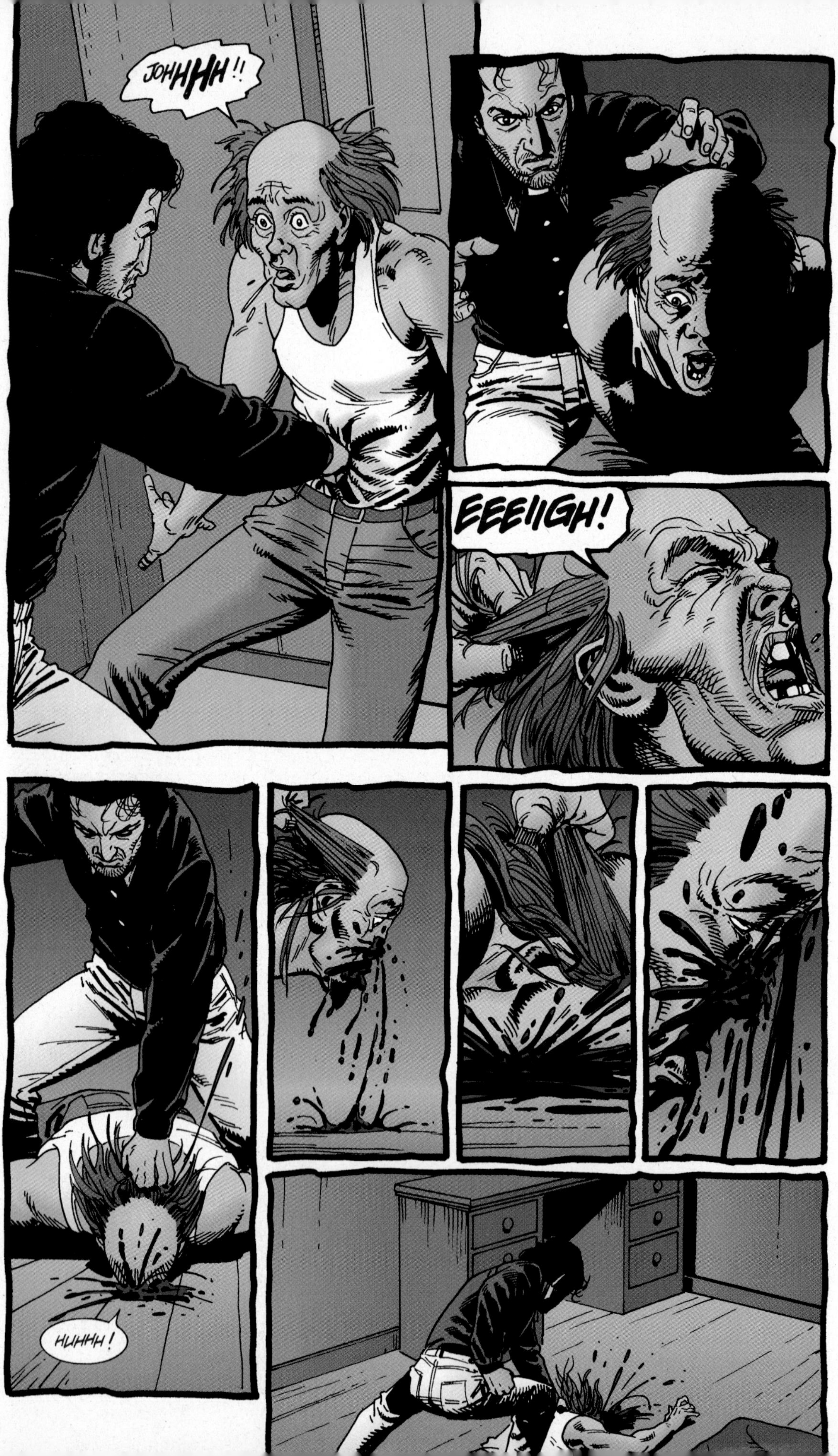
JOHHHH!!
EEEIIGH!
HUHHH!

HHHHRIGHT.

NO MORE QUITTIN'. I'M GONNA GO GET GRAN'MA AN' JODY AN' THE REST'VE THAT MOTHERFUCKIN' VERMIN, AN' I'M GONNA STAMP 'EM INTO THE *SHIT* THEY CAME FROM.

AN' THEN I'M GOIN' BACK TO LOOKIN' FOR GOD, AN' WHEN I FIND HIM--

HE BETTER HAVE A *FUCKIN'* GOOD EXCUSE.

GLAD TA HEAR IT, PILGRIM. 'CAUSE THERE'S A LITTLE GIRL LYIN' DEAD OUT THERE THAT NEEDS *AVENGIN'!*

YOU KIN TALK THE TALK--

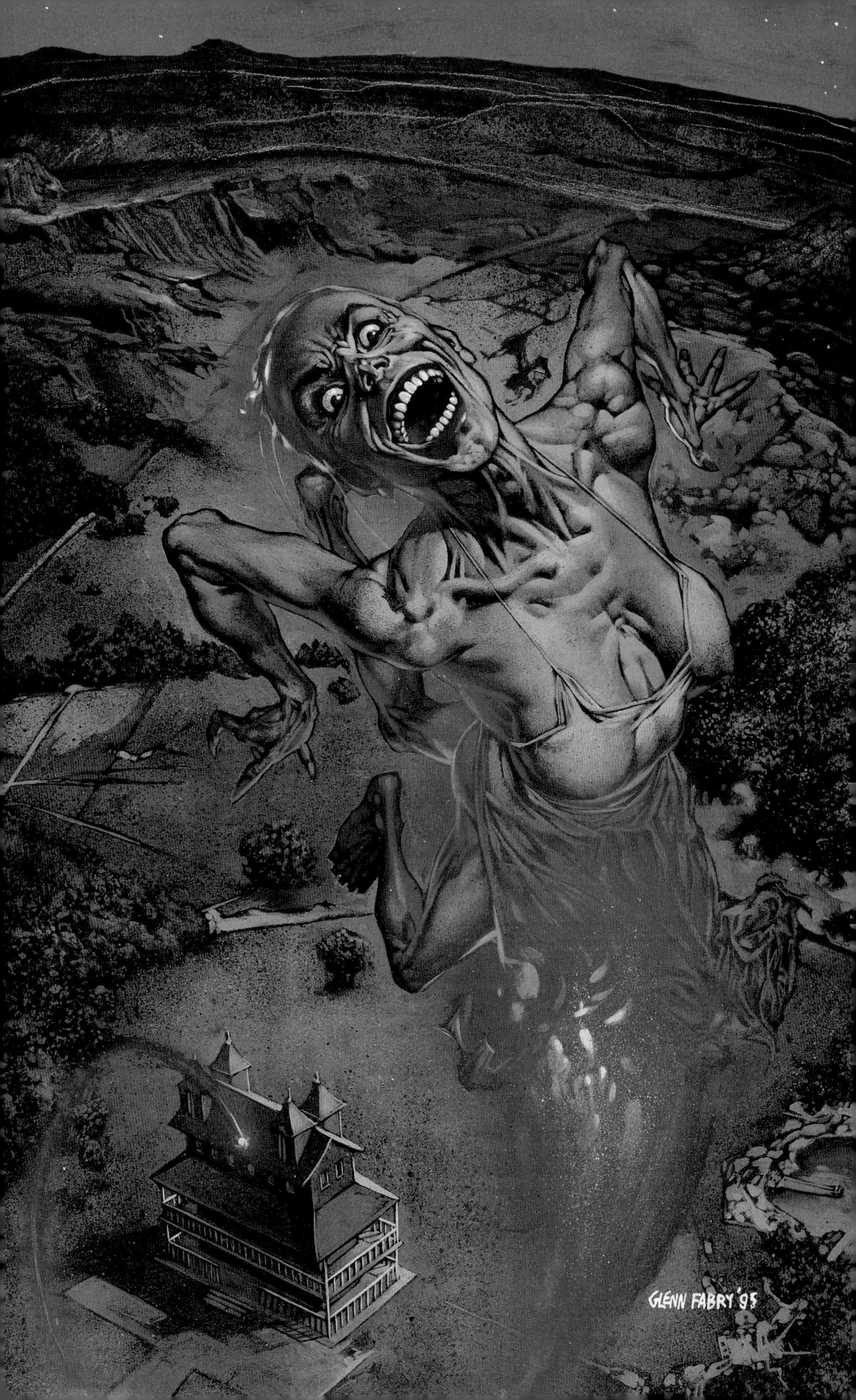
GLENN FABRY '95

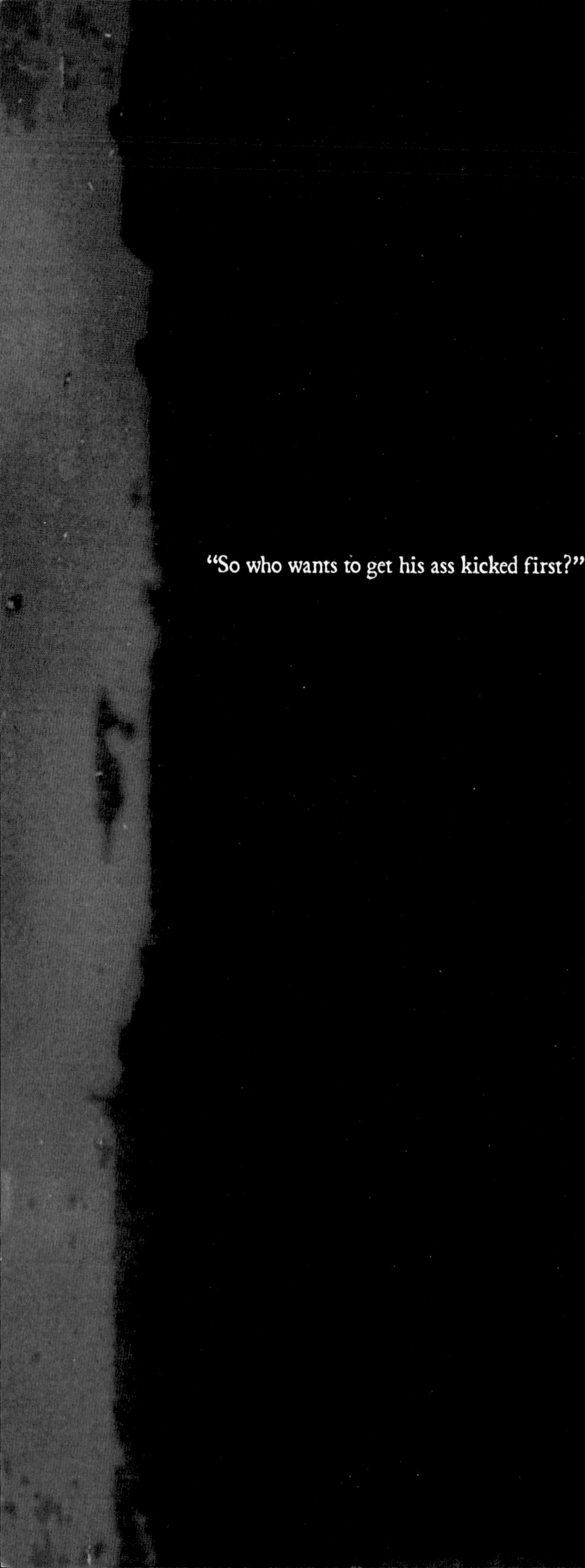
"So who wants to get his ass kicked first?"

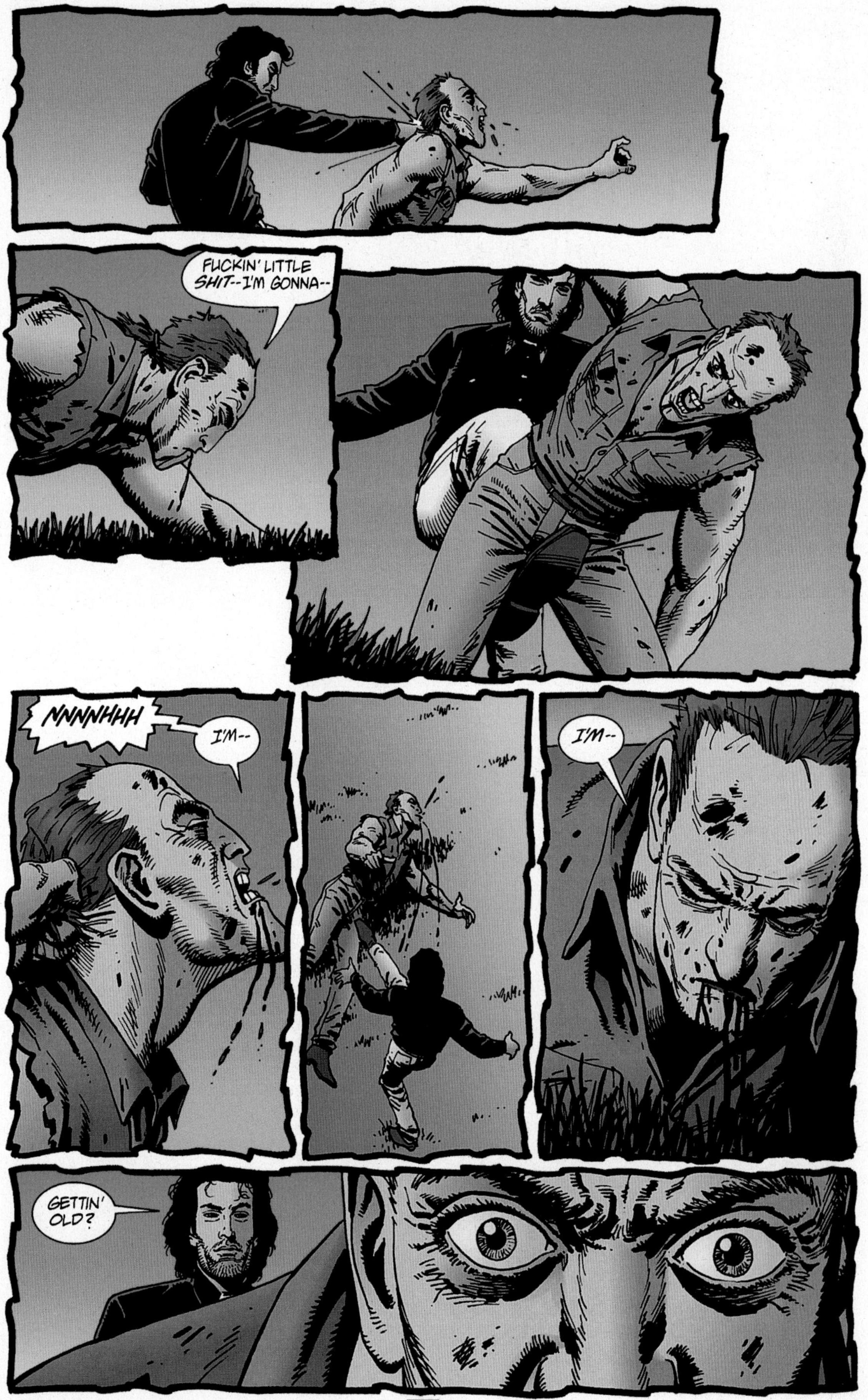
FUCKIN' LITTLE SHIT--I'M GONNA--
NNNNHHH
I'M--
I'M--
GETTIN' OLD?

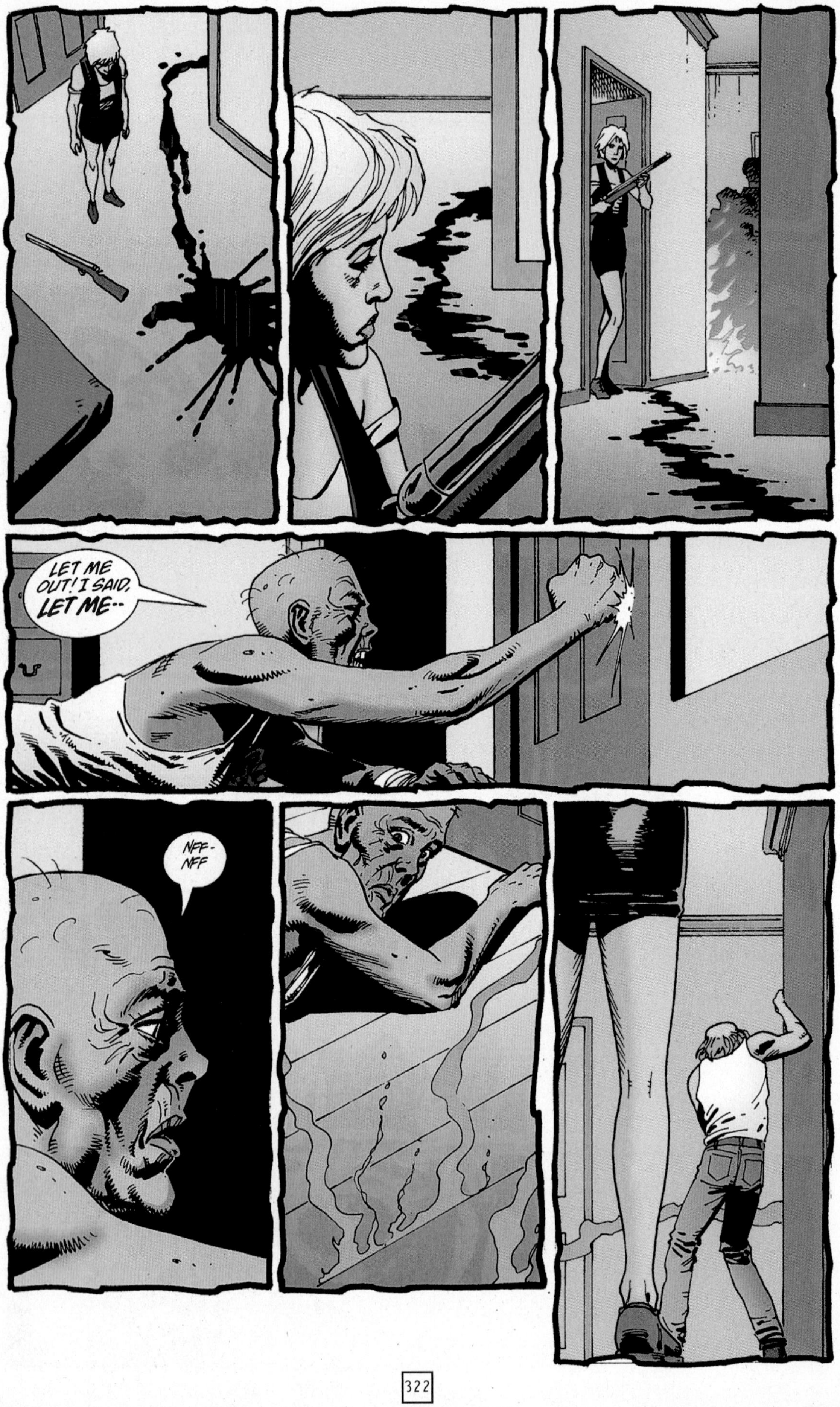
LET ME OUT! I SAID, LET ME--
NFF-NFF

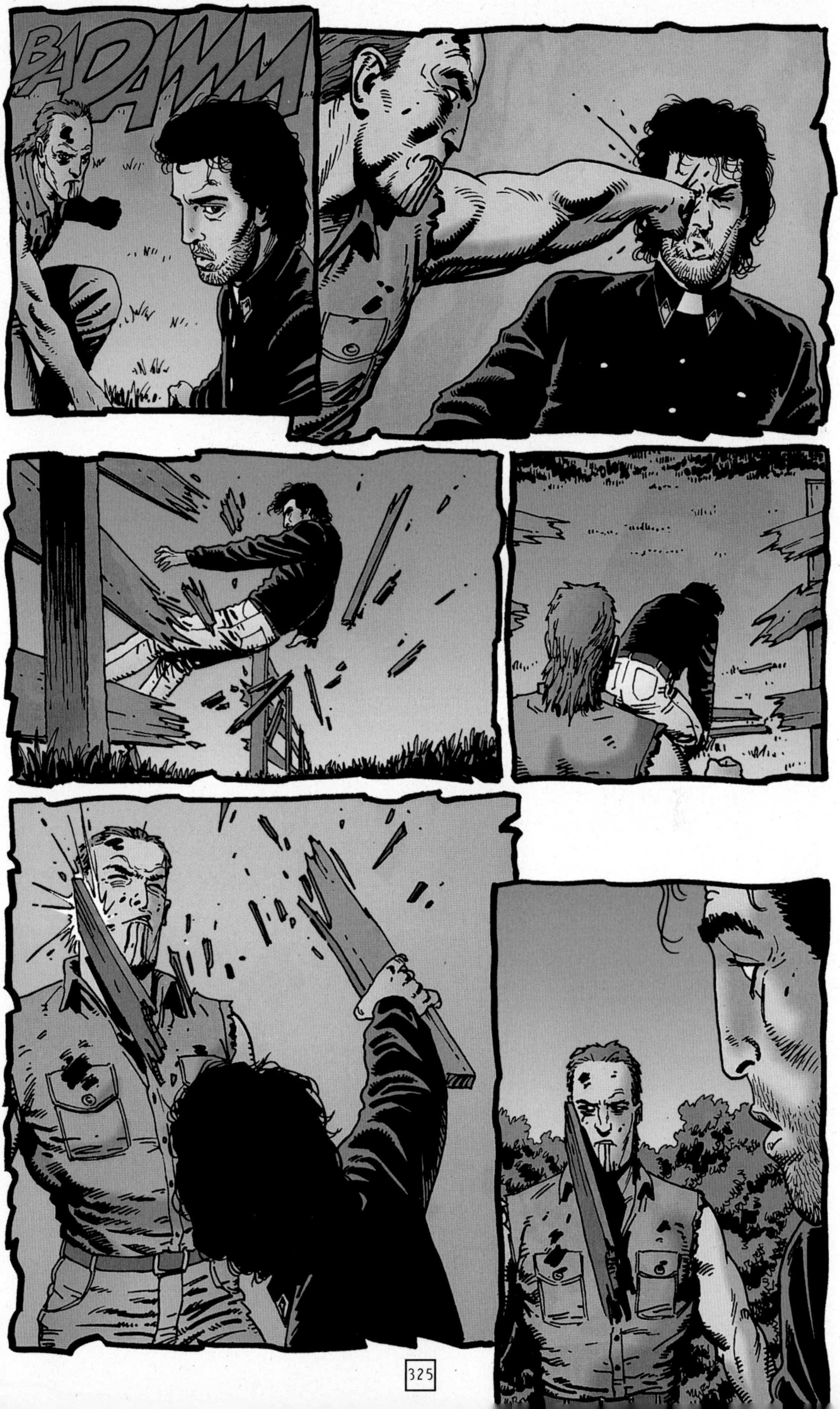
BADAMM

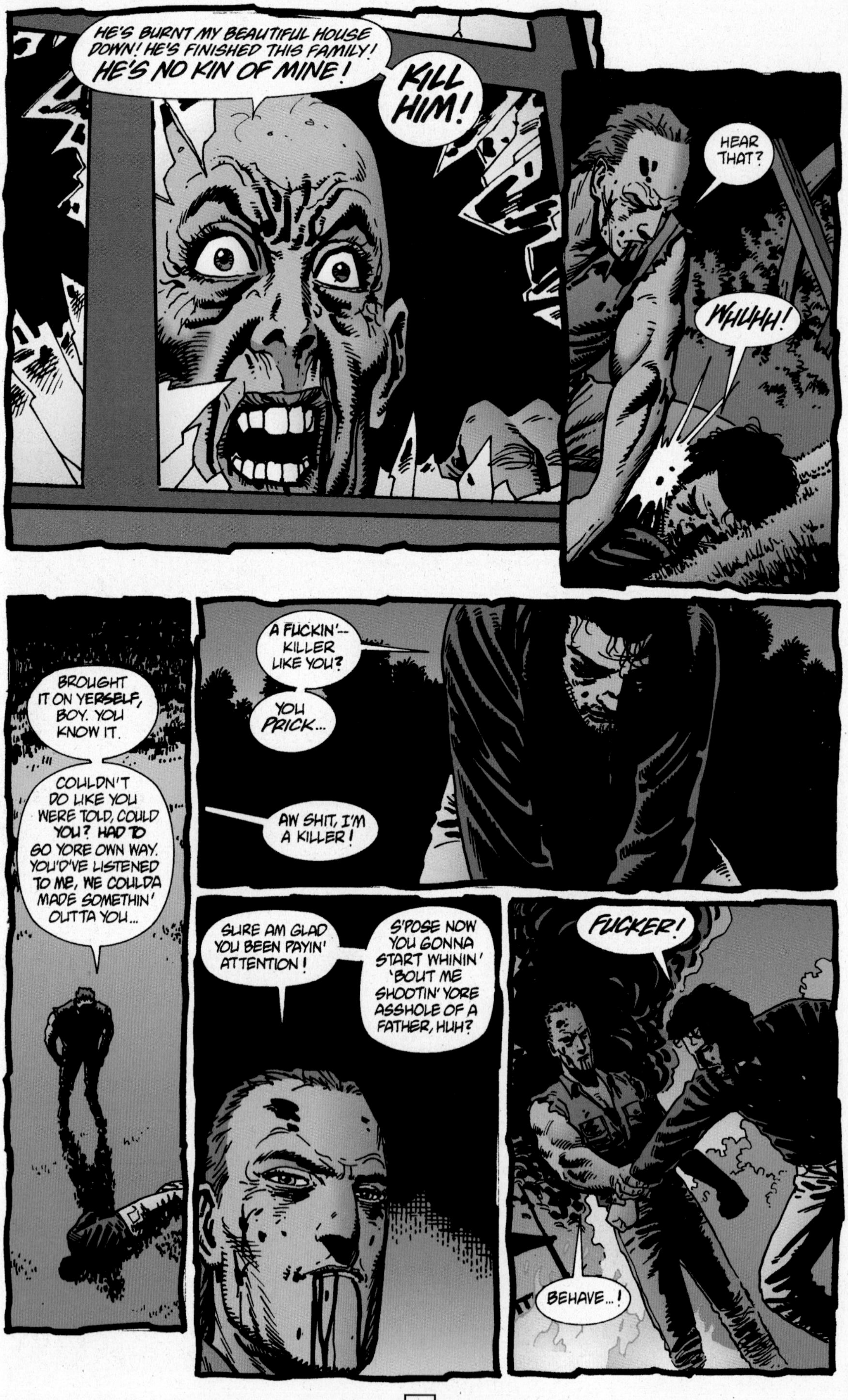
HE'S BURNT MY BEAUTIFUL HOUSE DOWN! HE'S FINISHED THIS FAMILY! HE'S NO KIN OF MINE!
KILL HIM!
HEAR THAT?
WHUHH!
BROUGHT IT ON YERSELF, BOY. YOU KNOW IT.
COULDN'T DO LIKE YOU WERE TOLD, COULD YOU? HAD TO GO YORE OWN WAY. YOU'D'VE LISTENED TO ME, WE COULDA MADE SOMETHIN' OUTTA YOU...
A FUCKIN'-- KILLER LIKE YOU?
YOU PRICK...
AW SHIT, I'M A KILLER!
SURE AM GLAD YOU BEEN PAYIN' ATTENTION!
S'POSE NOW YOU GONNA START WHININ' 'BOUT ME SHOOTIN' YORE ASSHOLE OF A FATHER, HUH?
FUCKER!
BEHAVE...!

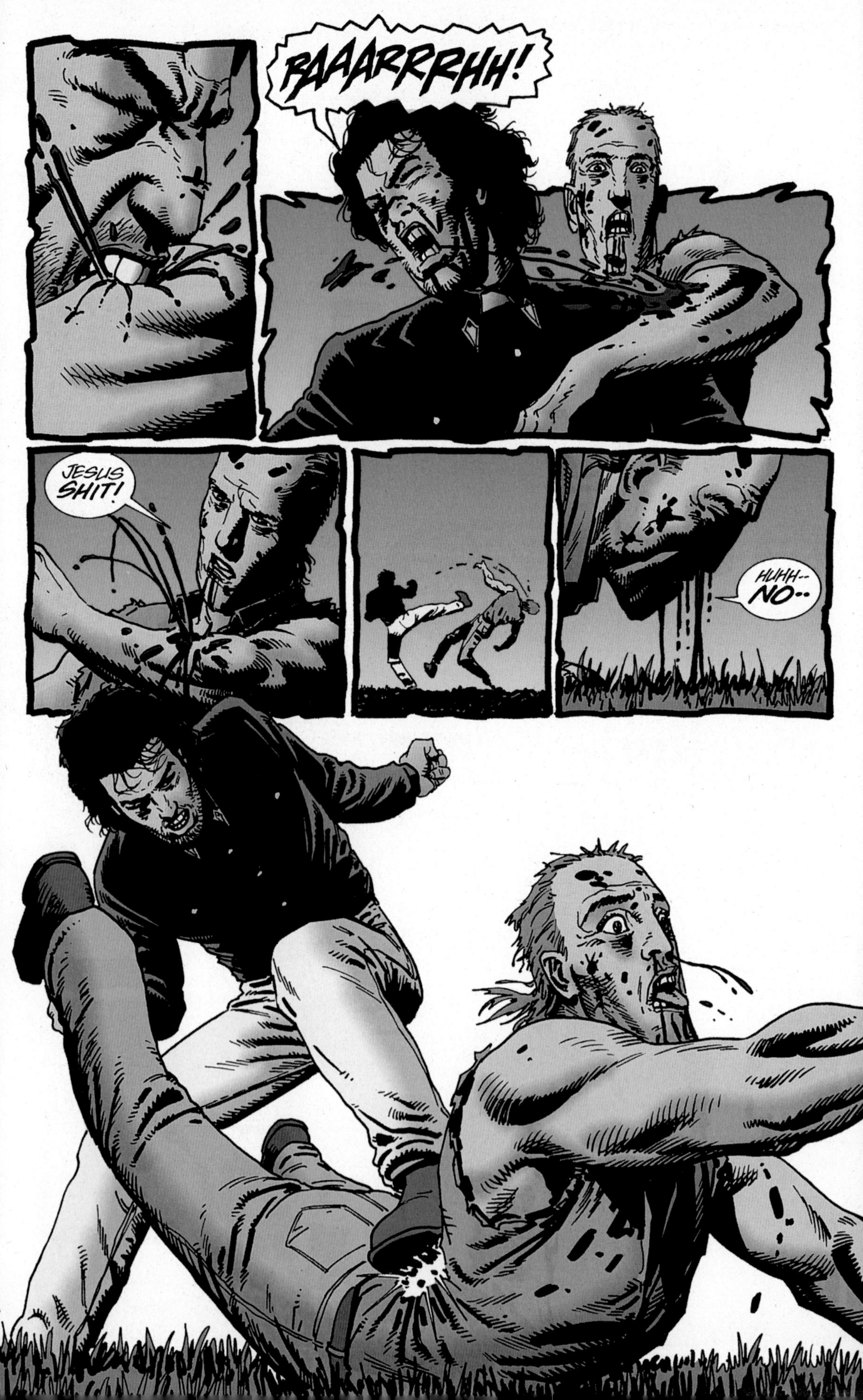
RAAARRRHH!
JESUS SHIT!
HUHH-- NO--

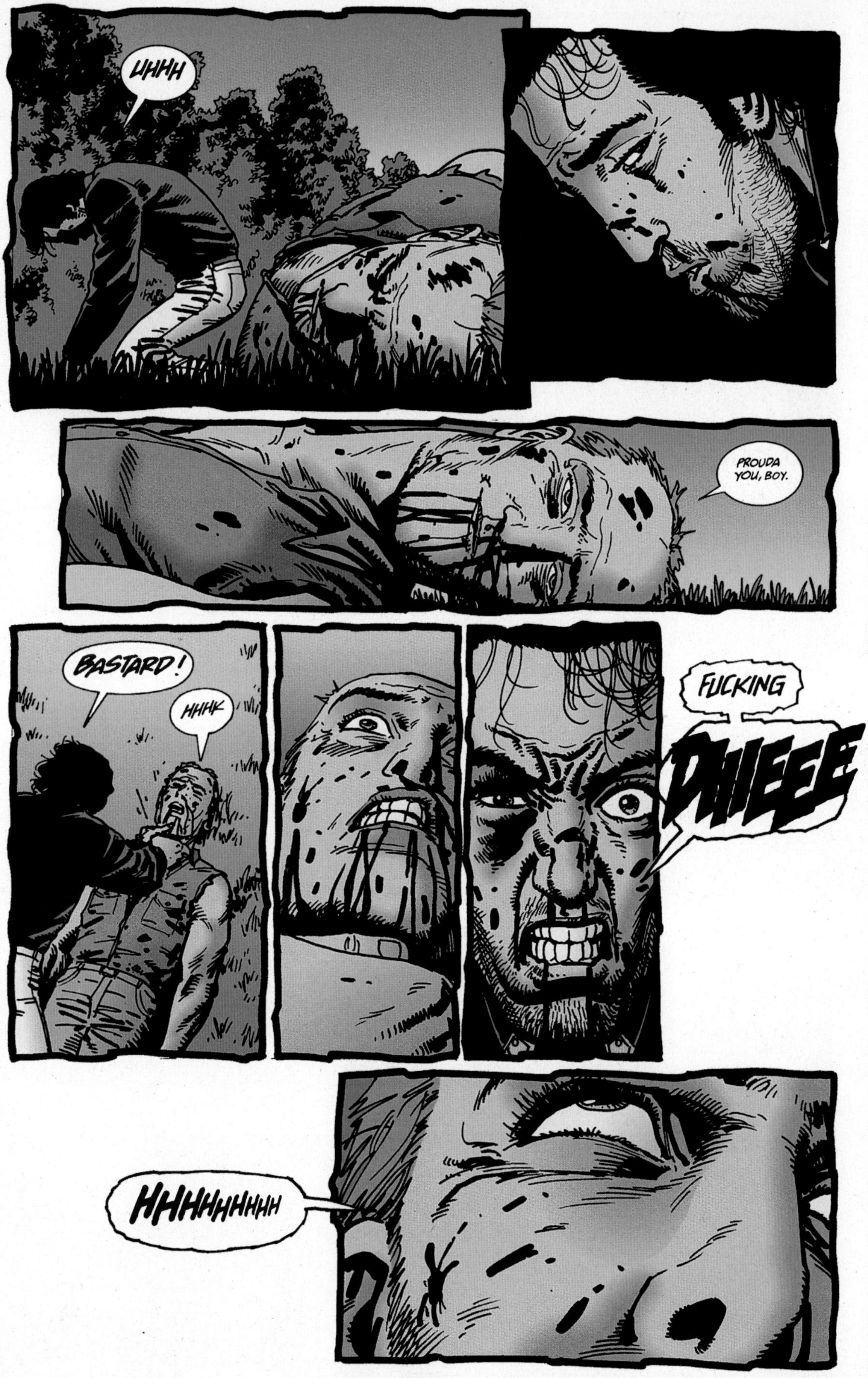
UHHH
PROUDA YOU, BOY.
BASTARD!
HHHK
FUCKING
DIIEEE
HHHHHHHHH

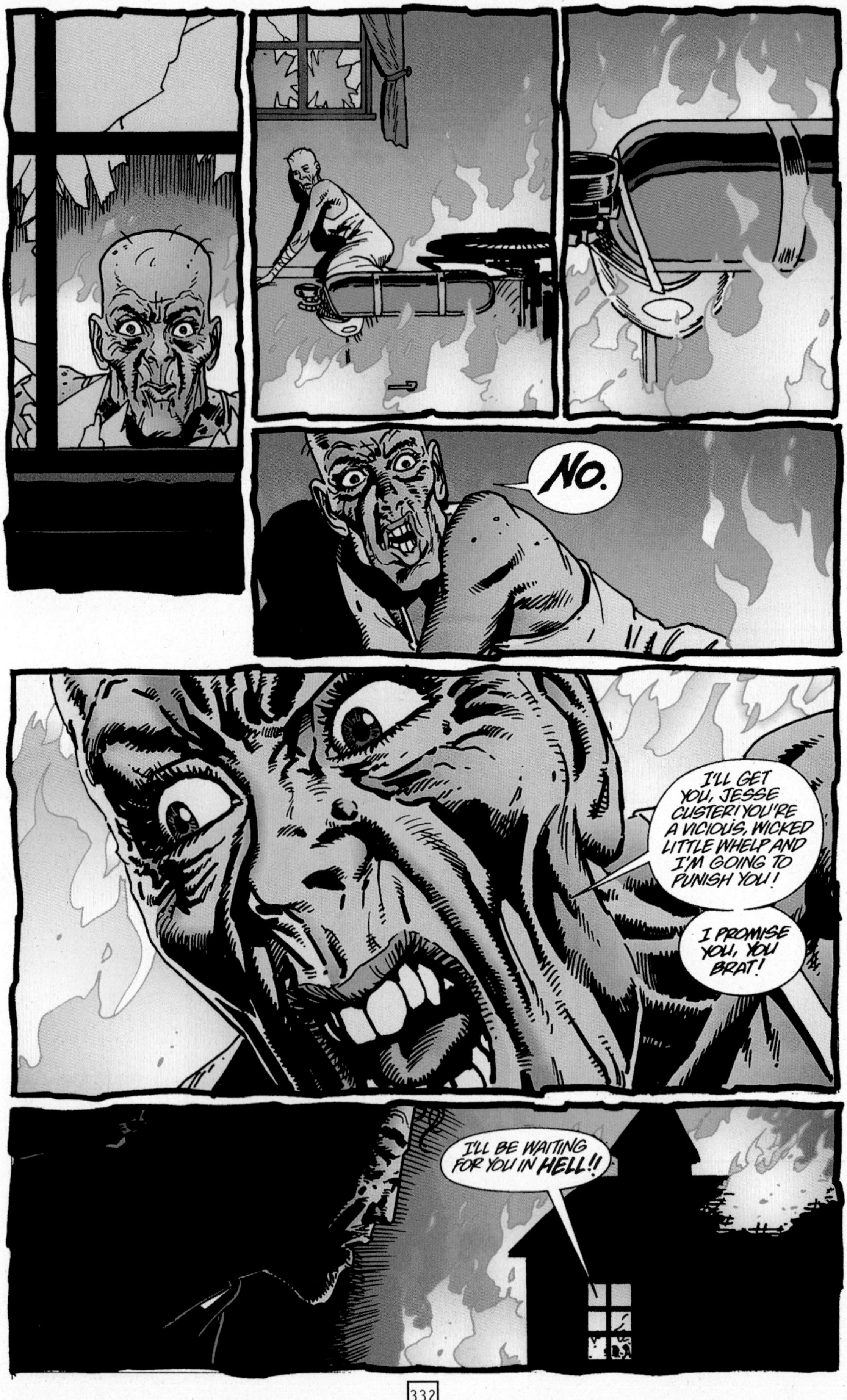
NO.
I'LL GET YOU, JESSE CUSTER! YOU'RE A VICIOUS, WICKED LITTLE WHELP AND I'M GOING TO PUNISH YOU!
I PROMISE YOU, YOU BRAT!
I'LL BE WAITING FOR YOU IN HELL!!

335

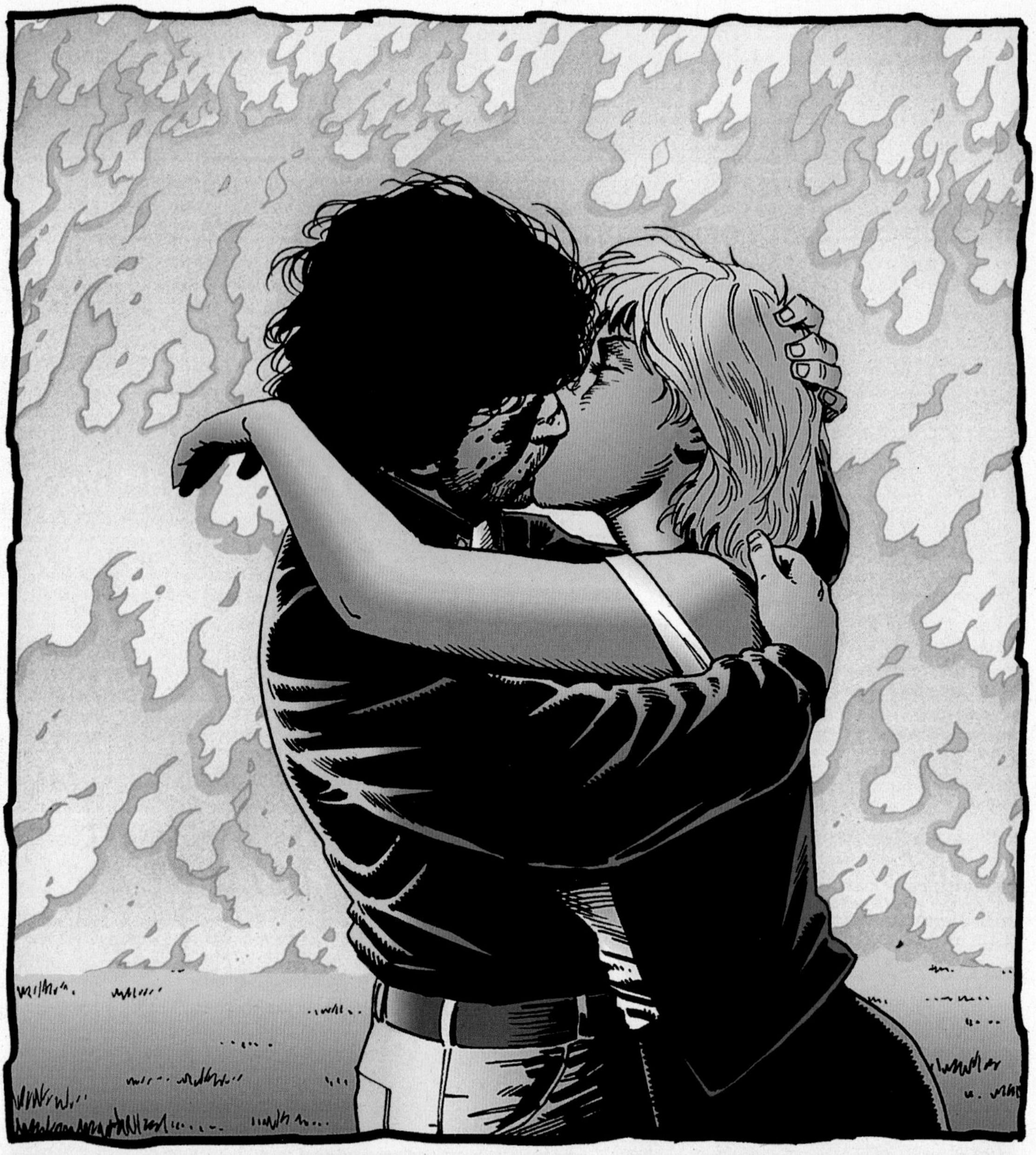

UNTIL THE END OF THE WORLD

GARTH ENNIS
WRITER

STEVE DILLON
ARTIST

MATT HOLLINGSWORTH - COLORIST

CLEM ROBINS - LETTERER

STUART MOORE
AND
AXEL ALONSO
- EDITORS

PREACHER CREATED BY
GARTH ENNIS AND STEVE DILLON

WANTED
A PREACHER Gallery

art by Tim Bradstreet
color by Matt Hollingsworth
338

art by Glenn Fabry
color by Matt Hollingsworth
339

art by John McCrea
color by Matt Hollingsworth
340

art by Doug Mahnke
color by Matt Hollingsworth
341

pencils by Joe Quesada · inks by Jimmy Palmiotti
color by Matt Hollingsworth
342

art by Kieron Dwyer
color by Matt Hollingsworth
343

pencils by Jim Lee · inks by Scott Williams
color by Tad Ehrlich
344

art by Dave Gibbons
color by Matt Hollingsworth
345

pencils by Amanda Conner · inks by Jimmy Palmiotti
color by Matt Hollingsworth
346

art by Carlos Ezquerra
color by Matt Hollingsworth
347

art by John Higgins
color by Matt Hollingsworth
348

art and color by Dave Johnson
349

art by J.G. Jones
color by Matt Hollingsworth
350

art by Brian Bolland
color by Matt Hollingsworth
351

art by Bruce Timm
color by Matt Hollingsworth
352

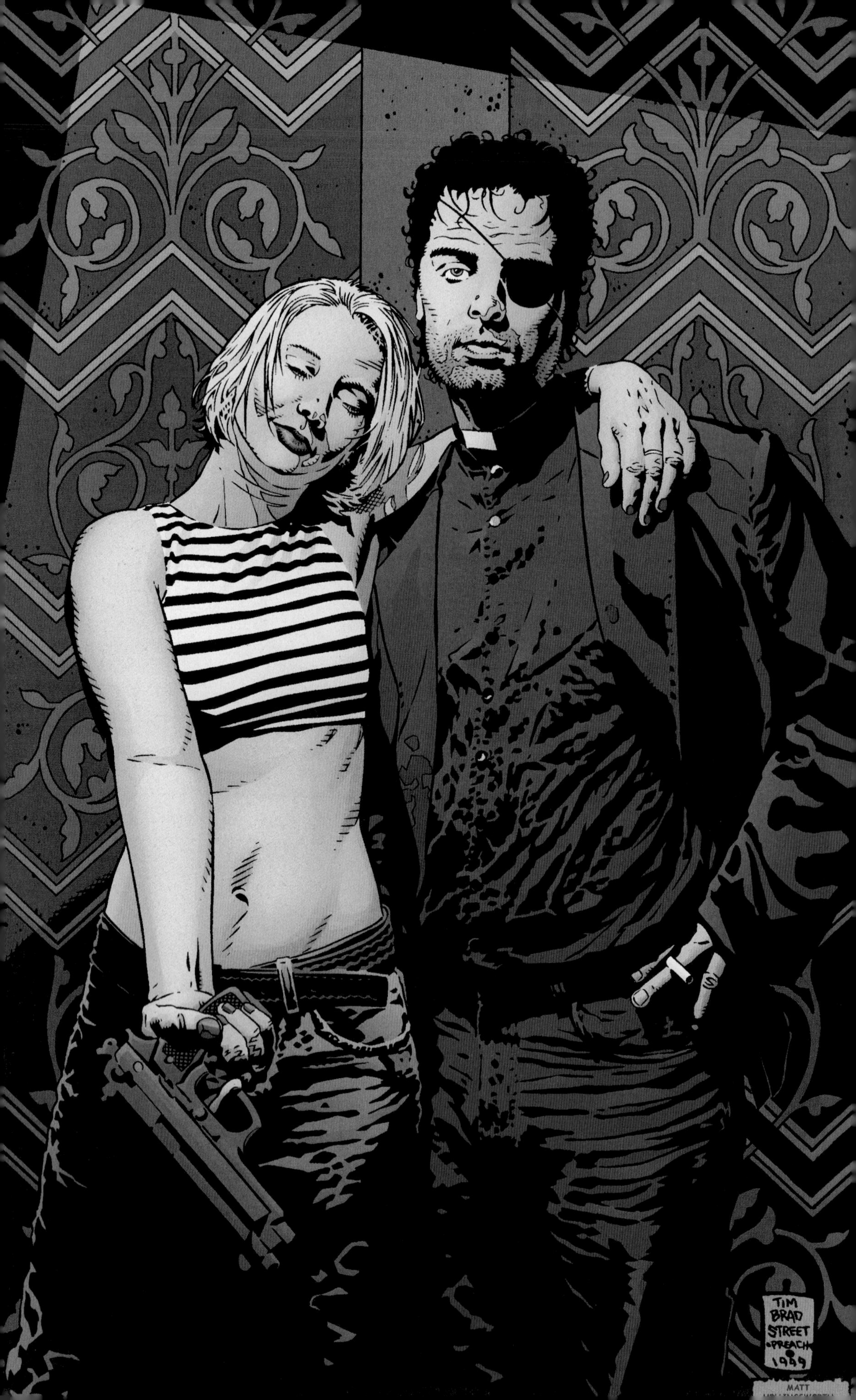
TIM BRAD STREET
•PREACH•
1999
MATT

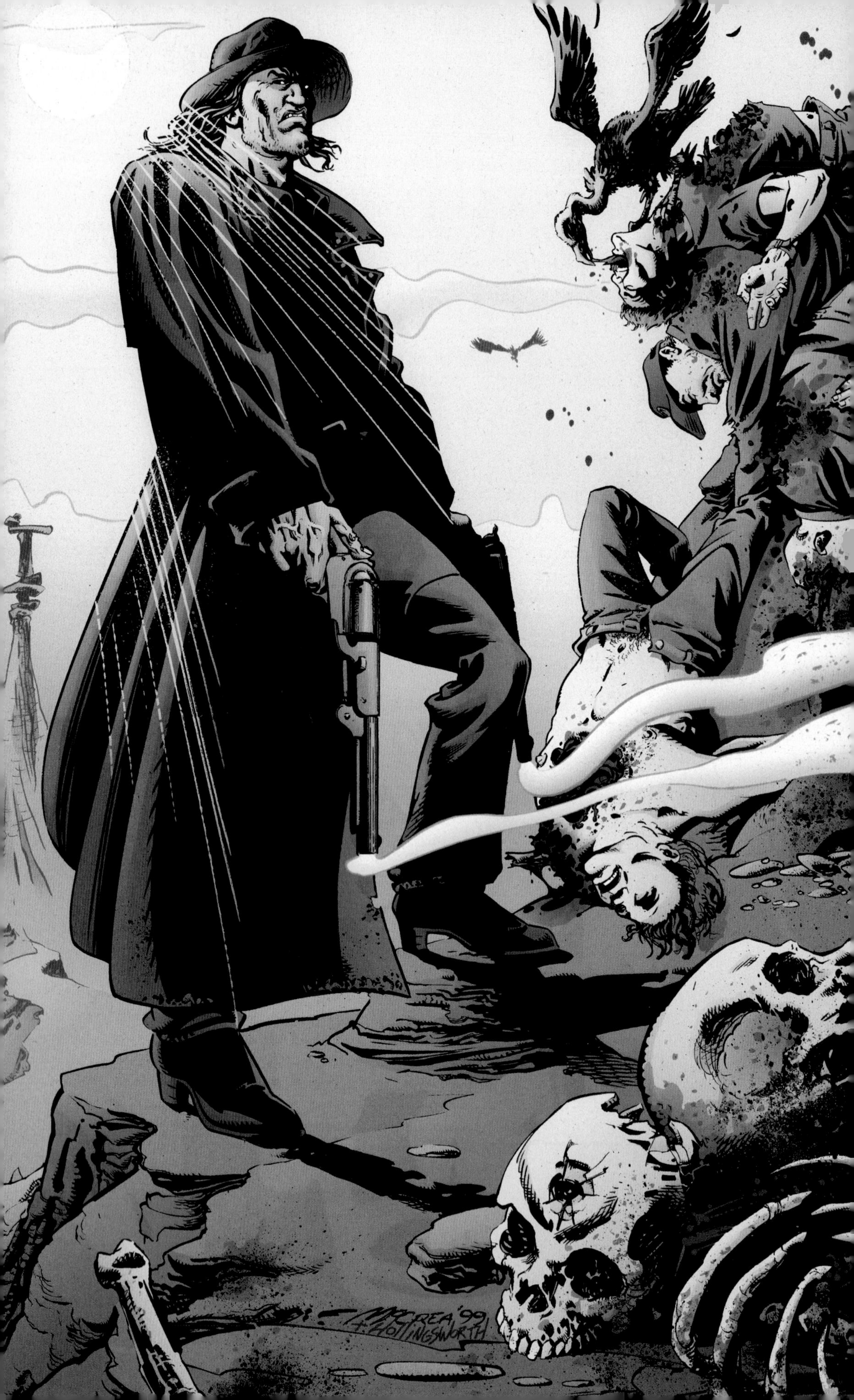
McCREA '99
+ HOLLINGSWORTH

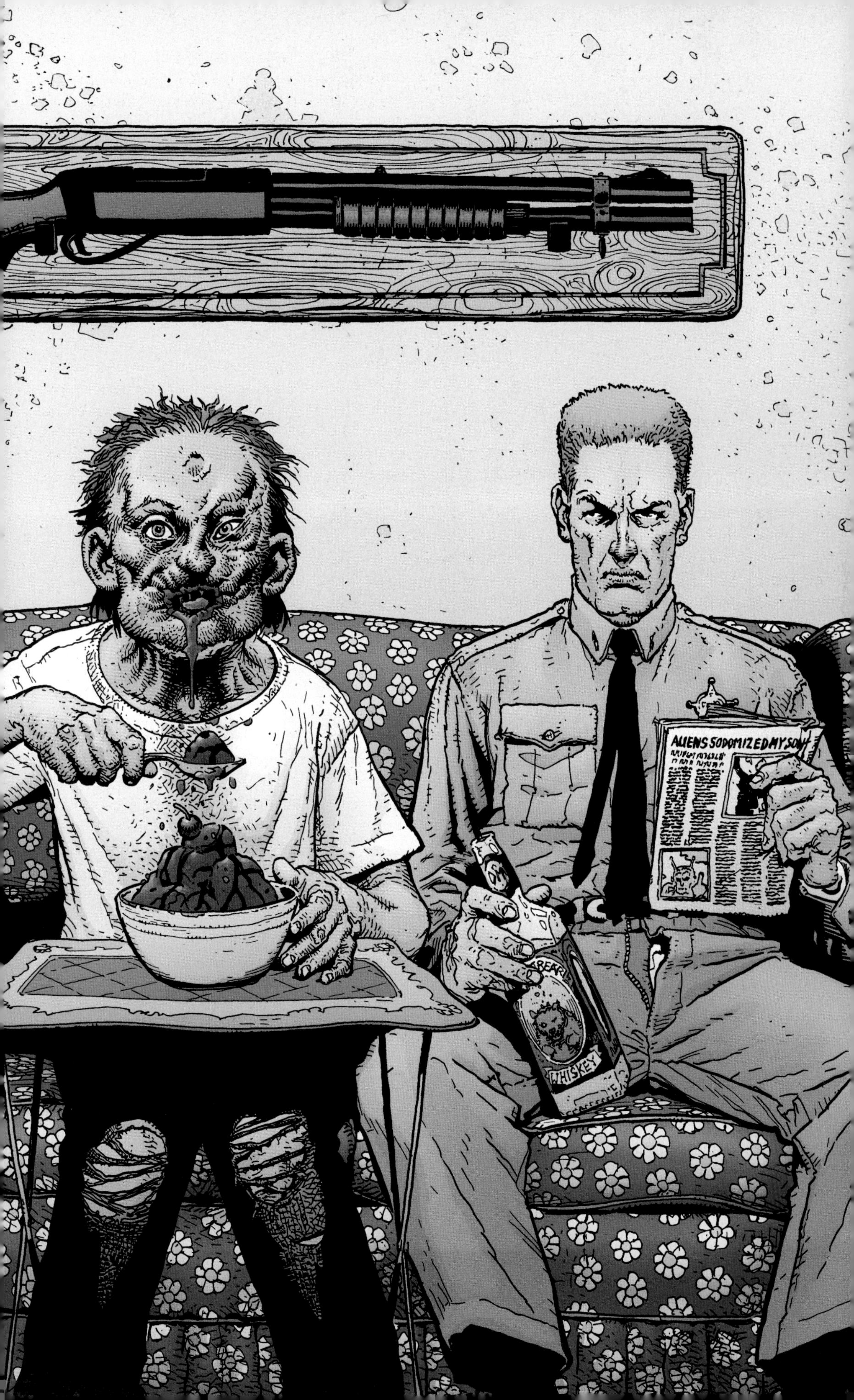
ALIENS SODOMIZED MY SON
WHISKEY

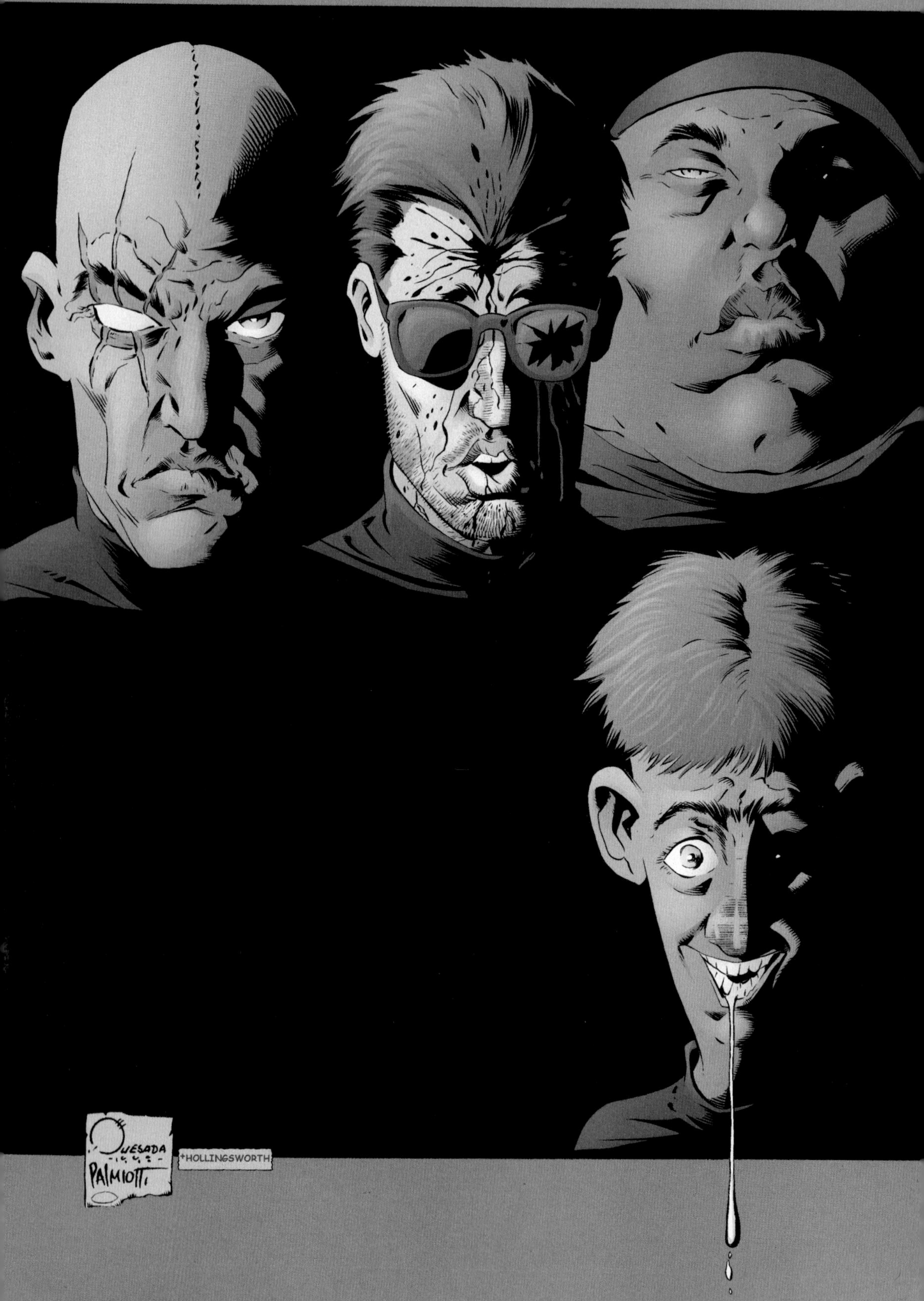
QUESADA
PALMIOTTI
+HOLLINGSWORTH

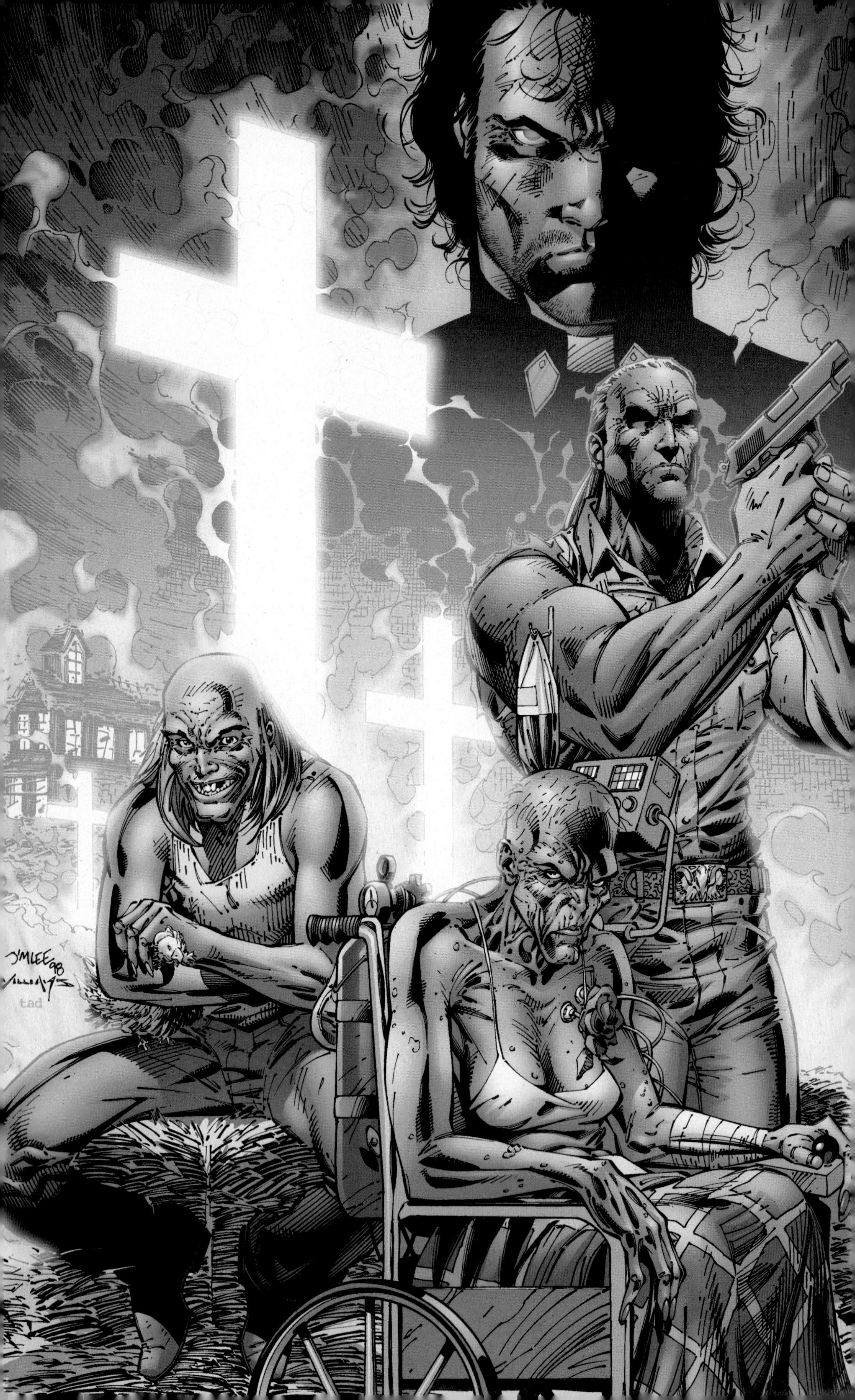
JIMLEE'98
tad

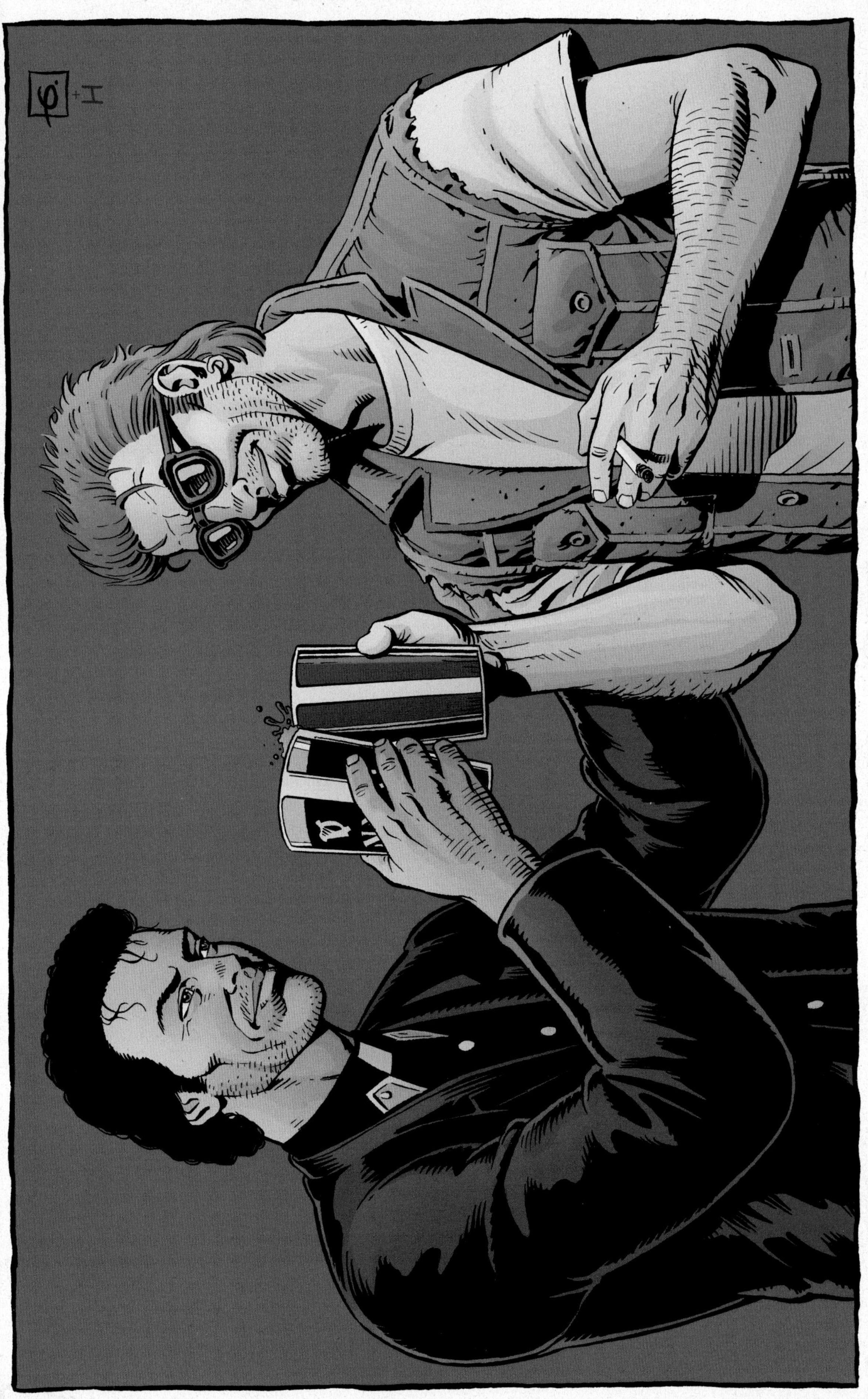

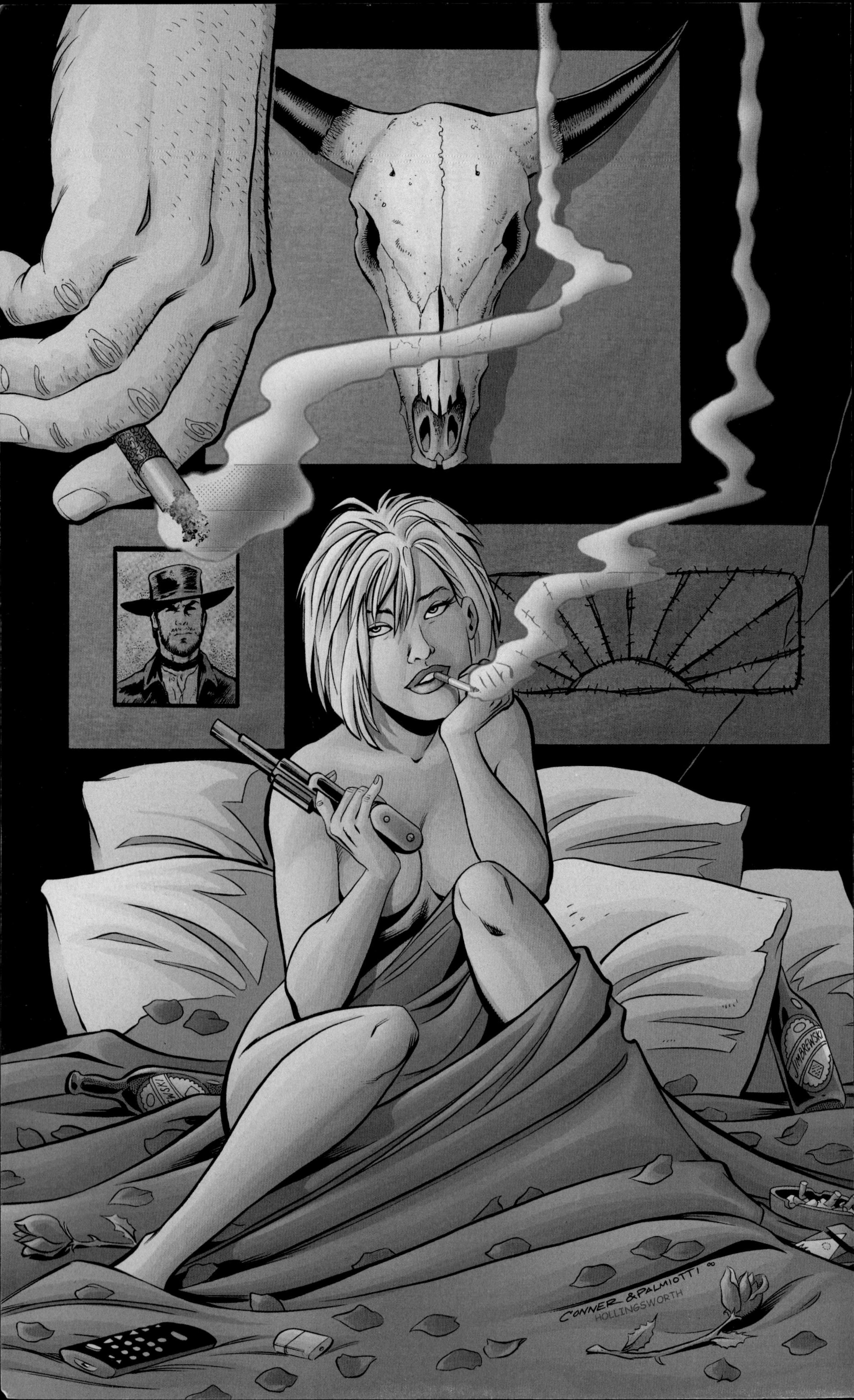
JIMBREWSKI
CONNER & PALMIOTTI 00
HOLLINGSWORTH

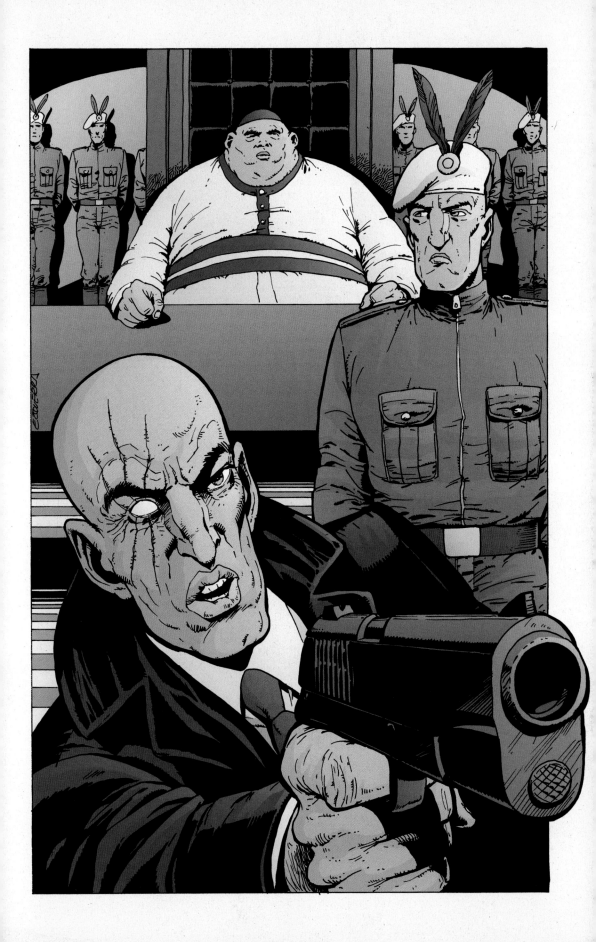

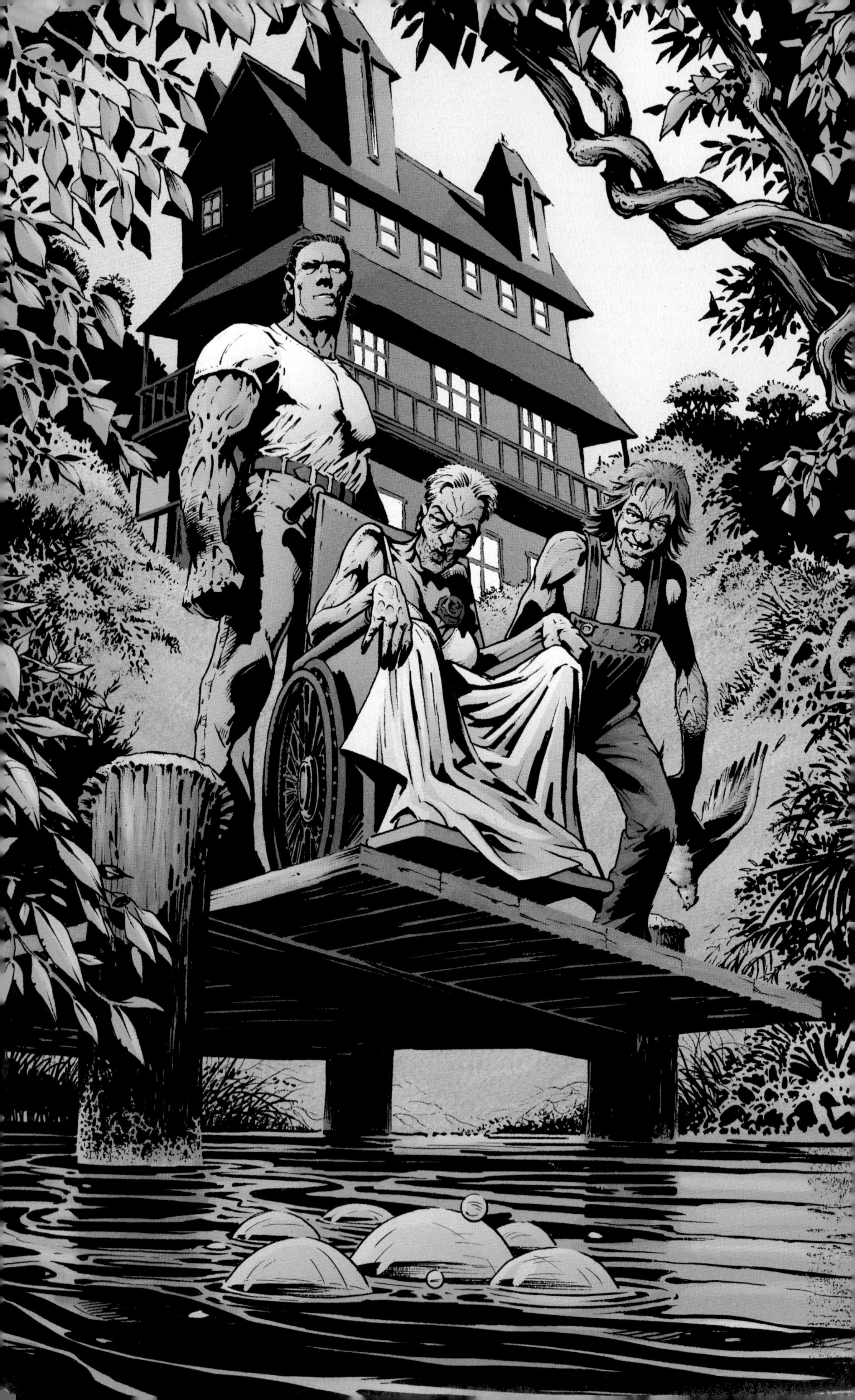

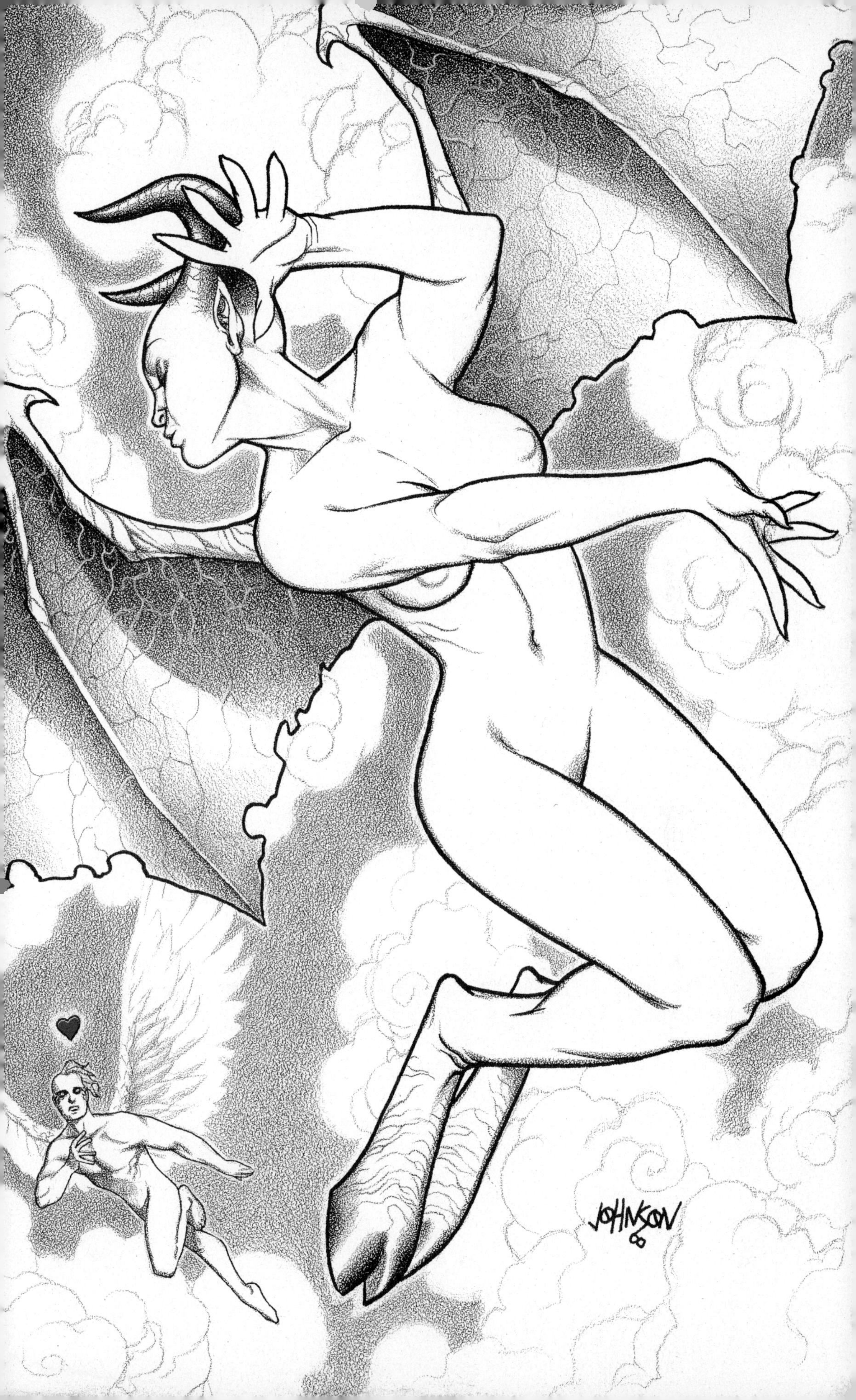
JOHNSON

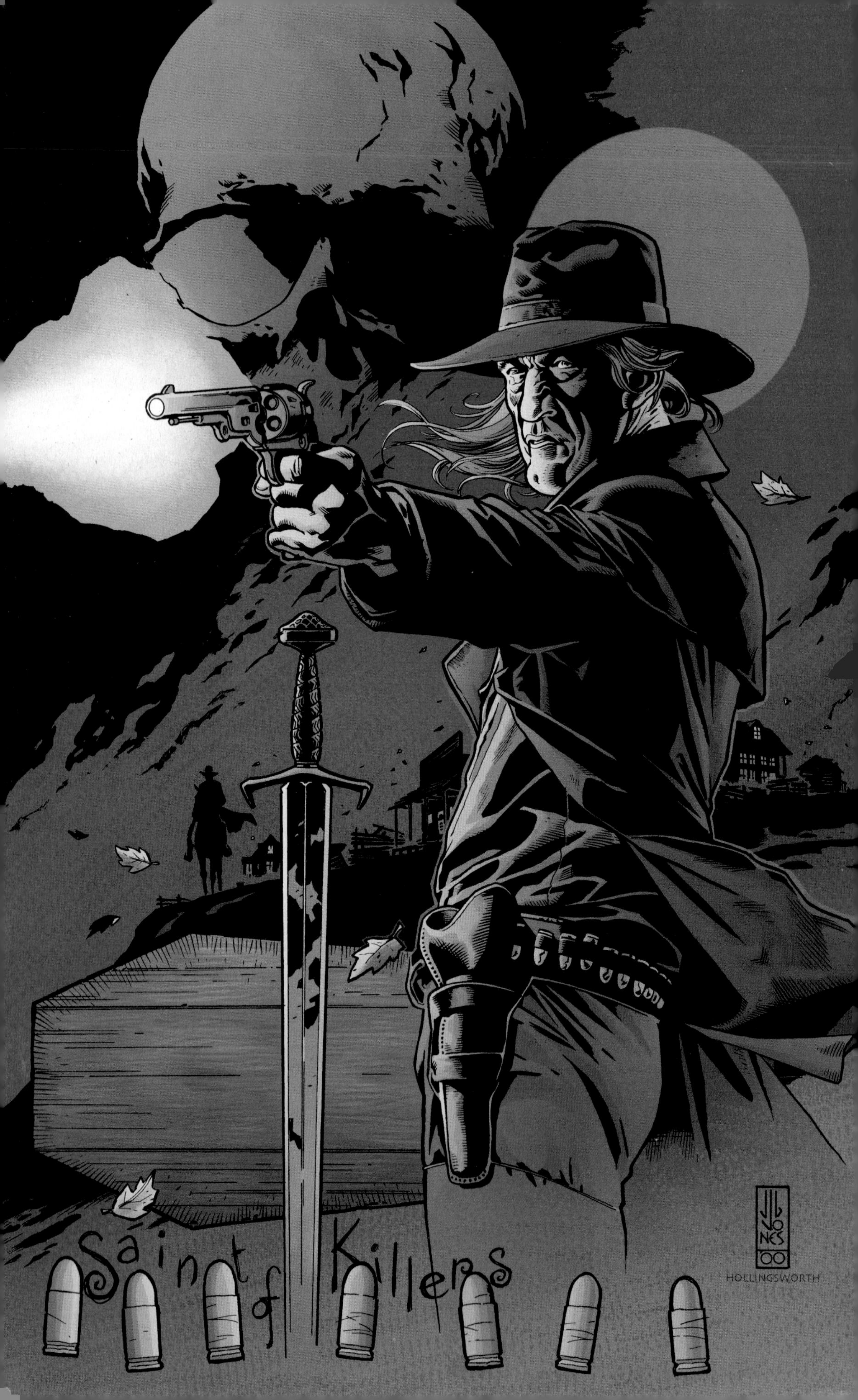
Saint of Killers
JG JONES 00
HOLLINGSWORTH

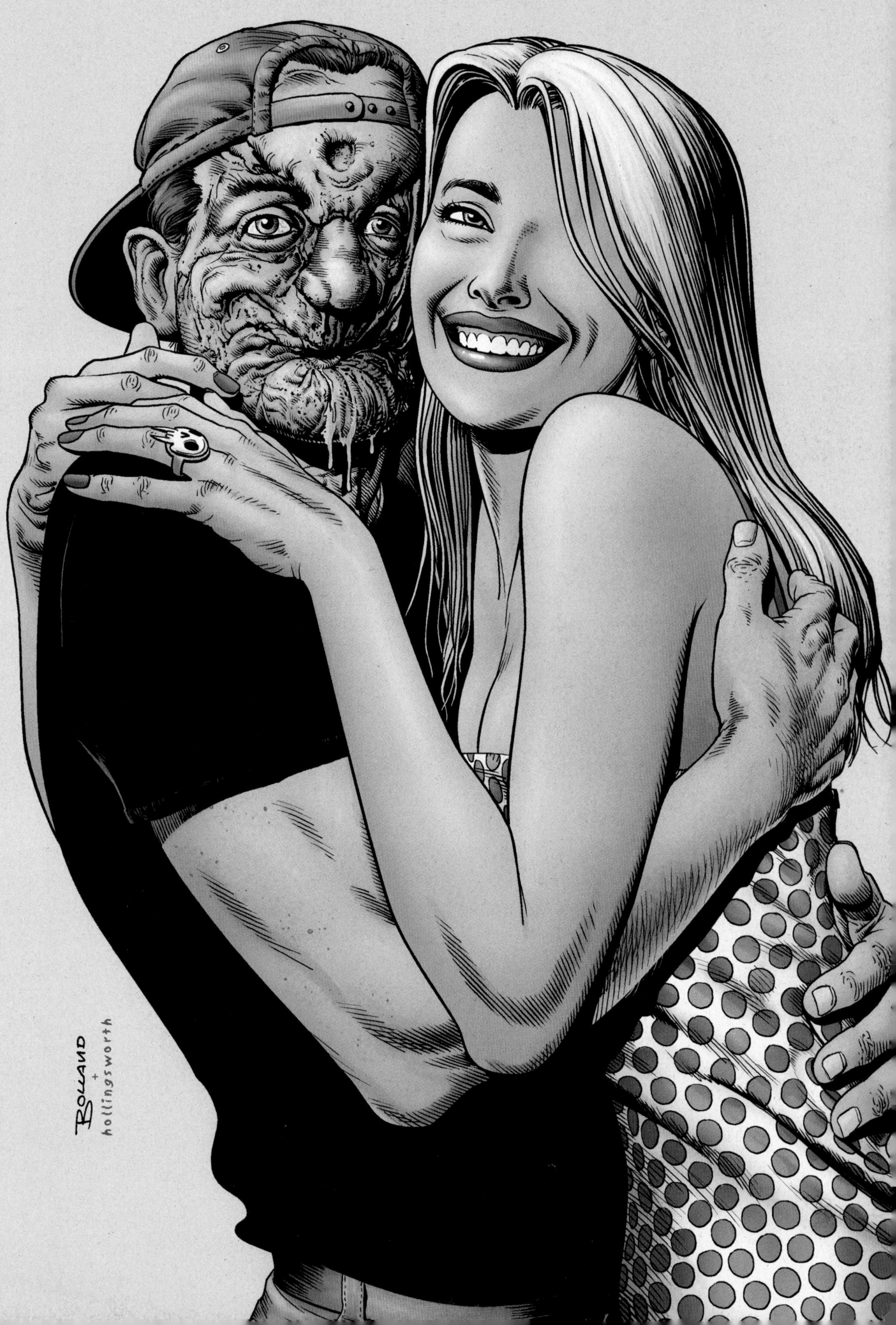
BOLLAND
+
hollingsworth

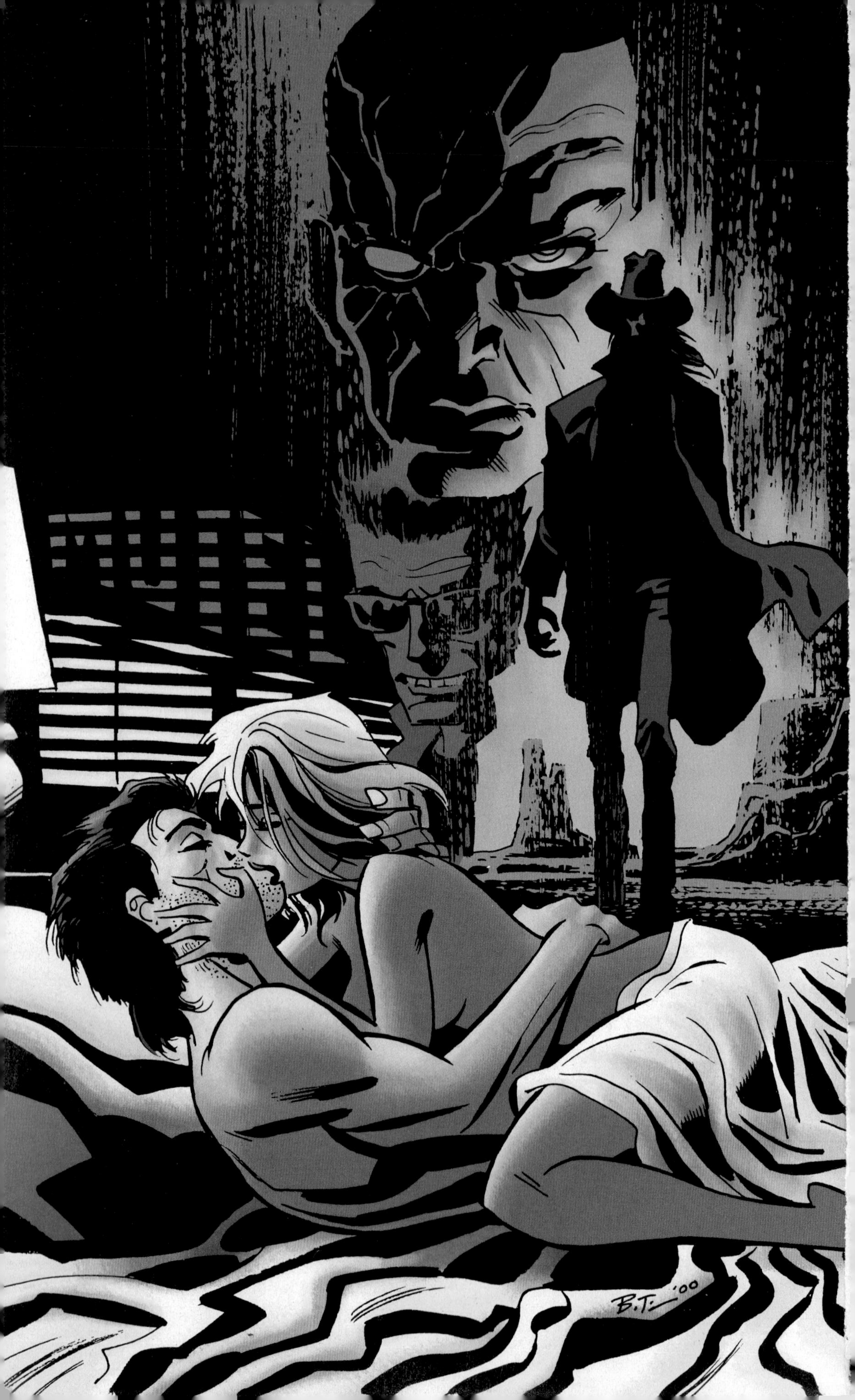
B.T. '00